POLITICAL, LEGAL AND MILITARY HISTORY OF INDIA

(Ancient, Medieval, Modern)

VOLUME 1

VEDIC AND ARYAN INDIA

Evolution of Political, Legal and Military Systems

NEW 3RD EDITION

By the Same Author

- Encyclopaedic History of the Sikhs and Sikhism (6 Vols.)
- European Women in India—Their Life and Adventures
- History of the Conquest of China
- International Law and Practice in Ancient India
- Legal & Political System in China
- Martial Law—Theory and Practice
- Military Dictionary and Encyclopaedia
- Military History of British India
- Origin & Development of Legal & Political System in India (3 Volumes)
- Political, Legal and Military History of India (10 Vols.)
- Portrait of a Political Murder—Trial and Execution of Z.A. Bhutto
- Rare Documents on Sikhs and Their Rule in the Punjab
- Studies in Islamic Law, Religion and Society
- Unity and Discipline through Law

POLITICAL, LEGAL AND MILITARY HISTORY OF INDIA

(Ancient, Medieval, Modern)

VOLUME 1

VEDIC AND ARYAN INDIA

Evolution of Political, Legal and Military Systems

Edited by

H.S. BHATIA

Founder Editor

Civil & Military Law Journal, New Delhi

Distinguished Scholar and Author

NEW 3RD EDITION

DEEP & DEEP PUBLICATIONS PVT. LTD.

F-159, Rajouri Garden, New Delhi - 110027

VEDIC AND ARYAN INDIA
Evolution of Political, Legal and Military Systems

(POLITICAL, LEGAL AND MILITARY HISTORY OF INDIA)

ISBN 978-81-8450-332-6 (Vol. 1)
ISBN 978-81-8450-342-5 (Set)

First Published: 1984/86
Second Edition: 1992
Reprint Edition: 2001
Third Edition: 2012

Typeset by THE LASER PRINTERS, 8/15, 3rd Floor, Subhash Nagar, New Delhi-110027.

Printed in India at MAYUR ENTERPRISES, WZ Plot No. 3, Gujjar Market, Tihar Village, New Delhi - 110 018

Published by DEEP & DEEP PUBLICATIONS PVT. LTD.,
F-159, Rajouri Garden, New Delhi-110027. Phones: 25435369, 25440916.
E-mail: ddpubs@yahoo.com • ddpubs@gmail.com
Sales Showroom: 2/13, Ansari Road, Daryaganj, New Delhi-110002
Phone/Fax: 23245122

Contents

Preface

It is said that History is not entirely a narration of events in order of their occurrence. Such narration would be Annals or Chronology not History. Neither it is a summary of salient events and facts in the lives of Kings or of famous or infamous men of any period. It might be Biography or Archaeology of a period, but no History. History is a record of causes and consequences of passions of body and soul of masses of men and women of a race or country. By the phrase "passions of body and soul" is meant ideas, impulses, and sentiments that affected the daily life of the people, or changed their old habits and customs, or induced them to go to war and over-run and settle in countries other than their own, or spread their culture, norms and religion in peace or which brought about changes or improvements in their science, literature, arts and defence preparedness.

History does not exclude Anthropology, lives and memoirs of distinguished men and women, chronicles of past ages and even Archaeology. History cannot do without them. Further it should extract from events, facts and dates, habits, customs and religions, such massive causes and large consequences of civil and military nature which had interplay on each other casting impact on the society. History does not ignore personal incidents provided they are of a representative person, a person who may be taken as a sample of a host of his contemporaries. Kings, warriors, statesmen, philosophers, writers and even holy men become representative men only when they embody in themselves the ideas and aspirations of a large body of their subjects, admirers and followers.

Some scholars and historians say that the Hindu has not been a chronicler, and with rare exceptions, has left us nothing similar to the monkish histories of medieval Europe or the works of the Muhammad an historians. But for practical purposes he has been a diligent recorder of particular facts and the records have survived even today. But for Asoka's edicts upon stone and copper, we would have known little of dynasties, chronology, geography, religious systems, taxation, land tenures, social organisation and languages. These and other inscriptions, 'Dharma-Sastras', religious literature (Vedas, Ramayana, Mahabharata, Tripitakas, Jatakas, Angas), sacred literature, (Puranas, Dipvamsa, Mahavamsa), historical literature (Arthasastra, Mudra Rakshasa, Rajtarangini), old monuments (Mohen-jo-daro, Taxila, Harappa, Patliputra), writings of foreign travellers (Megasthenese, Arrian, Fahein, Hieun T-sang, Alberuni) and other documents which extend over many centuries from the days of Asoka or perhaps earlier, down to the Muhammadan advent and even later, are valuable source material for recording political, legal and military history of those times.

In the present volume in the "Introductory" article, Dr. Narendra Nath Law considers the historical research for getting at the truth in a scientific spirit in Free India as a challenge and the highest national service. He then critically examines and compares different versions about the 'Deluge' including one recorded in Satpatha-Brahmana. According to him the Floods were not simultaneous. In India, Manu who survived the Flood is looked upon as a man, the progenitor of a race that ruled in India. Then follows the Royal genealogies of ancient India.

According to Professor Gulshan Rai the "Vedic Age" in India may be said to be already existing at the time of Manu, the son of Vaivaswata. The Vedic age had six definite landmarks and the writer proceeds to describe the important characteristics, chief political, legal and military events of those periods. Romesh Chunder Dutt divides the ancient history into five distinct epochs, e.g. Vedic Epoch, Epic Epoch, Rationalistic Epoch, Buddhist Epoch and Puranic Epoch and provides interesting details of each Epoch. The next research article by Dr. G.C. Pande deals with "Population in Ancient India". In "Aryan Expansion in the Post-Rigvedic Period" was involved a terrific war in which sixty-six thousand tribal warriors were killed. The Aryans had to fight with the local aborigines to colonise the area.

"Several types of states like republics, oligarchies, diarchies and monarchies were prevailing in India in ancient times but eventually monarchy became the order of the day," observes Dr. A.S. Altekar in his article "Apex and Distributories of Political Power" on polity of ancient India, while T.R. Sesha Iyengar outlines the history of the evolution of political institutions in South India in ancient times.

Law in ancient India meant *Dharma* in the broader sense and was based upon the twin roots of religion and agreement of men learned in sacred law. Gautama, the earliest of law-givers declared Veda as the source of Dharma, but Manu said, "Veda is the first source, tradition is the second and usage of virtuous men, the third source". "Conception of Law in Ancient India" by Radha Krishna Choudhary, "Ethico-Juristic Conceptions in Ancient India and the Austinian Doctrine" by N.C. Chatterjee and "Legal Literature of Ancient India" by A.A. Macdonell discover law in ancient India as of modern times, while "The Judiciary and Judicial Process in Ancient India" has been described by Prof. N.C. Tyagi and Ram Raj in Chapter 13.

Government and administration has been dealt with in "Government and Laws of Ancient India" (Indian Antiquities), "Royal Power in Ancient India" by Prof. Nilakanta Sastri, D.K. Ganguly's "The Yuvaraja in Ancient India", J.N. Samadar's "Kingship and Republics in Ancient India" and C. Hayavadana Rau's "Local-Self-Government in Ancient India". The article 14 reveals that India was a nation of panchayatdars and ancient Indians were well versed in the art of local government.

Article 15 by John Adam, Dr. Sures Chandra Banerji and Romesh Chandra Dutt throws interesting light on social, cultural and religious "Aspects of Ancient Indian Society", while Dr. M.M. Patkar deals particularly with "The Role of Gambling in Ancient Indian Society". Dr. P.N. Banerjee in his "International Law and Conduct in Ancient India" demolishes the often-held theory that International Law is the product of modern European culture. He establishes that *ancient Indians had a definite knowledge of the rules of International Law according to which they regulated their international conduct.* S.L. Malhotra in "Administration of Justice to Aliens in Ancient India" points out that ancient Indians evolved the mode of adjudication of cases involving aliens out of their own moral and legal norms. He then discusses the principles on which administration of justice was based in ancient India. In a thought-provoking article, "Kautilya and Machiavelli", Prof. Narendrakrishna Sinha compares the writings of these two world famous philosophers, statesmen and thinkers and concludes that "differences between Kautilya and Machiavelli are considerable".

In "The Game of Chess", Parmeshwar Lal examines the Chinese, the Persian and the Indian claims to be originator of this "Game of the Science of War". F.D. Douglas tries to prove that "Chess Originated in Moenjodaro". Lastly, Major S.P. Sharma in his informative article "Art of War in Ancient India" deals with the ancient Indian army, its morale and discipline, approach to war, organisation of the army, chariot corps, elephant corps, cavalry, infantry, commissariat, medical, equipment, armaments, nuclear weapons, and strategy and tactics and asserts that the Indian army was second to none in the world, and formed an efficient instrument of warfare.

With the political, legal and military life of a nation is linked the social, religious and the economic aspects also. India has witnessed through the ages, many wars, upheavals and armed attacks on its soil, thereby affecting its social, cultural, ethnic, and economic and religious life and military strength. What had been the action and reaction of such events on each other has been incorporated in these volumes. This first volume of the ten-volume monumental work may serve as an introduction depicting the origins and evolution of political, legal, military, social and moral systems of the grand panorama of Indian History which will unfold itself in the volumes which are to follow.

In compiling this work, which has taken several years, I have taken valuable help from the publications of several authors both civilian and military. List of books and journals which I have consulted and from which I have extracted are provided at the end of each volume. I am also grateful for the cooperation extended to me by various librarians and eminent historians and scholars.

New Delhi H.S. BHATIA

Hindu Names and Titles

Family and Personal Names

A system of surnames, especially among the middle and upper classes, has evolved in India under western influence, but Hindu surnames had existed earlier and became recognized, being listed, for example, under the later Mughal rulers in 'the chronicles of families'.

Hindu surnames, as one would expect, are largely drawn from religious, caste, sect and tribal names, and very frequently carry a functional sense. Personal (or given) names are chiefly drawn from attributes or appellatives of the deities, and of the epic and Puranic heroes. Hindu names may conveniently be analysed under the following headings :

Religious Names

The ancient Indian system of name-giving was not rigid, and although Hindu treatises laid down the most minute refinements, these were not in practice observed. A detailed scheme was formulated for the bestowal of astrological names, the child being called not only with reference to the month of birth, but also the presiding deity, appropriately masculine or feminine according to the sex of the child. Such names clearly were of good omen, giving the children a share in the attributes of the original bearer and providing also the opportunity of pronouncing holy names as frequently as possible. The personal (or given) names of most Hindus, male and female, are taken from the names of chief deities of the Hindu pantheon, like Shiva, Vishnu, Brahma, Indra and others and their consorts. Names invoking the protection of the gods are also common: Devaprasada, 'Favour of the Gods'; Indrapalita, 'Protected by Indra'; Mitradatta, 'Given by Mitra'; Devadatta, 'God-given'.

Caste and Sect Names

Such personal names, especially those connected with the founder or heroes of the caste, are frequently found. Vaishnavkes, for example, often use Vishnu as a component of their names, or one of his epithets (e.g.. Hari, Keshava, Narayana, Madhava) or the name of one of his incarnations, especially Rama and Krishna (with the synonyms Gopala, Govinda, Radhavallabha) or of his female counterpart (Lakshmi, Shri). Likewise, Shaivites assume the names of Shiva (Rudra, Shankara. Sharva) or of his female counterpart (Durga, Gauri).

Among the main case divisions the following name-components are common: for *Brahmans,* the ending -sharman, deva; for *Kshatriyas,* the endings -varman, -raja; for *Vaishyas,* the endings -gupta, -bhuti, -datta. While these endings are recommended in the ancient lawbook, *Manusmriti,* for the caste-groups under which they are mentioned, much confusion has taken place in practice and a modern name ending in one of these terminations is no infallible guide to its owner's class.

Occupation is usually a mark of caste, and many Hindu names carry an occupational sense, e.g. Mehta (clerk), Kulkarni (accountant), Patel (headman), Joshi (astrologer), Shroff (moneychanger), Chaudhari (headman).

Typical examples of Hindu names built up from divine and functional or family components are :

Surendranath ('Having as lord chief of the gods'), Banerjea (perhaps implying a Brahman teacher);

Keshab Chandra ('Having Keshava [Vishnu] as his moon') Sen (the family name).

Hindus in the north and east of India generally bear a given or personal name and a family or surname on the English model, the name Jawaharlal ('Darling jewel') Nehru providing a good example of this practice. But in the west and south of India names are rather more complicated. In the western Dravidian area a full name gives first the tribal and village name, secondly, the father's name, and thirdly, the personal name. In the Kanarese area where Maratha influence is strong we find the exact reverse. Among the Marathi-speaking and Gujarati people we have first the personal name, then the father's name, then a family name taken place or function with or without modifications. Thus the following names from west India, Ramakrishna Gopal Bhandarkar and Bal Gangadhar Tilak, and the

Gujarati name Mohandas Karamchand Gandhi, are formed as follows:

Ramakrishna (the personal name) Gopal (the father's name) Bhandarkar (a family name meaning 'treasurer');

Bal (the personal name meaning 'boy') Gangadhar (the father's name meaning 'Holder of the Ganges', i.e. Shiva) Tilak (the family name);

Mohandas (the personal name) Karamchand (the father's name) Gandhi (the family name meaning 'a perfume merchant').

The name Singh (Sinha), meaning 'a lion', borne by men of the princely or military castes, is now affixed to the personal name by nearly all Sikhs and many Rajputs and by some men of other castes, too.

Ancestral and Regal Names and Epithets

The Hindu concept that a forefather may be reincarnated in his descendants gives rise to the naming of a child after one of his ancestors, especially his grandfather. In the dynasties of ancient Indian kings a number of such instances occur; in the Gupta Empire, for example, Chandragupta I is first followed by Samudragupta and then by his grandson Chandragupta II. In ancient India appellatives were often changed especially to secure success or for distinction, and Hindu Kings frequently assumed names for these purposes; thus Chandragupta II was known also as Vikrama or Vikramaditya, and the first three Maurya Emperors, including Ashoka, bore the title Piyadasi ('of amiable appearance').

Female Names

On marriage a Hindu wife invariably takes the family name of her husband. In addition to what has been said in above, the basis of female personal names is often formed from the similar and gentler qualities of character and the softer and prettier natural objects, for example, Sarojini (lotus pool), Padma (lotus), Malati (jasmin), Moti (pearl), Usha (dawn).

Honorifics

Popular usage has created a number of designations, usually drawn from occupations or from social, literary or religious position, which in some cases are being accepted as surnames.

Among Hindus, Shri (Sri), Shrijut, Shrimat (fem. Shrimati) before a name denote the same as the English 'Mr.' or 'Esq.'. Ji (meaning 'life, soul') at the end of a name (for example, Gandhiji) denotes affectionate and deep respect. A similar meaning is given to Babu, at one time a title of respect, which now means no more than 'Mr.'. Among Brahmans the specialization of functions gave rise to such terms as Acharya (religious teacher), Pandit (Sanskrit scholar), Chaube (learned in the four Vedas); in Bengal, the name Tagore (from Thakur, meaning 'lord') has become the surname of one of the most famous Brahman families. Baba, literally 'father', is a mode of address to ascetics. Mahatma ('great soul') is especially applied to Gandhi of recently living men, implying that he had transcended the limitations of the flesh and the world. Lala ('writer') or Munshi ('writer'), both Persian terms are used by Hindus. To female names in general in south India, -amma is affixed as a respectful term of address meaning 'Lady' or 'Mistress': for example, Sitamma. To men -appa is sometimes applied.

Titles

The Hindu titles *Raja* and *Maharaja,* which imply sovereignty, were originally held in ancient India by important rulers, and in the period of the Mauryan Empire (4th-3rd centuries B.C.) the emperors themselves—for instance, Asoka—did not hesitate to use them; but in later ages, for example, in the Gupta Empire (4th-6th centuries A.D.), such titles were held only by subordinate princes; the more powerful rulers, like Chandragupta I, meanwhile assuming higher-sounding personal titles such as *Maharajadhiraja* ('Supreme King of Great Kings'). Moreover, as the emperors began to take on the attributes and character of divine beings—probably through Greek and Chinese influences—their personal titles faithfully reflected this development, and, whereas Ashoka was merely *Devanampiya* ('Beloved of the Gods'), the Kushan emperors of the first two centuries A.D. were named *Devaputra* ('Son of Heaven'), and later rulers *Parameshvara* ('Supreme Lord').

In the Gupta and post-Gupta periods hereditary feudal titles were common, the following, for example, being applied to feudatories: *Samanta, Mahasamanta, Mandalika, Mahamandalika.*

Under Mughal rule the titles of *Raja* and of its equivalents, *Rao, Rana* and *Rai,* were bestowed on Hindu civil officers of high rank (e.g., *Rai-raian),* whence they later became family designations, e.g. Ram Mohan Roy. Under the British Government these titles of nobility were also widely conferred on Hindu subjects, so that although the title of *Raja* may still denote a subordinate chief or prince, it is also often held by socially eminent persons, such as important landholders and officials; and *Rai* and *Rao* have been assumed by many men of position.

PLACE-NAMES AND GEOGRAPHICAL TERMS

A large proportion of Indian place-names are formed, as in English, by the addition of a suffix (or less frequently of a prefix) to a personal name or designation; the latter usually being the name of the founder or being, human or divine, in whose honour the place was founded. The linguistic source, whether Sanskritic, Dravidian or Persian, whence the suffix or prefix is taken usually indicates the age of the name itself, but clearly does not establish the history of the place. The name Allahabad, for example, made up by the addition of the Persian suffix -abad ('made populous by'), was given in the time of Akbar (1556-1605) to the long-established Hindu city of Prayaga.

The commonest suffixes from the Sanskritic languages are :

-gad, -gud, -gadi, -gadhi, -gadh, -garh, -gurh (a hill-fort)
-ghat, corruptly -ghaut or -gaut (river-crossing or mountain-pass)
-gram, -gaum, -gaon and corruptly -gong (a village)
-hat (market)
-kot, -kota (written also -cote), -koth, -kotta (fort)
nagar, -nugur, corruptly -nuggur and -nagor (town, city), e.g. Vijayanagar (City of Victory) and Chandernagore (Moon-city)
-pur, -pura, corruptly -poor and -pore (town), e.g. Serampur (Shri-ram-pur, i.e. Rama's town) and Cawnpore (Kanhpur, i.e. Krishna's town)

Common Sanskritic prefixes are Deo- (a god), Rai- (a king).

The Dravidian languages provide:

-konda (hill)
-pattanam, corruptly -patam (town or village), e.g. Masulipatam (Fish town). Also found in Sanskrit
-palle, -palli, -palliya (hamlet)
-pet (town)
-ur, -oor, -uru, -ura and corruptly -ore, e.g., Vellore, Coimbatore, Tanjore.

SYSTEMS OF DATING

Hindu

'Ages' lasting for thousands of years are frequently referred to in Sanskrit texts. One of the best known, though not one of those found in ancient documents, is the *Kali-yuga,* or Kali age supposed to be the last and worst of the four ages that make up a great age. Starting in 3102 B.C. from the death of Krishna, it is to last through 432,000 years of progressive deterioration until it ends in the general dissolution of existing forms. This era seems to have been a late invention. Scholars have also identified a considerable number of now-forgotten eras attributable to various conquerors of ancient India and usually dating from their accession to the throne. The idea of suzerainty over all the rulers of a large region is deeply rooted in Indian conceptions of government, and the establishment of this supreme lordship was usually marked by the foundation of an era. The two most significant Hindu eras of the historical period are the Vikrama or Samvat (year) and the Shaka (Saka), both of which are still used.

Vikrama Samvat era began in 58 B.C., and, according to Indian tradition, was established by Vikramaditya, a legendary king of Ujjain, who was said to have defeated the Shakas. Some scholars attribute its foundation to the Shaka king Azes I. Its use became widespread. The year A.D. 1948 may be said to be 2006 of the Vikrama era. Discrepancies occur because the era year is assumed to begin in March-April in eastern India and in October-November in the west.

The *Shaka (Saka) era,* which has obtained a wide currency in India, especially in the south, is believed by some to have been founded by the Kushan king Kanishka, and dated from his supposed accession in A.D. 78. Possibly, and more probably, it was founded to commemorate the accession of the Satrap Nahapana. The year A.D. 1948 is 1870 of the Shaka era. See also Saka in the 'Key to Important Terms' in Volume 3.

Buddhist and Jain

Two religious eras in common use are those of the Buddhists in Burma and Ceylon, said to date from the death of the Buddha (*c.* 483 B.C.), and of the Jains in north India, said to date from the death of Mahavira (*c.* 468 B.C.). The Buddhist era actually begins in 544 B.C. and the era of Mahavira in 528 B.C.

1

Introductory

Dr. Narendra Nath Law

Research, a National Service

The freedom of India lias brought new opportunities, and also new responsibilities to our historians for carrying on investigations. A new challenge has come to the historians to give of their best, true to the highest ideals of getting at the truth in a scientific spirit. Such research is the highest national service that an historian can render. Considering the vastness of this country, and the centuries covered by its history and recorded historical tradition, the necessity of research work among our historians cannot be over-emphasized.

THE FLOOD

It is stated that the Flood recorded in the *Satapatha Brahmana* was "the greatest landmark in the pre-dynastic history of India." The Flood has been proved to be a historical fact by Dr. Woolley's excavations. The area of the Flood was certainly the continuous land from Mesopotamia to Rajputana, and there is the common tradition at both ends of this area, embodied in the ancient literatures of the Semites and the Hindus. Our dynastic history in the Puranas almost begins from the Flood, and the Mohenjo Daro civilization is post-

Flood event". "The Puranas are amongst the most ancient documents on race-history, and the tradition and data embodied therein go back to the Flood and even earlier."

Biblical Deluge and Noah

These statements have a very important bearing on the royal genealogies, and dynastic histories of ancient India and researches relating thereto, and so, they require a close scrutiny. The ancient Flood-legends are numerous and are found recorded in many parts of the world. I have no space here to give summaries of even two or three of these accounts. I shall append here only the *Timetable* of the Biblical legend.

Timetable of the Deluge

The universal flood which happened at the time of Noah—2348 B.C.

"October	Noah and his family entered the Ark.
November	The fountains of the great deep broke open.
December 26	The rain began, continued 40 days and nights.
January, 2349 B.C.	The earth buried under the waters.
February	Rain continued.
March	The waters at their height till the 27th, when they began to abate.
April 17	The Ark rested on Mount Ararat in Armenia.
May	Waiting the retiring of the waters.
June 1	The tops of the mountains appeared.
July 11	Noah let go a raven, which did not return. He let go a dove, which returned.
July 25	The dove, being sent a second time, brought back the olive-branch.
August 2	The dove, sent put a third time, returned no more.
September 1	The dry land appeared.
October 27	Noah went out of the Ark."[1]

Beeton in his *Illustrated Dictionary of Religion, etc.* (p. 190) says (sv. "Deluge"): "Some of the ablest scientific and theological students are now disposed to regard the Biblical deluge as partial and local. It is true the language of the narrative in Genesis seems to imply its universality; but similar expressions are used in Scripture in cases where the meaning is evidently limited. For instance, we read that *'all* countries came into Egypt to Joseph for to buy corn, because the famine was so sore in *all* lands'. In 1 Kings, Obadiah tells Elijah that 'there is no nation or kingdom, whither my lord hath not sent to seek thee'. In the book of Daniel it is said that 'King Darius wrote unto *all* people, nations, and languages, that dwell in *all* the earth'. It is not to be supposed that these phrases are to be taken literally, and it is not quite unreasonable to suppose that the meaning of the word 'all', in the account of the flood, may be subject to a similar limitation."

Scientists and the Universal Flood

"The belief in a universal deluge has long been abandoned by well-informed writers."[2] The grounds on which the geologists and other categories of scientists oppose the historicity of a universal deluge are:—

1. Ethnology—The presence of various races of mankind, independent of the Bible system, cannot be explained if there had been a universal deluge.
2. Geology—The agencies that have operated to build up the world are shrinkage, gradual sinkings and upheavals, deposits by action of animalcules, *but not universal deluge.*
3. Zoology—This science proves clearly that there is no definite line of demarcation between the extinct species and those of the present day which would have existed if there had been a break in the continuity of the animal world.
4. Botany—The remarks made in connection with zoology apply to plant life and its history,—there are no indications of any break.

Babylonian Story of Deluge

At present, many scholars are of opinion that the story of the Biblical flood is modelled on that of the Babylonian. C.L. Woolley says in his *Ur of the Chaldees* (p. 30)[3]—"Taking into consideration all the facts, there could be no doubt that the flood (of Ur), of which we had thus found the only possible evidence, was the Flood of Sumerian history and legend, the Flood on which is based the story of Noah."

In the Babylonian story, an ancestor of Gilgamesh, King of Uruk, was advised to build a ship of certain dimensions to protect himself, his family and friends, as also his belongings and the seed of life of every thing against the fury of a Flood. For six days and nights, the flood and tempest overwhelmed the land. On the seventh day, they subsided, the sea rested, the hurricane spent itself, and the flood was at an end. He looked upon the sea, and all men perished. On the twelfth day, the ship grounded on a mountain in Armenia. He waited there for another six days, and sent out birds one after another to ascertain that dry land had appeared. Later, when land appeared, he with others came out of the ship.[4]

While excavations were progressing on the 40 ft. high rubbish around Ur, Woolley came upon a layer of 8 ft. thick clean mud. Its texture convinced him that it had been carried there by a Flood, which marked a break in the continuity of the history of Ur. Inundations were of normal occurrence in Mesopotamia, but an ordinary rising of the rivers could not have left 8 ft. of sediment. The flood must have been of a "magnitude unparalleled in local history. . . . A whole civilization, which existed before it, is lacking above the clay bank, and seems to have been submerged by the water."[5]

This flood was, according to Woolley, the flood of the Sumerian history and legend, on which the story of Noah was based. From a brick pavement 16 ft. below, it could be inferred that the Flood came sometime later than 3200 B.C. "Two or three Sumerian cities are said to have existed equally before the Deluge and after it. We may assume (therefore) that the historical break was not final, and that so far from the disaster being universal, some at least of the local centres of civilization survived it."[6]

As the result of his excavations for seven years at Ur, and surrounding places, Woolley comes to the conclusion that the "Deluge was not universal but a local disaster confined to the lower valley of the Tigris and Euphrates, *affecting an area perhaps 400 miles long and 100 miles across;* but for the occupants of the valley, that was the whole world!"[7]

Story of the Flood in the Satapatha-Brahmana

In the *Satapatha-Bruhmana* (1.8.1), the story of Flood is thus related:—

> When water was brought to Manu, son of Vivasvan (sun-god), for washing, a fish came into his hands, and said that he would protect

Manu in the devastating flood that is expected to come in a future year, if Manu would save him now. As desired by the fish, Manu kept him first in a jar, then in a pit, and afterwards took him to the sea, according as he grew in stature. According to the direction of the fish, Manu built a ship and when the flood came, he entered into it. The fish swam near when Manu tied the ship by a rope to its horn. The ship was then drawn by the fish to the northern mountain, where it was fastened to a tree. As the flood gradually subsided, Manu descended down the mountain. The flood had swept away all the creatures leaving only Manu alive.

These details along with some additional features and variations are found in the *Mahabharata* (Vana, 187, Burdwan edition) and in some of the Puranas.

It has already been pointed out that the historicity of a universal Flood has been ruled out by scientists of several categories on various grounds, which I need not repeat here.

Manu, who survived the Flood mentioned already, is looked upon as a man—the progenitor of a race that ruled in India. He is also believed to be the divine personality, who has been presiding over the world during the Manvantara allotted to him, i.e. a period of 71 Mahayugas (each of which is equal to 4 Yugas viz. Krta, Treta, Dvapara and Kali totalling 4,320,000 years'.[8] Of the present Vaivasvata Manvantara, 27 Mahayugas have already elapsed, and of the 28th Mahayuga, three Yugas have passed away, leaving Kali which is now current. At the beginning of the current Kali Yuga, there could not have been an end of a Manvantara, and so according to the mythological scheme of Yugas applicable to the ruling periods of Manus, no flood could be expected in 3102 B.C. This year has been taken by Arya-bhata I, and some other astronomers as the starting point of Kali Yuga, when the Bharata War took place.[9] His view may not be accepted, but in case of non-acceptance, it is not reasonable to substitute it by an important event—Flood.

Thus, the Floods dealt with above were not simultaneous, and could not have been linked up with one another into a vast sheet of water from Mesopotamia to Rajputana as stated by Jayaswal.

ROYAL GENEALOGIES OF ANCIENT INDIA

I shall now deal with some aspects of the royal genealogies of ancient India from Manu to Candragupta Maurya. The fixed milestone on the chronological highway of ancient Indian history is the accession of Candragupta Maurya to the throne of Magadha at about 322 B.C.

Nandas

The Puranic tradition is that 9 Nandas ruled in Magadha for 100 years.[10] The first king Mahapadma was the son of Mahanandin, who was the last king of the Sisunaga dynasty. There was therefore no break in the continuity of the rule. V. Smith has allotted to the Dynasty 91 years.[11] If 9 years more be added, the average length of reign per king comes up only to about 11 years. Hence: the Puranic total of 100 years for the Nandas should be accepted.

Sisunaga, the First King

According to the Puranas, 10 Sisunagas ruled in Magadha for 360 years (or 'better 163 years' according to Pargiter). The first king Sisunaga is introduced thus in the Puranic list: 'Sisunaga' will destroy all their (i.e. Pradyotas) prestige, and will be *king*. Placing his son in Benares, he will make Girivraja his own abode'.[12]

It is not known how Sisunaga occupied the throne, and why he left his son at Benares, but it is noteworthy that the Puranas do not speak of any bloodshed, or revolution, preceding the dynastic change in Magadha.

Sisunaga soon surpassed the glory of the kings of the previous Pradyota dynasty (हत्वा तेषां यशः कृत्स्नं). There is no ground for holding the opinion that Sisunaga eclipsed the glory of Pradyota Canda Mahasena of the distant Avanti.

W. Geiger's List for Sisunagas

On the basis of the Ceylonese Chronicles, W. Geiger introduces drastic changes in the Sisunaga list of the Puranas.[13] Bimbisara is made the first king and not the 5th as the Puranas do, and Sisunaga the founder of the dynasty is allotted the 7th place.

As regards Bimbisara's father Geiger states that "Bimbisara and the prince Siddhartha were friends, and friends likewise were the fathers of both .... *The virtuous Bimbisara was fifteen years old when he was anointed king by his own father.*"[14]

The name of Bimbisara's father is not mentioned by Geiger. It is given in the *Mula-Sarvastivada-Vinayavastu* (Gilgit MS.) as 'Mahapadma'. He was a king of Magadha and used to pay tribute to the king of Anga, which was resented by Bimbisara. He refused to pay the tribute and brought him under his sway by invading his capital Campa.[15] The aforesaid Chronicles represent 5 sons and successors from Ajatasatru to Nagadasaka as parricides. Smith in the earlier editions of his *Early History of India* mentioned Ajatasatru alone as parricide, but in the last edition (1924, p. 36), he does not believe that even Ajatasatru committed the crime.

Criticisms of Geiger's List

E.J. Rapson does not think the Buddhist genealogy of the Sisunaga dynasty to be above suspicion. For, says he, "each of the five kings from Ajatasatru to Nagadasaka is said to have killed his father and predecessor within a period of fifty-six years, and we are solemnly told that, after the last of these, Nagadasaka, has occupied the throne for twenty-four years, the citizens awoke to the fact that 'this is a dynasty of parricides', and appointed the minister Susunaga (Sisunaga) in his stead."[16]

T.W. Rhys Davids praises the list as very reasonable and scholarly, but says at the same time, "It must be confessed that the numbers (of years of reigns of the kings) seem much too regular, with their multiples of six and eight, to be very probably in accordance with fact."[17]

Referring to Geiger's preference for the Ceylonese Chronicles as against the Puranas, V. Smith says that "the authority of the Puranic lists as against the muddled account of the *Mahavamsa* is more dependable." Smith is reluctant to accept "any and every indubitable assertion of the Pali canon as *true*."[18]

Even Geiger himself admits in connection with the Ceylonese royal genealogy given in the *Mahavamsa* that "the last reigns were lengthened in order to make Vijaya and the Buddha contemporaries."[19]

In view of these remarks, the following statement of Geiger should lose a good deal of its weight viz. "If finally the choice lies between the list of the Puranas and that of the Ceylonese Chronicles, which seems to be more probable and trustworthy, I do not hesitate to give the preference wholly and unreservedly to the latter."[20]

The Puranic List of Sisunagas

All things considered, the list of names of the Sisunaga kings found in the Puranas has greater claim to acceptance.

On the analogy of English kings, Smith allots a maximum of 252 years to 10 Sisungagas and arrives at 664 B.C. as the beginning of the rule of the dynasty. He however does not use this maximum period but fixes the date of Sisunaga at 642 B.C. taking only 229 years for the total period for the dynasty instead of 252 years.

Bimbisara Reigned from 582 B.C.

Bimbisara occupies a more or less fixed position in ancient Indian chronology because of his synchronism with the Buddha. Smith has altered the life-span of the Buddha from 566—486 B.C. to 623—543 B.C. in the 4th the (last) edition of his book, and as a result of synchronism of the Buddha with Bimbisara, the latter's probable date of accession now stands at 582 B.C. To the four kings preceding Bimbisara in the Sisunaga list, only 60 years have been allotted at an average of 15 years per king. This average is too low. I shall discuss it later on.

Regarding the date of the Buddha's death Smith (*EHI,* 4th ed., p. 50) makes the following observations.

> "I do not believe that the date can be fixed with anything like certainty, and in opposition to the arguments in favour of 487 or 486 B.C. we now have the new reading of the Kharavela inscription which, if correct, obliges us to move back all the Sisunaga dates more than 50 years and therefore supports the Ceylon date for the death of Buddha, viz. 544 or 543 B.C. It may be argued that traditions preserved in Magadha should be more trustworthy than those recorded at a later date by monks in distant Ceylon; but there is ample evidence of the fact that Gautama Buddha was contemporary with both Bimbisara or Srenika, and his son Ajatasatru or Kunika, and this being so, I feel compelled until further light is thrown on the subject to accept tentatively the earlier date 543 B.C., based on the chronology disclosed by the Kharavela inscription."

Pradyotas

According to the Puranas, the Pradyota dynasty consisting of 5 kings[21] succeeded the Brhadrathas, and preceded the Sisunagas, on the throne of Magadha, and reigned 138 years (52 years according to Pargiter). *Rapson considers this as distortion of history, because in his opinion Pradyota Canda Mahasena and his successors ruled in reality in Avanti and not in Magadha, and Bimbisara occupied the throne of Magadha just after Ripunjaya, the last Brhadratha king.*[22]

But the Puranas record (in the prophetic future tense) that "When the Brhadrathas, Vitihotras and Avantis[23] have passed away, Pulika will kill his master and anoint his own son Pradyota, by force in the very sight of the kshatriyas."[24]

In *Gunadhya's Brhatka'ha,* substance of which is partially preserved in the derivative Sanskrit works of the *Brhatkathamanjari*[25] by Kshemendra and the *Kathasaritsagara*[26] by Somadeva, Pradyota is described as king of Magadha. Vasavadatta, the daughter of Canda.[27] Mahasena of Avanti was the first wife of Udayana, king of Vatsa, with his capital at Kausambi. Through the crafty designs of his Prime Minister Yaugandhrayana, Udayana was married to Padmavati (Udyayana's second wife) who was the daughter of the Magadhan king Pradyota.[28]

तो प्रद्योत-महासेनौ त्वयाबुद्धैयव वञ्चितौ।

(*Brhatkathamanjari,* p. 76)

(Those two,—Pradyota and Mahasena,—have been outwitted by crafty designs of you, i.e. Yaugandharayana, Prime Minister of Udayana). The detailed account is given in the *Kathasaritsagara,* Tarangas xv, xvi.

In the Paurava dynasty after Parikshita[29] (i.e. after the Bharata War), *Udayana is the 24th king. In the Magadha line of kings, counting from Samadhi, the first Brhadratha king after the Bharata War, Pradyota's son Palaka is the 24th king (22 Brhadrathas+2 Pradyotas). Hence, Palaka was ruling in Magadha at the same time as Udayana at Kausambi (Vatsa).* For this reason, *the synchronism between Udayana, and Palaka's sister* (i.e. *Pradyota's daughter*) *makes the marital relation possible.*

In the *Brhatkathamanjari* and *Kathasaritsagara,* Padmavati is the daughter of the Magadha king Pradyota. Bhasa in his *Svapnavasavadatta*[30] Budhasvamin in his *Brhatkathaslokasamgraha*[31] and the unnamed author in the *Binavasavadatta*[32] state that *Padmavati was the sister of Darsaka. They do not mention her father's name. If this Darsaka be the 7th king of the Sisunaga dynasty of the Puranas, his sister's marriage to Udayana is impossible. For, in the royal genealogy of Magadha after the Bharata War, Darsaka of the Sisunaga list is the 34th king from the aforesaid Samadhi, while Udayana is the 24th Paurara king.* There is thus an interval of more than 160 years between Udayana and Darsaka or Darsaka's sister, taking 18 years as average length of reign (9 × 18=162 years). *The king Darsaka mentioned by Bhasa should not be taken as identical with his name-sake of the Puranic list of the Sisunaga dynasty, but should be equated to Palaka, son of*

Pradyota of Magadha. The fact that Darsaka had another name is suggested in a passage in Bhasa's Svapnavasaradatta.[33] In a scene of the 1st Act, while announcing the arrival of Padmavati at a hermitage, the Kancukin of the Magadha king refers to her as the *"sister of the king who used to be Darsaka by his father"*. The announcement is unusual, unless Bhasa's Darsaka had another name.

An episode in the *Brhatkathaslokasamgraha* testifies to the fact that Udayana had marital relation with the royal family of Magadha as also with that of Avanti.[34]

Average Length of Reign

After examining 14 series of 20 to 30 kings of Western and Eastern countries, Pargiter finds the average to be 19 years, the longest being over 24 and the shortest 12 years. But as the average is higher in Western countries than in the Eastern, he considers 18 years for the Indian kings as "a fair and even liberal estimate". Pargiter, however, has used scarcely this average of 18 years. His averages vary, and to the kings before the Bharata War he has allotted only 12 years as the average.[35] My revered teacher R.K. Mookerji writes in his *Hindu Civilisation* (1936), p. 153: "the only point that can perhaps be urged against Pargiter's reckoning is that it is based on an average of eighteen years for each king, which may be considered as rather a low average for the number of kings counted in the reckoning."

V. Smith does not accept the years allotted by the Puranas for the Sisunagas. But Pargiter's 163 years for them is also rejected by him on the ground of its giving a low average of 163 years per king. He examines the reign of 10 English kings from Charles II to Victoria (inclusive) who reigned 252 years from 1649 to 1901 (two exceptionally long years of George III and Victoria included), and considers that on the analogy of English kings, 252 years should be the maximum possible average allowable to Sisunagas.[36]

A. Toynbee points out that in spite of the current controvercy over the dates of the kings of the First Dynasty of Babylon round about 2000 B.C., Eduard Meyer, Sidersky, Goetze, Sidney Smith, Albright, Poebel and seven other scholars are all agreed that 11 kings including Hammurabi ruled for 300 years in Babylon. This gives an average reign of 27.27 years per king.[37]

G. Bose takes several sets of English kings from William I to Edward VII and finds the average to range from 20.2 to 26.1 years.[38]

Omissions in the Puranas

An important fact to be borne in mind in connection with the average is the omissions of names in the genealogies. The Puranas themselves admit that the genealogies are not exhaustive. That there were omissions in the Puranic lists of kings can be inferred from the statements in the Puranas themselves. It is stated that mainly those kings of the Ikshvaku family who are important in the line are being spoken of here.[39] In another context, while successive names of kings from father to son are mentioned, there appears a sudden break in the successive list, and only a few kings of the 'great line' are given.[40] In other place,[41] the *Purana* expressly states that only the principal names of the Brhadratha kings have been recorded.

Pargiter admits that 'insignificant kings' have been omitted from the genealogies, but he says that no compensation need be made for the omitted kings. It will not be prudent, according to him, to increase the average of 12 years for the kings before the Bharata War to a higher figure of 18 or $13^1/_2$ years. To push back the antiquity of genealogies "to vast figures is to weaken *pro tanto* the trustworthiness of the tradition about them when everything depended on memory alone."[42]

It should be borne in mind that there were sets of people whose special duty was to commit to memory the names of kings of different dynasties, and their achievements. These people could certainly have been depended upon in regard to the accuracy of the genealogies.

Vamsa-vid in the *Vayu-Purana* ch. 88, sl. 69, denotes 'one who had acquired knowledge in the genealogies'.[43]

"The character of these men is emphasised by the superlative *Vamsa-viltama,* showing that there were men specially learned in genealogies, just as *Veda-vittamas* are alluded to, and these special genealogists were ancient and are cited as earlier authorities by *pauranikas.*"

Further it should be noted that the task of memorising king-names and their achievements would not have been heavy, because on the average of 25 years per reign, the number of kings in a thousand years is 40, which a professional narrator should not have found difficult to commit to memory. If 10% of the kings at the minimum were omitted, it works out to 4 names in 1000 years. The years covering the omissions are not being taken into credit of the total of years as a measure of caution.

In view of the average already considered and also in view of the facts that there were omissions in king-names, it will, I think, be reasonable to apply 27 years as average length of reign for 125 kings from Kshatraujas (of the Sisunaga dynasty) to Manu.[44] It works out as follows.

B.C. 3966	Accession of Manu		
93	kings before the Bharata War		
22	Brhadrathas after Bharata War		
5	Pradyotas		
4	Sisunagas (Sisunaga to Kshatraujas)		
Total 124	kings @ an average of 27 years per king	3375	years
B.C. 591	6 Sisunagas (Bimbisara to Mahananadin)	169	"
B.C. 422	9 Nandas	100	"
		Total 3644	"
Add		322	"
		B.C. 3966	"

Before concluding this section, I want to submit that the association of the Yugas (with their implications) with the genealogies leads to anomalies and difficulties. It is, therefore, necessary that the extent of the association should be kept at the minimum.

HISTORY OF INDIAN LAW OF MORALS

I now turn to another subject,—the history of Indian (mainly Hindu) morals, which, I think, offers a new field for research. An attempt may be made for carrying on studies for writing a history of Hindu morals, i.e. application of ethical principles to actions in practical life. In order to explore the possibility of writing such a history, its object and method should first be pointed out.

Writers on Principles of Hindu Ethics

Regarding the exposition of ethical principles, Hopkins, McKenzic, Buch, Maitra, Sivaswamy Aiyer and other scholars have made valuable contributions but their theses mainly are :

(1) To exhibit ethical teachings of the ancient Hindus including truthfulness, generosity, kindness, purity of soul, forgiveness, compassion, etc. (Hopkins);[45]

(2) To show non-existence of a philosophy of conduct or morality among Hindus, except in a crude form in the Rg-veda, the crudeness being due to Hindu moral life being based on (I.E.W. Hopkins, *Ethics of India* 1924) ideas which did not admit of a righteous over-ruling God (McKenzie);[46]

(3) To discuss the excellence of ethical ideas without reference to their practice in actual life (Maitra);[47]

(4) To find out the criteria of morality in Rta, Sastra, practices of the best people, in order to reach the highest goal *Moksha* (Buch);[48]

(5) To prove the mutability and change of Hindu moral rules and ideals in accordance with the changing environment (Sivaswamy Aiyer).[49]

Object and Method

The history of morals is different from what these scholars give us in their treatises. I have in view the example of Lecky's *History of European Morals,* in which the author defines his object as follows:

> "To trace the action of external circumstances upon morals.
> To examine what have been the moral types proposed as ideal in different ages.
> In what degree they have been realised in practice, and by what causes, they have been modified, impaired or destroyed."[50]

Criteria of Morals

An examination of the elevations and depressions in morals at different times should be preceded by an enquiry into their nature and foundation. Difficulties arise in settling the criteria by which morals are to be judged.

Lecky steers clear of such difficulties by reducing the criteria into 'intuitional' and 'utilitarian'. The former takes for granted that fact that man is naturally endowed with a power of perception of those qualities that he should prefer and cultivate, and of the opposites that he should repress. The latter criterion denies such power of perception and states that the notion of right and wrong is derived from the observation of the course of human life.

Criteria According to Manu, Yajnavalkya, etc.

With the above ideas of Lecky may be compared what is laid down in the codes of Manu and Yajnavalkya.[51] Sruti (Vedas), Smrti

(Manu, Apastamba, etc.), *Sadacara* (practices of virtuous men) and *svasya ca priyam-amanah* (actions agreeable to one's ownself) are the sources of principles by which human actions are to be regulated.

These four have been arranged in order of their superiority in regard to acceptance of moral rules derived from them in cases of conflict. In them are embedded the moral criteria of intuition and utilitarian experience. Sruti is the repository of injunctions revealed to seers. These injunctions are of the weightiest character.

For instance, it is enjoined in the *Taittiriya Upanisad*[52] that righteous conduct, reading, teaching, truthfulness, self-restraint and mental calm are to be pursued. The same *Upanisad*[53] also records the instructions which the teacher is to impart to his pupil at the completion of his study:

> "Speak the truth. Perform your duty. Do not neglect the daily reading (svadhyaya). Do not deviate from truth. Do not swerve from duty. Do not be careless about what is good. Do not be careless about your welfare . . . Regard your mother as a goddess. Regard your father as a god. The works which are unblamable ought to be performed and not any other."

The Moral Character of the Romans: How it Changed

Discussing the character of the Romans from Augustus to Constantine (i.e. from 1st century B.C. to 4th century A.D.), Lecky points out the influences that operated on the character of the Romans and the changes that were brought about in that character. Stoicism, says, he made the Roman austere, unselfish, fearless of death, and mindful of duties without expectation of reward. After the conquest of Greece by Rome, the sternness of the Romans underwent a change towards softness by coming into contact with cultured Greeks (including, in a large measure, emancipated slaves), exploitation of the colonies, influx of foreigners, facilities for travels, and the destruction of the power of the aristocracy. While the Roman character changed under different influences, the Roman society became corrupt and debased by despotism, slavery and atrocious amusements including gladiatorial shows.[54]

Afterwards came Christianity which combined the stoic feeling of brotherhood, Greek spirit of amiability and Egyptian sense of reverence and religious awe, and held the field for centuries.[55]

The above example gives an idea of how the moral character of a people has been traced through several centuries, and the same may be done by an historian of Indian morals.

Instances of Virtues

Instances of virtues and vices of individuals, mainly kings, are found in ancient Indian literature.

1. King Hariscandra (*cir.* 3102 B.C.) of the Ikshvaku dynasty is cited as *an example of the utmost generosity, truthfulness and patience.* To keep his promise, he gave away his kingdom and wealth to Visvamitra and became a destitute. Then to meet Visvamitra's demand for Dakshina he sold his wife and very young son at a price which fell short of the amount needed for Dakshina and supplemented it by giving himself away to Visvamitra, who in turn sold him to a man in charge of cremation ground. The most pathetic portion of the story is reached when Hariscandra's wife came to cremate his son but was unable to pay the necessary fee. At this stage the former recognised her. Then the husband and wife resolved to immolate themselves on the pyre lit for the son. At this time Visvamitra, highly pleased with his openhandedness, and devotion to truth, restored to Hariscandra, his wife and son.

2. King Dasaratha (*cir.* 2265 B.C.) of the same dynasty banished the heir-apparent Rama and agreed to instal Bharata in his place for the redemption of his two promises to Kaikeyi, his 2nd wife and Bharata's mother. This is an instance of *rigid adherence to veracity* which people of those days held in the highest esteem. Although the detriment to the kingdom due to non-installation of Rama as king was very great, yet the redemption of promises outweighed every other consideration. Another remarkable aspect of the incident is Rama's *great devotion to his father and his helpful attitude towards him to follow the way of truth.*

3. Karna (*cir.* 1455 B.C.) occupies a unique position among the personalities in the *Mahabharata. He earned a great fame by his extraordinary generosity. He used to grant wishes of every one who approached him.* Taking advantage of this, god Indra appeared to him one day before the Bharata War in the guise of a Brahamana and begged of him his armour and ear-rings, which made him invincible, in order to save Arjuna's life in the war that was soon to follow. Karna immediately complied, though he knew very well that thereby he made himself vulnerable to the deadly weapons of Arjuna. He had been forewarned that Indra would approach him for the purpose.

But his devotion to what he thought to be his duty was so great that he did not heed the warning and made the gift even at the risk of his life.

It would nat be reasonable to appraise virtuous acts of Hariscandra, Dasaratha and Karma from modern standpoint. Hopkings' accusation of Rama as betraying base suspicion and incredible brutality in regard to his acquiescence in Sita's fire-ordeal suffers from this drawback. Rama's conception of kingly duties viz. good government and happiness of his subjects outweighed all other considerations.

4. The Chinese traveller Hiuen Tsang records an episode of unparalleled sacrifice and munificence. During his stay in India, the king Harshavardhana (606-648 A.D.) held a great ceremonial at Prayuga which continued for 75 days. Large numbers of poor and religious men assembled there from all parts of the kingdom, and received gifts from the king.[56] The treasury was then emptied of all treasure, and even the personal belongings of the king including his jewels were distributed.[57] It is stated that six such ceremonials were held in 30 years, and each time the same programme was followed.

By the modern canons of public finance, the action of Harsha may not be justified, but it must be borne in mind that in his times, such munificence was an ideal virtue for which Harsha was held in great esteem.

Perfections Leading to Buddhahood

In this connection, mention may be made of the birth stories of the Buddha in the *Jatakas* and elsewhere, the moral significance of which cannot be missed. Though imaginary, they exemplify the virtues practised according to the conception of *Paramitas* or perfections leading to Buddhahood. The *Paramitas* are dana, sila, santi, virya, dhyana, prajna, etc.—virtues generally held in high esteem. Hopkins in his *Ethics of India* (p. 218) has referred, as an instance of what he thinks to be a moral aberration, to the story of prince Vessantara, who made a gift of his wife and children. Evidently, he has missed the spirit of the story, the object of which is to typify in its perfection the particular virtue of gift (dana) by a Boddhisattva whose attachment to worldly things was attenuated to an extreme point preceding the attainment of Buddhahood.

Examples of Vices

In the *Kautiliya,* and the *Kamandakiya,* kings have been advised to restrain the six senses. Jamadagnya and Ambarisa-Nabhaga are said to have ruled for a long time because of their ability to control the senses. Kings who failed to do so perished with their kingdoms, relatives and friends. The names of some such kings are given below:

Name of the king	*Place or dynasty*	*Demerit*
1. Bhoja or Dandakya	Videha	Lust (Kama)
2. Karala		
3. Janamejaya		Anger (Krodha)
4. Talajaneha		
5. Aila	Sauvira	Greed (Lobha)
6. Ajabindu		
7. Ravana		Self-conceit (Mana)
8. Durvodhana		
9. Dambhodbhava		Intoxication through Power (Mada)
10. Arjuna Haihaya		
11. Vatapi		Excess of self-Confidence (Harsa)
12. Vrsni		
13. Pandu		Addiction to hunting (Mrgaya)
14. Nala	Nisadha	Addiction to dice (Aksa)
15. Vrsni		Addiction to drinking (Pana)[58]

Dice as Cause of Rain

In the *Rgveda,* a gambler disillusioned too late relates his sad experience and warns: 'Do not play at dice, pursue tillage.'[59] Dice is mentioned as a *vyasana in Manu Samhita.*[60] Manu has advised the king to prohibit the play of dice in the kingdom,[61] but Yajnavalkya wants prohibition of deceptive dice only (Kutadyuta).[62]

Two glaring examples of ruination due to the play of dice are Nala and Yudhisthira.

The virtuous king Nala of the Nisadhas (Marwar) incurred the displeasure of Kali, because Damayanti, the princess of Vidarbha, selected Nala as husband at a Svyamvara in preference to the gods. Prompted by Kali (who felt frustrated), Nala's younger brother Puskara, an expert dice-player, made repeated challenges to Nala to play dice with him, which Nala could not refuse ultimately without prejuidice to his honour. Nala, who staked his kingdom, lost in the game, and left his kingdom with his wife and children. In consequence, he had to pass through untold miseries.

Yudhisthira (*cir.* 1455 B.C.) played dice on two occasions with disastrous results. On the first occasion, asked by Dhrtarashtra, he came with his brothers from Indraprastha to Hastinapura. Though at first very reluctant to play with 'that habitual winner Sakuni', he ultimately accepted the challenge on a point of honour.[63] The play began with stakes, and Yudhisthira lost in the game, one by one, his kingdom, wealth, the four brothers, himself, and even Draupadi. Taunts and abuses were heaped on the Pandavas and Draupadi by the Kauravas. Frightened by the threats of Bhima and Arjuna, Dhrtarashtra restored to Yudhisthira whatever he had lost. On the second occasion, the bet was the banishment of the vanquished from the kingdom for 13 years, of which the last was to be spent *incognito.* This time also Yudhisthira played with Sakuni, lost, and went into exile with Draupadi and the brothers.

These instances of challenge thrown out and accepted with the risks, taken on both sides, of dire consequences may well be compared to the practice of duels long prevalent in Europe and America. It is recorded in the *Encylopaedia of Social Sciences* (Vol. v, pp. 269-70) that in spite of repeated endeavours to prohibit duels in the different countries of Europe, and later on, in the U.S.A., they continued till the 19th century. During the last 400 years thousands of duels were fought. Henry IV of France granted 14,000 pardons to duelists. 4000 gentleman were killed in affairs of honour between 1589 and 1607. It was only after the International Anti-duelling Congress held in Budapest in 1908 that the practice of fighting duels was finally and effectively brought to an end.

Teacher and Pupil

The relation between the teacher and the pupil is an interesting and important subject in the history of morals. In ancient India, the Guru was held in high esteem. The pupil has been enjoined in the *Taittiriya Upanisad* to revere the Guru as a god.[64] Of the four *asramas* prescribed for the Hindus, the first Brahmacarya up to the age of 25 was to be spent as a student in the Guru's abode. Elaborate rules of conduct are laid down for the guidance of the teacher and the pupil.[65]

The narrative of Aruni and his Guru provides an outstanding illustration of the pupil's veneration for the teacher. One day, the Guru ordered Aruni to see that cultivated plots of land belonging to him were not flooded. Aruni, while watching, noticed a breach in the mound of earth around the plots, and as all his efforts to stop the rush of water through the breach failed, he laid himself down across the breach, and continued in that posture for hours till he was found out by the Guru. This gives as a glimpse of the nature of devotion shown by the pupils to the teachers. This helped to sustain the personal relation between the teacher and the pupil.[66]

An affectionate relationship used to grow up between the teacher and the student. This continued in the *catuspathis* up to the 19th century. The personal relationship extended even to universities like Nalanda, Valabhi, Vikramasila. R.K. Mookerji records in his *Ancient Indian Education* (1947), p. 565 that out of 10,000 monks residing in Nalanda 1,510 were teachers and 8,500 students. The average number was therefore 7 students per teacher.

The deterioration in the teacher-pupil relationship in the prevailing conditions in India has created a problem. This is attributable to various factors, such as impact of politics, limitations of economic resources, loose grip of religion and moral ideas upon the minds of the people, various distractions conflicting with single-minded devotion to studies.

There are many other virtues and their opposites,—individual or institutional,—which come within the purview of the history of morals. Lecky's work deals with many of them such as the advance of loans at interest, suicide, religious persecutions, celebacy, patriotism, philanthropy, infanticide, ascetism, and kindness to animals. A complete and fairly big chapter has been devoted by him to the treatment of the morals of women. This indicates that in India also, there is scope for a similar study if adequate efforts be made in that direction.

The 25th Centenary of the Buddha

The year 1956 has witnessed the 25th centenary of the Pari-nirvana of Gautama Buddha—the apostle of peace and love. Torn as the world is today by strife and violence in many places, the teachings of the great Buddha have a special importance for mankind.

The *Panca-Silas* inculcated by the Buddha have a great significance for the human society. They enjoin avoidance of (1) Killing, (2) Stealing, (3) Speaking falsehoods, (4) Incontinence, and (5) Intoxication. The *Neo-Panca-Silas* suggested by our Prime Minister for application to international relations owe their affiliation to the teachings of the Buddha regarding *Matri* (amity), *Karuna* (mercy), and *Upeksa* (equanimity). It is a matter for gratification that these precepts for the regulation of relations between nations have caught the imagination of many of them. The precepts are:—(1) Recognition of independence and sovereignty, (2) Non-aggression, (3) Non-interference in the internal affairs of other countries, (4) Mutual respect, and (5) Peaceful co-existence. The immense potentialities of the implementation of these *Silas* will have to pass through a course of trials through hard realities before they can actually transmit their beneficence. It is, however, hoped that in the long-run, success will result, and the combined efforts of the nations will lead to lasting goodwill and peace in these days of threats from the lethal use of atomic energy.

Handicap Due to Scarcity of Essential Books for Research

I want to point out that scholars are being very much handicapped for want of many books that are essential for research on ancient history. They have been out of print, and the World War has dislocated the trade in such books here as well as in Europe. It is fortunate that some publishers have already given their active attention of this inconvenience, and have recently printed books with original source material. Many other important works are in the process of publication. They should be printed as soon as practicable.

NOTES AND REFERENCES

1. *Calmet"s Dictionary of the Bible,* 1811, 3rd edition, vol. I, s.v. "Deluge".
2. *Encyclopaedia of Religion and Ethics,* ed James Hastings, 1911, 545 f.
3. Published by Ernest Benn Ltd., London, 1929. Cf. James Hastings' *Dictionary of the Bible* (1952), s.v. Deluge.
4. Suryakanta, *The Flood Legend,* Delhi, 1950, pp. 140-147.
5. *Wooley, op. cit.,* p. 27. Wooley's *Ur of the Chaldees* in the Pelican, vol. A. 27 (pp. 22-23) contains the same passages as quoted above. *Excavations at Ur* (1955) by the same author however mentions the depth of the silt as 11 ft. maximum and puts the area of the Flood as 300 miles x 100 miles— 30,000 sq. miles instead of 40,000 sq. miles as formerly stated in the Pelican volume, p. 24 (p. 35).
6. *Ibid.,* p. 22.
7. *Ibid., p.* 31.
8. 1 Krta = 4 × Kali)
2 Treta = 3 × Kali) = Mahayuga = 10 × Kali = 4,32,000 years.
3 Dvapara = 2 × Kali)
4 Kali = 432000 years)

   According to one astronomer, the annual rate of precession of the equinoxes is 49.8 seconds. The time taken by the earth for a revolution through a whole circle is $26024^{16}/_{166}$ years. This figure has been converted into an integer by multiplying it by 166. (See Cunningham's *Book of Indian Eras.* p. 4).

At the end of each Manvantara, a Flood (jalapalava) takes place.

14 Manvantaras = 1 Kalpa = 1 day of Brahma (the Deity)

Another Kalpa = 1 night of Brahma

At the end of each Kalpa, living beings meet with their destruction.

360 days (with nights) = 1 year of Brahma

100 such years = life span of Brahma

At the end of the Life-span of Brahma comes the dissolution of the Universe—Mahapralaya.

50 years of Brahma's life are over.

Of the present Kalpa, 6 Manvantaras are at an end and the 7th i.e., Vaivasvata Manvantara is on. Of the Mahayugas and Yugas of this Manvantara that are over, see the text above.

Surya-Siddhanta, I, 15-22 Slokas.

Vayu, ch. 5, 6 slk re. *pralaya* at the end of a kalpa:

Visnu, VI ch. 1, 2-6 slks. re. *pralaya* at the end of kalpa, and *Maha* (*Prakrita*) *pralaya* at the end of the life-span of Brahma.

9. P.C. Sen Gupta, *Anc. Ind. Chronology,* p. 45 *EI,* VI, pp. 11, 12; Fleet, *JRAS* 1911, p. 689.
10. Pargiter. *Dynasties of the Kali Age* (or *DKA* 1913), pp. 26 and 69. An Ancient Indian Historical Tradition (or *AlHT,* 1922), p. 287, he allots 80 years to Nandas (B.C. 402-322).
11. *Early History of India* (or *EHI,* 4th ed., 1924), p. 44.
12. Pargiter's translation, *DKA,* p. 68. For collated version, see p. 21.

हत्वा तषां यशः कृत्स्नं शिशुनागो भविष्यति।
वाराणस्यां सुतं स्थाप्य श्रयिष्यति गिरिब्रजम्।।

13. For convenience of comparison, the lists acccording to *Maliavamsa* (tr. *Geiger,* 1912, intro, p. XLVII) and *Matsya Parana* (Smith, *EHI,* 4th ed., p. 51) are given below:

Mahavmasa	*Years*	*Matsya P.*	*Years*
1. Bimbisara	52	1. Sisunaga	40
2. Ajatasatru	32	2. Kakavarna	26
3. Udayabhadda	16	3. Ksemadharman	36
4. Anuraddha	8	4. Ksemajit (or Ksatraujas)	24
5. Munda		5. Bimbisara	28
6. Nagadasaka	24	6. Ajatasatru	27
7. Sisunaga	18	7. Darsaka	24
8. Kalasoka	28	8. Udasin or Udaya	33
9. 10 sons of Kalasoka	22	9. Nandivardhana	40
10. 9 Nandas	22	10. Mahanandin	43

14. Geiger, *Mahavmsa* (tr.) II, 25-29, p. 12.
15. N. Dutt, *Gilgit Manuscripts,* Vol. III, pt. IV, intro. p. viii.

16. *Cambridge History of India* (or *CHI*), Vol. 1 (1955), p. 279.
17. *Ibid.*, p. 169.
18. *EHI* (4th ed.), p. 39, n. 1.
19. *Mahatamsa* (tr.), intro. p. xliv.
20. *Mahavamsa* (tr.), intro. p. xliv. See Appendix I.
21. The five Pradyota kings are:
    1. Pradyota
    2. Palka
    3. Visakhyayupa
    4. Ajaka
    5. Nandivardhan
22. *CHI* (1955), p. 277.
23. Haihayas comprised 5 families of whom Avantis were one (Pargiter, *AIHT*, p. 102). The territory called Avanti obviously took its name from the family. According to Rhys Davids (*Buddhist India*, 1955, p. 17):
    "It was called Avanti at least as late as the second century A.D. but from the seventh or eighth century onwards, it was called Malava."
24. Pargiter, *DKA*, p. 68.
25. प्रद्योतो मगधाधीशः
    (Pradyota the king of Magadha)—*Brhatkathamanjari*, Nirnayasagara ed., Sl. 99, p. 76.
26. प्रद्योतो मगधेश्वरः
    (Pradyota the king of Magadha)—*Kathasaritsagara*, Nirnayasagra ed., III, I, Sl. 19. p. 48.
27. Mahasena became distinguished as Canda Mahasena, because of his extreme austerities उत्कृत्याथ स्वमांसानि होमंकर्म स चाकरोत्।
    ...अतीव चण्डं कर्मेह कृतं चैतद् यतस्त्वया। अतश्चण्डमहासेन इत्याख्या ते भविष्यति।
    Kathasaritsagara Nirnayasagra ed. III, 37-40, p. 33.
    According to the same treatise, the genealogy of Mahasena is as follows:
    1. Mahendravarman
    2. Jayasena
    3. Mahasena
    4. Gopalaka and Palaka (king), pp. 33 and 40.
28. The ministers of Udayana deliberated thus :
    वयं राचहितं कर्मुः साधयामोऽस्य मेदिनीम्।
    परिपन्थी तु तत्रैकः प्रद्योतो मगधेश्वरः।।
    पार्ष्णिग्राहः स हि सदा पश्चात् कोपं करोति नः
    तत्तस्य कन्यकारत्नमस्ति पद्मावतीति यत्।
    तदस्य वत्सराजस्य कृते याचामहे वयम्।।
    KSS, III. 1 sls. 18-20, p. 48.
    (We are promoting the welfare of the king by expanding his territories. But

Pradyota the king of Magadha is an impediment on the way, as he can at any time attack us from the rear. For that reason, we would ask. for the king of Vatsa, his Pradyota's jewel of a daughter named Padmavati).

प्रद्योतो मगधाधीशो दूतेनाभ्यथर्य भूभुजे।
दातुं पद्मावतीमैच्छत् पार्वतीमिव शूलिने।।

Brhatkathamanjari, II, Sl. 93, p. 75.

(Pradyota, the king of Magadha, having requested the king, Udayana, through a messenger, offered Padmavati to him, as the offer of Parvati was made to Siva.)

29. I exclude Abhimanyu's name from Pargiter's Kaurava King-list (in the *DKA*, p. 4 because in Pargiter's royal genealogical table (AIHT, pp. 146-149), the 95th Paurava king is Abhimanyu who never resigned, and should therefore be replaced by Pariksit. So the Dynasty after the Bharata War began with Janamejaya from whom Udayana is the 24th king (inclusive of Janamejaya and Udayana).
30. ed. Ganapati Sastri, 1912, p. 4.
31. ed. Lacote, v. p. 286, p. 74.
32. ed. Madras Oriental Series, p. 9.
33. काञ्चुकीय: भो: श्रूयताम्। एषा खलु गुरुभिरभिहितनामधेयस्यास्माकं महाराजदर्शकस्य भगिनी पद्मावती वाम।
34. सान्त:पुरपरीवार: सदारसचिस्तत:।
सापौरश्रेणीवर्गश्च यानमध्यास्त भूपति:।। 284
पाक् प्राचीमगमद्दिशम्। 185
ददर्श दर्शकस्तत्र यानं यान्नगरोपरि। 286
पद्मावतीद्वितीयेन स च राज्ञाभिवादित:।। 287
इति प्रदक्षिणीकृत्य स भुवं सागराम्बराम्।
अवन्तिनगरीं प्रायात् प्रवृत्तोदकदानकाम्। 288
पद्योतस्य तदालोक्य रत्नप्रद्योतपिञ्जरम्।
किमेतदिति सन्देहदोलादोलमभून्मन:।। 290
सन्दिहन्मानसस्येति प्रद्योतस्य पुर: शरम्।
पातायामास वत्सेश: शनकैर्लेखिताक्षरम्।। 292
महासेनस्तमादाय चित्रमेतदवाचयत्।
राजन्नुदयनश्चौर: सदारस्त्वां नमस्यति।। 293
इति श्रुत्वा महासेनो जामातरममाषत।
चौराय दत्तमभयं तस्मादवतरत्विति।। 294

Brhatkathaslokasamgrah, ed. Lacote, V. 284-294, pp. 73, 74.

(The king was seated in the aero-vehicle with his spouses, members of the household, ministers, and some members of the city guilds, 284. At first he proceeded in the eastern direction, 285. *Darsaka saw the aero-vehicle moving over the city,* 286. *Hewas saluted by the king along with Padmavati,* 287. Thus while circling over the land girdled by the sea, he flew to the city of Avanti. 288. Looking at that shining jewelled framework of the vehicle, Pradyota's mind became agitated with the question as to what the thing was, 290. *In front of the inquiring Pradyota fell an arrow with a missive shot by the king of Vatsa,* 292. *The former took up the queer thing and perused it: 'Oh king, the pilferer Udayana with his wife is saluting you',* 293. *After this Mahasena shouted to his son-in-law: 'Pardon is granted to the pilferer. He may now come down',* *294*).

35. See Pargiter, *AIHT,* pp. 287 and 301, from which the following has been taken:

(From 322 B.C. to earlier times)

9 Nandas	80	years
10 Sisunagas (average 16$^{1}/_{2}$ years)	165	"
5 Pradyotas (average 10$^{1}/_{2}$ years)	53	"
16 Brhadrathas (Ripunjaya to Senajit, 6th king after Bharata War, 950 B.C. acc. to Pargiter,—average 14$^{1}/_{2}$ yrs.)	231	"
6 Brhadrathas (Brhatkarman to Somathi)	100	"
92 Steps up to Pururavas	1104	"
	1732	years
Accession of Candragupta	322	B.C.
Advent of Ailas	2054	B.C.

36. Smith, *EHI,* (4th ed.), p. 47.

37. A. Toynbee, *A Study of History,* vol. x (1954), p. 192.

38. Purana Pravesa (1934), p. 66.

1 William	I	1066-1087				
10 Edward	II	1307-1327	$\frac{261}{10}$	average	26.1	yrs.
19 Henry	VII	1485-1509	$\frac{202}{19}$	average	20.2	yrs.
28 Janus	II	1685-1688	$\frac{203}{10}$	average	20.3	yrs.
37 Edward	VII	1901-1910	$\frac{225}{10}$	average	22.5	yrs.
			$\frac{844}{37}$	average	22.8	yrr

39. एते इक्ष्वाकुदायादा राजानः प्रायशः स्मृताः।
बंशे प्रधाना ये ते स्मिन् प्रधान्येन तु कीर्तितताः।।
Vayu Purana, ch. 88, 213. See Pargiter. AIHT, p. 89.

40. तस्यान्ववाये महति महापौरवनन्दनः।
Matsya Purana, ch. 49, 72; *Vayu Purana,* ch. 99, 187.

Referring to the above, Pargiter writes: "In fact it will be found that gaps occur sometimes in the genealogies, and in one place it is frankly admitted that there is a *gap*".—*AIHT,* p. 89.

41. अत ऊर्ध्वं प्रवक्ष्यामि मागधेयान् वृहद्रथान्।
जरासन्धस्य ये वंशे सहदेवान्वये नृपाः।
अतीता वर्तमानाश्च भविष्याश्व तथा पुनः।
प्राधान्यतः प्रवक्ष्मामि गदतो मे निबोधन।
Vayu Purana, ch. 99, 294-5.
42. Pargiter, *AIHT*, p. 183.
43. *Ibid.*, p. 27.
44. See Appendix 11.
45. E.W. Hopkins, *Ethics of India, 1924.*
46. John McKenzie, *Hindu Ethics, a historical and critical Essay,* 1922.
47. S.K. Maitra, *Ethics of the Hindus,* 1925.
48. M.A. Buch, *The Principles of Hindu Ethics,* 1921.
49. Sivaswamy Aiyer, *Evolution of Hindu Morals,* 1935.
50. *History of European Morals* from Augustus to Chariemagne 1913 (London) in 2 volumes (468+372 pp.) written in 1869 at the age of 31, by the Irish scholar, E.H. Lecky, of remarkable ability.
Sivaswamy Aiyer (*op. cit.*, preface pp. ix and x) remarks that a good deal of study and research are necessary to write a history of Hindu Morals on the line of Lecky.
51. *Manu,* 2, 12; *Yajnavalkya,* 1, 7.
52. *Tain Up.* 1, 9: ऋतं च स्वाध्यायप्रवचने चा सत्यं च...।
दमश्च...। शमश्च...।
53. *Ibid.*, 11: सत्यं वद। धर्म चर। स्वाध्यायान्मा प्रमदः।
सत्यान्न प्रमदितव्यम्। धर्मान्न प्रमदितव्यम्। कुशलान्न प्रमदितव्यम्। भूत्यै न प्रमदितव्यम्। ...मातृदेवो भव। पितृदेवा भव। आचार्यदेवो भव। अतिथिदेवो भव। यान्यनवद्यानि मर्माणि तानि सेतिव्यानि। नो इतराणि।
54. Lecky, *History of European Morals,* Vol. 1, pp. 161-335.
55. *Ibid.*, p. 335.
56. *Smith, EHI.* p. 364:
"The assembly was attended by all the vassal kings and a Vast concourse of humbler folk estimated to number half a million including poor, orphans and destitute persons, besides specially invited Brahmans and ascetics of every sect from all parts of Northern India. The proceedings lasted for seventy-five days."
57. *Ibid.*, p. 365: "All being given away, he begged from his sister (Rajyasri) an ordinary second-hand garment."
58. *Kautilya,* 1, 3; *Kamandakiya,* ch. 1.
59. Rv, x, 34 1-14.

60. *Manu Samhita,* 27, 47.
61. *Ibid.,* 9. 221-227.
62. *Yajnavalkya Samhita,* 2, 202-06.
63. *MBh, Sabha* 58, 16; 59, 18.
64. *Taitt, Up.,* I, H.
65. *Manu Samhita,* ch. II.
66. K.M. Panikkar, *Hindu Society at Cross Roads,* 1955 (related portions), and *The State and the Citizen,* 1956, pp. 51 ff., 82 ff.

APPENDIX I

Chronology (Approximate) of Sisunaga and Nanda Dynasties According to V. Smith

(a)

S. No.	Kings	Col. 1 1st edition: 1904		Col. 2 2nd edition: 1908		Col. 3 3rd edition: 1914		Col. 4 4th edition: 1924		Col. 5 Acc. to N. Law		Col. 6 The Buddha
	Sisunaga Dynasty	*Probable Date of Accession*	*Length of Reign*	*Probable Date of Accession*	*Length of Reign*	*Probable Date of Accession*	*Length of Reign*	*Probable Date of Accession*	*Length of Reign*	*Probable Date of Accession*	*Length of Reign*	
		B.C.		B.C.		B.C.		B.C.		B.C.		B.C.
1.	Sisunaga	600		600		602		642		699		
2.	Kakavarna	For the 4 Kings together	81 years		72 years		72 years		60 years	108 years for the 4 kings @ 27 years each (average)		b. 693
3.	Ksemadharman											
4.	Ksemajit or Ksatraujas											
5.	Bimbisara	519	28	528	28	530	23	582	28	591	28	
6.	Ajatsaru	491	32	500	25	502	27	554	27	563	27	Nirvana 543
7.	Darsaka	459	25	475	25	475	24	527	24	536	24	
8.	Udasin or Udaya	434	33	450	33	451	33	503	33	512	33	
9.	Nandivardhana	401		417		418		470		479		
10.	Mahanandin		40		46		46		57		57	
	Total		239		229		230		229		277	
	Average		23.9		22.9		23.0		22.9		27.7	
	Nanda Dynasty											
11.	Mahapadma etc.	361		371		372		413				
12.	9 Kings: 2 Generations		40		50		50		91		100	
										422		
	Maurya Dynasty											
	Candragupta Maurya	321	24	321	24	322 (325?)	24	322	24	322	24	

APPENDIX II

Some Kings of the Royal Genealogies of Ancient India with Approximate Dates

(b)

Date of Accession	*S. No.*	*Ayodhya Ikshvaku Dynasty*	*Paurava Dynasty*
B.C. 3966	1	Manu	Manu
3939	2	Ikshvaku	Ila
3912	3	Vikuksi-Sasada	Pururavas
3858	5	Vena	Nahusha
3831	6	Prthu	Yayati
3804	7	—	Puru
3777	8	—	Janamejaya
3453	20	Yuvanasva	Tamsu
3426	21	Mandhatr	
3102	33	Hariscandra	
2913	40	Sagara	
2832	43	—	Dushyanta
2805	44	Dilipa I	
2778	45	Bhagiratha	
2481	56	Mulaka	
2373	60	Dilipa II Khatvanga	
2319	62	Raghu	
2238	65	Rama	
2103	70	Nala	
2076	71	Nabhas	Kuru
2049	72	Pundarika	Parikshit I
2022	73	Kshemadharman	Janamejaya II

APPENDIX II *(Contd.)*

Some Kings of the Royal Genealogies of Ancient India with Approximate Dates

(c)

Date of Accession	*Serial No.*	*Ayodhya Ikshvaku Dynasty*	*Paurava Dynasty*	*Magadha Dynasty*
B.C. 1860	79	Vajranabha	Aradhin	Brhadratha
1509	92	Amarsa	Vicitravirya	Jarasandha
1455	94	Brhatbala	Pandava	Sahadeva
		BHARATA BATTLE (1455 B.C.)		
1428	95	Brhatkshaya	Janamejaya III	Somadhi
1401	96	Urukshaya	Satanika	Srutisravas
1320	99	Divakara	Abhisimakrsna	Niramitra
1266	101	Brhadasva	Usna	Brhatkarman
1239	102		Citraratha	Senajit
861	116		Vasudeva	Ripunjaya
834	117		Satanika	Pradyota
807	118		Udayana	Palaka
699	122	Sumitra (End	Kshemaka	Sisunaga
591	126	of Dynasty)	(End of	Bimbisara
563	127		Dynasty)	Ajatasatru
479	130			Nandi-vardhana
422	132			Mahapadma
322	141			Candragupta Maurya

2

The Vedic Age

PROFESSOR GULSHAN RAI

INTRODUCTION

The Vedic Age in India may be said to be already existing at the time of Manu the son of Vaivaswata. He is a Vedic Rishi, and Suktas 27 to 31, invoked in praise of the Vishvadevas, in Mandala VIII of the Rigveda, are ascribed to him. Even at this early age the 33 gods of the Vedic Aryans are known. Manu Vaivaswata is supposed to be the first Aryan king of India after the Flood. I should think that the Vedic Age extended from the first settlement of Manu Vaivaswata in Northern India, right up to the time when the Nanda rulers of Magadha, in Bihar after destroying the Aryan kingdoms of Koshala, Kosambi, and Avanti, established an extensive empire in the country. From the dynastic lists given by F.E. Pargiter, in his Ancient Indian Historical Tradition, pp. 144-149, we find that there were 95 reigns or generations from Manu to Abhimanyu, son of Arjuna Pandva, and Somadhi, the Brihadratha king of Magadha. The Puranas then tell us that subsequent to the battle of Kurukshetra there were 22 kings of Brihadratha dynasty in Magadha. This dynasty was succeeded by the Pradyotas, who had 5 kings. They in their turn were succeeded by the Sisunagas, who had 10 kings. The last king of this dynasty was overthrown by Mahapadma Nanda. There are thus 37 kings from

Parikshita to Mahapadma Nanda. The Vedic Age may therefore be said to extend from Manu Vaivaswata to Mahapadma Nanda. During all this time there were 95 plus 37 or 132 reigns. This is a sufficiently long period.

Six Landmarks in the Vedic Age; Earliest after the Deluge

If we study carefully the events recorded in the Puranas during this long period of 132 reigns, we come across six definite landmarks in the traditional history of the Vedic Aryans. The first and the earliest landmark is the settlement of the Indo-Gangetic plains of India by Manu Vaivaswata after the Deluge, the story of which is first mentioned in the Satapatha Brahmana. After this the Suryavanshi kings seem to have established their kingdoms all over India. We do not know how long the Suryavanshis had exclusive domination over the country. The second great landmark in the traditional history of India is reached when the Chandravanshis come into India, under the leadership of Pururava; and established their headquarters at Pratishthana, near the confluence of the Ganges and the Jumna. From this time begins a struggle between the Suryavanshis and the Chandravanshis. The Puranas record a long Deva-Asura Sangrama, in which it is supposed as many as 12 wars were fought. These wars are supposed to have been concluded in the time of the Chandravanshi king Nahusha. The third great landmark in this traditional history is reached when Sasabindu, the Yadava king, destroys the other Chandravanshi kingdoms in the east, and north, and then later on the Haihaya kings Kritvirya, and his son Arjuna Sahastra-bahu, overwhelm the kingdoms of Kashi and Ayodhya. It was during these wars that Parusharama, the son of Jamadagni, comes into prominence. These destructive wars are concluded by the victories of the Suryavanshi king Sagar. The fourth landmark in the traditional history of the Vedic Aryans is when Rama Dasharathi, the Suryavanshi king of Ayodhya overthrows the power of Dashagriva Ravana, whose sway at that time, it seems, extended from Ceylon to the sources of the Godavri. A couple of generations after Rama Dasharathi, this period is brought to a close by the Dasha-ragya Sangrama of the Panchala king Sudas. The fifth landmark in this history is the Mahabharata War. After this War the Vedic Age begins to decay. This last period of decay is brought to a final close when the Vedic kingdoms are at length destroyed by Mahapadma Nanda. The birth of Buddha, and the rise of the Nandas in Magadha is the sixth and the last landmark in the long traditional history of the Vedic Aryans.

Manu was a South Indian King

The most important question for settlement is what was the original home of the Suryavanshis. If we study the story of the Deluge given in the Satapatha Brahmana, and the different Puranas, we find that Manu Vaivaswata whose personal name appears to be Satyvrata, was a South Indian king, and that when the Floods came he had abdicated from his throne, and was practising austerities in the Malabar country. We also find that the Dcccan was in the Vedic Age known as Dandeka Vana, after the name or Danda, one of the sons or Ikshwaku, the eldest son of Manu. In the Ramayana also, we find Rama asserting an ancestral claim on the South. If we can draw any inferences from these stories it is this that Manu Vaivaswata and his descendants came to Northern India from Southern India. Mr. Pargiter in his Ancient Historical Tradition comes to the conclusion that what we call the Suryavanshis were in reality the Dravidians. (*See* page 295 of his book).

Ten Suryavanshi Settlements in Northern India

According to the tradition recorded in the Puranas, the descendants of Manu Vaivaswata made ten settlements in Northern India. One branch, the Saudyumnas, established themselves in Orissa, Chhota Nagpur, and Southern Bihar. The second branch, the descendants of Nabhanedhishta, established themselves in North Bihar, and their settlement grew later on into the kingdom of Vaisali. The third son, not in the seniority of age, but in the order of settlements counting from the East, was Ikshwaku. He is supposed to have numerous progeny. Some of them, Danda and others, settled in the Deccan. One branch out of the descendants of Ikshwaku, settled in North-western Bihar, a tract well-known by the name of Mithila or Videha. The main branch, descendants of Vikukshi, remained at Ayodhya. The fourth son of Manu was Karusha, whose descendants settled in the Vindhyachal hills. The fifth son was Nabhag who is stated to have settled in the midlands, in between the Ganges and the Aravalis, in the one direction, and between the Saraswati and the Vindhyachals in the other direction. The sixth son was Dhrishta, who may be said to have settled in the Panjab. The ancient Balhikas and their subdivision the Jartakas (Jats) may be supposed to be a section of the descendants of Dhrishta. The seventh son was Narishyanta. He is stated to have, according to Matsya and Padma Puranas, a son, Saka. He settled in the trans-Indus regions. According to Manava Dharma Sasira, the Sakas became split up into four sections, the Paradas, the Kambhojas, the Pahlavas, and the Yavanas. If these statements record a correct tradition then the Paradas, or the Parthians, the Kambhojas or the modern Kambohs of the Panjab, the Pahlavas, or the ancient Iranian people, and the Yavanas, or the Ionians, or the Greeks, were all Suryavanshi Aryans, the descendants of Narishyanta, a son of Manu Vaivaswata. Then again if this tradition is correct then it appears that the Suryavanshi Aryans spread out of India, through Afghanistan, Iran, Mesopotamia, Turkey, to Greece; and that they did not come to India from the north-west. The eighth son of Manu Vaivaswata was Saryati, whose descendants settled in Gujrat-Kathiawar. The other two sons, Pramsu and Prasadra, may have settled in Rajputana and Malwa, respectively. In this way it seems the descendants of Manu Vaivaswata spread all over India, and the Middle Eastern countries, and from there one section, the Yavanas, penetrated Greece in Europe.

The Ten Suryavanshi Settlements and the Ten Rishi Families

There is one other point to be noted in this connection. It stems in each of these ten divisions or kingdoms, which were formed by the Suryavanshis, there arose a separate family of Vedic Rishis. In Vaisali, or Northern Bihar, we had the Angiras. The Brihaspatis who were an offshoot of the Angiras, established themselves, in the eastern lands of Bengal and Orissa. The Vasishthas attached themselves, to the descendants of Ikswaku in Mithila and in Ayodhya. The Agastyas were attached to the lands of the Karushas in Bundhelkhand. Kashyapa, the son of Marichi, settled in the Midlands, between the Saraswati, and the Vindhyachals. The Atris settled in the Panjab. The Bhargavas established themselves in Gujrat-Kathiawar, in the country of the Saryatis. These are the seven earliest families of Vedic Rishis. The other three were Kratu, Pulha, and Pulastya. The last named Rishi, is associated mostly with the Rakshsas and the other South Indian people. Pulha on the other hand is associated with the Kimpurushas, the Pisachas and people in the north-west. Valkhilyas who are supposed to be descendants of Kratu, may have belonged to Rajputana. It is curious, and quite significant that each section of the Manava or Suryavanshi race is associated with a separate family of Vedic Rishis. So long as the Chandravanashis do not appear on the scene; this division of territories among the descendants of Manu seems to have prevailed.

Origin of the Chandravanshis

The advent of the Chandravanshis was the first great landmark in the traditional history of Vedic India. They seem to have come into the Gangetic Doab like a wedge, may be from western Tibet and the lands where the Ganges and the Jumna have their sources. According to the stories given in the Puranas, the god Chandra had a son, Buddha, whose son was Gotama. This man Gotama is supposed to have married Ila, and their son was Pururava, the first Chandravanshi king in India. The Pauranic traditions point towards the mid-Himalayan regions as the original home of the Chandravanshi Aryans. The Matsya Purana connects Ila, the mother of Pururava with a country called, Ilavrita, which became known later on as Uttara Kuru. But it seems Ila was also assigned a place for residence at the confluence of the Ganges and the Jumna. It is just possible the original name of Allahabad may have been Ilabas, or Ilabad. Pratishthana, the first capital of the Chandravanshi king Pururava was near Allahabad.

Expansion of the Chandravanshis

But when Pururava established himself at Pratishthana, there was a powerful Suryavanshi kingdom of the Ikshwakus in the worth at Ayodhya, and a strong military power of the Suryavanshi Karushas in the south, in the hilly country of Bundhelkhand. So the new Chandravanshi power could not expand northwards into Oudh, nor southwards into Bundhelkhand. Naturally it could expand only in the east and in the north-west, into the Gangetic Doab, and Malwa and Eastern Rajputana. This is exactly what we find. On the death of Pururava, the new Chandravanshi kingdom is divided into two parts. The eastern and the home territories of Pratishthana are inherited by Ayu, the eldest son of Pururava, and the northern territories in the mid-Gangetic Doab come to the share of his second son Amavasu. Two generations after this, that is to say, after the death of Ayu and his son Nahusha, there is a further partition of the kingdom. The home territories of Pratishthana are inherited by Yayati, and his brother Kshatravriddha establishes a new kingdom in the east at Kashi or Benares.

Deva-Asura Sangrama

All Pauranic traditions agree that the Deva-Asura Sangrama, it contained as many as 12 wars, were concluded in the time of the Chandravanshi king Nahusha. Who were the parties to these wars? Were they between the Suryavanshis and the Chandravanshis? That is the opinion of Mr. Pargiter. (*See* his Ancient Indian Historical Tradition, pp. 305-307.) But if the Asuras are identical with Daityas and the Danavas, and the Rakshasas, then it is clear this Deva-Asura Sangrama cannot be a struggle between the Suryavanshis and the Chandravanshis, but between the Aryans and the non-Aryans. Was this a struggle between the Aryans and the Indus Valley people, or the Indo-Sumerians? We must in this connection collect all the details about the Deva-Asura wars, before we can give any opinion with regard to the racial particulars of the parties to this struggle. The Puranas are definite that the Daityas, the Danavas, and the Rakshasas, do not belong to the same race as the Devas, or the Aryans. But it is at the same time stated in many places that political and religious opponents are also very often given the name of Asuras. It is just possible there may have been religious and political differences between the Chandravanshis and Suryavanshis. There is one thing very significant in this connection. If we take up the dynastic lists of the different Suryavanshi kingdoms, we find that although the whole of India was distributed among the sons of Manu, yet we find dynastic lists only for the Suryavanshi kingdoms of Vaisali, Videha, Ayodhia, and to a very incomplete extent, of the Saryatis in Gujrat-Kathiawar. The dynastic lists of the kingdoms founded by the other sons of Manu; Nabhag, Dhrishta, Narishyant, Pramsu, and Prasadra, have all disappeared. What can be the explanation? If the Chandravanshi king Pururava, came in like a wedge from Uttara Kuru and Manasarover regions, directly into the Gangetic Doab, and established himself at Allahabad, and the Deva-Asura Sangrama was a struggle between the Suryavanshis and the Chandravanshis, in which the Chandravanshis, under the leadership of Nahusha finally came out victorious, then the disappearance of the dynastic list of the kingdoms established by Karusha, Nabhag, Dhrishta, Narishyanta, Pramsu, and Prasadra can be readily understandable. The Nabhagas had been established in the midlands of the Gangetic Doab. They were probably the first to be displaced by the Chandravanshi Pururava. As the Chandravanshis expanded in the time of Yayati and his sons, they must have displaced the Karushas in the south, the Pramsus, the Prasadras, and finally the Saryatis, in the west, the Dhrishtas in the Panjab, and the Narishyants in the north-west. With the destruction of these Suryavanshi kingdoms, it is natural all records concerning their dynastic lists disappeared. It may also be possible that the Suryavanshi kingdoms of the Dhrishtas and the Narishyantas in the north and the north-west may have, before the arrival of the Chandravanshis in the Gangetic Doab, been destroyed by the Daityas and the Danavas or the Indo-Sumerians, coming from the Middle East. It is also possible that the Chandravanshis who seem to have been allied in race to the Suryavanshis, may have been invited by the latter to help them in repelling the invasions of the Indo-Sumerians, and that after driving out the Daityas and Danavas, the former took possession of the whole of Northern India, west of the Ganges, and north of the Narbuda. In the absence of necessary material, it is useless to speculate on the nature of Deva-Asura Wars.

I. THE PRIMITIVE PERIOD 7350 B.C. TO 6400 B.C.

This first and the primitive period of the Vedic Age may be said to have lasted from the settlement of Manu at Ayodhya to the time of Nahusha. How long this first period of Vedic Age last ? Employing the method suggested by the late Mr. Bal Gangadhar Tilak, we should find out how many times has the list of Nakshatras been revised. The present list is headed by Aswini. The previous list was headed by the Krittikas, and the one previous to that was headed by the Mrigshira or the Orion. There was a list of Nakshatras earlier than that, which was headed by Punarvasu. The presiding deity of Punarvasu is Aditya. If the vernal equinox took place when the Sun was at the end of Punarvasu Nakshatra, that is to say 93°-20' of the Lanar Zodiac, and it was at the end of Revati, or zero degree, in 660 B.C. we can calculate backward. The annual precession of the equinoxes is supposed to be 50°-26'. The distance 93°-20' is equal to 336,000", which can be said to be covered by 6,685 years. Add to this, 660 years B.C. when the vernal equinox was at zero degree of the Lunar Zodiac. So the commencement of Aditya period can be put in this way in circa 7350 B.C. The Mrigshira or Orion period began when the vernal equinox was at 66°-40', that is say in 5440 B.C. So we may say that this primitive period of Vedic history began from 7350 B.C. I call this a Vedic period, because it was during this time that the Vedic gods, the children of the Adityas were born.

Moreover during this period too we have several Rigvedic Rishis. Among the Brahmanic Rishis, we had Brihaspati, Angira, Vasishtha, Agastya, Marichi, Kashyapa, Atri, Bhrigu, Chyavana, Puloma, and Prachetas. We have also during this period such Vedic Raj Rishis as Vivaswana, Yama, Yami, Manu, Nabhanedhista, Saryati, Pururava, Nahusha, and Yayati. Most of the hymns ascribed to these Rishis are in the tenth Mandala of the Rigveda, which is considered by the Western scholars to be later additions. But it is significant that the mantras in all these hymns do not mention any geographical names, or the names of persons belonging to ruling families which became well-known in later periods of the Vedic Age. No sufficient reasons have been given to show that most of the hymns in the first and the tenth Mandalas of the Rigveda belong to later periods. They may have been added later to the collection made by Krishna Dwaipayana Vyasa, but the subject-matter ascribed to the Rishis mentioned above seem to belong to a very much earlier age. Merely because the subject matter of these hymns is in a later style, and is difficult and obtruse, is no reason why they should be considered later. There are some Rishis in the tenth Mandala. such as Chakshu, Dhruva, Vena, and Prithu, which seem to belong to the ante-deluvian period. So it was during this primitive period of the Vedic Age. 7350-6400 that the earliest Rishis, who were mostly Brahmanas, and Suryavanshi Kings, lived, the gods and goddesses, whom the Vedic Aryans worshipped, were found and discovered; and again it was during this early period that persistent struggle against the non-Aryans, who may have been Indo-Sumerians, and between the Suryavanshis and the Chandravanshis, was carried on.

The Linguistic Survey of India Supports Indian Tradition

The linguistic survey of India made by Sir Grierson, shows that there is an inner ring of language, the Suraseni, which is surrounded by concentric circles of other allied languages. Towards the east of this innermost ring are Oudhi and Bagheli, in the south we have the Chhatisgarhi, and Bundheli. In the west we have the Malawi, and the Rajasthani, and in the north we have the Panjabi and the Pahari. All these languages in the first concentric circle are allied to one another, and are yet different from the innermost Suraseni. Beyond this first concentric circle there is another concentric circle of languages, Bihari and Uriya in the east, Marathi in the south-west, and Sindhi, Multani, Kekayi, Pothowari, and Kashmiri in the north-west and north. There is however an opening in Gujrat-Kathiawar in the west. This can be explained by the fact that the Suryavanshi kingdom of the Saryatis in this area was destroyed by the Chandravanshi Yadavas at a very early date. Beyond the second concentric circle of languages, there is Pashtu in the extreme north-west, and Bengali and Assamese in the east. This state of affairs can be explained satisfactorily, only when we accept the view that the people speaking the languages in the outer rings were the earlier inhabitants of the country, and that the people speaking the language in the innermost ring came into the country like a wedge. This people in the innermost ring could not have come from the north-west, because these areas are inhabited by people speaking languages of the outer rings, but from the mid-Himalayan regions, where the people speak Pahari languages, very much allied to the language in the innermost ring. The state of affairs exhibited by the linguistic survey of India supports the Indian tradition as exhibited in the Puranas. The primitive and the first period of Vedic history may be said to have ended with the conclusion of the Deva-Asura wars in the time of the Chandravanshi king Nahusha, in about 6400 B.C.

II. EARLY VEDIC PERIOD 6400 B.C. TO 5450 B.C.

Early Chandravanshi Kingdom

The early Vedic period may be said to have begun in 6400 B.C. with Nahusha and ended in 5450 B.C. with the victories of Sagar, the Suryavanshi king of Ayodhya. In the Ayodhya dynastic list given in Pargiter there are from Kakuststha to Sagar as many as 37 reigns. Kakuststha was a contemporary of the Chandravanshi Nahusha. Yati, the brother of Yayati, and the son of Nahusha was married to Go, the daughter of Kakuststha. It appears that the kingdom of Yayati was divided among his five sons. His eldest son Yadu obtained Malwa. His second son Turvasu received Bundhelkhand, which seems to have been conquered from the Suryavanshi Karushas. His third son Anu received territory in the north, probably in between Pratishthana and Kanyakubja, belonging to the Amavasu branch. The fourth son Druhyu may have obtained territories in between the Jumna and the Aravalis. So. Druhyus were towards the north of the Yadavas. Puru, the fifth and the youngest son of Yayati inherited the home territories of Pratishthana.

The Rise of the Yadavas

It is evident the first Chandravanshi power to rise into prominence was that of the Yadavas in Malawa. This kingdom is soon divided into two, that of the Yadavas and of the Haihayas. They seem to have first destroyed the Rakshasa power in Gujrat-Kathiawar, who are supposed to have overthrown the Saryati kingdom there. They then turned their attention towards the north, and drove their cousins the Druhyus across the Aravalis into the deserts of Marwar. From here they seem finally to have gone through Sind to Qandahar. Here they displaced the Suryavanshi Narishyantas, who were driven across the deserts of Seestan and the mountains of the Hindukush. Having reached the Middle Eastern countries the Narishyantas became divided into the four sections of the Parthians, the Kambohs, the Pahlavas and the Ionians. Having driven the Druhyus out of Eastern Rajputana, the Yadavas then turned their attention towards the east. Here they seem to have overthrown the power of their cousins the Turvasus in Bundhelkhand, and of the Pauravas in the midlands, near about Allahabad. Matinara, the Paurava king was a contemporary of the Yadava king Chitraratha. Gauri, the daughter of the Paurava king Matinara was married to Yuvanashwa II, the Suryavanshi king of Ayodhya. Their son Mandhatri of Ayodhya was married to Bindumati, daughter of the Yadava king Sasabindu, who is No. 20 in Pargiter's dynastic lists. The Yadava king Chitraratha, and his son Sasabindu were great kings. It is significant that after Tamsu, the son of Matinara, who is also 20th in the list, there is a great gap in the Paurava list. Probably Sasabindu had destroyed the Paurava kingdom. We also find that Gandhara, the grandson of Angara, in the Druhyu list are respectively 23rd and 21st in the list. It means that the Druhyu were driven out of Eastern Rajputana either by Chitraratha or his son Sasabindu. In the Turvasu list we find very few kings. They seem to have lost power at a very early stage. Then again in the Anavi list we find that in the time of the sons of Manamanas, 24th in the list, they are divided into two branches. Usinara, one of the sons of Mahamanas is found in the Panjab, and from his second son Titikshu, is descended the Anavi dynasties of Bengal. The only inference we can draw from this is that the Anavis who were established in the mid-Gangetic Doab, in between Kanouj and Allahabad were after their defeat at the hands of the Yadavas, split up into two sections. One proceeded northwards into the Panjab, and the other was driven to seek their fortunes in Bengal. In the Panjab, the Anavis displaced the Dharshtakas, the Suryavanshi descendants of Dhrishta.

Anavi Kingdom in the Punjab

Usinara the Anavi king, after his arrival in the Panjab, probably established himself at Multan. We are told that after the death of Usinara, his Anavi kingdom was divided among his five sons. His eldest son Sivi succeeded to the throne at Multan (Moolasthan). His other son Nrga established a separate kingdom in the present district of Montgomery, and northern parts of modern Bikaner State. This State was later on known by the name of the Yaudheyas. Their modern representatives the Panjabee tribe of the Joyas, still live in this part of the province. They were known to the Greek authors of the time of the Macedonian invader, Alexander the Great. They were also known in the time of the Guptas, as a Republican State. The third son of Usinara, founded the State of Navarashtra. It is not known where this Navarashtra was. The fourth son of Usinara, Krimi, founded the State of Krimila. The location of this State is also not known. The fifth son of Usinara was Suvrata, who is said to have founded the State of the Ambashthas. This State was probably in Eastern Panjab. Sivi Aushinara, king of the main branch of the Anavi kingdom in the Panjab, is a well-known Vedic king. King Sivi, son of Usinara is said to be a Vedic Rishi. Sukta 179 of Mandala X of the Rigveda is ascribed to him. But it appears the Anavi kingdoms did not remain strong military and political powers for long. With the rise of the Haihayas, under the leadership of Kritvirya and Arjuna Sahasrabahu, and with the subsequent victories of Sagar of Ayodhya, the military strength of the Anavas was destroyed. It seems after this the Anavi territories in the Panjab and Sind, continue to be split up into a large number of small monarchical and republican States. That continues to be the state of affairs right up to the time of Alexander the Great, and even after that. On his death his kingdom was divided amongst his four sons. The home territories of Multan seem to have remained under his eldest son Vrishadarbha, whose descendants continue to be called the Sivis. They were found in these parts right up to the time of Alexander's invasion His second son Suvira established a separate kingdom in Sind, which was called by the name of Sauvira. His third son Kekaya established himself in the northern parts of the kingdom, now represented by the Panjab districts of Gujrat and Shahpur in between the Jhelum and the Chenab. Madraka, the fourth son of Sivi Aushinara founded still another kingdom, with its capital at Sakala, on the banks of the river Apaka. This town still exists under the name of Sialkot (Shalyakot). This Madraka kingdom comprised the central districts of Lahore Division of the present day Panjab, and the Jummu province of Jummu and Kashmir State. The State of the Madrakas was a well-known Vedic kingdom Madri, a princess of this country was the mother of the Pandava brothers, Nakula and Sahadeva.

The Gandharvas and the Gandharas

It appears that the territories of Kashmir Valley, together with the Panjab districts north of the Salt Range, the present Frontier Province, and eastern districts of modern Afghanistan, formed the ancient land of the Gandharvas. I should think that the Gandhara of the classical times was not the Gandhara kingdom founded by the descendants of the Chandravanshi Druhyu, but the country of the Gandharvas of Vedic times. These Gandharvas were neither Suryavanshis, nor Chandravanshis. The Gandharvi, Urvashi, is said to have married Pururava, the first Chandravanshi king of Pratishthana. The kingdom of Gandhara, founded by the descendants of Druhyu, was more to the south, south-west of Ghazni, near about modern Qandahar and Quetta. They seem to have arrived in these parts, after they had been driven out of Eastern Rajputana across the Aravali hills, into Western Rajputana and Sind, by the Yadavas, and later on driven from Marwar and Sind by the Anavi Sauviras. Many of these Anavi and Druhyu kings are mentioned in the Rigveda.

Struggle Between the Suryavanshis and the Chandravanshis

Turning back towards the Yadavas, it appears the Yadava power decayed after the death of Sasabindu. But now Ayodhya under king Mandhatri, who was son-in-law of Sasabindu, became the most important king in upper India. He seems to have taken possession of Kanyakubja and Paurava kingdoms, and then proceeded through the Vindhyachals to the banks of the Nerbuda. He is said to have fought also against the Anavas and the Druhyus, in the north-west. Purukutsa, the son of Mandhatri seems to have continued the conquests of his father. But being connected by matrimonial alliances with the Yadavas they do not seem to have touched their dominions. Mandhatri had another son, Ambarisha, whose descendants known by the name Harita Brahmanas, are known as hymn makers. After the death of Purukutsa, the sons of Mandhatri, lose their paramountcy in upper India, and then the Chandravanshi kingdoms in the west again rise into prominence. Among the Yadavas, now the Haihayi branch, rises into prominence. They re-occupied Malwa, and Mahishmanta 23rd in Pargiter's dynastic list, founded the city of Mahishmati on the banks of the Nerbuda. Having taken possession of Malwa, the Haihayas, under the leadership of Bhadrashrenya, son of Mahishmanta turned his attention towards the east, took possession of the Paurava kingdom, round about Allahabad, and then invaded the kingdom of Kashi. The ancient Saryati kingdom of Anarta, in Gujrat-Kathiwar, was also, included in the Haihaya empire.

The Wars of Parashurama and Sagar

The Rishis of the Bhargava family who were residing in Anarta, being dissatisfied with the state of affairs there, left the country, and took up their residence in the territories of Kanyakubja. But some time after this the Haihaya king Kritavirya and his son, Arjuna Sahasrabahu invaded the kingdom of Kanyakubja also. We find that after this, the dynastic list of Kanyakubja State suddenly stops. The last king of Kanyakubja was Gadhi, and his son, Vishwaratha, becomes now a Vedic Rishi under the title of Vishwamitra. Harishchandra seems to be a contemporary of Arjuna Sahasrabahu and Vishwamitra. At length the Haihaya kings attack even Ayodhya, and king Bahu of this State is driven out of his kingdom, and is compelled to take refuge in the forest Ashrama of Jamadagni Aurava, belonging to the Bhargava family, in the Kanyakubja territory. King Bahu died in this Ashrama, and his widowed queen gave birth here to a posthumous son, known by the name of Sagar. In this old kingdom of Kanyakubja, Parashurama, the son of Jamadagni Bhargava organised a strong opposition against the Haihaya kings. The Bhargavas had at first been compelled to leave their ancestral home in Anarta, and now in their new home in the kingdom of Kanyakubja too they were not left in peace. So they now tried to strengthen their position by matrimonial alliances with ruling families. Richika Aurava, a Rishi of this family married Satywati, a daughter of king Gadhi of Kanyakubja. Their son was Jamadagni, who married a princess of the royal family of Ayodhya. As I have stated Sagara, the son of ex-king Bahu of Ayodhya was born in their Ashrama. Talajangha, a successor of the Haihaya king Arjuna Sahasrabahu had in the meantime, conquered Ayodhya, overrun the kingdom of Kashi, and was contemplating the invasion of Videha in the east. It was at this time that Parashurama, son of Jamadagni formed a combination of Vaisali, Videh, Kashi, and

Ayodhya, which put up a fight against Vitihavya, the successor of Haihaya Talajangha. The Haihaya king was defeated, and compelled to take refuge with another Bhargava Rishi. After this the dynastic list of the Haihayas practically stops. Vitihavya, the king, now becomes Vitihotra the Brahmana. Gritsmada, and his descendants, the celebrated Rishis of most of the hymns of the second Mandala of Rigveda, belong to the family of the Haihaya king Vitihavya. After the destruction of the power of the Haihayas, Yadava imperialism ends. King Vidarbha of the Yadava family retires into the Deccan, and there founds the kingdom of Vidarbha. The whole of Northern India, now acknowledges the sovereignty of Sagar. The Puranas tell us that the victories of Sagar and Parashurama conclude the Kritrayug, or the early period of Vedic Age. After these wars the older kingdoms of the Druhyus, the Panjab Anavas, the Turvasus, the Pauravas, and Kanyakubja, all disappear. The Yadavas retire into the Deccan. But in the east the kingdoms of Bengal Anavas, Vaisali, Videh, Ayodhya, and Kashi continue to exist. The wars of Sagar were really a victory for the Suryavanshis, and a defeat for the Chandravanshis. The most important Vedic Rishis of this period were Jamadagni (*Rigveda,* VIII, 101; IX 62, 65, 67; and X, 110, 138, 167); Vishwamitra, (3rd Mandala of Rigveda, his son Ashtaka (*Rigveda,* X 104); Ayasya (*Rv.* IX 44 46; and X 67-68); Gadhi of Kanyakubja (*Rv.* III 19-22); Gritsmada, son of Sunahotra, king of Kashi (*Rv.* II 17-27; and 30-33); Madhuchhanda, son of Vishwamitra (*Rv.* I 1-10; and IX 1); Sunnasepa, son of Ajigarta (*Rv.* I 24-30; and IX 3).

This early Vedic Period, called the Kritayug, lasted from 6400 B.C. to 5450 B.C. It was towards the end of this period that the list of Nakshatras which was headed by Punarvasu had to be revised. With the end of the Aditya Period also ended Kritayuga.

III. MEDIEVAL VEDIC PERIOD 5450 B.C. TO 4000 B.C.

The Bharatas and the Panchalas

After the victories of Sagara there was the beginning of a new order in India. On the destruction of old kingdoms new kingdoms came into existence. In the east, the Titikshu branch of the Anavas, who had been driven out of the Mid-Gangetic Doab, came and settled in Anga, modern Bhagalpur in Bihar. One of the descendants of Titikshu, known by the name of Bali founded a kingdom in these parts. On his death his kingdom was divided among his five sons.

They formed the five eastern states of Anga (Bhagalpur), Banga (Bengal), Kalinga (Orissa), Pundra (Rajshahi), and Suhma (Chhota Nagpur). These kingdoms carry on their existence right up to the close of this Vedic Medieval period. After the death of Sagara, the Paurava kingdom near Pratishthana (Allahabad) was revived. It appears that on the destruction of the Paurava kingdom in the previous period by the victories of the Yadava king Sasabindhu, and the subsequent occupation of their territories by the Haihayas and the Ikshwakus, the royal family of the Paurava kings took refuge in the hilly regions of Bundhelkhand. One of these princes Dushyanta was an adopted son of the Turvasu chief Marutta. After the death of Sagara, the hold of the Aikswakus on the Paurava territory became weak. Dushyanta got an opportunity to take possession of his ancestral kingdom which had been lost by his remote ancestors, more than twenty generations back. He was married to Sakuntala, who appears to be a daughter of Vishwamitra, and was brought up in the forest Ashrama of one Rishi, Kanwa, belonging to the family of Kashyapa. Bharata was the son of Dushyanta and Sakuntala. This king was a great conqueror. He extended his dominions northwards and the frontiers of his state extended right up to the banks of the Saraswati. From this time onwards the Pauravas begin to be called the Bharatas. One of the most important kings in this dynasty was Hastin, who is said to be the founder of Hastinapur, whose ruins still exist in Meerut District. He is No. 51 in Pargiter's list. After the death of Hastin, this kingdom of the Bharatas became divided amongst the different members of his family. One of his son, Ajamidha continued to rule at Hastinapur. His other son, Dwimidha, established his kingdom probably in Kumaon Division of present day United Provinces. This kingdom of the Dwimidhas seems to have continued throughout this Medieval Vedic period. But there is very little known about this kingdom. After the death of Ajamidha, his kingdom seems to have been divided into three parts, namely, North Panchala, South Panchala, and Hastinapur. So according to the Pauranic tradition, the Panchalas were separated out of the Bharatas. It appears that the kingdom of North Panchala comprised the territories of modern Rohilkhand in the United Provinces. The territories of South Panchala took the place of the old kingdom of Kanyakubja (Kanouj) and consisted of the districts of Agra Division in the Gangetic Doab, and of present day Cawnpore. The kingdom of Hastinapur consisted of Meerut Division of the United Provinces, and Ambala Division in the Panjab, together with the district of Delhi. But it seems the kingdom of Hastinapur was soon eclipsed by the more powerful kingdom of North Panchala. The most important kings in the North Panchala dynasty were Mudgala, Vadhryashwa, Divodasa, Srinjaya and Sudas. Divodasa appears to have been the contemporary of Dashratha of Ayodhya. It appears that the Hastinapur kingdom was split up into a number of small principalities. Most of the princes in this Hastinapur dynasty take to literary pursuits. After Ajamidha, for about twenty generations there is hardly any king mentioned in the Hastinapur line. The Kanwa family of Vedic Rishis is supposed to have descended from Ajamidha. Probably they belonged to the Hastinapur line, which is practically blank so far as their political power in this part of the country is concerned.

The Yadavas and the Deccan

The Yadavas after the victories of Sagar had withdrawn into the Deccan, and founded the kingdom of Vidarbha. But after the death of Sagar the Yadavas again spread out towards the north, and become masters of the territory which afterwards comes to be known by the name of Chedi. The most important king of Vidarbha was Bhimaratha. He was father of the celebrated Damyanti, who was married to Nala, king of Nishadha. Their daughter Indrasena was married to Brahmishtha, son of the North Panchala king, Mudgala. Some ten generations after Bhimaratha, we find the Yadavas to have spread out so far to the north that they are now masters of Mathura, which was founded by Madhu, who is 61st in Pargiter's list. But in the time of Rama, son of Dasharatha, it seems Mathura was taken away from the Yadavas. So it appears the Chandravanshi Aryans had occupied some parts of the Deccan some twenty-five generations before the time of Rama. It means that the Chandravanshis were in occupation of Vidarbha more than 800 years before Rama of Ayodhya goes to the Deccan. The kingdoms of Sugriva and Ravana must have therefore been south and west of the Yadava kingdom.

The Wars of Sudas

After the death of Rama, the power of Ayodhya again declined. The North Panchala kings again come into prominence. Some four or five generations after Rama, Sudas, the North Panchala king, undertakes great military operations. He fights against a confederation of ten powers. They are the five Chandravanshi powers of the Yadavas, the Turvasus, the Pauravas, the Anavas and the Druhyus, and the five trans-Indus powers of the Pakhtas (Pathans), the Alinas, the Bhalanas, the Shivis, and the Vishnanin?. These five latter tribes may have either been the remnants of the Suryavanshi Narishyantas, who in the earliest times occupied the trans-Indus regions, or they may have belonged to the Indo-Sumerian people. In these wars king Samvarana belonging to the Bharatas was defeated. He was compelled to give up Hastinapur, and take refuge on the banks of the Indus in the west. The confederate armies of the ten powers were defeated by Sudas on the banks of the Parusini (modern Ravi river in the Panjab). Kavasha Ailusha, the purohit of Samvarana was drowned in the Ravi. Sukta 33 of Mandala X is ascribed to this Kavasha. After many years' exile in Sind, Samvarana was able with the assistance of Samvarchas Vasistha, to recover his kingdom from Sahadava, a successor of Sudas. Kuru was the son of Samvarana. Kurukshetra is known after this king Kuru. His son Parikshila I succeeded to the throne of Hastinapur; and his son Janamejaya II was consecrated by Tura Kavesheya, who was very probably a descendant of Kavasha Ailush, the purohit of his great grandfather, Samvarana.

Date of the Wars of Sudas

The wars of Sudas bring to a close the Medieval Vedic Period, or Treta-yuga. These wars also bring about a new order of things in India, in the same way as the wars of Sagar had brought about a new order of things at the close of the previous Satya-yuga period. The dynastic list of Pargiter exhibits some 30 generations between the time of Sagara and Sudas. It appears that soon after the beginning of this Medieval period the Vedic Aryans discovered the different Nakshatras, and a regular Lunar Zodiac was formed. It may be calculated that in 5400 B.C. the Sun was in the Vernal equinox at the end of Mrigshira Nakshatra that is to say at 66°-40'of the lunar ecliptic. In 4250 B.C. the Vernal equinox was at the end of third quarter of Mrigshira, the winter solstice was at the end of the Purva Bhadrapada, the autumnal equinox was at the end of the 1st quarter of the Mula Nakshatra, and summer solstice at the middle of Uttara Phalugni. At that time the year began with the autumnal equinox, when the Sun was in the Mula Nakshatra. Hence the Mula Nakshatra was the first Nakshatra in the list of Nakshtras. That is why it was called "Mula". But when the Sun was in Mula, the full moon must have been in Mrigshira, that is to say the first month in the year was Mrigshira, and it was called Agrahayana (Aghana of Hindustani). So this list of Nakshatras with Mula Nakshatra at the head must have been drawn up between the years 4250 B.C. and 4000 B.C. As this year began with the autumnal equinox, it was called the Sharada year.

Separation of Parsis from the Aryans

There is another point to be noted in this connection. At this time when the year began with autumnal equinox, the Sun was in the Mula Nakshatra and the moon in the Mrigshira. Since at this time the Sun at the Summer solstice was in Purva Bhadrapada, it is clear the Dakshanayana, or the Pitriyana began with the Purnima of Bhadrapada. The Sharaddha ceremonies of the Hindus even today start with the Purnima of Bhadrapada. It is understood some sort of Shraddha for the ancestors is performed among the Parsis also. This shows that the Indo-Aryans and the Iranians were still living together, at the time when Shraddhas were instituted. The Iranians must have therefore separated from the Indo-Aryans after the wars of Sudas, at the end of Treta-yuga. I would allot about 1450 years to the 30 generations from Sagar to Sudas, that is to say 5450 B.C. to 4000 B.C.

IV. LATER VEDIC PERIOD, 4000 B.C. TO 3000 B.C.

New Order After the Wars of Sudas

After the wars of Sudas, new Chandravanshi kingdoms come into power. The old Suryavanshi kingdoms of Videha and Koshala continue to exist. The old Chandravanshi kingdoms of the Eastern Anavas, the Bharatas, the Dwimidhas, the North Panchalas, and South Panchalas, remain in existence, but in decayed conditions. The Yadavas become split up into the Andhakas and the Vrishnis. The Yadava kingdom of Chedi ceases to exist. The kingdom of Kashi is heard no more after the wars of Sudas. The most prominent kingdom that rises into prominence after Sudas is that of Kuru. After the wars of Sagar the ancient Pauravas recover their position under the name of the Bharatas. After the wars of Sudas, the Bharatas reappear as a great power under the name of the Kauravas. We are told that Kuru had three sons, or branches, known after Parikshit I, Jahnu, and Sudhanwan. Parikshit I was succeeded by his son Janamejaya II. But he and his brothers, and their descendants, for some sins, mentioned in the Vedic literature, lose all political power. The Rishi Yajnavalkya deplores the fate of this Janamejaya and his descendants. So his line suddenly ends. But this Janamejaya is by some of our historians mixed up with a later Janamejaya, who is a Post-Mahabharata king. This later Janamejaya, whom we may call Janmejaya III, lived some 20 generations after Parikshit I, the son of Kuru. I have discussed this matter in a paper I read before the Second Indian History Congress held at Allahabad. It has been published in the proceedings of this Congress.

Kingdoms of the Later Vedic Period

After the sudden ending of the line of Janamejaya II, Tahnu, the line of the second son of Kuru succeeded to the throne of Hastinapur. The line of the third son Sudhanwan, divided into two. One branch of the Brihadrathas, become master of Magadha, and the other of the Vasus, takes possession of Chedi, formerly in occupation of the Yadavas. The most important king of the Brihadratha line, towards the end of this period was Jarasandha; and the most important king of the new Chedi line towards the end of this period was Shishupala. The most important king of the Eastern Anavas was Karna, Ugrasena, and his son Kansa, who was a son-in-law of Jarasandha of Magadha, belonged to the Andhaka branch of the Yadavas, and Sri Krishna, son of Vasudeva, belonged to its Vrishni branch. It seems that during this later Vedic period the great rival of the parent Hastinapur power was the Chedi power, founded by Vasu. The descendants of Vasu had become masters of Magadha, Karusha, Kausambi, Chedi, and Matsya, countries. Under Jarasandha, the Magadha rulers, came into conflict with the Vrishnis, under the leadership of Krishna, son of Vasudeva. The Vrishni Yadavas were connected in matrimonial alliance with the Kauravas, through Pandu, the younger brother of Dhritrashtra, the Kaurava king of Hastinapur. The Vrishni branch of the Yadavas, and the Pandava branch of the Kauravas combined against the new imperial power of Jarasandha, who had now extended his empire right up to the banks of the Jumna in the west.

Mahabharata War

The Vrishnis had been forced to retreat from the neighbourhood of Mathura, and taken refuge in Dwarika, the ancient Kushasthali of Saryati kingdom of the Suryavanshis. With the help of the Pandava brothers, the Vrishnis were able to overthrow Jarasandha and his imperial power. As a result of this the Pandavas now became the paramount power in Northern India. In the Medieval Vedic period, there was rivalry between the two branches of the Pauravas, the Bharatas and the Panchalas. In the later Vedic period the Kauravas, the representatives of the ancient Bharatas became split up into the two rival branches of the Kauravas and the Chaidyas. The rise of the Brihadrathas, a section of the Chaidyas, to an imperial position, and their conflict with the Vrishni branch of the Yadavas, and their allies the Pandavas, led to the Mahabharata War. In this war the Chaidya power was destroyed, the main Kaurava branch disappeared, and one of their sections, the Pandavas, who became allied with the ancient Panchalas, came out victorious. It seems after his war the Pandava section of the Kaurava branch of the Bharatas became combined with the ancient Panchalas, and after this they are mentioned together.

Waves of Aryans Emigrants from India

It is probable that after the Mahabharata War, the Kauravas, the main branch of the Bharatas, left the country, and they became another wave of emigrants to the west. It seems at the commencement of each new order in India, there was an outflow of Aryans from India. The first outflow took place when the Suryavanshi Narishyants spread out beyond the trans-Indus regions. The second outflow took place during the Deva-Asura Sangrama, the struggle between the Aryans and the Sumerians. The third outflow from India took place when the Chandravanshis displaced the Suryavanshis in Northern India, in the territory in between the Ganges and the Hindukush, and the Himalayas and the Nerbuda. It was after this that this whole region occupied by the Chandravanshi or Induvanshis, began to be known as Indu-desha, or India, or Hindu-Sthana. The fourth outflow of the Aryans from India took place after the wars of Sagar; the fifth after the wars of Sudas, and the sixth after the wars of Mahabharta. There may have been some other subsidiary outflows also. There are five Aryan linguistic units in Europe, and the sixth in Iran, and Persia.

Introduction of Animal Sacrifices

On the conclusion of the Mahabharata War, Yudhishthira and Parikshit, grandson of his brother Arjuna, became kings of Hastinapur. I have discussed in Paper, "Two Parikshitas and Three Janamejayas in the Kaurava line of Hastinpur," and published in the Proceedings of the Second History Congress held at Allahabad, that there was an interval of 1000 years between Kuru and the Post-Mahabharata Janamejava III. So the fourth period of Vedic Age beginning after the Wars of Sudas and ending with the Wars of Mahabharata lasted from 4000 B.C. to 3000 B.C. It seems animal sacrifice began among the Chandravanshis, during this period. Vasu Chaidya seems to have been its advocate. We are told sacrifices or Yajnas, with fire, were originally introduced by Pururava, the first Chandravanshi king. The Suryavanshis, who were advocates of Ahimsa, remained at first content with Tapasya.

Construction of the Rigveda

It is interesting to note that the members of those royal families, which lost political power, subsequently became known as hymn makers. A large number of royal families had lost political power as a result of the wars of Sagara. The descendants of Vitihotra, the Haihaya king, became the well-known hymn makers, the Gritsmadas or the Saunakas. After Ajamidha, when the Bharatas at Hastinapur became eclipsed, their family gave rise to the Kanwa family of hymn makers. The Maudgalyas, a well known priestly family, rose from among the descendants of Mudgala, the famous king of North Panchala. The Gargyas belonged to the royal Paurava line. The Medieval Vedic period is distinguished with the greatest activity in hymn making. The greater portion of the Rigveda was constructed during this period. The hymn making activity continues during the later Vedic Period which is concluded by the Mahabharata War.

V. DECAY OF VEDIC PERIOD, 3000 B.C. ONWARDS

Post-Mahabharata Kingdom

After the battle of Kurukshetra, which on astronomical grounds I fix in October 3140 B.C. begins the decay of Vedic Age. The date given in the Mahabharata for the death of Bhishma Pitamaha enables us to fix the date of the battle of Kurukshetra. We are told that he died on 8th Shukla Paksha Magha, at noon, about 12 hours after the Uttarayana had begun in the preceding midnight, in the Rohini Nakshatra. At the present moment the Uttarayana begins in the Mula Nakshatra. So there has been precession of the Equinoxes from Shatabhija to Mula since the time of Mahabharata. The coronation of Yudhishtra took place in January 3139 B.C.; and the Pandava brothers retire to forests after the destruction of the Yadavas, 37 years after assumption of power, that is to say in 3102 February. From this time is supposed to begin the Kaliyuga. At the commencement of this period there is another new order in India. The Yadavas retire from Dwarika. The most important kingdoms of this period are those of Magadha, Koshala, Kausambi, Panchala, Surasenas, Avanti, and Chedi. The dynastic lists are given in Pargiters dynastic lists of the Kali Age. From the birth of Parikshit to the destruction of the Vedic kingdoms by Mahapadma Nanda, the years of reigns of the kings of Magadha, added together give 1504 years. The other dynastic lists do not give the periods of individual reigns.

Growth of Vedic Rituals

It appears that the Kauravas after the battle of Kurukshetra begin to be called the Pandavas. But the 5th king after Parikshit seems to have abandoned Hastinapur, and fixed his headquarters at Kausambhi, a few miles west of Pratishthana, the ancient capital of the Pauravas and the Bharatas. During this period there are three dynasties in Magadha, the Brihadrathas, the Pradyotas, and the Sisunagas. The great Buddha was a contemporary of Bimbisara, the fifth king of this last dynasty, and of Udayana, the Pandava king of Kausambi and of Prasenajit of the Koshala kingdom. It was during this period that the sacrificial ritual of the Aryans developed. The Brahamana granhas were composed, the Aranyakas or Forest Books, and the Upanishadas were produced, and then after this the Sutra literature grew up. On astronomical grounds the date of the Satapatha Brahmana can be fixed at 3000 B.C. The date of the Chhandogya Brahmana can be calculated at 2500 B.C. We know that the Sutra literature was contemporaneous with the time of Buddha.

Reaction Against Ritualism

It was about the time of the Upanishadas, that the list of Nakshatras was again revised. The old Mrigshira list gave place to Krittika list in about 2500 B.C. There was soon a reaction against animal sacrifices, and the creed of non-violence gained ascendency with Parasnath, the Jain leader and Siddhart, the Buddhist teacher. It is significant to note that both the Jain and Buddhist teachers belonged to the countries, where the Suryavanshis were predominent. As I have already stated the fire sacrifices and animal sacrifices were a peculiarity of the Chandravanshis. But is seems such practices had been adopted by the Suryavanshis also. But under the Jain and Buddhist reaction, they were given up. The period of animal sacrifices seems to have lasted from about 3500 B.C. to 1500 B.C. After 1500 B.C. the more important object of worship became the Surya, the presiding deity of

Ashwini. Among those who did not turn Jain or Buddhist, Surya worship was the most popular. With the end of the period of the sacrifices, ends the Vedic Age.

Conclusion

In this rapid sketch, I have tried to point out the existence of five distinct periods in the Vedic Age. We have so far neglected the information contained in the Puranas. But those statements in the Puranas which find corroboration in the Vedic, Jain, and Buddhist literature, should be accepted as trustworthy. I have tried to give above a connected and rationalised story of our political history of the Vedic Age as gathered from the Puranas. We can in this rationalised story trace not only our political, but also social, religious, and intellectual history of the Vedic Aryans. We can with the aid of the Puranas fill up the gaps, and reconstruct the entire history.

3

Epochs of Ancient Indian History

ROMESH CHUNDER DUTT

It has been observed, with much truth, that the early civilization of mankind was determined by natural causes, or, in other words, by the fertilizing power of great rivers and by the influence of a warm and genial climate, conducive alike to the production of crops and to the comfort of man. Other causes have exerted a greater influence in more modern times, and a temperate or cold climate has fostered the more robust civilization of these days; but in the remote past we shall seek in vain for the first glimpses of human civilization except on favoured spots, where Nature helped man by copious and fertilizing inundations, and a warm and genial climate.

Four Favoured Spots in the Old World

Modern researches have shown that between thirty and forty centuries ago civilization was not the common property of the human race, but was confined almost exclusively to four favoured spots in the old world. The valley of the Nile was the seat of a powerful empire, and of a very ancient civilization. The valley of the Euphrates and the Tigris similarly witnessed the civilization of powerful Semitic nations—the Assyrians, and the Babylonians—flourishing within its confines and imparting its light to surrounding regions. The valley of the Hoang Ho and the Yangse Kiang was similarly the home of an ancient Turanian civilization which flourishes to this day after the lapse of thousands of years. And lastly, the valley of the Indus and its tributaries witnessed the earliest form of civilization developed by a section of those Aryan races,[1] who in the present day rule the world, and carry civilization to the remotest portions of the globe. So universal is the fact of civilization, in these days, that it is difficult to conceive that it was confined to four isolated spots in the world only a hundred generations ago; and that the vast spaces between these favoured and very limited areas were filled by swarms of hunting and pastoral tribes, warring against each other, migrating in hordes with their tents and cattle from place to place, leaving no trace of their movements or their national existence in the records of history, leaving no mark in the annals of human progress, literature, and science.

Misty Dawn of Civilization

The history of civilization, of the infant civilization of mankind, belongs to these four countries. The light has broadened and expanded as the day has advanced, but mankind will ever look back with interest on the misty dawn of civilization, on the small beginnings of progress and knowledge, for which the enlightened and mighty nations of the modern world are indebted to the early shepherds and cultivators of Egypt and Babylonia, of China and India. To Greece and to Rome belongs the credit of catching the light from the East, and reflecting it with ten-fold lustre on the West.

In studying the history of the earliest civilized nations of the world, we are unable to fix dates, or to trace the course of events with the degree of accuracy which marks modern history, or even the history of Rome and Greece. But nevertheless we possess sufficient materials with regard to the earlier nations to ascertain the general course of events, to mark the great results achieved from age to age, and to trace the progress of knowledge, literature, and science, through the successive epochs of their national existence.

If this is true of Egypt, and Babylonia, and China, it is still more so in respect of India. The hieroglyphic records of the Egyptians tell us about ancient kings and pyramid-builders, of dynasties, invasions, and wars. The cuneiform inscriptions of Assyria and Babylon tell us much the same kind of story. And even the ancient records of China tell us more about kings and dynasties than about the progress and civilization of the people.

Ancient Hindu Works Provide Comprehensive History

The ancient Hindu works, with which Europe has become familiar within the last hundred years, are of a different character They tell us little of kings and dynasties; and even when such lists are available, they are bare lists of names, and have little value in a true historical sense. On the other hand, the copious literature which we possess, and which belongs to the different epochs of Hindu history, presents a faithful picture of Hindu life and civilization through the successive periods of their natural existence. And thus the ancient works form a connected and comprehensive history of the Hindu nation for four thousand years, so full, so clear, that he who runs may read.

Inscriptions on stone and writings on papyri are recorded with a design to commemorate passing events. The songs and poetry and religious compositions of a people are an unconscious and true reflection of their civilization and thought. The earliest effusions of the Hindus were not recorded in writing; they are therefore full and unrestricted—they are a natural and true expression of the nation's thoughts and feelings. They were preserved, not on stone or papyri, but in the faithful memory of the people, who handed down the sacred heritage from century to century with a scrupulous exactitude which in modern days would be considered a miracle. For several centuries this ancient literature was thus preserved in the nation's memory, until writing was introduced, and the literature was recorded; but even then teachers preferred to teach, and students to learn, by rote, and it was considered a sin to learn sacred texts from written works. Later literature sprang up in following ages, and lies strata upon strata, over the more ancient literature of India, as clearly distinguishable from each other to the historian, as the different strata of rocks are to the geologist. European antiquarians have during the last hundred years examined this great mass of literature, have sifted and classified it, and have assigned to each class of works its proper age; and thus classified and examined, the literature tells a continuous and most interesting story of a nation's life and progress through forty centuries. It is the story of an Aryan people, at first isolated by situation and circumstances from the outside world, and working out its own religious and social institutions, its literature, laws, and science; and it forms one of the most instructive and interesting chapters in the annals of human progress and culture.

This wonderful story divides itself into several well-defined Epochs or 'Periods' and five of these epochs belong to ancient history. It is desirable here to make a brief mention of these five epochs.

I. VEDIC EPOCH

Hindu Settlements on the Indus, B.C. 2000-1400

The history of the Hindus begins with their settlement in the Punjab and their conquest of that province from the dark-skinned aborigines. This war of conquest and colonization went on for centuries; and the obstinate and brave children of the soil were beaten back from river to river and from forest to forest. The interminable forests were gradually cleared, fair villages and hamlets surrounded by smiling fields of corn arose on the banks of the fertilizing streams, Hindu forms of worshipping the "bright gods" of Nature by oblations to the fire were established, and Hindu civilization at last spread itself thoughout the land of the "seven rivers", from the Indus to the Sarasvati. A great division had in the meantime broken out in the Aryan camp. A section of that race protested against animal sacrifices and the use of the fermented Soma wine, and these puritans retired from the Punjab westwards to the Iran, where they formed the ancient Persian race, and founded the Parsi religion.

It is not possible with any degree of accuracy to fix the dates of these events. "Four thousand years ago," says Professor Max Muller, "or it may be earlier, the Aryans who had travelled southwards to the river of the Punjab, called him (their Supreme Deity) Dyaush-Pita or Heavenly Father," answering to the Jupiter of the Romans. The hymns which were composed by the early Aryan conquerors of the Punjab to Dyaush-Pita and the other bright gods of Nature are still preserved to us in the compilation known as the *Rig Veda;* and we may safely fix the period between 2000 and 1400 B.C. as the approximate age of these ancient hymns. We may roughly accept these six centuries as the first epoch of Hindu history, the epoch of Hindu settlements on the Indus and its tributaries.

II. EPIC EPOCH

Hindu Kingdoms on the Ganges, B.C. 1400-1000

From the Punjab the Hindus began to pour down along the course of the Ganges, until in a few centuries the whole of the Gangetic basin, from the Northern mountains to Benares and Behar, became the seat of brave, martial, and civilized nations. Indeed, these vigorous colonists soon left their mother-land, the Punjab, in the shade; and the picture we possess of the cultured Gangetic, races with their brilliant courts and schools of learning, with their great tournaments and feats of arms, and with their elaborate social rules and religious rites, testifies to a state of civilization far in advance of that of their sturdy forefathers of the Punjab. Prominent among the Gangetic races where the Kurus, who settled on the upper course of the Ganges, to the east of the site of modern Delhi, and their great rivals the Panchalas, who settled lower down the stream, not far from the site of modern Kanouj. Lower down the same river lived the Kasis, near modern Benares; still further down the stream, and to the north of it, the Videhas dwelt in modern Tirhut; while between the Kurus and the Videhas lived the powerful Kosalas in modern Oudh. These and other races had their mutual jealousies, their varying alliances, and their internecine wars, but were nevertheless bound together by a common sacred language and literature, by a common religion and by common social and religious institutions. The student of Greek history is tempted to compare these flourishing and civilized Gangetic states with the Greek cities in their palmy days, while he would compare the sturdy but less civilized Hindu settlers on the banks of the Indus with the robust Greek warriors who fought with the Trojans. The ascendency and vigour of the Gangetic kingdoms lasted for four or five centuries.

III. RATIONALISTIC EPOCH

Hindu Expansion over all India, B.C. 1000-320

When Northern India as far as Benares and North Behar had been occupied, colonies began to be established in more distant places, and the whole of India became thus Hinduized in the course of some centuries. South Behar or Magadha was early civilized; schools of philosophy multiplied in this age, and in the sixth century before Christ, Gautama Buddha preached there the great religion which is now the religion of a third of the human race. Malwa or Avanti became a seat of culture or learning; while beyond the Vindhya mountains the Andhras had a great and powerful kingdom in the Dekhan, stretching as far down as the Kistna river, and boasting of a great capital and of celebrated schools of learning. Colonists from the banks of the Jumna and the Ganges settled in Gujrat and founded the ancient seaport of Dvaraka; and it is supposed that merchants from this place sailing to the extreme south of India helped to civilize the kingdom of Pandya. Certainly it is that by the fourth century before Christ, three sister nations, the Pandyas, the Cholas, and the Cheras, had established powerful kingdoms in India, south of the Kistna river. In the east, Anga or East Behar, Vanga or Bengal, and Kalinga or Orissa, also received the light of Hindu civilization, religion, and literature, while the distant island of Ceylon was conquered and Hinduized in the fifth century.

Thus all India, except wilds and deserts, had received Hindu civilization, manners, and religion, before the time of Alexander the Great. It is necessary, however, to make a passing remark about these southern Hindu kingdoms, as distinguished from the older northern Kingdoms. The Aryan races had penetrated in vast numbers into the Punjab and the Gangetic valley, and had all but exterminated or expelled the children of the soil, who were utter barbarians; and the population of Northern India therefore is, to the present day, more or less of pure Aryan stock. On the other hand, the latter and less numerous Hindu colonists who penetrated into South Behar and Bengal, to the Dekhan and Southern India, found the aboriginal races of those spacious regions possessing a more or less imperfect civilization of their own, and the extermination of those vast populations all over India by a handful of colonists was out of the question. The Hindu colonists were satisfied therefore with introducing Hindu civilization, language, and religion; and to this day the majority of the population of Southern and Eastern India are of non-Aryan stock who have adopted the higher civilization, literature, and religion of their Aryan Hindu conquerors and teachers.

The Hindu world of the third Epoch, i.e., of the sixth, fifth, and fourth centuries B.C., thus appears to us as a map coloured in two or three different shades, representing different degrees of Aryan enlightenment. Northern India is almost purely Aryan, while the Southern and Eastern Indian states are more or less non-Aryan, with a veneer of Aryan religion and civilization cast over them. It is remarkable that the ancient Hindu writers of the sixth and fifth centuries before Christ viewed India in this light, and one of them parcels out the Hindu world into three portions to indicate the degrees of their Aryan purity. Northern India comes first; South and East Behar, Malwa, Gujrat, and Dekhan are included by him in the second portion; while Bengal, Orissa, and India south of the Kistna are included in the last. If we were disposed to find a parallel to the

Hindu world of the third Epoch, we should compare it with the Greek world after the death of Alexander, when outside Greece proper, Macedon, Egypt, and the whole of Western Asia wore the livery of Greek civilization, religion, and literature.

IV. BUDDHIST EPOCH

Ascendancy of Magadha, B.C. 320-A.D. 400

If the first three epochs of Hindu history are epochs of the gradual expansion of the Hindus first over the Punjab, then in the Gangetic valley, and then all over India, the fourth is the Epoch of a union among these Hindu races under a great and dominant ruling power. Immediately after the departure of Alexander the Great from India, the Great Chandragupta founded a new dynasty in Magadha, and for the first time united the whole of Northern India under his vigorous rule. His grandson Asoka the Great, adopted Buddism as the state religion in the third century before Christ, even as Constantine the Great adopted the Christian religion in the fourth century after Christ. The dynasty of Chandragupta and Asoka declined in course of time; but the powerful Andhras of the Dekhan took possession of Magadha about the commencement of the Christian era, and down to the close of the fourth century after the Christ held the supreme power both in Northern and Southern India. After the fourth century the Andhras declined, and the ascendancy of the Magadha Empire was at an end.

We may consider the first three Epochs of the History of Ancient India as a preparation for the fourth Epoch. In the former, all India was gradually civilized and Hinduized; in the last, it was united under one great central power, even as Europe and Western Asia were united in the same age under the imperial power of Rome.

V. PURANIC EPOCH

Ascendancy of Kanouj and Ujain, AD. 400-800

The parallel between Hindu history and European history extends further than would appear at first sight. The supreme power passed from the rulers of Magadha to the emperors of Kanouj and Ujain in the fifth and succeeding centuries, but like the later Roman emperors they had to battle against hordes of barbarian invaders to save their country and their civilization. The war went on for centuries, and races of barbarians settled down in the west and south of India, and adopted Hindu manners, religion, and civilization. But the crisis came, and ancient Hindu rule was at last swept away from Northern India in the eighth century. Ancient Hindu history terminates at this date.

Dark ages followed in India as in Europe, and the history of Northern India in the ninth and tenth centuries is a perfect blank. Towards the close of the tenth century, a new power arose on the ruins of ancient civilization in Europe and in India; the feudal barons in Europe, and the Rajput barons in India. These new Rajput chiefs stepped into the vacant thrones of ancient and polished but effete nations, and adopted the Hindu religion and civilization, even as the mediaeval kings and conquerors of Europe embraced the Christian faith. And the new defenders of Hinduism and of Christianity had to fight in India as in Europe against the same rising power, viz. the Muhammadans. But here the parallel ends. After centuries of warfare, the Christian knights beat back the Moslems from France, from Spain, and from Austria. The Rajput chiefs of India offered an equally brave but not an equally successful, resistance; they struggled and they fell; and Hindu independence and national life terminated with the conquest of India by the Muhammadans.

Historical analogies are often misleading unless we constantly bear in mind the great differences in details, even when the resemblance in the outline seems most striking. But when instituted with due caution, such comparisons have their use; and they show us how the same historical laws rule the destinies and the progress of nations at the farthest ends of the globe, and how the same great historical causes often affect and control the march of events, simultaneously in the east and the west.

Note and Reference

1. Recent anthropological discoveries have proved that the nations which are known as the Aryan races in Europe and in Asia, viz. the Teutons, the Celts, the Slavs, the Halics, the Hellener, the Persians, the Hindus, etc. are not all actually descended from the same stock, although they speak languages derived from the same ancient tongue, of which the Sanscrit language is the oldest and nearest specimen. It is supposed that the primitive Aryans, dwellers probably of Central Asia and Eastern Europe, spread their conquests on all sides and imposed their language on nations whose descendants still speak modifications of the same tongue. It is convenient to speak of these Aryan-speaking nations of the modern day as Aryan nations. The Hindus claim that they are actually descended from the primitive Aryan stock.

4

Population in Ancient India*

DR. G.C. PANDE

Modern Perspective

Malthus argued in 1798 that there is a constant natural tendency to overpopulation in every society, for men increase at a faster rate than food supplies,[1] the necessary adjustment between the two being effected by preventive and positive checks. Since Malthus published his Essay, world population has increased enormously. The population of Western Eupore has passed during the last two centuries through a veritable 'demographic cycle' which has tended from a 'high stationary' to a 'low stationary' phase.[2] This has happened because the adoption of various preventive checks has decreased the birth-rate while the Agrarian and Industrial Revolutions and the improvement in public health measures have decreased the death rate. In India, however, only the earlier stages of the 'demographic cycle' have been operative yet. In the sixteenth century she is estimated to have had a population of about a 100 millions.[3] By the middle of the 19th century the population had increased to about 150 millions. It was 203 millions in 1871, 254 millions in 1881, 279 millions in 1891, 353 millions in 1931 and 389 millions in 1941.[4] In a century, thus, the population of India has more than doubled itself while it was practically stationary in the preceding three centuries.

*J.B.R.S., Vol. XXXV.

Pre-industrial Age

Before the Industrial and Scientific Revolutions human population appears to have remained on the whole in a 'high stationary' phase. Doubtless the adoption of settled agriculture at the dawn of civilisation must have meant a great rise in the level of population equilibrium. It is not certain if the later use of iron meant any significant change in this level. On the whole, "in unimproved peasant conditions, birth rates and death rates are both high and the population remains fairly steady, fluctuating up and down according to food-supplies, pestilences, wars, etc."[5] An illustration may be obtained from China which is the only country where a long tradition of census records has come down from ancient times. These records show that in Pre-Manchu times population tended to rise rapidly but was restrained by periodical destruction. Already in the 9th century B.C. China north of the Yang tze kiang is stated to have had a population of 21.7 millions.[6] Between A.D. 2 and 155 the average of the census gives 63.5 millions. In A.D. 180 it was 23.1 millions, in 606 it doubled, increased rapidly and then declined to 43.2 millions in 733. By A.D. 1097 it had risen to 101.2 millions but in the Mongol and Ming periods it declined by 40 to 50 per cent.[7] In other words, for nearly 2500 years the population of Pre-Manchu China fluctuated between 20 millions and 100 millions.

It is probable that for India in ancient times a similar state of affairs held good. Although census records were not unknown then,[8] none have been preserved for the sceptic to doubt. The available evidence is indirect and scanty but it may be eked out with considerations of general probability in the light of the demographic perspective indicated above.

Pre-historic India

Since food supply, security of life, and the social attitude towards the size of the family are the chief determinants of population, it must have been small in the Stone Age but must have increased greatly with the discovery of agriculture and the domestication of animals. Thus north-western India in the third millennium B.C. had at least two large cities—of which the present sites have a circumference of more than three miles and of which at least one probably covered a square mile of well-inhabited area—several smaller towns, and numerous villages.[9] This civilized society of chalcolithic India with developed agriculture, commerce and town-life extended over a thousand miles from the foot of Simla hills to the Arabian Sea. Assuming the urban population to have been 50,000, we may estimate the total population of Harappan India at half a million to a million persons.[10] This would be a fairly conservative estimate. In the second millennium B.C. town life declined in this area but had again recovered by the middle of the next millennium. Although a gradual desiccation of Baluchistan, Sindh and W. Rajputana took place in ancient times, Sindh remained prosperous and populous throughout, as is indicated by later Greek and Arab accounts. The Aryan expansion in the second millennium B.C. brought the greater part of N. India from Kabulistan to Bihar under the plough. The Vedic attitude towards the family reflects the need and trend of this period of agricultural expansion. The Vedic Aryans fervently prayed for progeny and larger numbers and would have blessed every mother with ten children.[11] Wilh such a social attitude and fresh cultivable land easily available, population must have tended to increase in geometric progression.

From Bimbisara to Asoka

By the fifth century B.C., the whole of Northern India except for Bengal had been settled and town life was flourishing. Expansion to the south had also clearly begun. Herodotus writing about the middle of the century described the Indians as the most populous nation in the known world and so prosperous that they paid to the Achaemenian Empire the huge revenue of 360 talents of gold dust, which was equivalent to more than a million pounds sterling and was one-third of the total levy on the Asiatic provinces.[12] Since this description relates only to that part of north-western India which formed the twentieth satrapy of Darius, we may turn to Buddhist records for contemporary north-eastern India. We are told that Magadha including Anga, had 80,000 villages.[13]

The Sakyas are supposed to have had at least 160,000 families.[14] The population of Vaisali has been given as 168,000,[15] the assembly of the Licchavis consisting of 7707 rajas.[16] Buddhist records speak of six great cities at the time of Buddha's death—Campa, Rajagrha, Sravasti, Saketa, Kausambi and Varanasi—all lying between modern Allahabad and Bhagalpur. For Varanasi a circumference of 12 yojanas was claimed! (*Jataka* I, 125). According to Hsuan Chwang the circumference of ancient Vaisali was 70 li, which would be near that of Alexandria in the first century A.D. as reckoned by Pliny. (*Life of Greece,* pp. 592-3). Rhys Davids has estimated the population of northern India as fifteen to twenty millions in this period.[17] This would appear to be a conservative estimate.

In the fourth century B.C., the Greeks who came with Alexander have left behind certain observations regarding the population and armed forces of some Indian states. We are told that the Kingdom of Taxila between the Indus and the Jhelum was very fertile and densely populated.[18] Again, between the Jhelum and the Beas there were nine nations and 500 cities that were conquered by the Macedonians. None of these cities was less than Cos Meropis.[19] Between the Jhelum and the Chenab lay the Kingdm of Poros and upwards the territories of the Glausai or the Glauganikai. The former contained 300 cities,[20] the latter at least 37 towns the smallest of which contained over 5,000 inhabitants and many contained more than 10,000.[21] The army of Poros consisted of 50,000 foot, 3,000 horse, about 1,000 chariots and 130 elephants.[22] Since even in 1914 France and Germany could only mobilise one in thirty, the population of the Kingdom of Poros could not have been less than 1,680,000. The Glausia with an urban population of at least 200,000 could not have been less than a million and a quarter. East of the Ravi lay the Kathaioi. When their stronghold Sangala was stormed, 17,000 were killed and 70,000 taken captive.[23] These casualties were much heavier than those suffered by Poros. We would be safe in regarding the Kathaioi as at least a million. The Agelessoi who lived in the lower part of the Chenab-Ravi doab had an army of 40,000 foot, and 3,000 horse.[24] The Oxydrakai and the Malloi lived below the confluence of the Chenab and the Jhelum. They had an army of 90,000 foot, 10,000 horse and 900 chariots.[25] This suggests a population of over three millions. The Abastanoi dwelling on the lower Chenab had an army of 60,000 foot, 6,000 cavalry and 500 chariots.[26] This indicates a population of over two millions. We are told that the banks of the river were most thickly studded with their villages.[26]

Thus seven states of the Punjab, viz., that of Poros, the Glausai, the Kathaioi, the Agelessoi, the Oxydrakai, the Malloi and the Abastanoi, occupying some of the territories between the Jhelum and the Beas had a population of more than ten millions. In this very region, there were several other states like Abisares, Gandaris, Adraistai, the realm of Sophytes of Phegelus, the Siboi, the Xathroi and the

Ossadioi about whom we do not get any figures. The states in the Sind were fairly populous, for the Greeks in their campaign in these parts killed 80,000 and sold multitudes into slavery.[27] Similarly, the territories west of the Indus contained powerful state like Peukelaotis in the Peshawar district and the Asvakas on the Swat. The Asvakas had an army of more than 30,000 foot, 20,000 horse and 30 elephants.[28]

From these accounts it is clear that to the Greeks who had come with Alexander and had seen the ancient countries of Egypt and Western Asia, north-western India appeared full of populous states and the numbers they give for these states and the figures they mention for the armies of some of them suggest that an estimate of twenty millions for north-western India extending up to the Hindukush and including Sindh would not be exaggerated.[29]

Over north-eastern India sprawled the Magadhan Empire. It was reported that the "country was exceedingly fertile, and that the inhabitants were good agriculturists."[30] The empire had an army of 80,000 horse, 200,000 foot, 8,000 war chariots, and 6,000 war elephants. When Candragupta mounted the throne he increased the army to 600,000 men and with it "subdued the whole of India."[31] From this the population of northern and North-eastern India may be estimated to have been at least twenty millions.[32]

In the Deecan and the South we hear that the Andarai had thirty walled towns and an army of 100,000 foot, 2,000 cavalry, and 100 elephants.[33] The Calingai had 60,000 foot, 1,000 horse and 2,700 elephants.[34] The Pandae had 300 cities, 150,000 foot and 500 elephants.[35] These large figures get some confirmation from the fact that according to Asoka (R.E. XIII) in his war against Kalinga 100,000 persons were killed, 150,000 taken captive and many times that number wounded.[36] Later, in the first century B.C., Kharavela declared that in his twelfth year of rule he led forth an army of 100,000 from Kalinga to intimidate the rulers of the north.[37] Andhra and Kalinga both belonged to eastern Deccan but there were several states in western Deccan for which we have no figures. Similarly, from the grammarian Katyayana we know that by the side of the Pandyas there were the Colas and the Keralas. The population of the Deccan and the south, thus, must have been at least ten to twelve millions.

We may conclude, then, that by the end of the fourth century B.C., the population of India was at least fifty millions. It is likely that the Greek figures show exaggeration but this would be offset by the fact that in calculating from them we have attributed to ancient states in India the efficiency in military organisation possessed by west European states in 1914.[38]

The foregoing account would suggest that from the age of Bimbisara to that of Candragupta Maurya the population of India probably doubled itself. This should hardly surprise us if we reflect over the territorial, political and economic development which took place during the period. During the third century B.C., under the peace and welfare activity of the Maruryan state, population must have tended to grow further rapidly. The *Arthasastra* even discusses the contingency of over-population in certain areas and suggests that the state should undertake to bring fresh land under cultivation, establish new villages and encourage suitable migration.

After the Mauryas

The fall of the Mauryan Empire was followed by three centuries of political turmoil when several waves of foreign invaders came in through the north-west. Apart from the positive check to population which such conditions of political insecurity imply, the growth of the ascetic attitude must have acted as a kind of preventive check. Formerly the Brahmanical lawgivers were not favourable to the ascetic doctrines which Buddhism and Jainism preached.[39] The *Arthasastra* was definitely hostile to the influence of such heretical mendicants and sought to restrain the tendency of indiscriminately renouncing the world.[40] But now Buddhism was more popular than ever and Manu is fully reconciled to the claims of asceticism. He upholds the ideal of a small rather than a large family.[41] It is of course true that the ideal of continence in marriage must have been largely ineffective in practice and while the gradual lowering of the age of marriage of girls must have added to the birth rate, the disappearance of *Niyoga* and gradually of the remarriage of widows must have acted in a contrary direction.

From about the first century A.D. the Kusanas, the Westen Satraps, and the Satavahanas established strong states and must have lessened insecurity. At the same time there was a remarkable growth of maritime trade with the West and Roman gold poured into India.[42] From the east coast proceeded commercial and colonial enterprize towards south-east Asia. Similarly in the north-west under the Kusana empire trade with central Asia flourished and the northern highway winding from Mathura to Purusapura and beyond was brisk with caravans from far away. If the breakdown of the Kusana Empire in the third century inaugurated a long period of political confusion in the north-west, the rise of the Gupta Empire revived the ancient glories of Magadha and established a period of peace and prosperity which included the whole of northern India from sea to sea. Population must have been on the upgrade.

It has even been contended that the increased pressure on land in the Gupta period led to the fragmentation of holdings and the reduction of their size.[43] The account of Fa-Hsien certainly indicates a very prosperous and popular Madhyadesa. In the eighty Yojanas before the pilgrim reached Mathura he passed monasteries containing in all about 10,000 priests. Mathura was clearly a large city, for it had twenty monasteries with some 3,000 priests.[44] Magadha had the largest number of towns and cities of all the countries of Middle India.[45]

After the Guptas

The fall of the Gupta Empire and the invasion of the Hunas doubtless spelled disorder especially in the north-west. In the seventh century the account of Hsuan Chwang indicates that many changes had occurred since the days of Fa-Hsien. In northwestern India Kashmir, Multan, Sindh and Jalandhara were prosperous and populous, but Gandhara, Udayana, Simhapura, Urasa, Pun-nu-tso, and Rajapura were not so well developed. The towns and districts of the ancient Madhyadesa continued to prosper. Sthanesvara, Mathura, Govisana, Kanyakubja, Kausambi, Varanasi and Chen-Chu (Ghazipur!) are mentioned as especially rich and well populated. Even Brhmapura (Garhwal and Kumayun) is stated to have been prosperous and populous. The Buddhist towns of north-eastern U.P.—Sravasti, Kapilavastu, Ramagrama, and Kusinagara had, however, become desolate. In Bihar the picture had altered much since Fa-Hsien. Walled cities like Vaisali and Pataliputra were in ruins and had few inhabitants but the towns or villages were thickly populated. An idea of what Hsuan Chwang means by a town may be gathered from the fact that speaking of the Vrji capital which was in ruins but still had about 3,000 houses he expresses the opinion that it might be called a town or a village. The soil of Magadha was rich and fertile but it was low and damp and used to get flooded in rains when boats remained the only means of communication and transport. Bengal certainly had made much progress since its debut in the Gupta period.

Pundravardhana, Tamralipti, and Karnasuvarna were prosperous and thickly populated. The Deccan and the south were full of forests. Kalinga which formerly had a very dense population was now sparsely populated. So were the territories of Dhanakataka, Colas and Mala-Kuta. Southern Kosala, however, was well populated with towns and villages close together. Kanci was a big town and so were the capitals of Konkana and Maharahstra. It appears that the richest and most densely populated parts of India were in west—Gujrat, Kathiawar and Malwa.

In short, in the seventh century A.D. population had declined in the NWFP, northwestern Punjab, north-eastern U.P., Bihar (at least the urban population) and eastern Deccan. Madhyadesa, Malwa and Gujrat, Sindh and Multan continued to flourish. Kashmir and Bengal had become more important. Big forests were particularly noticeable only in the Deccan and the south. In the territories of Udyana too thick forests are mentioned. We may presume the same for the northern mountaneous and the north-eastern frontier areas.

Arab Accounts

In the Arab accounts of the 9th, 10th and 11th centuries India appears as one of the four great Kingdoms of the world, the other three being the Caliphate, China, and the Eastern Roman Empire.[46] The Arab merchant Sulaiman of the 9th century mentions the realms of Balhara, Jurz and Ruhmi as the most important in India, all three being mutually at war.[47] These arc the realms of the Rastrakutas, the Gurjaras and the Palas. The King of Ruhmi or the Pala ruler had 50,000 elephants and the very big number of the washermen in the army amounted to ten or fifteen thousand.[48] Al Masudi in the 10th century stated that Bauura, King of Kanauj, had four armies each of which numbered 700,000 or 900,000.[49] Multan is stated to have had around it 120,000 towns and villages.[50] Debal and Mansura were the other two most important cities in Sind. Mansura was a mile long and a mile broad.[51] The capital of Balhar was Mankir or Manya-kheta. Rashidud-Din stated on the basis of Al Biruni that Gujrat comprised 80,000 flourishing cities, villages and hamlets.[52] Ten thousand villages maintained the temple of Somanatha.[53] The country of Sawalak, i.e., Sapadalaksa comprised 125,000 cities and villages.[54] Malwa had 1,893,000 villages.[55] These same figures occur in the Tarikhi Wassaf. The *Kavyasiksa* of Vinayacandra also gives 70,000 villages for the Guijaradesa and 1,892,000 for Malava-desa.[56] The

Prabhavakacarita of Hemacandra describes Arnoraja as the lord of Sapadalaksa. According to an inscription, a King of Medapata or Mewar possessed 1,000,000 tracts of land (*Laksa-Ksitisa*).[57] According to *Prabandhacintamani,* Prthviraja was the lord of 125,000 tracts of land (*Sapadalaksa-Ksitipati*). Telangana in Alauddin's time had 30,000 'tracts of country'.[58]

Like Vinayacandra, *Aparajitapircha* also mentions 1,892,000 as the number of villages in Ujjayini. It gives 36 lacs of villages for Kanyakubja, 18 lacs for Gauda, 66,063 for Kasmira and $3^1/_2$ lacs for Maru. In many inscriptions from the Deccan and the South exceedingly large figures are similarly associated with certain regions, viz., Vanavasaka 12,000, Nolamavadi 32,000 and Gangavadi 96,000. The three Maharastras are stated to have had 99,000 villages.[59] The Kavadidvipa or northern Konkana was called Iakh-and-a-quarter, while the territories of the Western Calukyas were called seven-and-a-lakh country. (Fleet: *Bombay Gazct.* I, pt. II, p. 298, n. 2). These and other similarly large figures have excited much controversy and it has been suggested that they stand not for villages, but for estates or revenue or population.[60] All these interpretations are remedies of despair and appear far-fetched. To reconcile these figures with probability, we have to remember in the first place that the recent increase of population in India should not be supposed to have meant an increase in the total number of villages. On the contrary, the fact that in divided India small villages with population less than 500 number more than 380,000 and yet contain only 26.5% of the rural population, suggests that the recent phenomenal growth of population in India has been due to the growth of the medium and large sized villages and towns. In many cases these bigger villages must have grown by the amalgamation of smaller villages scattered in the neighbourhood, these smaller villages becoming the hamlets or 'purwas' of the bigger village. Thus the actual number of villages instead of increasing would decrease with any marked increase of population. This would be clear if we reflect over the fact that while the number of villages in central India is nearly $2^1/_2$ times that in Western India, its population is hardly 10% more. Besides we have to remember that the proportion of urban population must have been much less than now. We may thus expect that villages in ancient India were probably more numerous though smaller and more scattered than now.[61]

In the second place, there is probably a great deal of overlapping in the numbers of villages given for states like Kanauja, Gauda, Malava and Gurjara. The numbers probably refer to these states at their maximum extension. It is well known for instance that the kings of Kanauja and Gauda were long rivals and claimed the imperial title and on occasions the rulers of Gauda came up to Kanauja. Besides, it is possible that in estimating these figures, many conventional titles conferred on feudatories or assumed by ambitious rulers may have been taken realistically. Similarly, on occasions, territorial divisions may have been assumed to have had the number of villages required in them by convention.[62] In fact, it is likely that the figures of villages for the different states were reached from counting its major territorial divisions and feudal lords and then assuming that for each their conventional connotation in terms of the number of villages comprised in or ruled by them actually held good. Such assumptions are likely to lead to 'inflated' figures and these would get further 'conflated' on account of the overlapping of Empires and imperial claims. This also explains why the figures for definite territorial divisions like Konkana are more modest and reasonable than for imperial states like Kanauja or Gauda.

Arab accounts thus confirm the directions of population growth discernible in Hsuan Chwang. Kashmir and Sindh, Kanauja and Gauda, Gujrat and Malwa became the leading states in northern India in the 9th, 10th and 11th centuries. From inscriptions it appears that Maru or Rajputana gradually emerges into importance, and in the south under the Eastern Calukyas, the Colas and the Pandyas there was a remarkable expansion of political activity and accumulation of wealth. We may suppose that the growth of population kept pace *pari passu.* Rashidud-Din calls Malabar or Coromandel coast, 'the Key of Hind', possessing many cities and villages and engaged in a brisk and profitable trade with Chin and Machin, Hind and Sindh.[63] Of the country about Cape Comorin it was earlier declared that 'no Kingdom has a more dense population'.[64]

Whether we look to the general impression of Arab travellers or to the number of villages in different parts of India reported by them and by literary works and inscriptions or to the large armies then maintained, it appears probable that while Northern and Western India under the Gurjara-Pratiharas, Palas and Rastrakutas had not declined in population since earlier times, Deccan and the South were more densely populated under the Rastrakutas, Calukyas and Colas than before. If the population of the Deccan and Vijayanagara in the sixteenth century was about 30 millions,[65] it could not have been much less under the Colas, and the same equivalence probably held good of India as a whole which in the 12th century could not have been far behind the 100 million mark.

NOTES AND REFERENCES

1. Malthus, *An Essay on Population,* Vol. I, pp. 5ff. (Everyman's Library Ed.).
2. S. Chandrasekhar, *Hungry People and Empty Lands,* pp. 27ff. (Baroda, 1952); E. John Russel, *World Population and World Food Supplies,* pp. 18-19 (London, 1954).
3. Moreland, *India at the Death of Akbar,* p. 22 (London, 1920).
4. S. Chandrasekhar; *op. cit.,* pp. 152 ff; Baljit Singh, *Population and Food Planning in India,* p. 3 (Bombay, 1947).
5. E. John Russel, *op. cit.,* p. 18.
6. This is based on Ma-Tvan-Lin's account of the 13th Century A.D. who refers to a census of those times. It has been utilized by several modern writers, e.g., Latourette.
7. *Ibid.*
8. *Arthasastra,* II, XXXVI.
9. Wheeler, *The Indus Civilisation,* pp. 15, 36.
10. The population of ancient Egypt in the 13th century B.C. has been estimated from 3 millions to 4.5 millions.—Will Durant, *Oriental Heritage,* p. 214; cf. J.A. Wilson, *The Culture of Ancient Egypt,* p. 271 (Phoenix Books).
11. Cf. *Rgvedasamhita* X, 85.45.
12. Herodotus, *The Histories,* p. 215 (The Penguin Classics); cf. *CHI,* I, p. 335. In the 5th century B.C. the population of Attica had been estimated at 315,000 (Will Durant, *Life of Greece,* p. 255); Laconia had 376,000 (*Ib.* p. 74).
13. Rhys Davids, *Buddhist India,* p. 24. Modern Bihar has 71,378 villages (*Times of India Directory for 57-58,* p. 345).
14. *Ib.* p. 18,
15. *Mahavastu,* I. p. 214 (tr. J.J. Jones); cf. K.P. Jayaswal, *Hindu Polity,* p. 51, fn. 5; cf. *Mahavastu* I, p. 216—84,000 Brahmanas of Magadha.
16. Rhys Davids, *op. cit.,* p. 41.
17. *Ib.* p. 34.
18. McCrindle, *Ancient India, its Invasion by Alexander the Great,* p. 343, 94. Philostrates described the cily of Taxila as being about the size of Nineveh. (A.N. Bose, *Social and Rural Economy of Northern India,* II, p. 169).
19. McCrirdle, *op. cit.,* p. 112, fn. I. Plutarch mentions 15 tribes, 5,000 considerable cities, and villages without number (*Ib.,* p. 309); Arrian speaks of 7 nations and 2,000 cities, (*Ib.,* p. 133).
20. *Ib.,* p. 309, fn. I; cf. *CHI,* I, p. 360.
21. McCrindle, *op. cit.,* p. 112.

22. *Ib.*, p. 274. The figures vary in different accounts.
23. *Ib.*, p. 119.
24. *Ib.*, p. 285.
25. *Ib.*, p. 234.
26. *Ib.*, p. 252.
27. *Ib.*, p. 254.
28. *Ib.*, p. 66.
29. In the 2nd century A.D. Egypt had a population of 8.5 millions, Syria 10 millions and Palestine 2.5 millions. Cities like Alexandria and Antioch each contained over half a million (Will Durant, *Caesar & Christ,* pp. 495-500, 510-11,535). Jerusalam had 100,000, Carthage and Ephesus over 200,000 (*Ib.*, pp. 535, 515, 40).
30. McCrindle. *op. cit.*, p. 121.
31. *Ib.*, p. 310. Candragupta also had 30,000 horses and 9,000 elephants beside the chariots and the infantry of 600,000 (Smith, *Early History of India,* 4th Edition, p. 131). This was not a militia but a standing army "drawing liberal and regular pay and supplied by the government with hone, arms, equipment and stores". (*Ib.*)
32. Patliputra was 9 miles long and 1 1/2 miles broad (*Ib.*, p. 127). Strabo described Alexandria in the 1st century A.D. as only 3 miles long and 1 mile broad. Its population exceeded half a million (*Life of Greece,* pp. 592-93; *Ceasar and Christ,* pp. 295-500). In 189 B.C. the city of Rome had a population of 257,000 (*Caesar and Christ,* p. 81). In 1941 Patna had nearly 2 lacs, but though at the same site it is not a continuation of the ancient city.
33. McCrindle: *Ancient India as described by Megasthenes and Arrian*, p. 141.
34. *Ib.*, p. 138.
35. *Ib.*, 151.
36. R.K. Mukherji estimates the population of Kalinga at 25 millions! (*Asoka Inscriptions : A Commentary,* p. 23, Allahabad, 1942).
37. Barua, *Old Brahmi Inscriptions,* p. 32.
38. The population of the Roman Empire in its early centuries has been estimated by Beloch as 54 millions, by Gibbon as 120 millions,—Gibbon, *Decline and Fall of The Roman Empire,* I, pp. 37-38 (Modern Library); *Caesar and Christ,* p. 364. The Han Empire exceeded 60 millions.
39. See the .author's *Studies in the Origin of Buddhism* (Allahabad, 1957), Chapter IX.
40. *Arthasastra* (tr. Shamasastry), p. 47.
41. Cf. *Kulluka on Maim,* 3.45.
42. Gibbon, *op. cit.* I, pp. 49-50. Rome's annual loss is estimated at 800,000 pounds sterling (ft).
43. R.S. Sharma, *The Sudras in Ancient India,* pp. 230-31, 234.
44. Fa-Hsien, *Travels,* tr. Giles, p. 20.
45. *Ib.*, p. 47.
46. Eliot and Dowson, *Early Arab Geographers,* p. 3 (Pub. Susil Gupta).
47. *Ib.*, pp. 4-6.

48. *Ib.*, p. 6.
49. *Ib.*, p. 29.
50. *Ib.*, p. 30.
51. The Estates and Villages Dependent on Mansura amount to 300,000 (*Ib.* p. 31).
52. *Ib.*, p. 93.
53. *Ib.*, p. 134.
54. *Ib.*, p. 95.
55. *Ib.*, p. 96.
56. Pran Nath, *Economic Condition of Ancient India,* pp. 35-36.
57. *Ib.*, p. 38; *E.I.* II, No. XXXII, pp. 415-17.
58. *History of Ghazni,* pt. II. *Elliot & Dowson,* pp. 53-54.
59. Pran Nath, *op. cit.,* p. 35; Altekar: *Rastrakutas and their times,* p. 139.
60. Pran Nath, *op. cit.,* p. 26 ff; Rice, *Bhandarkar Comm. Vol.;* Altekar, *op. cit.* 139 ff; V.S. Agarwal, *Journal of the U.P. Historical Society,* 1951-52, pp. 290-91; B.N.S. Yadav, *Aspects of Society in Northern India in the Twelfth century A.D.* (umpublished thesis in the Allahabad University); Nilkantha Shastri, *JOR.,* 1930.
61. According to *Sukraniti,* Grama of a Krosa; *Agnipurana,* Grama of six families (vide Yadav,. *op. cit.*) cf. Altekar, sizes of 30 gramas granted by Rajaraja (*op. cit.,* p. 148); Kautalya, 100 to 500 families, boundaries of a Krosa or two. (l.c.).
62. Altekar, *op. cit.*, p. 149.
63. *Early Arab Geographers,* p. 96.
64. *Ib.*, p. 10.
65. Moreland, *op. cit.,* p. 10.

5

Aryan Expansion in the Post-Rigvedic Period

R.C. GAUR

According to *Baudhayana*[1] the land lying to the east of *Vinasana,* to the west of *Kalakavana,* to the north of *Pariyatra* and to the south of Himalaya was known as *Aryavarta* or the country of the Aryas.[1a] *Vasistha's*[2] account is also more or less the same with the only difference that instead of making a reference of *Vinasana,* he places the *Aryavarta* to the east of the region where river *Sarasvati* had disappeared. However, from *Mahabharata*[3] we learn that *Vinasana* was a holy place (*Tirtha*) where *Saraswati* had vanished,. Thus both the accounts of the *Sutra*-authors are identical. *Vasistha's* statement that *Pariyatra* and Vindhyan ranges were in the south of *Aryavarta* has made the identification of *Pariyatra* with the Aravali range[4] much easier and the southern limit of the Aryan country more precise. In spite of the fact that the western, southern and northern boundaries of the *Aryavarta* are quite distinct in the *Sutra* literature, the eastern limit of the region could not be ascertained so far finally for the simple reason that the identification of the *Kalakavana,* mentioned in the east is not yet beyond dispute. However, Manu's[5] account of the *Madhyadesha* provides some clue to determine the location of the *Kalakavana.* Though Manu has extended the limit of *Aryavarta* to the whole of the Northern India, his definition of *Madhyadesha* tallies more or less to the *Sutra* account of *Aryavnrta.* According to him, the country lying between *Himavat* (Himalaya) and the *Vindhya* and the west of *Prayaga* and to the east of *Vinasana* is *Madhyadeshal.* Since the three boundaries of north, west and south given by Manu are identical to those of *Sutra* literature, the fourth one, eastern, could also not be much different.

It may, therefore, be presumed that *Kalakavana* of the *Sutra* literature would have been somewhere in the near vicinity of *Prayaga* (Allahabad). The possibility of its identification with the *Kalakarama* of the Buddhist texts seems more plausible. The *Anguttara Nikaya*[6] tells us that the Buddha once had stayed at *Kalakarama* in *Saketa* and there he had delivered his *Kalakarama-Suttanta.*[7] Thus *Kalakarama* perhaps was somewhere beyond *Prayaga* though not far away in the outskirts of Kosala country, perhaps between rivers Rapti and Gandaka. It is possible that it was a western extension of *Mahavana* which has been mentioned in the neighbourhood of *Vaisali.*[8] However, its identification with the *Anjanavana*[9] on the basis that the words *Anjana* and *Kalaka* are synonyms seems wrong as the word *Kaluka* may mean terrific or fearful but not black.

We know that even in our times the eastern rivers of the Ganga plain such as Ghagra, great Gandaka, Burhi-Gandaka and Kamla and above all Kosi are devastating. 'Their Khadar flow plain are wider than in the upper Ganges...which develop into vast and intricate chain of temporary lakes during the rainy season, one such chain, an old course of the Great Gandaka, covers 140 sq. miles when full'.[10] Thus it would have not been possible to cross this area easily unless it was deforested and dried up on a large scale. It is quite convincing that the Aryan expansion as mentioned in *Sutra* literature could not go beyond Rapti. It would be better if we refer to other details of Manu about the Aryan land to understand the problem of Aryan expansion. Although Manu's work belongs to a much later date, it appears that the earlier traditions (as is indicated by the use of past perfect tense)[11] have been recorded accurately in it. It mentions four geographic regions which were under Aryan occupation, *viz.,* 1. *Brahmavarta,*[12] 2. *Brahmarshidesa,*[13] 3. *Madhyadesha,*[14] and 4. *Aryavarta.*[15]

Most Holy Centre

According to Manu the most holy centre of pure Aryan culture was the *Brahmavarta* country lying between the two divine rivers, the *Sarasvati* and *Drishadvati.* Adjacent to it was the land of the

Brahmarshis comprising the countries of *Kurukshetra, Matsya, Panchala* and *Saursena.* The country of *Madhyadesha* has already been discussed above. However, it may be observed that Manu's *Madhyadesha* was divisible into three provinces, *viz.,* (1) the region between *Sarasvati* and *Drishadvati,* (2) the region between *Drishadvati* and the Ganga up to Mathura and (3) the region between Mathura and *Prayaga.* Finally, he describes *Aryavarta* which includes the whole of Northern India lying between the two mountains of *Himavata* (Himalaya) and Vindhya and extending between eastern and western oceans. Rest of the land according to him belongs to the *Mlechchhas* or non-Aryans.[16] But as is evident *Baudhayana*[17] referred to an earlier stage of the Aryan expansion as he attributed the countries of *Avanti, Anga, Magadha, Saurashtra, Dakshinapatha, Upavrita, Sindhu* and *Sauvira* to the people of mixed castes, *viz.,* non-Aryans (*Varna-sankara*). Thus he excludes not only south India but also considerable part of eastern and western territories of Manu's *Aryavarta.* This statement more or less is also corroborated by an earlier reference of *Atharvavcda.*[18] According to it the countries of *Mahavrishas, Valhikas, Mujavants* and *Gandharas* in the west and *Anga* and *Magadha* in the east were the land of *Sudras.* Strangely enough these references exclude a considerable part of *Sapta-Sindliu* land also from their definition of the Aryan land. Why and how the land in the west of *Sarasvati* was de-Aryanised? Was this due to sudden or constant influx of new people from the west? Or was it the result of non-Aryan effort to oust the Aryans? Though it is not easy to answer these questions we may try to probe into the problem. We know that the Aryans, particularly the Bharata tribe in the latter stage of the Rigvedic period, were losing their hold in the west of *Sarasvati.* The battle of the Ten Kings[19] on the banks of Parushni shows an organised effort of the non-Aryans to oust the Bharatas from the land of *Sapta-Sindhu.* In their effort they succeeded in getting the support of the weaker Aryan tribes also. It must have been a terrific war in which sixty-six thousard and sixty-six warriors[20] belonging to the *Anu* and *Drhyu* tribe were killed by king *Sudasa* the leader of the Bharatas. But unfortunately very soon the Bharatas had to fight another crucial battle on the east of their territory with *Bheda,*[21] another leader of the non-Aryans on the bark of *Yamuna.* Though, the Bharatas were victorius in this battle also, it appears that after the death of *Sudasa,* they also began to lose power. The internal strife of the Aryans on one hand and their light with the non-Aryans on the other, left them weaker and perhaps only two groups, *viz.*, Purus a branch of the Bharatas who were known as Kurus[22] later on and the Yadus were left to organise themselves subsequently in the Kuru and Mathura (Surasena) regions respectively.

Sacrifice to the Fire God

It has already been discussed that there was a regular shifting from the west to the east throughout the Rigvedic period so much so that the land between the *Sarasvati* and *Drishadvati*—Brahmavarta of the later text—had become the home of the Bharatas. Their invasion on the bank of *Yamuna* had created greater urge among the Aryans to move further into the Ganga plain. Virtually there was no natural hindrance, such as desert, mountain, etc. to withhold their onward movement except the thick forests coupled with marshy stretches of land due to heavy rains in the region. There are frequent references to dense forests in the *Satapaiha Brahmana*[23] as well as in the *Aitareya Brahmana.*[24] These forests could not be cleared without iron except for a narrow strip on the low .watershed between the Punjab and the Ganga basin.[25] This factor would have detained the Aryans for some time in the region between *Sarasvati* and *Yamuna* with its centre at Kurukshetra,[26] bounded on the south by *Khandava,* on the north by *Turghana* and in the west by *Parinah.* A detailed account of clearance of the Khandava—the region around Delhi—by the traditional method of burning is given in the *Mahabharata.*[27] The clearing was conceived as a grand sacrifice to the fire god (Agni), which continued for fifteen days and in which every living creature—sparing only six —that tried to escape was slaughtered.[28]

Fight with the Local Aborigines

This event was not merely a grand devastation by fire, but it also indicates a battle, which Aryans had to fight with the local aborigines to colonise the area. Among the six non-Aryan survivors were *Asvasena,* son of *Takshaka,* a *Naga* chief, *Maya,* an *Asura* and four persons belonging to unknown *Sarangoka* tribe. Maya's association has been shown with prominent *Dasa* chief *Namuchi*[29] of the Rigvedic period. Of all these tribes the *Nagas* appear the greatest enemy of the Aryans in the subsequent period. The *Mahabharata* records that king *Janamejaya* III performed a great *Yajna* (sacrifice) for the total destruction of the *Nagas,* when one of them killed. *Janamejaya's* father Parikshita II. *Naga's* stronghold is also recorded in the *Puranas* in the Mathura region under their leader *Kaliya.* He would not allow others to use the water of *Yamuna* and this ultimately led Krishna to trample him down. However, he was not killed. All these events indicate that it was not easy to suppress them. Consequently, we see that in due course all the prominent religious sects of India, in one way or the other, had to assimilate the *Naga* cult to harmonise the situation. This is evident from the fact that the *Naga* (serpent) has been used as the canopied bed of *Narayana* in the ocean, put as an instrument in the hand of Ganesha and used as Siva's ornaments. It also becomes many-headed canopy over the head of two prominent Jaina *Tirthamkaras, viz., Parshvanatha* and *Suparshvanatha,* and is associated in many ways with the Buddha and his *stupas.*

Discovery of Iron Helps Advance

With the discovery of iron, the Aryans were in much better position to advance eastward. By this time we get specific references of iron in almost all the principal texts of this period. In *Vajasaneyi Samhita*[30] *'Loha'* and *'Shyama'* and in *Atharvaveda*[31] *'Lohayas'* and *'Shyama'* words have separately been used to distinguish the copper (*Lohayas*) from the iron (*Shyamayas*). The earlier view[32] that iron was not in general use in India earlier than the sixth century B.C. holds no longer. The excavation at Atranji Khera in district Etah of UP has pushed the antiquity of the iron to C. 11th century B.C. in northern India. This date has been ascribed to the metal on the results of Radio Carbon analysis carried out by the Tata Institute of Fundamental Research at Bombay.[33] Subsequently iron was reported from a number of sites including Hastinapur[34] (District Meerut); Noh[35] (District Bharatpur); in association with the Painted Grey ware identified with the Aryans. All these evidences led us to infer that the people of this culture had settled down in the Ganga valley around 1200 B.C. It is likely that iron could have been introduced in India much before that date.[36]

Pastoral to Settled Agricultural Life

With the help of the iron tools and implements, it became very easy for the Aryans to penetrate in the Upper Doab of the Ganga-Yamuna plain and soon after the Kuru kingdom was established roughly comprising modern Thaneshwar, Delhi and the greater part of the Upper Ganga Doab with its capital on Asandivanta probably Hastinapur of the Epics and the *Puranas.*[37] Another important country was that of the *Panchalas* which roughly comprised the Bareilly,

Budaun, Farrukhabad and the adjoining districts of Rohilkand and the central Doab in the modern Uttar Pradesh. The Panchalas, as their name indicates, probably consisted of five clans—the *Krivis,* the *Turvasas,* the *Kesins,* the *Srinjayas* and the *Amakas.* They appear to be the descendants[38] of those Aryan groups who were defeated in the battle of the Ten-Kings. The tradition of interval war and alliance[39] seems to continue in the later periods also. Since we do not get any mention of the *Sarasena* of Mathura belonging to the Yadu family in the vedic literature, it may be supposed that this state grew later on out of the *Panchala* kingdom itself and existed in its west. This assumption is possible on the basis that the *Yadus* have been shown closely associated in the *Rigveda,*[40] with the *Turvasas,* one of the five founder classes of the *Panchala* country. Just outside the Doab was the country of the *Matsyas*[41] being bounded in the north by the territory of the *Kurus* and in the east by the country of the *Surasenas* comprising parts of Alwar, Jaipur and Bharatpur. According to Manu it was the land of these four territories which the Aryans occupied first when they moved from the land of *Brahmavarta* or the region between the *Sarasvati* and the *Drishadvati.* This statement of Manu is fully corroborated by the archaeological evidence. Extensive exploration[42] of this region coupled with large scale excavations of such sites as Hastinapur, Noh, Ahichehhetra, Sonkh and Atranji Khera, have confirmed that the Painted Grey Ware industry of the Aryans had its longest duration in this part of our country ranging between 1200 B.C. to 500 B.C. Two main factors probably were responsible for the long survival of the Aryans in this area, *viz.,* (1) change from pastoral to settled agricultural life, and (2) mastery over the iron industry. Copious references[43] are available in the later Vedic texts to show that how concerned the Aryans were to their agricultural profession.

Protest by Local Natives

But all did not go peacefu'ly always. A reference to Naga strife has already been made. It appears that in due course the priestly class of the Aryans grew stronger[44] in this region and they began to emphasise too much on the necessity of the sacrifices which involved a large scale animal killing. The above situation naturally would have irritated the cattle-herd commune of the region. Their displeasure has well been preserved in the famous lore in which Krishna is said to have asked the people to defy Indra, the god of sacrifice and to offer worship to Govardhana. This indicates that there was a direct and strong protest by the local natives against the *Brahmanic* system of *Yajna*. Further the word *'Govardhana'* indicates their desire to develop the cow progeny a necessary part of the agricultural life. The *Brahmanas,* it appears ultimately had to yield for there is a categorical statement against beef eating in the *Shatapatha Brahmana.*[45]

Painted Grey Ware Culture

It is not that the entire period of the Aryan occupation in *Brahmarshidesa* was prosperous and without difficulty. Soon after *Janaincjaya* there was continuous deterioration in the economic and social set-up of the Kuru country. Ultimately in the reign of *Nichakshu,* the great grandson of *Janamejaya,* the city of Hastinapur was washed away by the Ganga and the King is said to have transferred his residence to *Kausambi*.[46] *Chhandogya Upanishad*[47] also makes a reference to a great devastation of the crops in the Kuru country by hailstorms or locusts (*matachi*) which forced the people to abandon the town completely. The literary reference of the great devastation of Hastinapur by the Ganga has almost been confirmed by the flood evidence revealed during the course of excavation[48] at Hastinapur, which destroyed the Aryan settlement represented by the Painted Grey Ware industry in about 800 B.C. This is actually the period of the beginning of the Painted Grey Ware culture at *Kausambi*[49] which further proves the literary reference convincingly that the Kuru Capital was transferred from Hastinapur to *Kausambi.*

Flood Caused Large Scale Mirgation

However, the flood which brought a great disaster would not have been confined to one place alone, but would have affected a larger area. Atranji Khera excavations[50] also have brought to light the evidence of flood belonging to the same period. This tragedy followed by the devastation of crop, would have caused a large scale migration of the Aryans towards east and in some cases towards south[51] also. Since it was a period of decay and trouble we do not get rich sites of the Painted Grey ware in the lower area of the Doab, and the sites found are sporadic. However, *Kausambi* in the south-east and Sohgaura[52] in the north-east (District Gorakhpur) on river Rapti, mark the eastern limit of the Painted Grey Ware industry. Virtually rivers Rapti and Kalakavana were the natural barriers which the Aryans could not or did not like to cross. This archaeological evidence fully corroborates the *Satapatha Brahmana*[53] account which tells that till the time of Videgha *Mathcrva,* river *Sadanira* was not crossed by the Aryans since the land beyond it was uncultivable and marshy and was not burnt down. Puranic traditions also confirm this fact. It is said that the famous *Bhagiratha* marched towards east from his ancestral kingdom, hundreds of miles, with his army and reached the river Ganga. To the east of Ganga he founded a kingdom named Kosala which was bounded in the east by *Sadanira.*[54]

River *Sadanira* has usually been identified with the modern Gandaka which does not seem a correct view if geographical factors are taken into account. Moreover, in *Mahabharata* as pointed out by Oldenberg,[55] Gandaki and *Sadanira* have been referred to as separate rivers. Pargiter, therefore, identified the *Sadanira* with the Rapti which seems more reasonable view, more so because the Painted Grey Ware has not been found beyond Rapti.[56]

East India Included within Aryan Fold

It appears, that by the time of *Satapatha Brahmana,*[57] the people of the east had become quite strong and new states were gradually coming into power. It seems a period of tussle between two types of people with different ideologies, customs and beliefs. While the tyrants were trying to colonise the east, the eastern people probably known as *'Vratyas'* in *Atharavaveda,* were dashing eastward and perhaps were successful in occupying the land between *Prayaga* and *Saketa,* where the *Kashi* state emerged. The tradition does not regard the *Kashi* monarchs as belonging to one and the same dynasty.[58] According to *Jatakas*[59] some of the kings hailed from Magadha and several others were of Videhan origin. Many of *Kashi* princes bearing the cognomen 'Brahmadatta' were of Videhan lineage and a few originally belonged to Magadha. Ajatsatru of the Upnishadas, a contemporary of Uddalaka, most probably was also a Brahmadatta. This assessment is perfectly borne out with the archaeological evidence also. In spite of the best efforts, the Painted Grey Ware, the distinctive pottery of the Aryans has not been found in the *Kashi* (Varanasi) region. However, the ceramic tradition of this region represented by the black and red, the black slipped and N.B.P. wares, has an overall affinity with that found in territories of Videha, *Anga,* Magadha, etc. situated in the east beyond Rapti. This observation leads us to presume that *Kashi* and Videha were included much later within the Aryan fold. Virtually this extension would have been of cultural nature rather than actual colonisation by the ethnic movement. In *Satapatha Brahmana*,[60] Videha *Mathava* is said to have asked the fire god (Agni) to abide to the east of river *Sadanira* (Rapti). This reference is of much importance since it indicates an attempt on the part of the Aryans under the guidance of their priests, to bring the people of the east (the *Vratyas*) under the influence of the Brahmanic cult. *Atharvaveda Book XV* is known as *Vratya Book* and its connection with the *Vratyastoma* is well established. According to Bloomfield,[61] *Vratyastoma* of the *Srauta* books makes it possible for an unruly half savage community to become *Brahmana*. The details of *Vratyastoma*[62] show that it was virtually a conversion *stoma* and perhaps was politically motivated to admit particularly non-Aryans to Aryan way of life from the east and it was not simply a religious ritual, because it implied the ability to pick up the Aryan speech after conversion and not actually the ability to pronounce it correctly.

However this would have been resisted to a great extent which ultimately gave birth to the *Upanisadic* doctrines. Most probably this new philosophy was the creation of the *Vratya Rajanyas* of the east, particularly of the Videha and the *Kasi* kingdoms, who were quite close to the Aryan states. This was virtually a revolt not against the whole of the Aryan society but its priestly class which was striving hard to keep the entire society particularly the ruling-class, under its influence.

Ethnic and Cultural Expansion

Various references available in the later Vedic texts, show that there already existed a similar resentment within the Aryan society. With the result that the *Satapatha Brahmana*[63] declared that the sacrifices were useless without the spiritual knowledge and for the first time it also declared that the *Kshatriyas* were higher[64] in position than the *Brahmanas*. On the other hand, *Taittiriya Brahmana*[65] laid emphasis on one's *Karma* (deed) than the rituals. Ultimately came the *Upanishadas* condemning the supremacy of the *Brahmanas* and decrying the utility of the *Yajnas*.

All this indicates that in the changed set up the ruling class of the Aryan Society probably also joined its hand with the rulers of the non-Aryan community to minimise the influence of the *Brahmanas*. Ultimately *Brahmanas* seemed to change their rigid outlook and gradually they were converted to Upanishadic theosophy and in turn became the missionary preachers of this Neo Aryanism which subordinated the faith and belief of the *Brahmanas* to the theosophic doctrine of the Eastern *Vratya Rajanyas.*

In the light of the above discussion it may be concluded that till the period of the compilation of the *Satapatha Brahmana,* the eastward Aryan movement up to river Rapti, was actually an ethnic one, but immediately after beyond Rapti, synchronising with the Upanishadic period, it was a cultural expansion.

Notes and References

1. *Baudhayana Dharma Sutra* : 1. 1. 27, sacred Books of the East, XIV, 147.

1a. *History of Culture and the Indian People,* Vol. I, p. 215 shows that there was no Aryan invasion of India and the first man in the world was bom at Multan = Multhan = Mulasthana, on the bank of the river Devika, a tributory of the Ravi in Punjab, where the Nrsimha (man-lion) incarnation took place.

2. *Vasistha Dharma Sutra* : 1. 8. 13. (B.E. XIV 2-3).

3. *Mahabharata,* (Vanparva) 82, 111.

4. Cf. H.C. Chakladar : *Aryan Occupation of Eastern India,* Calcutta, 1962, p. 8.

5. *Manusmriti:* II. 21.
   हिमवद्विन्ध्योर्मध्यं यत्प्राग्विनशनादपि।
   प्रत्यगेव प्रयागच्च मध्यदेश: प्रकीर्तित।।

6. *Anguttara Nikaya :* II. 24 ; cf. Chakladar *op. cit.*, p. 8.

7. *Mahabodhi Vansa* Vide PT.S., pp. 114-15.

8. Cf. Chakaladar, *op. cit.*, p. 9.

9. Rhys Davids : *Buddhist India,* p. 39.

10. O.H.K. Spate : *India and Pakistan* (A General Regional Geography), London, 1957, p. 516.

11. Manu. II. 22. विदुबुर्घा: used in past perfect tense (root विद्)

12. *Ibid.,* II. 17.

13. *Ibid.,* II. 19.

14. *Ibid.,* II. 21.

15. *Ibid.,* II. 22.

16. *Ibid.,* II. 23.
    म्लेच्छदेशस्त्वत: पर:।

17. *Baudhyayana Dharma-Sutra* 1. 1. 31.

18. A : V. V. 22. 14.

19. Rv. VII. 18. 8 ; VII. 83. 8.

20. Rv. VII. 18. 14.
    निगव्ययो नवो द्रुह्युवश्च षष्टि शता सुषुषु षट सहस्त्रा:।
    षष्टिवीरीसी अधिषड् दुवोयु विश्वेदिन्द्रस्य वीर्माकृतनानि।।
    Cf. Rv. VII. 18. 6. 12.

21. Rv. 18. 19.

22. *Kurusravana* was one of the famous kings of the Puru tribe and it appears that the Kurus got their name after him, cf. Rv. X. 33. 4.
23. S.B. 13. 3. 7. 10.
24. Ait. Br. 3. 4. 4.
25. Cf. D.D. Kosambi: *The Culture and Civilization of Ancient India in Hist. Outline;* London : 1965, p. 11.
26. *Vedic Index* I, pp. 169-70; cf. H.C. Raychoudhuri, P.H. A. I., Calcutta, 1953, pp. 22-23; R.K. Mookerjee; *Hindu Civilization,* Bombay, 1957, p. 110.
27. Mbh. : Khandavavandah Parva, I. 222-34; I. 2-316, *vide* S. Sorensena : Index to the Names in the Mahabharata, Delhi, 1963, p. 738.
28. D.D. Kosambhi: *op. cit.*
29. Rv. X, 73. 6-8.
30. Vaj. San. 17. 2. 1.
31. Atharva : X 5. 4.
32. Cf. Martimer Wheeler : Civilization of the Indus Valley and Beyond, London, 1966, p. 112.
33. D.P. Agrawala : *Indian Prehistory :* 1964, Poona, 1965, p. 209; T.F. 191.
34. B.B. Lal : *Ancient India,* Nos. 10-11.
35. *Indian Archaeology*—A Review : 1963-64; 1964-65.
36. R.C. Gaur : *Indian Prehistory* : 1964, Poona 1965, p. 145.
37. Cf. Vedic Index. Vol. I.; cf. H.C. Raychoudhuri, *op. cit.,* p. 23.
38. Cf. H.C. Raychoudhuri, *op. cit.,* pp. 70-74.
39. Mahabharata 1.166; I. 93. 54.
40. Rv. I. 108. 8. cf. Raychoudhuri, *op, cit.,* p. 138.
41. Raychoudhuri, *op. cit.,* p. 66.
42. Cf. the volumes of Indian Archaeology—A Review.
43. Cf. Atharvaveda : IV. 13; VII. 18. 39; VIH. 7. 20; XII. 2. 54 Vaja. Sam. 18.12; 19. 22. di.
44. In *Satapatha Brahmana,* the priests were termed as the human god cf. S.B. II. 2.2.6.
45. S.B. 3. 1. 2. 3.
46. Cf. Pargiter: Dynasties of the Kali Age, p. 5.
47. Chh. Up. 1. 10:1, मरची हतेषु कुरू:
48. B.B. Lal: *op. cit.*
49. Cf. G.R. Sharma: Excavations at Kausambi, Allahabad, I960.
50. The excavation of Atranji Khera in District Etah (U.P.) has been conducted by the Department of History, Aligarh Muslim University, under the direction of the author of the present paper.
51. The Painted Grey Ware has been found at Ujjain which is the southern limit of this industry; cf. Indian Arch, A. Review, 1956-57.
52. I.A.R. 1961-62, p. 56.
53. Cf. P. L. Bhargava : *India in the Vedic Age,* Lucknow, 1956, pp. 142-43.
54. *Ramayana,* II. 49; 11-12.
55. Mbh: II. 27; Oldenberg : *Buddha,* p. 398 n. *vide* Rajchoudhuri, *op. cit.* p. 52.

56. J.A.S.B. 1897, p. 87.
57. *Atharvaveda:* XV; R.K. Choudhary, *Vratyas in Ancient India* (Benaras, 1964).
58. Cf. Raychoudhri, p. 75.
59. Cf. Jatakas, 378, 401, 529 *vide* Raychoudhuri, *op. cit.*
60. S.B. 1. 4. 1. 17.
61. M. Bloomfield : The Atharvaveda and the Gopalha Brahmana. *Ency. of Indo.-Aryan Research,* Vol. II, Part I. B. cf. N.N. Ghosh: *Indo·Aryan Lit.* and *Culture* (origed.).
62. Cf. N. N. Ghosh : *op. cit.,* p. 12.
63. S.B. 60. 8. 3. 10; 10. 2. 6. 19.
64. *Ibid.,* 12. *9.* II; eli.
65. *Taitt. Br.* 3. 12. 3.

6

Polity of Ancient India

I
APEX AND DISTRIBUTORIES OF POLITICAL POWER

DR. A.S. ALTEKAR

Several types of states like republics, oligarchies, diarchies and monarchies were prevailing in India in ancient times but eventually monarchy became the order of the day. This phenomenon was not peculiar to ancient India; it repeated itself in Greece and Italy, where republics were being gradually supplanted by monarchies and empires. Representative government was not known both to the ancient East and West, and so republics could prosper only when the state was small and a meeting of its Assembly, consisting practically of all the senior members of its privileged order, was possible. As in the ancient republics of Greece and Rome, political power was vested not in the whole population, but in the members of a small privileged order, mostly consisting of Kshatriyas and perhaps of the Brahmanas also, in a few cases. The ancient Hindu polity worked in a society that had accepted the principles of the caste system, which laid down that government was primarily the function and duty of the Kshatriyas, assisted to some extent by the Brahmanas. Franchise in the ancient Indian republics could, therefore, not be extended to the whole population. In the modern age, which does not believe in the predetermination of one's functions by birth, it will naturally have to be extended to all.

Democracy is the order of the day at present and we have a full-fledged republic in India. It will be, therefore, necessary to understand the causes that led to the disappearance of the republics in ancient India. Generally speaking, republics could function successfully in ancient India in smaller states. They also presupposed a kind of tribal unity in the governing class; republics failed to develop into a purely territorial stage of large dimensions. Distances are annihilated now; the principle of representative government has been discovered and is in universal practice. Tribal stage has been passed away long ago and we have now developed a national consciousness. There is therefore no reason why India should not function and flourish as a large republic.

Growing veneration for a hereditary ruler fostered by the principle of the divinity of king was also partly responsible for the disappearance of the ancient republics. When presidents, generals and members of the council became hereditary in republics, their polity could not be much differentiated from monarchy. Divinity of king is now a dead doctrine and we need not apprehend that it will prejudice the development of the republican spirit of institutions in the modern times, except perhaps in the Indian states, where the monarchical traditions are still nourished. Ancient Indian polity, however, conceded divinity only to virtuous, conscientious and able rulers, who acted as real trustees for their subjects, and who were prepared to sacrifice their own interests, comforts and funds to promote the well-being of their subjects. Monarchy can continue in Indian states only if their subjects are convinced that their monarchs belong to the above category. Our political thinkers, it should not be forgotten, condemn incapable, vicious and tyrannical kings as demons incarnate and permit their subjects to dethrone them, and even to kill them.

Ancient Republics Lacked Harmony and Concord

A study of ancient Indian history and polity shows that our republics flourished as long as there was harmony and concord among the members of their Assemblies. There was, however, a tendency among them to quarrel. In some republics every member of the Assembly was given the title of raja; often he was not inclined to accept the leadership of fellow member, because it presupposed his own inferiority. Neighbouring kings used to send spies to foment quarrels and dissensions among the members of the republican bodies. Groups and parties were often formed in the republican assemblies and they spent their time and energy in bringing each other's downfall and incidentally paving the way of an outside conqueror. Many of the ancient Indian republics were destroyed by the neighbouring kings and emperors by encouraging feuds and dissensions among the members of their Assemblies. The party defeated in the Assembly would often seek outside help and thus seal the ruin of the state. Modern India, which seeks to develop republican traditions and institutions, may well carve on the gate of its future Parliamentary House the prophecy of the Buddha about the Lichchhavi republic. The republic of the Lichchavis, said the Buddha, will prosper as long as the members of their Assembly meet frequently, show reverence to age, experience and ability, transact the state business in concord and harmony and do not develop selfish parties engaged in eternal wrangling for their narrow and selfish ends.

Emergence of Monarchy

In the course of time, monarchy became the order of the day owing to the causes already explained. It cannot be denied that our political writers have placed the highest possible ideals before the kingly order; they can be, hardly improved in modern times. The king was to be dhritavrata, pledged to maintain and defend law, order, justice and morality; he was not above the law, but subject to its jurisdiction. He was to be something even more than a trustee for his subjects; a trustee has merely to abstain from taking any undue advantage of his position, while promoting the interest of the trust; the king, according to the ancient Indian ideals, has to sacrifice his own personal comforts and interests in order to secure the prosperity of the kingdom. Divinity was conceded not to the person but to the office of the king. The theory that a king can do no wrong and is accountable to none but God was almost unknown to ancient India. Attention of the king was pointedly drawn to the great necessity, of a proper training, the absence of which was sure to land him into numerous pitfalls, that do not come across the path of an ordinary individual. The doctrine of the divinity of the king's office was intended merely to inspire respect for authority; and not to encourage autocracy or irresponsibility in the kingly order.

It must be however admitted that in actual practice many kings failed to live up to the ideal. The percentage of vicious or tyrannical—

kings in ancient India was however by no means higher than in medieval Europe. It would be however useful to understand the causes that were responsible for the non-realisation of the ideal of kingship in a large number of cases.

Failure to develop proper secular and constitutional checks on the power of the king was the main reason for the kingly ideal not being frequently realised in practice. Like some medieval political thinkers of Europe, most of our ancient Indian thinkers did not doubt nor say that a bad king was accountable to God alone. Nevertheless, in actual practice the fear of hell was the only effective deterrent in the case of a tyrant. Our writers no doubt permit subjects to migrate en masse from the country, if the king became oppressive; ancient inscriptions supply some instances of kings being brought to their sense by this method. This remedy, however, is a very impracticable one and could not be easily resorted to. They also sanction regicide in extreme cases. Regicide, however, presupposes an open and successful rebellion, as a remedy against day-to-day petty cases of tyranny; it is altogether impracticable and inapplicable. Ancient Indian polity failed to develop secular and practicable remedies which could control the actions of a king who was inclined to disregard the ideal and become tyrannical.

This failure was largely due to the disappearance of the samitis or popular Assembly in the post-Vedic period. As long as these Assemblies functioned, they could effectively control the actions of the king in the day-to-day administration. The Vedic literature makes it quite clear that a king could succeed in maintaining himself on the throne only so long as his samiti or Popular Assembly was in agreement with him. If there was a disagreement, the views of the Assembly generally prevailed, and kings had to submit or abdicate and go into exile.

Central Assemblies, however, gradually disappeared in the post-Vedic period, not because democracy became more and more unsuitable to the Indian temperament, but because the state became bigger and bigger in size, rendering the meetings of a Central Assembly more and more impracticable. Had Asoka, Chandragupta or Harsha revived the Central Assembly, its members would have had to spend several weeks in reaching the capital in order to attend the Assembly meetings, and an equally long time in returning to their homes. The principle of representation was also unknown in those days both in the East and the West.

It is possible to try the experiment of a limited and constitutional monarchy in the modern Indian states, if the popular and Representative Assemblies are allowed to function as in the Vedic period. Members of the princely order will have to remember that they will have to submit or abdicate and go into exile if they cannot carry their Assembly with them.

Decentralisation of Powers

Effective popular Central Assemblies being found impracticable in the case of larger kingdoms, ancient Indian political thinkers tried to protect the interests of the people by recommending and bringing about a great decentralisation of the functions of the government. Large powers were vested in the district, town and village administrations, which could be effectively supervised and controlled by local non-official councils. In the Gupta period, the sale of even the waste lands owned by the state required the sanction of the popular district council. The powers of town and village councils in ancient India were probably more extensive than those of similar bodies in any other polity, eastern or western, ancient or modern. They collected the revenues on behalf of the Central Government, refused to collect oppressive taxes, settled village disputes, organised works of public utility, and often maintained and financed hospitals, poor houses and educational institutions. It would be worthwhile in the new Indian constitution to entrust larger and larger power to the district boards and local and village councils. A word of warning, however, must be given. The village councils worked successfully in the past because the people had a high regard for truth and character and were instinctively inclined to respect age, experience and ability. Members of the village councils were not elected; they were raised to that position by the consensus of public opinion. Democracy of the modern type involving voting and party alignments did not exist, and is new to India. It presupposes widespread of education, which must be immediately brought about. Fear of God and hell which has now disappeared most be replaced by the sense of civic duty, which alone can now induce our elected representatives to place the good of the people they represent above everything else.

Village Panchayats Exercised Wide Powers

Village Panchayats of ancient India exercised wide judicial powers. They decided practically all cases excepting those of serious crimes.

Life in ancient times were simple and the law to be administered was known to and understood by all. Modern law is complex and complicated, and presupposes technical knowledge and assistance; parties to a dispute may often belong to distant places. Village Panchayats in modern times cannot, therefore, successfully exercise that wide civil jurisdiction which they did in the past. Nevertheless a beginning must be made by investing them with a limited civil jurisdiction. It will be difficult for witnesses to tell brand lies in the presence of their fellow residents in the Panchayat courts, with reference to events and transactions well-known to the locality. The revival of the village Panchayat courts will no doubt secure speedier justice. There will be, however, some uphill task. The faith in God and the dread of hell that helped the cause of justice in ancient times are rapidly dying out. Party factions are cropping up in villages due to illiteracy and selfishness. So until a proper sense of civic duty and responsibility is developed to replace the faith in God and fear of hell, there will be some difficulty in the successful working of the village Panchayats.

Ancient India sought to solve the problem of the finance of the local bodies by localising a part of the land revenue. Most of the villages could get back about 15 to 20% of the proceeds of land-tax, which they collected for the Central Government, as its contribution to the funds of the village councils. This experiment is well worth trying in modern times.

Excellent Principles of Taxation

There can be no doubt that ancient Indian political thinkers had evolved excellent principles for taxation. The grounds on which remissions were sanctioned and exemptions granted were also as a rule sound. All will agree that the state should gather the taxes like the bee which sucks the honey without damaging the flower, that trade and industry should be taxed not on gross earnings, but on net profits, that an article should not be taxed twice; that the raise in taxation when inevitable, should be gradual and so on. The principles of exemption were also sound. The original idea was to grant exemption only to learned but poor Brahmanas, who used to impart free education. In some cases this privilege was abused, but the State usually did not fail to levy taxes on Brahmanas, traders and government servants. The cases where the whole Brahmana class was exempted were far and few between; we cannot and should not revive in modern times such a concession to any wholesale class determined solely by birth.

The taxation was usually determined by the local customs and traditions. In the later times, however, when the Samiti disappeared from the scene, governments would often impose high and arbitray taxes. We often find tugs of war between the central governments, which wanted to levy new and oppressive taxes and the village committees, which would refuse to collect them. Very often, however, power prevailed and justice went to the wall; we find villagers migrating en masse to escape unbearable taxation. There can be no doubt that in later times, the interests of the average man in the sphere of taxtion were not adequately protected when a greedy tyrant was on the throne. This, however, happened primarily because there was samiti or popular assembly in later times. The importance of a strong and vigilant popular assembly as a champion of popular rights and interests cannot be overemphasised.

Nation-building Activities

The ancient Indian state was not merely a tax-gathering corporation, interested only in preserving in law and order. It is pleasing and surprising to find that the state in ancient India should have interested itself in a number of ministrant activities of the nation-building type, which are being undertaken by the modern governments only in relatively recent times. Individual enterprise and initiative were, however, not usually affected by the activities of the state, because it would usually utilise the services of commercial and industrial guilds to carry out its policy. Freedom was also given to experts to chalk out their own plans within certain reasonable limits, and the state would give them substantial subsidies to carry them out, if they contributed to further its nation-building activities. This undoubtedly is a pleasing characteristic of the ancient Indian polity. State for instance helped education merely by giving liberal grants to non-official colleges and universities; it did not care to dictate their policy or courses through a Director of Public Instruction. The growing sphere of state socialism threatens to create a conflict between the individual and the state in modern times. If the state seeks to materialise its plan and policy through the local bodies and trade guilds and organisations, as it did in ancient India, the interests of both are likely to be harmonised.

Welfare of the Whole Community

The ideals of the ancient Indian state were undoubtedly very high and all-comprehensive. It sought to promote the moral, material, aesthetic and spiritual progress of the whole community. Human ideas about the progress in those different spheres go on changing from age to age, and it is no wonder that we may not be able to agree with all that the state in ancient India did or countenanced in order to achieve progress in this four-fold field. For instance, it gave a general support to the varnasramadharma, which was undoubtedly iniquitous, especially to the Sudras and untouchables. We must not, however, forget that a state is but the spokesman of the society it represents; if certain iniquitous practices were tolerated by the state in ancient India, the society is as much to blame as the state. We should not judge ancient customs and institutions by modern standards and ideals.

Status Predetermined by Birth

People in those days had a burning and living faith in the doctrine of Karma. Even the Sudras and Untouchables believed that they were born in their particular caste as a natural result of certain sins committed by them in past lives. As a further consequence of the same, classes have certain religious and social disabilities imposed upon them in this life as well, under the sanction of the divine sastras. It was impossible for the ancient Indian state even to think of disallowing these disabilities much less of removing them. Equality of all citizens before the law did, therefore, not exist in ancient India to a great extent. It is no doubt a sad spectacle. We would all have felt prouder of our civilisation if the Smriti writers had imposed a higher punishment on the Brahmana culprit than on the Sudra one, since they recognised the sin of the former to be greater than that of the latter. We should, however, not forget that such iniquities and inequalities existed in all civilisations, eastern and western and have not completely disappeared even in modern times. If the fine for murdering a Sudra is lighter than that for murdering a Brahmana, we should not forget that the wergild for the head of a slave or serf was much smaller in Europe than that for the head of a knight or landlord. Limited exemption from taxation sometimes sanctioned by the ancient Indian state to the Brahmana had its counterpart in the European polity, where the church and nobility enjoined many more unjust exemptions down to the 18th century. Ancient Indian state did no doubt not believe in affording opportunities to the son of a cobbler to become a premier; but such a phenomenon rarely occurred in ancient times, both in the West and the East. It will have to be admitted, however, by the impartial critic that the ancient Indian state was not solicitous only for the interests of the Brahmanas; it tried to promote the material and moral interests of all the castes; only it did not encourage one progession to trespass on the field of another; for society honestly believed that these fields were predetermined by birth.

All-India Emperor not at the Cost of Local Autonomy

The ideal of an all-India state under an emperor ruling over the territories from the Himalayas to the sea was recognised as early as c. 1000 B.C. if not earlier. There were, however, only few occasions in ancient Indian history when it was actually realised. The recognition of the ideal was probably a natural consequence of the realisation of the fundamental unity of India—geographical, religious and cultural. The ancient Indian polity, however, laid down that the empires should not be at the cost of local autonomy, culture and institutions; it, therefore, laid down that the chakravartin or the emperor should remain content if his imperial status is recognised by the offer of a suitable tribute. He was not to annex the local, provincial or district kingdoms; even if the heads of the latter had been defeated or had died fighting, some relations of theirs were to be put on the throne on condition that they were willing to recognise the conqueror's suzerainty. Local laws, customs and traditions were never to be interfered with by the conqueror.

An all-India state powerful enough to bring about the unity of the country and to defend it from foreign aggression through a co-operative effort under the aegis of the Central Government but generous and considerate enough to permit the existence of local governments following their own customs, traditions and fostering their own culture and ideals was thus the ideal of the ancient Indian polity. Curiously enough it is very much allied to our present ideal of a strong and united India with full autonomy to province. Let us therefore analyse a little more closely this idea and find out its strong and weak points as disclosed by our ancient history.

Ideal of Unitary India with Autonomous Provinces Examined

The insistence of the political thinkers that a conqueror should allow the conquered king or state to retain his or its individuality in the feudal capacity undoubtedly produced many good results. It permitted local culture, traditions and political institutions to develop more or less unhampered. It toned down provincial dynastic jealousies and animosities; for a province or a kingdom, could at most aim at imposing its more or less nominal suzerainty over its neighbour; it could never aim at crushing its culture or wiping out its independent existence. Warfare also tended to remain humane; neither side had the danger of being completely wiped out, if it was defeated; it, therefore, did not stoop to unchivalrous and unapproved methods to avert a defeat or win a victory.

While recognising that this ideal of an ernpire with a number of composite units governed by feudatory kings or republics had many good points about it, we cannot remain oblivious to certain injurious results that sprang from it. The recommendation to recognise local autonomy by permitting the conquered king or state to continue in the feudatory capacity eventually stood in the way of effective unification of India. Most of the ancient Indian empires were merely loose federations of a number of feudal kingdoms held together by masterful personalities for a few decades. Most of his feudatories were usually entertaining imperial ambitions; for the political thinkers recognised that it was but a natural thing that each feudatory should aspire to the imperial status for himself. As a consequence big kingdoms and empires in ancient India were never in a state of equilibrium for a long time. There was a constant tussle going on for the coveted position of a chakravartin. It was the duty of each king to secure the expansion of his kingdom by attacking his neighbours when they were weak. Feudatories were therefore usually on the lookout for an opportunity to rebel against the imperial power. Ninety per cent of the wars in ancient Indian history would have not been recommended to every feudatory, and if its successful realiser had not been prevented from annexing the conquered state and compelled to permit it to continue to rule in the feudatory capacity.

Ancient Indian political thinkers probably thought that there was nothing wrong in this ideal. Probably they felt that each king, state or province should have a sporting chance to be the leading state in the country at some one time or another. Frequent wars no doubt thus became inevitable; they were, perhaps, felt to be necessary to keep up the martial spirit and traditions of the Kshatriyas. It did not matter whether it was to be Pataliputra, Kanauj or Avanti which was to be the imperial capital of India. Whatever province may be at the head of the empire, the culture, religion and language of the subordinate provinces did not suffer; for the conqueror was expressly required to respect and encourage local traditions, cultures and institutions.

Ancient Indians began to become growingly indifferent in the course of time to the necessity and desirability of a strong and stable central state. As monarchies became the order of the day from c. 400 A.D. the interstate struggles became dynastic wars for hegemony; people were not much interested in them because they knew that their local culture, laws and institutions would not be much affected, whatever may be the outcome of the struggle. Contending armies also fought not so much for their provinces as for their kings. There was hardly any patriotism in the real sense of the word. This ideal of a federal-feudal empire, with full liberty to each constituent state to strike for the imperial status but without permission to forge a unitary empire after the conquest thus produced a state of continuous instability in ancient India. There were frequent wars, but they did not lead to the emergence of a strong and unitary state. The energy of the nation was unnecessarily wasted in interminable feuds, which only weakened the combatants. The country as a whole became weak and fell an easy prey to the Muslim invaders.

II
ANCIENT SOUTH INDIAN POLITY

T.R. Sesha Iyengar

It would be possible in this article to attempt only an outline of the history of the evolution of political institutions in South India in early times. All that is possible to accomplish here is to pass in review the history of South Indian polity during one most remarkable but nonetheless forgotten period of its development. The early centuries of the Christian era form an important landmark in the development of political institutions of the peoples of peninsular India. An attempt will be made to deal with the political thought of ancient South India during the early centuries of the Christian era as exhibited in ancient Sangam works, and to present a picture, however dim and shadowy, of the state and its duties during the period under review. It may also be unhesitatingly affirmed that the political organisation portrayed in these Sangam works was not simply an ideal sought after by the thinkers and writers of the day but also an actual achievement. That there was phenomenal progress achieved in the field of polity, that the Government in that distant age was not an undiluted, unmitigated despotism but was subject to checks and counterchecks, that the ancient monarch carried on the Government in consonance with high ideals and lofty principles, that he invariably sought the advice of a council of elders and certain popular assemblies and that he had a great regard for public opinion which reigned as supreme as the law guarded by himself, these indisputable facts will, it is hoped, be apparent from a perusal of this article.

The reputed works of the third Sangam like Ahananuru, Purananuru, Sillappathikaram, Manerulkalai, Kalethokai, the Ten Idylls, Puraporulvenbamalai, and the Kural which are now acknowledged by the generality of scholars to have belonged to the period under review throw much interesting light upon the polity of this time.

The Word State

According to Valluvar, the constituent elements of a State are the minister, people, resources, allies, army, and fortresses. That is a great country which never fails in its need of harvest which, is the abode of sages, which attracts men to itself by the greatness of its wealth and which yields abundantly being free from pests, which is free from famines and plagues, and which is safe from the invasions of enemies. The country which has known no devastation at the hands of its foes and which, even should it suffer any, would not bate one whit in its yield will be called a jewel among the countries of the world. The waters of the surface, the waters that flow underground, rain water, well situated mountains, strong fortifications, these are indispensable to every country. The nation, which is not divided into warring sects, which is free from murderous anarchists and which has no traitors within its bosom to run it, is truly great.

Fortresses

Fortresses are helpful not only to the weak who think only of their defence but also to the strong and powerful. Water courses, deserts, mountains, thick jungles—all these constitute various kinds of defensive barriers. Height, thickness, impregnability, these are the requisites that science demands of fortresses. That is the best fortress which is venerable in very few places, which is spacious and capable of breaking the assaults of those that attempt to take it, which affords facility of defence for the garrison, which is filled with stores of every kind, which is garrisoned by men that will make a brave defence, which cannot be reduced by a regular siege, by storm or even by mining, which has been rendered impregnable by works of various kinds and which enables the defenders to fell down their adversaries. The poet Mulamkirar of Aiyur in referring to the different parts of a fortification says, 'there was first of all a most so deep that it reached down to the abodes of demons; this was crowned with turrets from which the archers shot forth their arows; there was an impervious wood that surrounded small forts at every angle'.

The Prince

Regarding the qualifications of the prince, we are told that he must have courage, liberality, wisdom, energy, alertness, learning and decision. He should not fail in virtue, should not sin against the laws of valour, should know how to develop the resources of his kingdom, how to enrich his treasury, to preserve his wealth, and spend it worthily. He should be accessible to all his subjects and be never harsh of word. He should have the virtue to bear with words that are bitter to the ear. Parsimony, over-confidence, and excessive armour, these are the faults which a prince should avoid. The ideals that a king should place before himself are also described. He should give with grace and rule with love. He must administer impartial justice and consult the men of law. The prince shall devote himself assiduously to works that are commended by the wise. If he neglects them, he will suffer in all his future births. Men look up to the sceptre of the prince for protection. His sceptre is the mainstay of the Brahmans and of righteousness. In the land of the prince who wields the sceptre—in accordance with the law, seasonal rains and rich harvests have their home. It is not the lance but the sceptre that brings victory to the prince. The prince who is not easy of access, who judges not causes with care will fall from his place and perish even when he has no enemy. In poem 35, Purananuru, the poet says addressing the king, 'Be easy of access at fitting time as though the lord of justice sat to hear and decree right. Such kings have rain on their dominions at their will: Kings get the blame whether rains fail or flow copiously and lack the praise; such is the usage of the world'. The prince that guards his subjects from enemies both within and without may punish them when they go wrong. It is not a blemish but his duty. Punishing the wicked with death is like the removing of weeds from the cornfield. It is pleasing to note that these high ideals were completely realised. When Pandiyan Neduncheleyan was told by pilgrims that some North Indian princes insulted him and other Tamil princes, he is reported to have exclaimed, 'I shall defeat those princes and make them carry stones; otherwise let me be known as the king who tyrannised over his subjects'. Thus oppression of the people by a monarch was considered most abominable in those days and unworthy of the ancient Tamil rulers. The prowess of the king in war, his immutable justice and accessibility, his protecting hand over the poor, his liberality and piety, are all set forth in Puranuru and Puraporulvenbamalai.

Evils of Weak Monarchy

The author of the Kural is aware of the dangers of incompetence on the part of the monarch. The sovereignty of the prince who does not oversee the administration everyday and remove the irregularities will wear day-by-day. The evils of tyranny have not escaped the penetrating eye of the immortal author of the Kural. The prince who oppresses his subjects and does iniquity is worse than an assassin. The thoughtless prince whose rule swerves from the ways of justice will lose his kingdom and his substance. We know for instance, from Silappathikaram, the tragic end of Pandiyan Neduncheleyan when he realised that he had unjustly put to death Kovalan. The tears of those groaning under oppression wear away the prosperity of the prince. Unjust rule darkens the glory of the prince. Repression of the rich, forgetfulness by the Brahman of his science, failure of the heavens to send showers in their season, premature and abrupt close of the reign, these are the characteristics of tyranny.

Functions of the King

The king's position in the early centuries of the Christian era was hereditary. He was the head of society. He was the supreme priest, the first to offer sacrifices when seasons fail and the supreme commander. He was also the supreme judge in civil and criminal cases. We have interesting details as regards the administration of justice in that remote age. A thief arrested with stolen property was beheaded. A man caught in the act of adultery was killed. Justice was administered free of charge to suitors. There were special officers who performed the duties of judges. Crimes were rare since punishments were very severe. Though the king was the repository of the executive and judicial powers, these powers were harmoniously combined in him. He carried out the law which had been formulated by the great men who had gone before him. His function was to administer, not to make the law. The king was not an autocrat but a constitutional ruler.

The Minister

As the eyes of a prince are his own ministers, he should use his discretion and choose them wisely. The minister should be a man of affairs, clever, pure-minded, devoted to the prince and skilful in reading the hearts of men. The man who is able to develop the resources of the kingdom and cure the ills that may befall it should be made to manage the affairs of the state. The man who is endowed with kindness, intelligence, decision, and who is free from greed, should be selected for service. Work should be entrusted to men in consideration of their expert knowledge and capacity for patient exertion, and not of their love towards the person of the prince. The prosperity of the prince who will not take counsel with his councillors will wane.

Council of Elders

According to Puraporulvenbamalai, the council of elders which existed in the Tamil country should possess the eight qualities and should always look to success after duly weighing the chances of victory and defeat and after debating justly the questions raised and the objections urged. The eight qualities of the councillors stated to good birth, learning, good character, truthfulness, purity, ornament of even mindedness without being envious and being covetous. These are ideal characteristics which, if possessed, would bring glory to the land. The power of the king was restricted not merely by the council of elders but also by the five great assemblies.

The Five Great Assemblies

These consisted of the representatives of the people, priests, physicians, astrologers or augurs, and ministers. The council of representatives safeguarded the rights and privileges of the people, the priests directed religious ceremonies, the physicians attended to all matters affecting the health of the king and his subjects, astrologers fixed auspicious times for public ceremonies and predicted important events. The ministers attended to the collection and expenditure of the revenue and administration of justice. Separate places were assigned in the capital town for each of these assemblies for their meetings and transaction of business. On important occasions, they attended the king's levee in the throne hall or joined the royal procession. The power of Government was vested in the king and in the five great assemblies. According to Mr. R.G. Majumdar, the so-called five assemblies were really the five committees of a great assembly. The representative character of these bodies and the effective control which they exercised over the administration are clearly established. It is interesting to note also that the ministers formed one of the assemblies. The assemblies taken together may justly be compared with the Privy Council, the assembly of the ministers corresponding with the cabinet composed of a selected few.

Influence of the Poets

Besides the constitutional checks explained above, there were additional safeguards to the wayward actions of the king in the class of poets who were the sages and wise men of those days. They were a privileged class and they tendered their good counsel without fear or favour and the King dared not injure them as their person was considered sacred.

Irrigation

The ancient Tamil kings realised that the great remedy against famine was irrigation. Very extensive irrigation works were carried out by these rulers who had at their disposal large treasures and an immense amount of forced labour. The embankment thrown on the Cauvery by Karikal Chola is an instance in point. Then Tamil kings thoroughly understood the importance of agriculture to this land. The writers of the age were also keenly alive to the need for fostering agriculture. In 35, Purananuru, the poet exhorts the king to lighten the load of the tillers of the soil. An old lyric (No. 18, P.N.N.) says:

" . . . . therefore O Cheliyan, great in war, despise this not
Increase the reservoirs for water made
Who bind the water and supply to fields
Their measured flow, these bind
The earth to them: the fame of others passes swift away."

Land Revenue

The king collected as state revenue one-sixth of the produce from the people. The Tamil princes were enjoined not to levy arbitrary taxation. There was a young prince called the learned Pandyan Nambi. He was disposed to be tyrannical. He was advised by the poet Pisiranthayar not to follow evil methods of rule in the following words:—

"If an elephant take mouthfuls of ripe grain on it the twentieth part of an acre will yield it food for many days but if it enter a hundred fertile fields with no keeper
Its foot will trample down much more than its mouth receives
So if a wise king who knows the path of right take just his due
His land will prosper yeilding myriad fold
But if a king not softened by his knowledge take just what he desires
Nor heed prescriptions, rule, feasting with song and dance
Amid his court and kindred and show no love to his subjects
Like the field that elephant entered
His kingdom will perish and he himself will lose his all."

The Army

Public defence was highly organised. Elephants, spears and swords, bows and arrows, cavalry and infantry, chariots, all were utilised in war. The army of a prince should be well organised and puissant. It should contain veterans who could hold out in desperate situations with grim determination regardless of decimating attacks. It should know no defeat, should be incapable of being corrupted, should have a long tradition of valour behind it and should face valiantly even the god of death if he were to advance against it in all his fury. It should not be inferior in numbers to that of the enemy, should have no implacable jealousies and should not be left to starve without pay and should be led by capable chiefs. Our ancients knew the different ways of fighting an enemy by siege and in the open battlefield. They employed spies. According to the teachings of the Kural, the power of the prince who has tact to convert enemies into allies will last without end. If he has to contend alone and without allies against two enemies, he must try to gain over one of them to his side. Valluvar says:

"Form a wise plan, consolidate thy resources, provide for thy defences. If you do this the pride of your enemies will soon be humbled to the dust. They shall not last long who humble not the pride of men who defy them. The prince should take into consideration the output, the wastage, the profit that the undertaking will yield and then put his hand to it. He must weigh justly the difficulty of the enterprise, his own strength, the strength of his enemy and the strength of his allies and then he should enter upon it. To make war without planning every detail of it before hand is only to transplant your enemy on carefully prepared soil. Bend down before your adversaries till the day of their decline, when that day arrives, you may easily throw them down."

Though the ancient Tamils were implacable in their rage, still no one ventured into a war unless forced by sheer necessity and without deeply considering all the horrors of war. The Puraporul-venbamalai gives us an idea of the political organisation of the ancient Dravidians. According to it, all their science of public or state affairs was summarized chiefly under the head of war which consisted of various branches. Battle lifting was the beginning of warfare. The raid was followed by the rescue and this by the organised invasion of the enemy's country for which a particular wreath was assumed. This led to the systematic defence and the defenders assumed a different wreath. The seige and protection of forts, each demanded its appropriate garland. Then came war in general and for that another wreath was borne. Finally, the victors who had gained supremacy had another wreath which they wore as the proud token of victory. This work relates to the expeditious in which these eight different chaplets were worn by the combatants according to the character of those undertakings and the feelings of those engaged in them. These garlands were intended to strike awe into the minds of the opposing hosts and to some extent supplied the place of military uniforms.

Laws of War

The rules of warfare may then be briefly touched upon. The capture of the enemy's cattle was carried out with a view to remove the useful and sacred animals from the scene of war. The invader was equally humane to the aged, the infirm, the childless, the women and the Brahamans. 'Touch not the temples where sacrifices were offered; spare the dwellings of the holy ascetics; enter not the houses of the sacred Vedic Brahamans; let all the rest be abandoned to our warriors.' But the ancients were merciless to the vanquished. The war usually ended with the death of the King and the overthrow of his Kingdom. The inhabitants of the invaded country would flee on everyside. The country would be ravaged with fire. 'The beautiful homes with pictured halls are levelled with the dust. Assess are yoked to plough up the soil with spears; while worthless plants are sown on the foundations.'

Such was the system of Government followed in the three great kingdoms of the Pandya, Cherla, and Chola in the early centuries of the Christian era.

7

Law in Ancient India

I

CONCEPTION OF LAW IN ANCIENT INDIA

RADHA KRISHNA CHOUDHARY

Law Based upon Religion and Agreement of Learned Men

The idea of evolution of property finally brought in its train certain implications and social complications, the remedy for which was to be found in forms of legal justice.[1] The stability of human society depends upon harmonious inter-relationship of the profoundest ideas of all its members, which can be easily striven for! Though the primitive Aryans had no such organised state and system of administration, we find that they wanted order everywhere and the projection of this idea into all departments of human life and the natural procedure for the early thinkers. They valued the norm of humanity and conceived the notion that "order dwels amongst men, in truth, in noblest places."[2] The moral and political theories determine origin and development of law. The foundation of law was laid on this basis. There is no denying the fact that the Vedic people, though not backed by any definite democratic theory, were democratic in practice and Zimmer admits that the Vedic polity was limited everywhere by the will of the people. The early Aryans looked upon law as based upon the twin roots of religion and agreement of men learned in sacred Law[3] and the general conception was that the Samiti or Sabha had authority to declare laws. In the Vedic period it was the law that created State. The Purohitas were generally regarded as law-makers and their judicial authority was highly valued in the Vedas and the later literature.[4] Law in the Vedic period was the outcome of social and economic conditions and the expression of its intellectual capacity for dealing with those questions. The basis of law was democratic. Law expressed the truth underlying conduct and was a standard or ideal. It was correlated with justice. The Sanskrit term "Dharma" or the Pali, Dhamma, has been translated into English as "religion or law". The legal historians have accepted the latter, i.e., Law, Dharma is from the root "Dhṛi"—"to hold Dharma is so-called because it holds all beings with reference to society." Dr. Thomas has rightly observed, "Such a conception must have arisen very early with formation and growth of the association of individuals in societies . . . covering every form of human action."[5] Ethologists believe that when man adopts identical or common peaceful means of interchanges he creates also laws or rules of exchange. Dharma is that which produces harmony of work between dualism of human nature yoking the horse of egoism to the care of altruism.[6] Dharma keeps the whole and inorder as reins do the horses.[7]

Dharma as the Foundation of Social Order

With the development society and its complications the inner impulse of the living beings marched towards reasonable standards of life and as a creation of social forces Dharma emanated from the whole to be impressed on the individuals. Dharma is the foundation of social order.[8] Law is a means for realising in a particular way some ends derived from the different interests of life. The object of law (Dharma). . . is the maintenance of peace and order in the community according to the Manava-code.[9]

Principles about Law Established

During the Vedic period, law was the sublime them of the people. It brought together social and ethical ideas and reflected itself in the social aspect. The ascendency of the priest or the Purohitas, whose importance in judicial matter can in no way be ignored, idealised the practical conception of law but even that idealisation did not deter it from disclosing the world order as a whole. To maintain in its wider sense, all its legislative activity had to be guided and controlled by the existence of law.[10] Law covered all fields of human activity and indicated the regulative principles of nature and society. The word "rita" in the Vedic hymns signifies the order of the heavenly movements.[11] Sir Radhakrishnan is of opinion that it stands of "law in general and the immanence of justice."[12] To the Vedic people there was but one "rita" for both nature and men. To them, there was no dualism between nature and man. "Rita" may also be taken to mean "Standard". The Vedic people thought that some sort of Standard must be maintained to carry on the principles of law into practice. The Vedic experts did not leave a single stone unturned to develop the abstract side of law philosophically, and they established certain principles about law. Law led to everlasting truth.[13] The Vedic conception was that "by law they came to truth."[14] Philosophically, law and truth are regarded as two sideds by one reality.[15] Atharvaveda says, law is above the gods—"the home and life of gods."[16]

'Dharma' and 'Rita' (Law and Order) Intimately Connected

The Upanishadic legal experts started with pure philosophy and enunciated the principles that truth is the one reality and law and order are its different phases. The word "rita" is replaced by "Dharma" though the conception is the same. The conceptions of 'Dharma' and 'rita' (law and order) are intimately connected and tend to merge in each other for Law in scientific sense of sequence and coexistence is another name for order, and harmoney.[17] Upanishadic period was the time for the solidification of law. Law is the King of Kings . . . nothing is higher than law."[18] Law and truth are one and the same thing. In this period the priests wanted to maintain their ascendency by adding some virtues in their name. They made law such as to suit their own interests. They gave a philosophical interpretation of law, Moral authority imbedded in law was metaphysical in character. Vedic seers conceived of order in the very heart of the world but that ideas is spiritualised in the Upanishad when it puts the matter pithily in short sentence, "So the whole world has truth as its soul—that is reality."[19] The theological and metaphysical conception of law is a fine combination of objectivism and subjectivism. The ancient Indian Philosophy of Law was absolute and universal but the relativity of codes applicable to particular communities and guilds was recognised and the underlying principle was based on the universal Dharma.

Buddhist Conception of Law, Moral in Nature

The Buddhist law-givers were also influenced by the metaphysics of the Upanishad. Buddha declared: "Truth eternally exists whether he had appeared in the word or not". This clearly explains that the Buddhist philosophers deepened the conception of law and accepted, if not whole, at least a part of the metaphysical theory. The Buddhist conception of law was moral in nature. Dr. Barua, while discussing the relation between truth and law and explaining the implications of truth observes that "if a man declares what is true they say he declares law, and if he declares law they say he declares what is true". Dharma is not simply law but that which includes or underlies law.[20] Dharma meant norm, necessary or eternal order and it stood in place of theodicy or cosmos created and carried on by a first and final cause.[21] Stcherleab sky is of opinion that Buddhism is a metaphysical theory and that Dharma is transcendental.[22] According to the Buddhist conception, Dharma and law are the same. We find a similar conception in the Mahabharat. Dharma is protected by truth.[23] Truth is the container of Dharma and is Dharma itself.[24]

Approach to Law Transformed into Metaphysical

The realist approach to law was finally transformed into metapysical stage. The nature of law is highly generalised in the later period and it is said to be based on law and justice.[25] The social ideals of the community materially influenced the character of the law. Law has been interpreted as the means to secure Abhyudaya i.e., welfare in this world. Kulluka speaks of it as "relating to what has to be done to secure visible goods."[26] In the words of Mahamahopadhyaya Kane, the average Aryan conception of Dharma was that it represented privileges, duties and obligations of a man. It was a sociological concept. The end of law was to promote the welfare of men both individually and socially, and in order to make the law applicable, it generally encouraged obedience by reward and discouraged disobedience by awarding penalty. The conception of law is mainly based on a contract between the state and the people. Dharma is created to put a stop to the harm done by the harmful natured men. Whatever the King shall fix as Dharma is to be considered as actual law. The dictates of good men and superiors are the foundations of law. The epic law-givers favoured the rise of monarchical power. The King is the cause of prosperity and progress. King and Dharma are reciprocally protective. The authority of the court was invoked for the preservation of rights and liberties and deviation from the path of Dharma brought in its train the award of punishment. In the later period, state came to be recognised as the highest authority and it is from the state that Dharma and Artha resulted. But this does not signify that the King was the propunder of law. The duty of the state was to make the people conscious of their Dharma. The metaphysical side of law is widely developed. Nil Kantha has rightly pointed out that the metaphysical conception of Dharma in the Mahabharata is clearly manifested when they conceived of Dharma as the-very "cause of Kaivalya." Dharma rose out of Narayan (meaning thereby "God") and merged back into him.

Puranic Conception of Law

The Puranic conception is that Dharma arose out of the human necessity and an urge for a peaceful life and hence they enunciated that "Dharma is create according to the nature of men." The Puranas give a realistic touch to law. By that time society had also developed and they realised that there are different types of men in this world and hence different types of law must be framed by them in order to suit their interests.[27] That different classes of Society should be governed by different laws was the motto of the Puranic legal experts. We cannot ignore the fact that there was a marked difference between the Common Law and the Dharma Law. According to the Common Law the culprit was to be punished by the king and under the Dharma law was also to be punished for the sin implied in the crime. In the Brahmanical period the rule of law was not discriminated from the rule of religion.

Kautilya's Empirical Conception

Kautilya's conception of law was empirical but he, too could not throw off the shackles of metaphysics. By Dharma he not only meant the practical law but also the righteous law and declared that law was the eternal truth holding away over the earth.[28] In his time we find "the oriental counterparts of the Greek, Stoic, Roman and patriotic conception of law."[29] Law was a human creation, a creation of Society and of thinkers.[30] The realist approch to law was not lost sight of even in later period. Being convinced of the fact that law was a social creation, Mitra Misra gives a practical approach and says, "the confusion of right and wrong is the creation of law."[31] Kautilya's conception of law is definitely Austinian and we find the echo of

Epic conception in Kautilya. According to Kautilya, "law is a royal command enforced by sanction."[32] From the Greek sources we learn that if the king could make laws, he passed only regulatory laws and not making him arbitrary. Kautilya is of opinion that destruction befalls an arbitrary king.[33] Explaining the royal commands, he mentions "thirteen purposes" for which royal writs are issued, i.e.—"Writs of command, of information, of guidance, of remission, of license, of gift, or reply, of general proclamation."[34] Kautilya's conception of law was chiefly remarkable for giving definiteness and permanence to the best traditions of a people, so well-trained in the art of government. He applied the standard of Dharma to the individuals, Society and the State. The ancient Indian conception of Cosmic perfection was highly developed in Kautilya's time and the law manifested that if the ruler and the ruled were both responsible, nothing worse was to follow. Kautilya like Keats had a romantic view about the State,[35] which helped every individual, in realising his own end in a most organised manner and without any injury being done to the State. Law must be all-embracing and its operation must be intelligent. The law according to the Roman ideas rested on double foundations of divine revelation and human advance[36] and according to another competent authority law rested on the twin foundation of the law of Nature and the law of Revelation. All societies place at the centre of their conception the idea of the guidance of providence.[37] According to Kautilya, Dharma (Sacred Law), Vyavahar (evidence), Charitra (History) and Rajasasana (Edicts of the King) are the four legs of law. Dharma is the eternal truth, Vyavahar is the evidence of the witnesses, Charitra is the tradition and Rajasasana is the order of the King. We find a similar theme in Narada, according to whom, Virtue, Judicial proceeding, documentary evidence and an edict from the King are the four feet of Law. According to Narada, virtue is based on truth, judicial proceeding is based on the evidence of the witnesses and edicts depend upon the pleasure of the King. The Arthasastra of Kautilya revealed a Code of Law proper purely secular with the express provision that royal Law could supersede the Dharma Law.[38]

The secular laws or King's laws in the Sutra period were different from the Dharma Law. The Dharma Law cannot be treated as the real origin of Hindu Law. In the Manava Dharma Sastra, we find the Dharma-Sastra invading and approaching the province of the Artha-Law and making the latter only an apendage to its own System.

The reason was that the Sacerdotal power became also the political power in the country. The Law of the politicians got mingled with the Law of Sacerdotalists.[39] Asoka promulgated different laws establishing equal treatment of all subjects in the matter of Law and punishment.

Conception of Law in Smrti Literature

The conception of Law in the Smrti literature attains its highest perfection in the realisation of unity of the individual and the Society. Law must mean the normal condition and progress in a most organised fashion. One remarkable thing in the Smrti literature is that the institution of castes permeates the law and the judicial system of the time. Jolly says that the Smrtis were written by the Brahmins for their own use, and in these books their class demands have been clearly expressed. The Smrtis imply human authorship and thus introduced human agency in the declaration of Law. The Smrti-Jurists believe that the law arose out of agreement (Samaya-Charika)[40] and according to Haradatta, Dharma consisted of customs settled by human agreements. Jayswal is of opinion that Dharma rules originated in "Samaya" or the communal rulers agreed upon the assemblies and that the vedas were then only of secondary importance. Apastamba says, "conventions of the people conversant with Dharma are authority; also the vedas."[41] The importance of the man in determining the character of Law is recognised. Virtue is that which is applauded by many.[42] Paley defines virtue as 'doing' good to manking in obedience to the will of God and for the sake of ever-lasting happiness. In the Smrti period Law is a contract based on the agreement between the ruler and the ruled. Law is what is unanimously approved in all countries by men of the Aryan society.[43] Law is whatever is practised and cherished at heart by the virtuous and the learned who are devoid of prejudice and possion.[44] Law is the practice of the Sisthas, i.e., those whose hearts are free from desire,[45] Law is necessary to make a man honest.[46]

'Positive Law' Different from 'Dharma'

In the Smrti literature, we find the development of positive law or vyavahar. Vyavahar is not the same thing as Dharma. Whenever the people are unaware of their rights and duties and do not know their laws they follow a system, generally the traditional laws based on custom and that is what is called vyavahar. Vyavahar arose out of the neglect of duty on the part of men.[47] Vyavahar also means the promulgation of laws by the King.[48] Brhaspati, while supporting of the Vyavahar theory, also enunciates the principle of flexible law by saying that "a decision must not be made solely by the latter of the written Code" but the "reason of law" and "immemorial usages" must also be taken into consideration.[49] Manu says that the king must, in the first instance, refer to the sacred texts and then to the old customs.[50] The Mimansa philosophy supports the theory of positive law. Dharma is the "desired-for objective which is characterised by Command" (Jaimini).[51] According to the **Mimansa** philosophy, Dharma is the scheme of right living. Happiness is the goal recognised by the Purva-Mimansa. Activities which result in loss are not Dharma. Dharma leads to happiness. Command corresponds to Vidni, duty to Dharma and sanction of *phala*. Sir Radhakrishnan has rightly observed: "Mimansa rules are very important for the interpretation of Hindu law."[52] Narada states, "Royal order over-rules such law." "Wherever the King . . . of his own accord passes a sentence, it is called an edict."[53] According to Manu, custom, dictated by Sruti and Smrti, is the highest Dharma.[54]

Custom—An Important Source of Law

Another development is the interpretation of law as good conduct or Saachar.[55] The violation of Dharma is taken to mean the destruction of Justice.[56] Justice consists in the application of law to all cases arising amongst the members of the State. The custom of the majority of the people (Lokachara) was treated as the common law of the country. Later on, it came to be treated as an important source of Law. Custom was the determining factor and the original foundation of law. The important position given in this respect to the customary law is thoroughly in conformity with facts and renders it a duty to those who deal with the history of Law to search after the traces and survivals of the Indian customary Law. The class-interest of the Brahmanas so much influenced their judicial literary activity that their rules of Law cannot be accepted without criticism.[57] In the Smriti literature Law was all powerful and above the king.[58] The conception of Law was not merely sacerdotal but had a strong aesthetic background as in the case of the Greek idea of Law. Law was the part and parcel of the great principles guiding the universal phenomenon.[59] Theology had a prominent place in the evolution of Law.

II
ETHICO-JURISTIC CONCEPTIONS IN ANCIENT INDIA AND THE AUSTINIAN DOCTRINE

N.C. CHATTERJEE

Ancient India Legal History in the Light of Austinian Doctrine

The greatest obstacle to a comparative study of the legal history of ancient India is the influence of the Analytical School of Jurists of which John Austin was the most conspicuous representative. The present generation has consciously or unconsciously imbibed the Austinian doctrine—that Law is a command of a determinate political superior to an inferior enforced by sanction. Every serious student of comparative legal history who studies the evolution of law, from the earliest germination of legal consciousness in ancient societies, realises the various inconsistencies in the doctrine of the great jurist. The main plank in Austin's theory— that sovereignty must reside in a determinate body—is inconsistent with the modern conception of popular sovereignty, ignores the power of public opinion and takes no account of "political sovereignty." His theory has been criticised by a formidable array of distinguished historical jurists like Maine, Clark, Sidgwick, Lowell, and others. As Sir Henry Maine has pointed out, it is a historical fact that sovereignty has often been in the hands of persons not determinate. The Austinian theory of law as a command emanating from a determinate superior—has been criticised on the ground that it ignores the great body of customary law which has never had its origin in the will of a determinate political superior. It errs in treating law as merely command. It identifies sovereignty with legal despotism. It exaggerates the single element of force in law to the neglect of all other historical facts and the force and influences which contribute to the evolution of legal norms. But Austin theory is not wholly defective. The contents of legal systems may be complex and variable, but the idea of law is compartively simple. Despite all criticism Austin's main position is unassailable, regarded as a summary of existing facts. What the States wills, that the individual can be compelled to obey by means of coercive sanctions.

When the eovlution of Jurisprudence reached 'a comparatively mature stage in ancient India' we find that amidst the labyrinths of secular and ceremonial rules and rituals positive law gradually differentiated itself from religious and semi-religious injunctions. When the state became the determining factor in the administration of law and justice, positive law secured for itself a definite postion and established its sway by virtue of the punishment which the State would inflict in case of its infringement.

In the later Smritis the main principles of Austinian theory are noticeable:—

> Smrity-achara-vyapetena margen-adharshitah paraih
> Avedayati ched-rajne vyavahara padam hi tat.[1]

If a person, molested by others in the way which contravenes the Smriti or established usage, complains to the King, that gives rise to a topic for judicial proceeding." As pointed out Dr. P.N. Sen,[2] this injunction of Yajnavalkya implies three elements, *viz.* :

1. transgression of law as laid down in the Smriti or established by usage,
2. injury to some one other than a transgressor, and
3. intervention of the king in his judicial capacity.

The Hindu conception of positive law was not very different from the Austinian theory thereof.

(1) It emphasis that "law was added because of transgressions."
(2) It show that the intervention of the King is called for because and in so far as these transgressions cause injury to people other than the transgressors.
(3) It indicates that whether a transgression be of some rule of action laid down in the Smritis or of some established usage, in either case it is the intervention of the King, who is the protector of the people and dispenser of justice, that converts religious or customary law into positive law.

Points of Difference

This comparison also shows some points of difference as well. According to Austin, law, in its normal form, consists of commands emanating from the Sovereign in the State and the duty of enforcing the same is a self-imposed duty. But according to the great Hindu jurist, Law issues from a source: superior to the Sovereign and the duty of enforcing the same is cast upon him from above. Thus the Brihadaranyaka Upanishad lays down:

"Sa n-aiva vyabhavat-tech-chhreyorupam-atyasrijat dharmam
Tad-etat kshatrasya kshatram yad-dharmas-tasmad-dharmat-param n-asti
Atho abaliyan bhliyansam asamsate dharmena yatha rajnaivam
Yo vai sa dharmah satyam vai tat
Tasmat satyam vadantam-ahur-dharmam vadat-iti-dharmam
va vadantam satyam vadat=iti
Etad-dhy-ev-aitad-udhayam dhavati.[3]

"He......created still further the most excellent Law (dharma). Law is Kshatra (power of the Kshatra, therefore there is nothing higher than the Law. Thenceforth even a weak man rules a stronger with the help of the Law, as with the help of a king. Thus the law is what is called the true. And if a man declares what is true, they say he declares the Law, and if he declares the Law, they say he declares what is true. Thus both are same."[4]

In the Dharma-Sutras we find that the protection of all created beings as well as the infliction of lawful punishments was the primary duty of a King.[5] Manu went so far as to identify the King with punishment and laid down that the enforcement of coercive sanctions was a Dharma:

So raja purusho dandah sa neta sasita cha sah
Chaturnam-asramanam cha dharmasya pratibhuh smritah
Dandah sasti prajah sarva danda ev-abhirahshati
Dandah supteshu jagarti dandam dharmam vidur-budhah.[6]

Punishment Identical with Law

"Punishment is (in reality) the King (and) the male, that the Manager of affairs, that the ruler, and that is called the surety for the four orders' obedience to the law."

"Punishment alone governs all created beings, punishment alone protects them, punishment watches over them while they sleep; the wise declare punishment (to be identical with) the Law." (S.B.E., Vol. XXV, p. 219.)

The author of the Sukraniti like the earlier Smriti writers also enjoins the King to administer justice by the infliction of punishment:

Dushta-nigrahanam kuryyad-vyavahar-anudarsanaih.
Sv-ajnaya varttitum sakta sv-adhina cha sada praja.[7]

"The King should punish the wicked by administering justice.

The subjects who are made to observe his orders are always under his authority." (S.B.H., Vol. XIII p. 183)

Thus the idea of sanction[8] as an essential element of law was emphasised by the Hindu jurists specially by the author of the later Dharma Sastras.

The system of law prevalent in ancient India grew not out of legislation but was based on religion. The old Roman definition which the jurisconsults preserved even up to the time of Justinian—*Jurisprudentia est rerum divinarum atque humanarum notitia*—also points to the same conception Like other ancient people, the ancient Indians believed that their laws come from the gods. The divine origin is referred to in the a bove passage of the Brithadaranyaka. The ideal King in ancient India was also accounted semi-divine.

Arajake hi loke-smin sarvato vidrule bhayat
Rakshartham-asya sarvasya rajanam-asrijat prabhuh
Indr-Anila-Yam-Arkanam-Agnes-cha Varunasya cha
Chandra-Vittesayos-ch-aiva matra nirhritya sasvatih.[9]

"For, when these creatures, being without a King, through fear dispersed in all directions the Lord created a King for the protection of this whole (creation), taking (for that purpose) eternal particles of Indra of the Wind, of Yama, of the Sun, of Fire, of Varuna, of the Moon and of the Lord of Wealth (Kubera)." (S.B.E., Vol. XXV, p. 216.)

The ancient Cretans attributed their laws, not to Minos, the actual law-giver, but to Jupiter. The Lacedaemonians believed that their legislator was not Lycurgus, but Apollo. The Romans believed that Numa wrote under the inspiration of the celebrated Goddess Egeria. The Etruscans believed that they had received their law-giver laws from the God Tages. The ancient Indians believed their was Varuna—the great upholder of order, physical and moral (Rita) who punished the transgressors of his commands.[10] Thus the Vedic seer sang with characteristic candour:

Yat kim ch-edam Varuna daivye jane-bhidroham manashyas-charamasi
Achitti yat-tava dharma yuyopima ma nas-tasmad enaso deva ririshah.[11]

"Whatever the offence which we men commit, Varuna, against

divine beings, whatever law of thine we may through ignorance violate, do not thou, divine Varuna, punish on account of that iniquity." (Wilson's translation, Vol. IV, p. 181.)

Ancient Laws Based on Religious Belief

This the ancient people thought that Manu, Lycurgus Minos or Numa might have reduced the laws of their time to writing, but they could not have made them. The ancient laws were never invented by any one nor were they created by any legislators in the modern sense of the term. As Coulange has pointed out, there is truth in all these traditions as they indicate that the veritable legislator among the ancients was not a man, but religious belief which men entertained.[12]

But the facts showing that State justice was ultimately enforced by means of coercive sanctions, suggestive and interesting as they are, should be regarded in their true historical perspective, as the final outcome of a long unconscious process of evolution, fraught with infinite moment to the human race. For as we go back upon the history of Law, we very soon reach a point at which the theories of Austin are helpless to explain facts. Take for instance, the Smriti—a source of law, an authority which great masses of men feel themselves bound to follow, not because they choose but because they must. But certainly it is not a command of the Sovereign in a State, direct or indirect. The conception of command was not unknown to the ancient Hindus, for example, Jaimini in his Mimamsa-Sutras says:

Chodana lakshano-rtho dharmah.[13]

"Dharma or duty is that which, being discernible, is indicated by Vedic injunction." (S.B.H., Vol. X, p. 3.)

This injunction was not the command of a political superior to a political inferior but it emanated from a source which was superior to both and which was equally binding upon all. Dharma was above the king and bound him equally as it did the meanest object. Upon critical examination ancient laws may turn out to be the work of private persons. We find the Code of Hamurabi or the Code of Manu, or other ancient Code, often purely impersonal documents, compiled no one exactly knows how, or by whom. Yet it is the controlling force which shapes the daily conduct of large masses of men. They do not even consider the propriety of challenging its authority or disregarding its provisions. It is not the work of the State; it may not even be recognised by the State. We may even go further back in the primitive slages of humanity, there may be no State to recognise it. Yet the essential ideas of law, the evident ancestors of our modern juristic notions, are clearly there. Hence, the Austinian conception of law has proved to be historically incorrect, almost useless in considering the ancient systems of Jurisprudence. As Lawrence Lowell has remarked, the definition of Austin is not universally true of law in general.[14] The Neo Austinian School has also pointed out the great mistake of Austin in regarding law as the commnnd of the Sovereign to the subjects, the theory of Austin thereby giving countenance to the inference that law is the arbitrary creation of the ruler; whereas it is a command not of the ruler but of the State comprising both the ruler and the ruled. The Austinian theory has proved even pernicious as men under the influence of the Analytical School have disputed the existence of Hindu Law except as "a mere phantom of the brain imagined by Sanskritists without Law and lawyers without Sanskrit."

Ancient Society Based on Pre-existent Custom

In primitive systems of law where custom had inherent force and could even supersede the edicts of the King or statute law of the realm, the definition of Austin cannot hold good. A custom has its binding effect because the people observe it, not because it has been set by a political superior to a political inferior. Law is not really what the Sovereign enacts but what the subjects observe. The Austinian theory, although more accurate at the present day, is absolutely inaccurate when applied to primitive societies, in which law was mostly based on pre-existent custom.[15] It would serve very little useful purpose in our study of ancient Indian jurisprudence. It is historically untrue, as Sir Henry Sumner Maine has pointed out, in the case of countries where the king is not law-making but merely tax-gathering. Take, for instance, the injunction of avoiding forbidden food which is so constantly repeated by the Hindu jurists, e.g., "All intoxicating drinks are forbidden."[16] Vasishtha,[17] Vishnu,[18] and Manu,[19] also laid down the same injuction in the strictest possible terms and made the breach of it a *mahapataka.* We cannot deny the above rule the title of law simply because it deals with the private conduct of a person and not in his dealings with others. If the British Parliament or the French Legislature would pass a bill embodying such provision and interdicting the use of specific articles, Austin would unhesitatingly accept the same as law. But that would be really laying too much stress on the method of law-making in western countries and on the peculiarities of modern jurisprudence. Fustel de Coulange[20] has dwelt upon the omnipotence of the ancient state of Greece and Rome and the far-reaching nature of the legislation which included the minutest details of private life. The Athenian law forbade men to remain single. Sparta punished not only those who remained single but even those who married late. At Athens the States prescribed labour, and at Sparta, idleness. At Locri the law forbade men to drink pure wine, at Rome wine was forbidden to women. It was a common thing for the kind of dress to be invariably fixed by each city; the legislation of Sparta went so far as to regulate the headdress of women and that of Athens forbade them to take with them on their journey more than three dresses. At Rhodes and Byzantium the law forbade men to shave the beard.[21] Thus in the ancient world law was at first a part of religion. The ancient codes were collections of rites, liturgical directions and ceremonial rules joined with legal regulations. The laws regarding property and succession had to be picked out of a mass of rules for burial, worship of the dead and sacrifices. The ancient codes regulated penances, marriage rite and the worship of the dead. In those times law and religion were both blended together.

Primitive Punishment of Animals not Existed in Ancient India

Some primitive systems of law were administered not only to rational beings but also to animals and inanimate objects. There was a court at Athens which tried animals and inanimate objects guilty of injuring human beings. Plato, the great philosopher, recommended the trial and punishment of animals and lifeless objects ("Laws," IX, 12). The Exodus says, "If an ox gore a man or a woman that they die; then the ox shall be surely stoned and his flesh shall not be eaten; but the owner of the ox shall be quit" (XXI, 28). Many cruel punishments were also inflicted upon animals on the code of the Zendavesta, and we notice the survival of this primitive custom in mediaeval Europe.[22] Although we do not notice any such absurd instance of the trial and punishment of animals and inanimate objects in the history of Hindu Jurisprudence, it is clear that some primitive systems of law did not satisfy the Austinian test of being confined merely to rational beings. The Hindu Law, of course, made a distinction between sense of responsibility and its absence in the culprit for purposes of punishment and provided for compensation of loss and injuries suffered by persons in consequence of negligence of the owners of animals.[23]

The Austinian definition of law, therefore, based either on the source of command or its contents or the being to which it is addressed is bound to be inapplicable to ancient systems of law. By describing juridical norms as orders emanating from the State, it looked upon law as exclusively State product. Consequently, there can be no law where there is no State. In other words, neither customary law nor international law is true law. The essential mistake was the confusion of law with legislation. Comparative jurisprudence and comparative politics have clearly established this important fact—that constraint by State is not the fundamental attribute of the law, nor is it an element common to legal phenomena. Korkunov has justly observed: "The law of each people is a result of a continuous evolution throughout its history. Every historic epoch, however, brings its own moral notions, its own conditions of life, which determines the matter of its laws. So the law of a people is built up in historical layers."[24] The only universal conception in law is that there is a command-not necessarily by a determinate political superior in a State—with its consequent sanction in case of disobedience, whatever the source of the command or the nature of such sanction may be and whoever may put the sanction in force, either the State Judiciary, or a formidable theocracy, or the communal assembly.

Ethico-juristic Consciousness of Ancient India

Thus it is clear that to the question—what is law?—no categorical or comprehensive answer can safely be given. Not only do systems of law change their contents but the conception of law itself changes with the progress of society. As we want to look at the history of laws and of their administration, we must glance at the evolution of the idea of law itself. And this glance will show us something of the secret places of human thought. For man in his earlier stages at least, is a very material creature; and law concerns his material interests. He is, likewise, a creature of strong and ill-regulated passions; and law is the force which controls them. Therefore, men's ideas of law are very genuine; they are the expression of his inmost feelings, the truest possible index to his character and culture. The study of law as a mass of arbitrary rules is surely, one of the most repulsive persuits in which a man of intelligence can engage. The study of a legal system, as a deliberate attempt to cover and regulate the material activities of man, appeals only to the logical faculties of a student and creates but a limited horizon. But the scientific study of a Law as a record of human progress, as the golden deposit of the stream of Time, is worthy of the highest intellect and stimulating to the most gifted imagination. The study of the genesis and growth of law in ancient India and its practical administration by the clan and the state is as fascinating as it is interesting. We shall follow the evolution of the law which has "the oldest pedigree of any known system of jurisprudence," and in these days of national renaissance the study and investigation of the gradual emergence of the ethico-juristic consciousness of the ancient Indian is of the highest importance.

Evolution of the State and Law in Ancient India

The earliest glimpse of Indo-Aryan society in the Rig Veda reveals to us a tribal state—based on the family as the unit bound together by the tie of consanguinity and the worship of common ancestors. The Rig Veda presents to us joint families of the patriarchal type founded generally on the principle of agnation. The earliest type of Roman polity closely resembled the ancient Indian. The Vedic polity was in its early stage a tribal state (*jana*) made up of number of clans (*vis*)[25] which were again aggregates of village (*grama*). Similarly, the *tribus* of the ancient Roman City-State was made up of a number of clans (*gens*) which were aggregations of families, bearing a common name and tracing their descent from a common ancestor.[26] Even in the developed political life of Italy there was a survival or the *pagus*—a tribal or ethnic unit composed of a number of villages (*vici*), which seems to resemble the *tribus* of the fully formed City-State.[27] This interesting analogy shows that the earliest form of State both in ancient India and in ancient Italy was a confederation of smaller units, bound by the tie of kinship. From such evidences derived from comparative politics certain political philosophers have concluded that the family was the germ from which higher forms of social organism have been gradually evolved. There is a verse in the Rig-Veda which describes the different organisations in the Vedic polity and shows that the tribe was the highest political unit.

> Sa ij-janena sa visa janmana sa putrair-vajam bharate dhana nribhih Devanam yah pitaram-avivasati sraddhamana havisha Brahmanaspatim (II. 26, 3.)

'Wer den Vater der Gotter fur sich zu gewinren sucht, glaubigen

Sinnes durch Opfer Brahmanaspati, der erlangt Beute Reichthum durch die Manner: durch Stamm (*janena*), durch Gau (*vica*), durch Verwandtschaft (*janmana*), durch Familie (*putraih*)." (Zimmer. *Altindisches Leben*, p. 160.)

The Vedic tribes had no words for their countries. They were mostly known as the Alinas, or Usinaras, Kasis, etc. The "Pancha janab" or "five tribes" are often mentioned in Vedic literature; both Zimmer *Altindisches Leben*, 119-23) and Macdonell (*Sanskrit Literature*, 153-54) have identified them with the Purus, Turvassas, Yadus, Anus and Druhyus, who are all mentioned in one hymn of the Rig Veda:

> Yad-Indragni Yadushu Yad-Druhyushv-Anushu
> Purusha stah atah (I, 108, 8.)

We get sometimes indirect descriptions of their geographical settlements like "Sapta Sindhu," i.e., a tract which was traversed by seven rivers. We have of course a few names of countries like Gandhara, Sindhu, etc. which show that particular tribes occupied these regions; but there was no abstract nation of territorial states. These Vedic tribes were ultimately coalesced into nations with new names.

Modern researches have established that the family was the initial society among the different races of mankind and that at a very early ethnical period the family often became patriarchal.[28] From the Scriptural example of Jacob and Esau as well as from evidence of ancient Indo-European history of Sir Henry Maine pointed out that primitive communities were but expansions of single families into larger bodies of kindred, connected by common subjection to the highest male ascendant and by the bond of kinship, supposed or real. According to him the aggregation of these families formed the Gens or House; the aggregation of Houses made the Tribe; the aggregation of Tribes constituted the commonwealth or State. The State was thus the result of the expansion of its primordial cell, the family. From the patriarchal family have been successively evolved all the higher forms of politcal orgnisation and genealogical organisation of society preceded the territorial.

Main's Celebrated Theory

We must not fail to notice the luminous criticisms of the different writers who adversely commented upon Maine's celebrated theory. Of them the first was the great philosopher, Herbert Spencer, who accused

Maine of ignoring the great mass of barbarous and uncivilized peoples among whom parents exercise little or no control.[29] McLennan also subjected Maine's theory to critical examination and pointed out that the Hebrew scriptures, where Maine perceives "the chief lineaments" of patriarchal society, far from revealing the patria potestas and agnation bear witness to polyandry and the recognition of kinship in the female line.[30] According to him abundant evidence of original promiscuity and of the maternal system of kinship is disclosed among the ancient races.[31]

Certain verses in the Rig Veda and the Atharva-Veda has been cited as evidence of the custom of polyandry in Vedic India, and from certain verses (passages) in the different Smritis it has been argued that polyandry was in vogue for a very long time in ancient India. The following verse in the Rig-Veda,[32] which is also repeated in the Atharva-Veda:[33]

Tubhyam-agre pary-auahae guryam vahatuna saha
Punah patibhyo jayam da Agne prajya saha

"Mayest thou, O Agni, give to us husbands our wife, together with progeny. . ."[34]

Apastamba speaks of the forbidden practice of delivering a bride to a whole family (*kula*):

Kulalra hi atri pradiyata ity-vpadipanti
Tad-indriyadaurbalyad-vipratipannam[35]

Brihaspati refers to the same custom (*kule kanya pradanam*) almost in the same terms.[36] An ambiguous passage of Narada has also been constructed in favour of the polyandrous theory:

Dve bharye ksoatriyasy-any vaisyasye-aika prakirttaita
Vaisyaya dvau pati jneyav-eka-nyah kshatriya-patih[37]

A well-known rule of Manu[38] has also been construed in favour of this theory as an instance of "Gruppen-ehen" or group marriage.[39] Manu in this verse lays down that the son of one among several brothers should be looked upon as the common son of all:

Bhratrinam-eka-jatanam-ekas-chet-putravan-bhavet
Sarvam-stam-stena putrena putriao Manur-abravit

The Vedic passages quoted above are no indications of polyandry in the Vedic period. The whole adhyaya, if read carefully, proves that such inferences are untenable; as the very next verse in the Rig-Veda would clearly show:

> Punah patim-ahnir-addad-ayusha saha varchasa
> Dirghayur-asya yah patir-jivati saradah satam

"Agni gave the wife back again with life and splendour; may he who is her husband enjoying long life live a hundred years."[40]

Apastamba, Manu and Brihaspati were averse to the practice of *Niyoga;* hence they have been interpreted as obviously referring to something different from *Niyoga.* But the text of Apastamba refers to an ancient custom which was enjoyed by the early sages but had been obsolete by his time. Manu merely repeats the dictum of Vasishtha (XVII, 10) which is also given in Vishnu Smriti (XV, 42). The true meaning of Manu's rule is quite clear from Buhler's translation and docs not refer to survivals of polyandry:

> "If one among brothers, sprung from one (father), one have a son, Manu has declared them all to have male off-spring through that son."[41]

The statement of Brihaspati occurs in a long text in which various iorbidden practices, prevailing chiefly in South India, are recorded.[42] The laconic text of Narada, properly understood, disproves the polyandrous theory. The literal translation of the text as—"A Vaisya woman may take a husband of two different castes; and a Kshatriya woman may take a husband of one different caste,"—lends itself easily to mis-interpretation. But Jolly has paraphrased the original text as follows—"A Vaisya woman may either take a Vaisya husband, or she may wed a Kshatriya or a Brahman. A Kshatriya may either take a Kshatriya husband, or she may marry a Brahman."[43] The true import of this passage is thus clearly against the polyandrous theory.

According to Maine "relationship is exactly limited by the patria potestas. Where the potestas begins, kinship begins; and therefore adoptive relations are among the kindred. Where the potestas ends, kinship ends; so that a son emancipated by his father loose all rights of agnation. And here we have the reason why the descendants of females are outside the limits of archaic kinship."[44] The basis of the patriarchal family was the potestas, but the patria potestas was not and could not be durable institution.[45] Yet its former universality may be inferred from certain derivative institutions, such as the perpetual tutelage of women, the guardianship of minors, the relation of master and slave, and specially from agnation which is, as it were, a mould retaining the imprints of the paternal powers after they have ceased to exist. Applying this test Maine finds evidence of the existence of the potestas among the primitive Aryan people which were "originally organised on the patriarchal model."[46] In Hindu genealogies the names of women are generally omitted and even in modern times kinship is agnatic in the Mitakshara law. The custom of the Salian Franks excluding females from governmental functions had an agnatic origin. The Normans excluded uterine brothers and, when Norman law was transplanted to England, brothers of half-blood were prevented form succeeding to one another.

Notes and References

I

1. Emerson, "Representative Mao", p. 32.
2. Rgveda IV. 40 (Datta's Translation).
3. Sen Gupta, Sources of law at Society in Ancient India, p. 4.
4. Raj Dharmanusasana Parva, 77, Manu, VIII, 391.
5. Thomas, "Life of Buddha", p. 173.
6. Adi Parva, 41.
7. Rajdharmanusasan Parva, 65.
8. Dr. Beni Prasad, "Theory of Government in Ancient India", p. 9.
9. Jayswal, Manu and Yajnavalkya—p. 80. Manu, VII, 22; 18; 20.
10. Aiyanger, Ancient Indian Policy, p. 63.
11. Maxmuller, Hibbert Lecture (1878), p. 235.
12. Radhakrishnan, Indian Philosophy, Vol. I, p. 78, 79 C 109.
13. Rigveda, VII, 49. IX. 74.
14. *Ibid*, VII, 56.
15. *Ibid*, X, 190.
16. Atharva Veda, II, I, X, 65.
17. Sen, "Studies in Hindu Political Thought", p. 97.
18. Brb, Upanishad. 1-4-11-14.
19. Chandogya, Upanishad VI, 6-13.
20. Rhys Davids, Buddhism, p. 45.
21. Rhys Davids, Buddhism, p. 35.
22. Stecherleabtsky, "Central Conception of Buddhism", pp. 73-75.
23. Udogya Parva, 33.
24. Moksadharma Parva, 162.
25. Udogya Parva, 33. Rajdharmanusasana Parva, 85.

26. Bhagwata Purana VII, 14.
27. *Ibid.*, VII, II. Parasar 1-33. XI, 50.
    Dr. B. Prasad, Theory of Govt. of Ancient India, p. 180.
28. Arthasastra, p. 191.
29. Sen, Studies in Hindu Political Theories, p. 112.
30. Sukraniti, IV. 5-164.
31. Viramitrodaya, p. 3.
32. Arthasastra, p. 82.
33. *Ibid*, p. 11.
34. *Ibid.*, p. 83.
35. State, "as a vale of Soul-making". Ketas.
36. Robson, Civilisation and Growth of Law, pp. 31-34.
37. Virognadoff, "Collected Papers", Vol. 2, p. 348.
38. Jayaswal, "Manu and Yajnavalkya", p. 12.
39. *Ibid.*, pp. 13,17,3.
40. Apastamtba 1-1-1. Gautama VIII, 11.
41. Apastamtba 1-7-20.
42. Sukraniti, p. 264.
43. Apastamba 1-7-20.
44. Manu II.
45. Vasistha 1, 5, 6, Baudhyan, I. 1. 1, 4, 6.
46. Manu, VII, 18-24.
47. Narada 1, 2, Brahaspati 1, 1.
48. Sukraniti, p. 38.
49. Brahaspati, VII, 13.
50. Manu, VIII. 13.
51. Jaimini Mimansa Sutra, 1-1-2-2.
52. Sir S. Radhakrishnan, Indian Philosophy, Vol. 2, p. 148.
53. Narada, XVIII. 24. II. 27.
54. Manu, 1-108, 110,
55. Yajnavalkya, 1-7.
56. Manu, V.I. 14-15.
57. Jolly, Hindu Law and Custom, pp. 3-4.
58. Manu VIII, 336.
59. Indopadhaya—Hindu Polity, p. 287.

II

1. Yajnavalkya, II, 5, Stenzler's Edition (1849), p. 45.
2. "Hindu Jurisprudence" (Tagore Law Lectures, 1909), p. 29.
3. 1, 4, 14; Sacred Books of the Hindus, Vol. XIV, p. 93.
4. Sacred Books of the East, Vol. XV, p. 93.
5. Gautama, X, 7, 8; and XI, 28. Apastamba, II, 5, 10, 6. Vasishtha, XIX, 1. Cf. Vishnu, 111, 2.
6. VII, 17 and 18 ; Cf. VII, 27.

7. IV, 5,1.
8. The Hiudu Jurists, however, constantly reminded the King to administer justice and to enforce coercive sanctions with great circumspection and with an eye to all the surrounding circumstances, like the status of the criminal, the nature of the crime, etc.; e.g., Gautama, XII, 51 ; Apastamba, II, II, 27, 18; Vasistha, XIX, 9; Vishnu, III, 91, Manu, VII, 16, 19, 27-32 and Yajnavalkya, I, CCCIX-CCCXI, CCCLIV.
9. Manu, VII, 3 and 4.
10. In the Atharva-Veda illimitable knowledge is also ascribed to this omniscient Varuna: "The great superintendent of them sees, as it were, from close by; whoever thinks to be going on in secret, all this the gods know. Whoso stands, goes about, whoso goes crookedly, whoso goes about hiddenly—what two sitting down together talk. King Varuna, as third, knows that. Both this earth is King Varuna's and yonder great sky with distant margings (anta); also the two oceans are Varuna's paunches ; also in this petty water is he hidden. Also whoso should creep far-off beyond the sky, he should not be released from King Varuna; from the sky his spies go forth hither; thousandeyed, they look over the earth. All this King Vargna beholds ; (vi-caks)—what is hidden between the two firmaments, what beyond; numbered of him are the winkings of people ; as a gambler the dice, (so) does he fix these things." (IV, 16. 1 to 5 ; Whitney's Atharva-Veda, pp. 167-77).

    "The might and greatness of eternal highest beings, their wisdom and justice, their sublimity and kindliness are united in the chief Aditya, Varuna... They (the hymns of the Veda) picture the god as the all-wise creater, preserver and regent of the worlds, the omniscient protector of the good and avenger of the evil, holy and just, yet full of pity," (Dr. Kaegi's "The Rigveda," translated by Dr. Arrowsmith, pp. 61-62). As Dr. Kaegi has pointed out, it was in later times that Varuna was lowered to a more god of the waters, which stream down from the sky to the earth. "Varunaopened for thee, O Sindhu, paths to flow" (X, 75, 2.) "Without trouble Varuna set the waters free" (X, 24, 7.) (Vide Kaegie's "Rigveda," pp. 154-5.)
11. Rigveda, VII, 89, 5. Vide Afrecht's Ed., Vol. II, p. 67. Varuna frequently spoken of as a king (raja Varunah), as a king of the universe (visvasya bhuvanasya) and as an universal monarck (samrat). (Muir's Sanskrit Texts, Vol. V, p. 122.
12. "The Ancient City," Bk, III, Ch. XI.
13. 1, 11, 2.
14. "Essays on Government," p. 197.
15. Frederick Harrison has pointed out that even in modern states there are some laws which can hardly be made to exhibit the characteristics of a command, obligation and sanction; e.g., enabling Statutes, rules of interpretation, and judicial construction and procedure, etc. ("Fortnightly Review," 1378.)
16. Apastamba, 1, 5, 17, 51. S.B.E., Vol. II, p. 63.
17. 1, 19, 20. S.B.E., Vol. XIV, p. 5,
18. XXXV, 1, S.B.E., Vol. VII, pp. 132-3.

19. IX, 235, S.B.E., Vol. XXV, p. 388.
20. "The Ancient City," Bk. Ill, Ch. XVII.
21. The ancient State sometimes commanded a father to whom a deformed son was born to but him to death. This law is found in the ancient codes of Sparta and of Rome as well as in the ideal codes of Aristotle and Plato. On the strength of a passage in the Kathaka-Samhita (XXVII, 9) : "Tasmat-striyam jatam parasyanti na pumamsam," Weber, Deldruck and Zimmer asserted that girl infants were exposed by the Vedic Indians (Altindishes Leben, pp. 319-20 and Z.D.M.G., Vol. XLIV, pp. 494-6). It is now clear after Bohtlingk's explanation that Zimmer, Weber, Delhruck and others misunderstood the above passage which merely referred to the laying of the child aside (legt mou bei Seite) while a boy was lifted up Z D.M.G., Vol. XLIV, pp. 494-6). As remarked by Macdoneli the passage described the innate sentiment of primitive people looking down with disfavour upon the birth of daughters. (Vedic Index, i, p. 395.) The Atharva Veda distinctly invokes the birth of a son and deprecates that of a daughter. "Prajapati, Anumati-Sinivali hath shaped; may he put elsewhere woman-birth; but may he put here a male" (VI, 11, 3; W.A.V., p. 289). It may be noted that Bohtingk's view referred to above had been accepted later by Roth and Delbruck (Z.D.M.G., XLIV, 496).

    We notice the expression of the same sentiment in a later hymn of the Atharva-Veda which prayed for keeping the male child safe in the embryonic stage; Pinga, defend thou (the child) in process of birth; let them not make the male female; let not the egg-eaters injure the embryos; drive thou the kimidins from here." (VII. 6, 25; W.A.V., p. 498.)

    The Aitareya-Brahmana contains an old verse (VII, 15) which says that a daughter is a misery (kripanam), while a son is a light in the highest heaven.
22. In the English Law of Deodand, which survived up to the middle of the 19th century, there is a relic of the ancient custom that anything injuring or killing a man must undergo religious purification. A beast which killed a man or a tree which fell upon a man was deodand, i.e., was confiscated and sold for charity—a somewhat humanised version of the old Athenian process whereby the axe that killed a man was brought to trial, and, if found guilty, solemnly thrown over the boundary of the city. Similarly animals were considered as amenable to Laws up to very recent times on the continent of Europe and an elaborate process was followed specially by the French courts in the trial and the punishment of domestic and wild animals; the last instance of the enforcement of this absurd law was in the year 1748, when a cow was hanged.
23. The question whether the animals and the gods have any share in the duty of practising Vedic observances is discussed in Katyayana's Srauta-Sutras (I, 1,4). Katyayana concludes that animals have no such duty as they only look to what is near at hand not to the rewards of a future world, i.e., on account of the absence of rationality and conscience.
24. "Theory of Law," Bk. I, Ch. II, Sec. 10.
25. The expression vis is of doubtful significance. As Keith and Macdoneli have

pointed out, in many passages of the Rig-Veda the sense of "settlement" is adequate and probale; in other passages it means "subject" or "people." (V.L., II, pp. 305-6). There are other passages where it means "clan" a sub-division of the Jana or the whole tribe; e.g., the above passage shows that Vis was different from Jana, Janmana and Putra. In another passage (X, 91, 2) it again differentiated from both griha and jana:
Sa darsata-Srir-atithir-grihe grihe vane vane sisriye takkavir-iva
Janam-janam janyo nati-manyate visa a ksheti visam-visam
Atharva-Veda (XIV, 2, 27,) uses vis as a division less than the whole people in the sense of can (W.A.V., p. 758). Zimmer also takes vis in this sense (All Leben, p. 159) as 'Gan,'

26. "Roman Law," Muirhead, p. 6.
27. "Roman Public Life," Greenide.
28. It is to be noted, however, that Sir Henry Maine was not quite correct in holding that the primitive family of the Roman type was the "primosdial of social development," when he said that "'the effect of the evidence derived from camparative jurisprudece is to establish that view of the primeval condition of the human race which is known as the Patriarchal Theory." (Ancient Law, Pollock's Edition, 1912, Ch. V, p. 131.)
29. "Principles of Sociology," I, pp. 713-37.
30. "The Patriarchal Theory," edited by Donald McLennan.
31. Maine revised his opinion in his later works—'Early Law and Custom, Village Communities, and Early History of Institutions'. Sir Frederick Pollock has justly remarked, "much trouble and confusion might have been avoided, if Maine had in the first place expressly confined his thesis, as for all practical purposes it was confined to the Indo-European family of nation," (Ancient Law, Pollock's Edition, p. 177). Whatever might be the case with other races, it is certain that at the earliest period of which we have any distinct knowledge—the patriarchal family was the condition of the Indo-European family of nations:
32. X, 85, 38.
33. XIV, 2, I.
34. Wilson's tr, Vol. VI, p, 230.
35. II, 10, 27. 2-4; S.B.E., Vol. II, p. 164, Buhler's ed. (Bombay), p. 93
36. XXVII, 20; S.B.E., Vol. XXXIII, p. 386.
37. XII, 6; S.B.E., Vol. XXXIII, p. 166; Bib. Ind., p. 173.
38. IX, 182; S.B.E., Vol. XXV, p. 365.
39. 'Recht und Sitte', Jolly, p. 47.
40. Rv. X, 85, 39; Wilsan's tr., Vol. VI, p, 230.
41. S.B.E., Vol. XXV, 365.
42 S.B.E., Vol. XXXIII, p. 389.
43. S.B.E., Vol. XXXIII, p. 166n.
44. "Ancient Law," Ch. V, p. 155.
45. "Patria Potestas in Ancient India," N.C. Chatterjee, J.A.S.B.
46. *Ibid.*

8

Legal Literature of Ancient India

A.A. Macdonell

Dharmasastra is the designation of legal literature in Sanskrit. Here the word dharma has a much wider connotation than 'law' for it includes religion, custom, good conduct, duty, in fact all that comes within the sphere of right. The oldest treatises on this subject are the dharmasutras which grew up in close connexion with the works on ritual (kalpa). They are not compendia of law, but deal with the religious duties of man. They proceeded from the Vedic schools and were used by Brahmins for the purpose of instruction, not for practical application in law courts. They form part of Vedic literature, giving directions regarding daily religious rites, purification penances, duties, and rights of householders, Brahmins, kings, ascetics, forest-hermits, besides discussions on cosmology and eschatology. It is only where the duties of kings are concerned that sections occur on family law, legal procedure, civil and criminal law (vyavahara). They are written in the sutra style but in all of them, verses, generally in the sloka, often in the tristubh metre, are interspersed.

Dharmasutra of South India

The best preserved of these works is the Apastambiya dharmasutra, belonging to the school of Apastamba of the Black Yajurveda in south India. On grounds of language and subject-matter it can hardly be estimated to date from later than about 400 B.C. A little later, and attached to the school of Hiranyakesin, is a sutra which differs but slightly from that of Apastamba. Somewhat older than Apastamba's is the sutra of Baudhayana, also representing a south Indian school of the Black Yajurveda. But this work has not been well preserved, for some of its sections are certainly latter additions to its original form.

Dharma-sastra of Gautama

Most probably the oldest of this class of treatises is the Dharma-sastra of Gautama, which belongs to a school of the Samaveda. Though quoted by some of the earliest Dharma-sutras, it seems to contain some interpolations. Later than Gautama is the Vasistha-dharma-sutra, which probably belonged to a north Indian school of the Rigveda. This, too, contains a good many interpolations. It quotes a dharma-sutra of Manu, which was probably the basis of the famous Manava-dharma-sastra. The latter work once quotes the Vasistha-dharma-sutra, which probably dates from some centuries before our era. A more extensive legal work than any of those mentioned is the Vaisnava-dharma-sutra, also called the Visnu-smrti. It is founded on an old Dharma-sutra of the Kathaka school belonging to the Black Yajurveda. The Vishnuite redaction, in which form it has come down to us, cannot date from earlier than about 200 A.D., as is proved by the occurrence of the names of the seven days of the week, including the term jaiva, for Thursday, which is based on the Greek name zev's. The passages in which widow-burning is recommended belong to the same time. But the oldest parts of the work must go back to a very early period, for the texts of the Kathaka school, with which the Vishnu-smrti is connected, are among the oldest remains of Vedic literature.

A very early and extensive Dharma-sutra, which belongs to the Maitrayaniya school of the Black Yajurveda, is that of Harita, quoted by both Apastamba and Baudhayana. As is the case both in the Baudhayana-sutra and in the Vasistha-dharma-sastra, the sutras are interspersed with slokas and with tristubh stanzas.

Oldest Legal Literature

Although the chronology of the legal literature is uncertain, it can be assumed with probability that the older Dharma-sutras belonging to the Vedic schools date from between 800 and 300 B.C.

At any rate, they represent the oldest phase of the legal literature, because they characteristically deal with religious duties and rites to a far greater extent than with secular law. Thus the juristic part of the Apastamba-dharma-sutra amounts to only about one-seventeenth of the whole work.

The leaching of dharma in Vedic schools early gave place to general law schools meant for all classes. It was in these legal schools that the metrical Dharma-sastras and Smrtis arose. These were no longer handbooks for the narrow circle of a particular Vedic school, but for the teaching of the religious and secular rights and duties of all the three twice-born classes. These manuals naturally became more extensive, and treated law in the strict sense in much greater detail. The sutra style was no longer adequate for the purpose, and the metrical form, especially the sloka verse, long familiar as the vehicle of the simple epic, as well as of the didactic poetry so closely akin to the epic, was adopted. This sententious poetry was indeed one of the chief sources of the Dharma-sastras. The teachers of dharma themselves as its sources, besides sruti and smrti, the practice of the cultural (sistah) and customary law (acara). These rules of the latter two authorities were early expressed in slokas, many of which go back to the time of the Dharma-sutras or even farther. Much old material is thus preserved in the Dharma-sastras, which are themselves chronologically later productions. Numerous ethical and legal maxims in metre are found in the epics, especially the Mahabharata. Hence, the epic (itihasa) is stated to be a fifth source of dharma.

These metrical law-books have been studied as authoritative for centuries all over India down to the present day. Though claiming validity for all castes they are primarily written in the interests of Brahmins. But they deal to a much larger extent with the rights and duties of the king.

Manu-smrti Enjoys Great Reputation and Authority

No work has enjoyed so great a reputation and authority throughout India for centuries as the Manava-dharma-sastra, also called the Manu-smrti, or 'Code of Manu'. Not only in India, but among early European Sanskrit scholar fantastic views were held regarding the age of this work. Thus Sir William Jones attributed it to the thirteenth century B.C., and A.W.V. Schlegel to not later than 1000 B.C. It has been shown to be based on an antecedent Dharma-sutra, which was later versified. It is in fact probably one of the earlier examples of the transformation of the old Dharma-sutra into a metrical Dharma-sastra. Even yet the limits of time within which it must have come into being have not been narrowed down to a shorter period than about four centuries; between 200 B.C. and 200 A.D.

The relation of the Manu-smrti to the Mahabharata is of some importance in investigating its date. In the latest sections of the Mahabharata, especially Book XIII, passages of a Dharma-sastra of Manu are quoted and actually occur in our Manu-smrti. On the other hand, a larger number of identical verses occur in both works without being designated as quotations. As the varieties of reading are sometimes better in the one text, sometimes in the other, the conclusion is that such verses have in both texts been derived from the floating sententious poetry which we have seen to be one of the sources of the metrical Dharma-sastras, and of which it would be vain to attempt to assign the priority in the one text or the other. We seem to be justified in inferring that the oldest parts of the Mahabharata are older than our Manu-smrti; that its latest parts quote a work which was virtually identical with our Manu-smrti; and that both texts borrowed a considerable amount of identical material from the sententious poetry that was the common property of the educated. No more definite chronological conclusions are justified in the present state of our knowledge.

Literary Style of Manu-smrti

The contents of the Manu-smrti show that the interval between it and the oldest Dharma-sutras, which, like Apastamba's have remained unmodified by interpolation must be considerable. The purely legal parts of the Manu-smrti amount to rather more than one-fourth of the whole work. Owing to the sources from which a considerable portion of the book is derived, it produces on the whole the impression of a didactic poem, in which imagery, similes, and elevated diction abound. The author evidently aimed at producing a literary work rather than a dry manual of jurisprudence.

Manu Influenced Laws of other Countries

A testimony to the widespread fame of Manu is the number of commentaries composed on it in every part of India. Medha-tithi, who lived in Kashmir, probably in the ninth century, was the author of the oldest surviving commentary; he frequently refers to predecessors, some of whom he speaks of as ancient. Another commentator, probably belonging to the twelfth century, is Govindaraja, whose work is distinguished by accuracy and is valuable for its explanations of difficult passages. The best known, because most frequently printed, commentary is that of Kulluka, written at Benares in the fifteenth century. It is of little independent value, being virtually a plagiarism of the earlier work of Govindaraja. The reputation of Manu extended to Burma, Siam, and the islands of Java and Bali, whose law has been greatly influenced by this code.

Next Oldest is Yajnavalkya-smrti

Next in age to Manu is the Yajnavalkya-smrti, the Dharma-sastra of Yajnavalkya. It is probably based on a no longer extent Dharma-sutra belonging to eastern India and attached to the White Yajurveda; for it has been shown to have affinities with the Grhya-sutras of that Veda. It is evident that Yajnavalkya represents a more advanced stage than Manu, for it is more concise, more clearly arranged, and more systematic. While Manu confines the sphere of evidence to the statements of witnesses, and in the matter of ordeals treats only of those by fire and water, Yajnavalkya deals exhaustively with written documents as evidence, and knows five kinds of ordeals. This law book also contains far fewer passages resembling didactic poetry than Manu. Many indications appear in it that it dates from no earlier than 300 A.D. The most famous of the many commentaries on Yajnavalkya is the Mitaksara of Vijnanesvara. This is, however, more than a commentary, being really a juristic work based on Yajnavalkya. The author was a south Indian who lived between 1050 and 1100 A.D. His work early acquired a great reputation in Benares as well as the Deccan, and as late as the beginning of last century acquired a new importance within the jurisdiction of British India through Colebrooke's translation (1811) of its section on the law of inheritance. Quite a number of commentaries were written on this authoritative work.

Narada-smrti

The date of the Narada-smrti seems to be somewhat later still, as would appear from internal evidence. It is much more advanced in its treatment of law than Manu. Thus it emphasizes written procedure and documentary evidence. It has much more elaborate sub-divisions under various heads. Thus, Menu's eighteenth titles of the law have in Narada 132 subordinate divisions. The occurrence of the word dinara (the Latin denarius), as the name of a gold coin, shows that the Narada-smrti could not have come into being before the second century B.C., and that it was probably not composed before the fourth century A.D. because though Roman gold coins were already in abundant use in India in the first century A.D., the word dinara is not met with till 400 A.D. in inscriptions.

Brhaspati-smrti

The Brhaspati-smrti, of which only fragments have been preserved in medieval quotations, is still more closely connected with Manu than Narada; for it resembles a commentary, which, always starting from the dicta of Manu, supplements and extends them. It deals exhaustively with legal documents, and recommends widow-burning which is not done in the earlier law-books. Representing, taken in all, a more advanced stage of development than Narada, it probably came into existence a century or two later.

Other Dharma-sastras

There are numerous other Dharma-sastras which also are known only in a fragmentary way from quotations. Many other later Smrtis, preserved in manuscripts or printed in collections, deal not with the whole of dharma, but only with parts. One of the more important and comparatively old legal works is the Parasara-smrti, which was commented on by Madhava in the fourteenth century. It is uncertain whether the Parasara is identical with the one mentioned by Medhatithi in the ninth century.

Of great importance that the later law-books are the Dharma-nibandhas, which are systematic and sometimes very extensive works on dharma. This type of legal literature began to be produced from about 1100 A.D., and continues to appear even at the present day. Many of these works are important on account of the numerous quotations they contain from older works that have since been lost. One of the earliest books of this class is the Smrti-kalpataru by Lakshmidhara, the minister of a king who is identical with Govindachandra of Kanuaj (1105-43 A.D.).

Between 1260 and 1309 A.D. Hemadri wrote a bulky work entitled Caturvarga-cintamani, which in five chapters deals with vows, almsgiving, places of pilgrimage, salvation, funeral rites (sraddha) and the sacrificial calendar. It also terms with quotations from the Puranas and the Smrtis. Other compendia treat of law in the strict sense (vyavahara). One of these is the Dharma ratna of Jimuta-vahana, written probably in the fifteenth century. A portion of this work, the Dayabhaga, on the law of inheritance, is the chief authority of the Bengal school of law, and was translated into English by Colebrooke.

In the eighteenth century several Dharma-nibandhas were compiled by pundits who were commissioned for the purpose in the interest of the law-courts.

References

Jolly, Recht and Sitte, in Buhler's Encyclopaedia, II, Part 8, 1896.

Macdonnel, History, 428-30, Winternitz, Geschichte, III, 479-504 (bibliography down to 1922).

9

Government and Laws of Ancient India

There are various versions on the subject of the original form of government, laws and legal system in ancient India. In the following article reproduced from the 'Indian Antiquities' (published 1806), the English author presents a 'general survey of the ancient and wonderful code of Indian jurisprudence and the spirit that breathes through it.' In India, the ultimate traditional source of all law and jurisprudence are the Vedas, the Rigveda being the oldest. Then come the Upanisads, Srauta and Griha Sutras, Dharmasutras and Smrti, in that order. The development of law and jurisprudence in Ancient India was the outcome of not merely the Hindu sacred books as mentioned above, but the customs and usages of many races, besides the Aryan race, contributed considerably towards this development. Hindu Law proper as known to us is a product of the middle ages, applied and developed by British Indian Courts (Ed.).

Not absolutely relying on what classical writers have written concerning government, laws and jurisprudence in ancient India, let us consult the more accurate accounts which British diligence and zeal, in India, have recently procured for us of that country in its earliest periods, either from books or living authorities of the highest rank; let us inquire what actually was that government so celebrated for its wisdom and equity, and in what manner it was conducted to render it at once so lasting and so respectable.

Monarchical System of Government

It certainly was, in the strictest sense *monarchical,* but with very just and severe checks to guard against the possible abuse of the powers entrusted to the ruling sovereign. The Indian monarchy, as originally established, at the same time exhibits to us in a more marked manner than most other countries of Asia glaring vestiges of the original *patriarchal* mode of government, founded on the model of the *paternal,* in which the chief of each family exercised the sovereign jurisdiction over the individuals of it, even to the infliction of death, when merited; continuing to flourish unviolated for a long succession of ages. With the regal, in him were combined the sacerdotal dignity, and a kind of prophetic sanctity of character, supposed to have descended to him from that vener abie personage who was the grand fountain of all post-diluvian honours; the KING, PRIEST, and PROPHET, of the regenerated world! A band of holy Brahmins, who, like the Magi of Persia were the hereditary counsellors of the Indian crown, constantly attended in the palace, and around the sacred person of the prince, to give him their advice in the most important concerns of his empire, to inculcate upon him the duty of a just and wise sovereign, at stated periods to chaunt the solemn hymns of devotion, to assist at the frequently returning rites of sacrifice, and explain the omens of the blazing altar.

Brahmin—The Real Ruler

Though the functions of government, by the laws of Menu, devolved on the Khettri or Rajah tribe; yet it is certain, that, in every age of the Indian empire, aspiring Brahmins have usurped and swayed the imperial sceptre. A whole nation of Brahmins was found by Alexander in the western districts of India, on whom, for their obstinate opposition, the conqueror exercised the greatest severity, and even crucified their king. But, in fact, there was little necessity for the Brahmin to gasp at empire: he ruled both the empire and the monarch: he was greater out of the purple than in it. Without the immediate sanction of that tribe, in no event of national consequence did the sovereign dare to embark, either in the season of profound peace, or amidst the turbulence of the embattled field. He was invested with equal power in the palace and in the camp. He elevated alternately the olive peace, or wielded the thunderbolt of war. Strabo positively asserts, and his assertion is confirmed by the results of modern inquiry, that the code of Brahmin law was not originally *committed to writing:* in fact, the very name of that code, which is MENUSMRTI or *institutes remembered from Menu,* proves this representation to be just. Till the age of Vyasa they were deposited solely in the memory of the Brahmins; and to them the prince applied in all matters of difficulty. On occasions of extreme national urgency he visited them in the dread of the night, and their answers were given in all that gloomy pomp and profound solemnity attendant on the midnight hour. By an overstrained conception of the high sanctity of the priestly character, artfully encouraged for political purposes by the priest himself, and certainly not justified by any precept given by Noah to his posterity, the Brahmin stood in the place of the Deity to the infatuated sons of Indian superstition the will of heaven was thought to be uttered from his lips, and his decision was reverenced as the irrevocable fiat of destiny. Thus, boasting the positive interposition of the Deity in the fabrication of its singular institutions, guarded from infraction by the terror of exciting the divine wrath, and directed principally by the sacred tribe, the Indian government as originally formed may justly considered in the light of a THEOCRACY; a theocracy the more terrible, because the name of God, by this perversion, was made use of to sanction and support the most dreadful species of despotism, a despotism which, not content with subjugating the body, tyrannized over the prostrate faculties of the enslaved mind.

Four Classes

We are informed by Strabo, that the great body of the Indian nation was divided into *seven* distinct classes, but we know from more authentic sources, that this division was only four-fold that is to say, into the classes sacerdotal and regal, the tribe agricultural and mercantile; and that of artificers, mechanics, and servants. These, however, are again subdivided into an infinite variety of inferior castes, and in these, by the arbitrary mandate of their great legislator, they are bound to remain without hope of removal or possibility of exaltation. The apparent impolicy of this division has been often descanted upon, and justly anathematized as a barbarous attempt to chain down the powers of the human soul, to check the ardour of emulation, and damp the fire of genius. On that ground, it certainly deserves the severest reprobation; yet, by this arrangement, it should be remembered, the happiness and security of a vast empire was preserved inviolate during a long series of ages under their early sovereigns, by curbing the fiery spirits of ambitious individuals, intestine feuds were in a great measure prevented, the wants of an immense population amply provided for by the industry of the labouring classes, and the several branches of trade and manufacture were carried to the utmost degree of attainable perfection. Though the stern ferocity of Mahommedan despotism hath insulted their religion and overturned their government, yet they have not been able to rend from them the superior palm of excellence to which the curious productions of the Indian loom are so highly entitled, and the exquisite work in gold and jewellery, that passes through the pliant fingers of the Indian artist, remains still unrivalled in any commercial region of the earth.

Chinese Migrated from India

The wide diffusion of the Sanscreet sciences, language, and mythology over the whole eastern quarter of Asia, appears fully to justify the Brahmin assertions that the empire, in very remote periods, extended from the mouth of the Indus, west, to the Sea of China, east, and from the Thibetian mountains, north, to Cape Comorin in the south. These are the vast lines of demarcation which Sir William Jones, from the Brahmin records, sometimes assigns to the ancient empire of India; and, if Mr. Halhed's assertion be correct, "that he found the Sanscreet characters, and emblems allusive to the Sanscreet mythology, so universally engraved on the coins of Assam, Nepaul, and Cashmere, as well as on those of Bootan and Thibet," their claims to that wide domain seem to be indubitably established; and it should not be forgotten that the very same books record the migration, near four thousand years ago, of the heretic Chinese from the bosom of the mother-country, towards the regions lying nearer the rising sun.

Emperor and Kings

This mighty empire was governed, according to their own annals, by one supreme monarch, the Maha Rajah, or Great Rajah, to whose sovereign control through its whole extent a numerous class of subordinate rajahs was obedient, and wisely to govern such an immense territory, it will readily be granted, required the full exertion of all the sacerdotal, regal, and prophetic functions with which this superstitious people have invested their first venerated sovereigns, after the flood of Satyaurata Menu. These princes, therefore, formed a chain of feudatories, governing vast kingdoms, governed, in their respective districts, by the same laws that bound the sovereign, and equally restrained by the presence and power of Brahmins from abusing the office and chief magistrate delegated to them by supreme Brahma and the sacred tribe, who in the order of creation, sprang from his head, like Minerva from the head of Jove.

Nothing could have prevented the ancient Indian kings, exalted and revered as they were by their subjects, from becoming despotic tyrants, but this salutary restraint upon their power, added to the powerful ARISTOCRACY which the inferior, but valiant, nobility of their own tribe composed. The Brahmin might be faithless to the trust reposed in him by his god; but the inferior rajah disdained illegal and dishonourable submission: he well knew, and, at the hazard of being and fortune, would assert, the rights of his caste. The truth is, that, whatever arguments may be urged against an overgrown aristocracy in a highly monarchical government, they constitute still the great barrier against the exorbitant power and usurpation of the crown itself. Were the natural jealousy, the combined influence of a high-minded nobility, in a government, destroyed; the liberty, or rather the remains of liberty, in that state would be quickly annihilated, and complete despotism establish itself upon its ruins.

By his high office, the Maharaja had the sole power of directing the national vengeance against the common foe, and of summoning all the inferior rajahs to the field, at the head of the quota of troops which every separate province was compelled, by stipulation, to furnish.

The imperial army of India, therefore, when assembled together, must have consisted of an immense body of horse, foot, and elephants; and we ought not to consider as so highly exaggerated, the account given in classical writers, that Sandrocottus, or, in Sanscreet, *Chandragupta* who had usurped the throne of the ancient Maha Rajahas on the Ganges, had raised an army, to oppose the Greeks in that quarter, of 600,000 men. This number is in perfect unison with the immense extent, power, and population, of India, at that period, and greater armies have been since brought into the field of Indian war. Strabo, indeed, from Megasthenes, informs us, that, in his time, the great Indian empire consisted of one hundered and eighteen nations, each of which was governed by its own peculiar prince, a descendant of Porus afterwards wrote to Caeasar, then at Antioch, soliciting his alliance, and boasting, that he, at that time, reigned over 600 tributary princes, but most of these could have been governors of cities, or chiefs of small cantons, dependent on his power. The regal honours in their families, as in the chiefs, were hereditary, they had the power of life and death, but were compelled, by tremendous obligations and their forfeiture of caste, to regulate their decisions by the grand legislative code of Menu. An assembly of the Brahmins, sitting in judgment on a vicious or tyrannical king, may condemn him to death, and the sentence is recorded to have been executed: but no crime affects the life of the Brahmin, he may suffer temporary degradation from his caste, but his blood must never stream on the sword of justice, he is a portion of the Deity, he is inviolable, he is invulnerable, he is immortal!

So profound, so inextinguishable, was the respect, with the dawn of life, inculcated, and, through every period of it, paid, both by prince and subject, to that code, so perfectly did every member of the four classes know and, from dread of the horrible punishment denounced against the breach or omission of them, perform the duties incumbent on his peculiar station, that, while piety and fortitude reigned at the helm, while the Maha Rajah himself continued faithful to the awful trust reposed in him, while the Brahmins remained vigilant and uncorrupted, the utmost tranquillity could not fail of pervading every quarter of the empire. Strabo, with his usual correctness, informs us, that the Indian sovereigns were obliged to shew themselves publicly to the people once a day, to hear petitions, to redress grievances, to determine differences arising among subjects, nor could they rise from the tribunal till all were heard, and every claim adjusted: the descendants of Timur religiously adhered to this Indian rule. In all negotiations, the public faith when once plighted in any treaty was inviolably preserved. The figure of an anchor, the sacred symbol of truth and stability, was engraved upon the grand imperial signet used upon those solemn occasions.

Central Authority Weakened

While the main spring of this vast political machine performed its functions with undeviating regularity, all the inferior movements were in perfect unison with it, but, when the repeated invasion of Tartar and Persian warriors had at length shaken to its centre their ancient throne, and weakened their enormous power, a general relaxation, both in discipline and morals, took place in all the subordinate branches of the monarchy. The inferior rajahs renounced their accustomed obedience, to their chief, and, aspiring to independence, in their respective districts, forget equally the laws of Menu, and reverence for the Brahmin who ought to have enforced it; and the well-poised empire of Hindostan tottered to its foundations. Internal divisions added to the convulsion of the empire from foreign assaults, and the hostile rajahs endeavoured in the field, to which they had been trained, to wrest from each other the provinces which their treachery had usurped.

The Indian nations seem to have continued in that happy and envied state, before described, from the foundation of their empire, under Rama, till within about 700 years of the Christian era when the first Tartar and Persian invasions commenced, and were at first vigorously resisted, but India and the uncounted treasures of its peaceable monarchs, accumulated during a series of centuries, afforded too strong a temptation to those valiant marauders to be relinquished after only one or two repulses, the attack was therefore renewed by both with numbers vastly increased and with tenfold vigour, and the Maha Rajah, if not wholly conquered, was subjected at least to tributary dependence: thus they continued to the time of Alexander's invasions. The great bond of union, by which so vast an empire had been holden together, was already broken, and, both in its eastern and western quarters, the inferior rajahs had usurped authority and privileges unknown to the principles and original constitution of the monarchy. The situation of things, however, at the period of the Greek irruption, fully verifies the preceding representation both of the affairs of India and the characters and pretensions of the rajahs. It demonstrates that the great feudatory princes of India, though they retained their martial spirit and their usurped dominions, no longer obeyed the summons of the Maharajah as their supreme chieftain to the embattled field, no longer elevated those united banners against the foreign invaders of their country which, in ancient periods, formed around his throne an impregnable bulwark. Their conduct to their chief was perfidious, and, that they no longer cherished that harmony, even among one another, which might render them fromidable to the common foe, is evident from the motives which Strabo assigns for the junction of Taxiles, whose dominions spread for a great extent along both the shores of the Indus, with Alexander. The reason alledged for the ready assistance which he afforded Haephestion, in preparing the bridge of boats on which he passed that river, was the rooted enmity he bore to Porus, his rival, whose dominions lay on the east of the Hydaspes, and the noblest species of glory which that conqueror obtained in India was his uniting those rival chiefs in bonds of lasting friendship.

Alexander's Invasion

Of the nations at that period inhabiting the western region of India, and of the rajahs that governed them, we have just ground to entertain the most elevated and honourable nations, since they fought with the most undaunted firmness against the veteran troops of Alexander,—against troops that were the flower of the armies of Greece, conversant, from long and severe experience, in all the various movements and all the intricate business of war, as well as furnished with every dreadful and effective engine for carrying it on with vigour and success. Yet, neither the terror of the new arms which assailed them, nor the intrepidity of a new enemy whom they opposed, could, damp the ardour of their fortitude. In the desperate siege, the novel and terrific appearance of the immense battering machines prevented not the invested garrison from making the most spirited efforts against their invaders, and it was with hardly any remains of life that adventurous invader himself was borne on his shield from a principal city of the Oxydracae, whose name, by concealing it, it would seem as if they were afraid of immortalizing. Every new river which he crossed, every new province which he attempted to subjugate, his hardy Indian adversaries still disputed, with a fortitude that shrunk from no danger, with an ardour which no fatigue could abate, and with a perseverance that must have been crowned with success against an enemy not deemed invincible. Again and again driven from the field, they still continued to rally their dispersed forces and although the Oxydracae were defeated at Sangala, they renewed the engagement near the shore of the Indus. It may be urged that the veracity of the Greek historians stands upon a suspicious foundation, and that they who could degrade themselves so far as to compliment Alexander with the honours of divinity would not scruple at a falsehood to enhance his celebrity, but would naturally be led to magnify his enemies, with intent to increase the glory which victory, under such circumstances, must infallibly bring along with it. The Khettri, or war-tribes of India, however, have not less in modern than in ancient periods indubitably established their right to the distinguished character of heroic fortitude. The Mahrattas, one of those tribes in particular, may contest the plam of undaunted valour with the finest and best disciplined troops of Asia, and bid fair, at some future auspicious period, effectually to liberate their country from the galling yoke of their Mahommedan tyrants.

Law of Land

Having taken the above general survey of the duties and functions assigned to the first and second class of the Hindoos, it would be unpardonable to omit mentioning the guardian, the parternal attention extended by the ancient legislature of India to the two inferior castes, who while they contributed so materially by their industrious exertions as merchants, husbandmen, mechanics, and in the still humbler servile capacity, to the support, the comfort, and even the luxury, of the superior orders, had a right to expect, and fully enjoyed, the protection and fostering care of the government under which they toiled. It must here be noticed, that the sovereign of India has been immemorially considered as the sole proprietor of the soil, and, under ancient grants from the crown, the great Zemindars hold their lands on the easy terms of paying a sixth part of the annual produce to that sovereign for his support and the subsistence of the national armies. Ancient writers say, that a fourth was the sum stipulated between the sovereign and the renter of the land but I have elsewhere produced a passage to prove that it was only a sixth, which is a still more lenient deduction from his profits. It might be called a perpetual lease, for, the punctual payment of that sixth ever secured the possession of the farm to the family who rented it, and, in the ancient areas of the empire, it descended from father to son in the third cast by a kind of hereditary right.

To so important a member of the community as the cultivator of the ground, in a country where the inhabitants subsist principally on vegetable productions, it was but consistent with the highest policy to render his situation comfortable and his property inviolably secure from invasion. This is done in a most ample manner, by a series of wise and humane laws in the chapter of the code that concerns the third class, and which we shall presently more particularly notice. By those laws, he was for ever exempt from all the burthen of public service, military and civil, he saw, but felt not, the tempest of battle which raged around him, hostile squadrons in the ardour of pursuit and victory respected the property and the person of the husbandman. In the ancient periods of the empire, Strabo tells us, it often occurred, that, while in one field the flames of war spread havoc and destruction in that adjoining, the unmolested husbandman was beheld in security tilling the ground, and providing by his industry against its disastrous ravages. There was, indeed, one apparent burden under which the husbandman laboured, but his devotion to the religion of his fathers forbade him to esteem it as such. The king had his *sixth* by law allotted to him, but *all,* if he were disposed to take it, was the Brahmin's. Among the fruits and grain of the earth he selected the choicest for his own use and the service of the temple. It was a sacred claim beyond the arbitration of man, and the infatuated devotee, instead of withholding the boon demanded, however great, exulted to be thought worthy of the partial favour of heaven in accepting it.

Law and Order

The merchant was equally protected in his property with the husbandman, a moderate tribute paid the government, for liberty to exercise his employ, secured him that protection. The artisan, the labourer upon the same terms, shared similar advantages. Every name was enrolled according to his occupation, and his rank in that cast. A most rigid and vigilant police pervaded equally the city and the country. Innumerable officers were appointed in every district of the empire to collect those tributes, to inspect the state of the public roads, and those object of high importance in a country occasionally subject to droughts from defective inundations, the *tanks,* or reservoirs, to make out anew the boundaries of lands desolated by the more violent and destructive ones, to superintend the public inns, or *choultries,* destined by this hospitable nation for the accommodation of pilgrims and strangers, to preserve, free from annoyance or obstruction, the passages through forests and over the great rivers in a country where a vast internal commerce vigorously flourished, and, finally to transmit to the fountain of government constant and faithful reports of whatever fell beneath their jurisdiction, in which the least fraud or prevarication was punished with death. The legislative code sanctioned and fortified the vigour of the police with all its authority, minutely pointing out to every class its peculiar duties and alternately uttering, as the party seemed most likely to be affected by it, the soothing language of reward or the menaces of vengeance.

Thus the merchant is animated to liberality in dealing by the noblest precepts and incentives, the mechanic is deterred from injustice—the false weight and the deceitful balance, by the most dreadful denudations of the vengeance of heaven against extortion while the menial servant and labouring *cooley* are comforted with the cheering hopes that diligence in their respective stations will procure them favour in the sight of the all-seeing Brahma, and that their abject situation in this transitory world is only meant to prove their virtue and integrity amid the pressure of reproach and poverty. In truth, the situation of all the inferior classes is attempted to be made easy to them by perpetually impressing the maxim that they are only doing penance in those humble stations for crimes committed in a former state of being, and, though the limits assigned their sphere of action in this stage of existence are irrevocably fixed, yet the path is open for persevering virtue and piety to gain the summit of perfection in another stage of it,—even to be born again in the lofty Brahmin caste and rule the race of monarchs at whose nod they now tremble. The tribe of Chandalah, or *the outcast tribe,* awakens horrible ideas in the human mind, but, as I have nothing new to offer on the subject, I must refer the reader to what I have related in a former volume concerning that despised and misserable race.

Punishments

In every retrospect on the ancient Hindoo government it will be observed, that, while its politic legislator held out to presevering virtue and patient obedience the most alluring rewards, it assumed the most inflexible aspect towards criminals of every description. To temporal punishments the most dreadful, and to corporeal mutilations the most sanguinary, in order to impress his mind with deeper reverential awe, added all the terrors of the spiritual anathema, tormenting daemons and the *gehenna of gnawing serpents;* for this is the true Hindoo hell, and demonstrates the intimate connection of its theological system with our own, of which in its leading features, it is an evident perversion. What is not a little singular in this code, these present punishments and future terrors are often denounced against crimes comparatively trivial, with as much violence as against offence of the deepest enormity, as will hereafter be sufficiently manifest, in short, the stern dogmas inculcated by it, sanctioned by the combined authorities of heaven and earth, allowed of no relaxation in the severe discipline which it enjoined whether in moral on civil concerns. It was the awful manifesto of the deity, and both in its, sublimest and least important injunctions, the strictest obedience was alike indispensable. "PUNISHMENT," says the Hindoo code is the magistrate; punishment is the inspirer of terror; punishment is the defender from calamity; punishment is guardian of those that sleep; punishment with a black and a red eye terrifies the guilty." Consonant to this maxim the laws of Draco himself were not more deeply engraved in blood than many of the precepts in this tremendous code. These sanguinary maxims it is impossible to ascribe to Menu: what was *remembered* from that legislator was, we may conclude, only *severely just* but not cruel, we may reasonably refer to him all that is mild and humane in these Institutes, and some necessary precepts of a more rigorous nature, but, as his progeny degenerated; as the people gradually became more corrupt, the princes more despotic and the Brahmins more powerful it was thought necessary to add new and more terrible laws to those which in the primitive ages well deemed sufficient to control the disturbers of the public tranquillity. The hypothesis on which this work and that of Mr. Bryant have constantly proceeded and both of which record the invasion of India in early periods and the virtuous Shemites by the daring and nefarious Cuthite race will sufficiently point out to the attentive reader the period of this great national change and the fatal cause of this general depravity.

Liberal and Humane Laws

It should still be remembered however that many of the laws inculcated in the Brahmin code are in a high degree liberal and humane founded on the practice and decisions of the earliest ages when as yet no system of jurisprudence was committed to writing. Many also of the civil institutions enumerated in it go back to the days of Noah though most have been dreadfully perverted; for I must repeat in this place what has been frequently asserted in this work, and, indeed, forms in some degree the basis of it, that in the ancient world there were certain grand and primitive customs diffused universally over all nations, customs founded on the general consent and original creed of mankind, confirmed by immemorial laws and sanctified by pious traditions, customs which probably flourished in their full vigour and purity, under the domestic patriarchal roof of Noah, before the dispersion, which passed into all nations with the first colonists, and were observed in their vigour and purity, or debased and degraded in every country, according to their rectitude in adhering to, or depravation in receding from, the institutions of their primaeval ancestors. For the aspect of unrelenting severity assumed in general by legislative codes of very high antiquity, it may be urged as some degree of palliation, that the crimes, against the commission of which they were principally meant to guard, are not such as generally spring up among mankind in an associated and civilized state, but such dreadful offences as men scarcely emerged from barbarism, and under the influence of all the unbridled passions which agitate to tempest the human bosom, may be supposed capable of perpetrating, incest of the deepest dye, plunder and robbery, midnight murder, and the violation of virgin beauty. Against these crimes, so fatal to infant states, it was necessary, to raise the strongest rampart which the terror of regal authority could erect against them, and extreme necessity of the occasion will too often justify their being *written in blood.*

In eastern climes, where despotism has ever reigned in its meridian terror, in order to impress the deeper awe and respect upon the crowed that daily thronged around the tribunal, the hall of justice was anciently surrounded with the ministers of vengeance, who generally inflicted, in the presence of the monarch, the sentence to which the culprit was doomed. The envenomed serpent that was to sting him to death, the enraged elephant that was to trample him beneath his feet, the dreadful instruments that were to rend open his bowels, to tear his lacerated eye from the socket, to impale alive, or saw the shuddering wretch in sunder, were constantly at hand to perform their destined office. The audience-chamber, with the same view, was decorated with the utmost cost and magnificence, and the East was rifled of its jewels to adorn it. Whatever little, credit may in general be due to Philostratus, his description of the splendid palace and regal pomp of Musicanus too nearly resembles the accounts, given us by our own countrymen, of the magnificence which at present distinguishes those more powerful rajahs, who still retain a portion of their ancient hereditary rights and domain, to admit of doubt, especially in those times when, as yet, the hoarded wealth of India had not been pillaged by the avarice of successive Mahommedan plunderers; the artificial vines of gold adorned with birds of various colours in jewellery, and thick set with precious stones, emeralds, and rubies, hanging in blusters, to resemble grapes in their different stage towards maturity, the silver censers constantly borne before him, as a god, in which continually burned the richest perfumes of the East; the robe of gold and purple with which he was invested, and the litter of gold, fringed with pearls, on which he was carried in a march or to the chase. The Mahommedan sovereigns, doubtless in imitation of the splendour in which the ancient Indian monarchs lived had also their vines of gold, thrones encrusted with diamonds, and ceilings plated with silver.

Obedience to Law

In short, whatever could warmly interest the feelings and strongly agitate the passions of men, whatever inflames hope or excites terror, all engines of a most despotic superstition and of a most refined policy were set at work for the purpose of chaining down, to the prescribed duties of his cast, the mind of the bigotted Hindoo, to enforce undeviating obedience to the law, and secure inviolable respect for the magistrate. Hence his unaltered, his unalterable, attachment to the national code and the precepts of the Brahmin creed. As it has been in India from the beginning so will it continue to the end of time and the dissolution of nature: for the daring culprit who tramples on either, heaven has no forgiveness, and earth no place of shelter or repose.

10

Royal Power in Ancient India

PROF. K.A. NILAKANTA SASTRI

The power and prerogative of the king in ancient India which have formed the subjects of some controversy and discussion, which require elucidation. The first relates to the nature and extent of the validity of the royal edict; the second touches the apparently endless debate on whether ancient Indian king was the owner of the soil of the state or not.

A Law-guardian, not a Law-maker

It is common knowledge that the king in ancient India had little or no legislative power as we understand it in modern politics, he was more law-guardian than law-maker, and any orders issued by him had to have a due regard to the principles of common equity (Dharma) and defer to local customs and usages. One writer Katyayana, goes so far as to say that a royal order which did not satisfy these tests was not a properly made rule. He says this in a verse which has become the plaything of ignorant scribes and baffled editors who have fallen victims to them and which in its correct form should, I think, read as follows:

nyaya-sastra-(a) virodhena desa-drstes-tathaiva ca
yam-dharmam sthapayed-raja nyayyam tad-rajasasanam

Both in the reading and interpretation of this verse there it no difference between Professor Rangaswami Aiyangar and myself.[1]

But then, to this position upheld by the generality of writers on Hindu polity, there is an important exception, and that is the view put forward by Kautilya in his *Arthasastra.* I have no desire to open the question of the date and authorship of this work here, but would only say that I regard it in the main as the production of the celebrated Chancellor of Chandragupta Maurya. I consider, further, that the position taken up by Kautilya for the first time in India on the place of the royal edict in the Indian state is better accounted for on this supposition than on any other.

Four Legs of Law

Kautilya holds that royal edict (rajasasana) has an independent validity of its own; not only is it valid by itself because of its very character of being an order of the king, and without having to undergo or satisfy any tests regarding its conformity to *nyaya,* usage, and so on, but its validity is of such superior and overriding character that all other sources of law and right go under when they come into conflict with it. Here is Kautilya's text setting out the law of the matter:[2]

dharmasca vyavaharasca caritram rajasasanam
vivadarthascatuspadah pascimah purvabadhakah
atra satye sthito dharmah vyavaharastu saksisu
caritram samgrahe pumsam rajnam ajna tu sasanam

which may be rendered thus: *Dharma,* contract, custom and royal decree are the four legs of Law (determinants of litigation). Of these each later item is of superior validity to its predecessor. *Dharma* is rooted in truth; contract in witness; custom in the tradition of the people; and the decree in the command of king's. Nothing can be clearer, as an absolute exaltation of the king's power, legislative as well as executive, above all other sources of law.

And Kautilya does not stop here. He goes further and lays it down that whenever the Sastra is in conflict with any specific rule of reason finding expression in a royal decree the latter shall prevail, and the reason he assigns is startingly modern—the text must be corrupt.[3] It is noteworthy that the phrase *dharmanyaya* employed by Kautilya in this context was understood by Dr. Shama Sastri as meaning the king's law; I think that is the most natural way of understanding this phrase in the context. The verse reads :

Sastram vipratipadyeta dharma-nyayena kenacit
nyayastatra pramanam syat tatra patho hi nasyati

i.e. where the *sastra* is found to conflict with a rule of reason, there reason shall prevail, for the text indeed may be corrupt (*lit.* perishes). In the face of these statements of Kautilya exalting royal authority and reason above the canonical books and their precepts Yajnavalkya, who is often found versifying the text of the *Arthasastra* seems to have felt the need to mark his emphatic dissent from Kautilya on this matter, and he roundly asserts :

arthasastrat-tu balavad iharmasastram it[2] sthitih

And he was not far wrong; the general trend of Indian political thought was to exalt the code above the king and bind the king's discretion with its precepts. But Kautilya is the exception, and a very significant exception. Only one subsequent writer ventured to follow him in the view he took of the place of the royal edict in the constitution of the state; that was the author of the Smrti now going under the name of Narada who held along with Kautilya, that among the four determinants of a subject in dispute, the royal decree had the highest validity and overruled everything else.

Kautilya's Views

For Kautilya's sentence: *pascimah purvabadhakah,* Narada substitutes: *uttarah purvabadhakah* without any change in the meaning. Prof. Rangaswami Aiyengar however renders Narada's words by 'what precedes over-rides what follow', a rendering which by the way; he attached once to the words of Kautilya in the same context; and Dr. U.N. Ghoshal has cited him with approval.[4] Prof. Rangaswami thus imagines a conflict on this matter between Kautilya and Narada which does not exist.

It should not be supposed that Kautilya threw *dharma* overboard and advocated an unrestrained autocracy on the part of the monarch. He was too well rooted in Hindu tradition and had too little faith in the unaided intelligence of even the ablest monarch to have followed that course. In the midst of the discussion from which our extracts come, Kautilya affirms :

rajnah svadharmah svargaya praja dharmena rakshituh,

i.e. the king who fulfils his peculiar duties and protects his subjects in accordance with *dharmic* ways attains heaven. The king's obligation to keep to the path of virtue is thus asserted clearly; and his orders therefore embodied the rules of reason and justice as commonly understood of men, and were thus *dharma nyayas;* their high importance, and overriding validity in cases of conflict with other determinants of right is hinted at first in one verse which repeats the four determinants in the same order as before but puts them on the wider ground of general administration, instead of conforming them to litigation (*vivadartha*):

> anusasaddhi dharmena vyvaharena samsthaya
> nyayena ca caturthena caturantam mahim jayet

Here *samtha* and *nyaya* stand for *Caritra* and *rajasasana* respectively; then follows a verse on cases of conflict in which *artha* is to be subordinated to *dharma,* and lastly the verse already cited on the higher validity of a reasonable law of the king when it is in conflict with *sastras* (canon). It is clear therefore that while Kautilya keeps to tradition, he introduces a new element the effect of which is to attach to royal edicts a degree of importance they had never before possessed.

Age of Royal Absolutism

Now how are we to explain this exaltation of royal power by Kautilya which clearly runs against the main current of Indian tradition and in the end makes no tangible impression on Indian political thought as reflected in the subsequent literature on polity? The explanation must be sought in the general historical conditions of the age of Kautilya. It was an age of great monarchies, and the great Hellenistic kingdoms particularly Syria and Egypt, were perfecting the traditions and institutions of royal absolutism they inherited from the Persian empire of the Achamenids. And in these states we find the same exaltation of the royal edict above all other forms of law and convention, and the growth of a new and uniform civil law promoted by the active exercise of royal authority either directly in royal decrees or indirectly by the decisions and awards of the king's officers acting in his name. The position is well summed up for all the Hellenistic kingdoms in these words by Rostovtzeff:[5] 'This variety of juridical systems was dominated by the royal legislation and jurisdiction. It is evident that a royal law, order, or regulation if it conflicted with other laws, was always regarded as over-riding them, and that the royal verdict in law suits was final. The same may be true of the decisions of certain royal officials, who often rendered justice in the name of the king concurrently with the regular courts. It is clear that the royal authority was actively exerted in the sphere of civil law'. The Mauryan state was in active contact with its western neighbours, and the probability is great that the developments that were taking place under the Selecuids and Ptolemies were not altogether unknown to Kautilya who stated in so many words that he wrote his treatise for the use of his monarch basing it not only on all the extant *sastras* on the subject of polity but after having collected the contemporary practice of different states (*prayogan upalabhya ca*).[6]

Mimamsa Doctrine of Royal Ownership of Land

On the question of royal ownership of all land in the state the *locus classicus* regarding Indian tradition is of course the well known comment of Sabarasvamin on Jaimini VI-7. But Megasthenes and modern Anglo-Indian Jurisprudence hold the opposite view that all land is the property of the king (State), and that the cultivators are only tenants, not owners. Students of this question have fallen under the influence of this idea and traced it even in texts which are susceptible of another interpretation in conformity with Indian tradition. I shall examine the texts discussed by Dr. Ghoshal first, and then seek to explain how Megasthenes' view of the subject may be accounted for. Dr. Ghoshal's discussion[7] takes the form of a polemic against Jayaswal's contentions put forward in his work on *Hindu Polity*, and I find myself more in agreement with Dr. Ghoshal in his critique of Jayaswal's interpretations, and with this observation I take leave of the polemical part of this study, and turn to consider the true import of the texts cited in that paper with a view to determine how far they are opposed to the *mimamsa* doctrine laid down by Sabarasvamin that the king does not differ from any other man as regards proprietary rights in the soil, except that he is entitled as king to a share, usually a sixth part, of the produce from it.

The first text is from Manu on treasure troves and mines enjoining a half-share to the king in either case on the ground that the king offers protection to the land and is its overlord—*ardhabhag-raksanadraja bhumeradhipatir hi sah.* The main point at issue here is the import of the expression *adhi-pati,* lord or sovereign; and despite the high authority of Buhler who sees in this 'a distant recognition of the principle that the ownership of all land is vested in the king', I venture to question this statement. There is much difference between an overlordship (*adhi-patya*) which confers a right of regulation and control, and proprietorship with absolute rights of disposal of the property; the *mimamsa* position admits the former for the king in land, but not the latter, and I do not think Manu's statement means anything more. It says that the main reason for the royal share lies in the protection he affords; and Medhatithi discusses the nature of this protection in the case of treasure-troves and minerals. He raises the issue that the king can hardly be said to protect these as no one knows what is hidden underground, and answers it by saying that he guards it from being seized by a stronger person and thus affords real protection. And the general overlordship of the king over the land seems to be affirmed more to justify the larger share of this hidden wealth when it comes to light, than falls to the king in the case of produce raised by the exertions of the owners of the land. Manu's text can be understood in a sense that does not imply the royal ownership of all land, and I think that is the correct way to understand it.

Likewise in the verse cited by Bhattasvamin in his commentary on Kautilya II 24.

raja bhumeh patir-drstah sastrajnairudakasya ca
tabhayam-anyattu yad-dravyam tatra svamyam kutumbinam

Here it seems to me that the general control over land and water (*patitva*) that vests in the king as the head of the state is contrasted with the full proprietorship of other property vesting in their owners (*svamyam*). The utmost that this passage can be taken to imply is that land and water were subject to the eminent domain of the head of the state and could not ever become the absolute property of his subjects in the sense in which other things can. And Bhattasvamin cites this verse to justify the water rates laid down by Kautilya. It is still a far cry to the royal ownership of all land in the state.

The verses cited from the *Mcnsollasa* are a late echo of the early *arthasastras* which vest the king with a monopoly in mines, and the second verse is a loose justification of the monopoly as part of the divine order in the universe. It reads :

dhananam-isvaro raja hrahmana parikalpitah
bhugatanam visesena yato'sau vibudhadhipah

This is not sober political theory, but an extravagance of the nature of *arthavada.*

Cultivator—A Qualified Owner of Land

Lastly the extract from Mitra Misra who cites two verses from Katyayana and comments on them does not seem to put the matter in any different light. Here Dr. Ghoshal has been guided by the high authority of Mahamahopadhyaya P.V. Kane who writes: 'The idea underlying these verses seems to be the king is the owner of all lands in the state... The actual cultivators of the soil have only a qualified ownership of the soil'. The last sentence is to my mind the correct position; the hesitant tone of the first sentence is more than justified, though Kane's doubts are ignored by Ghoshal; in fact if the last sentence is correct, the king could not be 'owner of all lands', but at best only, like cultivators, 'a partial owner'. As a matter of fact both Katyayana and Mitra Misra do not assert anything more than the overlordship of the king in the land of the State, and as the whole passage is a closely reasoned statement of the position, I shall reproduce the text and offer my translation :

> "bhusvami tu smrto raja nanyadravsya sarvada
> tatphalasya hi sadbhagam prapnuyan-nanyathaiva tu
> bhutanam tannivasistvat svamitvam tena kirttitam
> tatkriyabalisadbhagam subhasubhanimittajam iti

Asyarthah raja bhuvah svami amrtah anyadravyasya bhumi-sambaddha dravyasya na svami anyatha bhumisvamyabhave bhutanam praninam tannivasitvat bhunivasitvat svamitvam rajna iti sesah ityatah tatkriyabalisadbhagam prapnuyat."

"Katyayana (has:) 'the king is declared the lord of the land, and not of any other wealth, as otherwise he would not get the sixth part of its fruits. As beings inhabit the land, the lordship (of the king) has been declared; hence he shall get a sixth part of the results of their work as tax, subject to exigencies good and bad'. This means: the king is declared lord of the land. Of the other wealth related to the land he is not lord. *Anyatha* means in the absence of the lordship of the land. *Bhutanam* means: of beings. *Taunivasitvat* means because they dwell on land. *Svamitvam,* that is, of the king (understood). Hence he shall get as *ball* (tax) a sixth part of (the results of) their work'."

Buhler and Kane are great names; but I am unable to help

thinking that they have been influenced by current notions in their interpretation of Manu and Mitra Misra. When it is possible to interpret them in line with the *mimamsa* tradition, and I think I have shown that this can be done, I believe that it is proper so to interpret them and in no other way. If my view is correct, the contradiction among authorities that Dr. Ghoshal discovered ceases to exit, and there stands revealed the continuity of tradition that is to be expected in so vital a question of constitutional law from a race of writers who were no mean masters of juristic argument.

Megasthenes' Version

To turn finally to Megasthenes. His statement as reproduced by Diodorus is clear and definite[8]: 'The husbandmen pay a land-tribute to the king, because all India is the property of the crown, and no private person is permitted to own land'. In saying this Megasthenes was clearly mistaken; but his mistake was most natural in his circumstances. He was a Hellenistic diplomat who had held other offices before he was deputed to Pataliputra and was presumably thoroughly familiar with the administrative systems of Egypt, Syria and other Hellenistic states. In them the State was the absolute property of the king. To cite Rostovtzeff again[9]: 'Absolute rule meant, alike from the Egyptian and from the Macedonian point of view the ownership of the State, of its soil and subsoil, and ultimately of the products of the soil and the subsoil. The state was the 'house' (*oikos*) the king, and its territory his estate. So the king managed the State as a plain 'Macedonian or Greek would manage his own household'. Now this view was never accepted in India, and there is no statement is Kautilya that even remotely resembles it, as has been admitted by close students of the *Arthasastra,* who like, Stein and Breloer, have studied it from different points of view.

At the same time the *Arthasastra* adumbrates a vast scheme of detailed control of the agrarian operations in the whole state including the marketing of produce, undertaken by a well organized bureaucracy comprising a vast host of officials, great and small. There are many sections in the *adhyaksapracara,* the unique contribution of Kautilya to *Arthasastra,* which bear out this statement, and it is not at all unlikely that they derived their inspiration from the contemporary practice (*prayoga*) prevalent in states outside India. And if the actual machinery of administration was anything like what is envisaged in the great work of Kautilya, and I presume that there was a close correspondence between the great Chancellor's theory and practice, Megesthenes who spent some time in Pataliputra and surely travelled along the whole length of the royal road from the frontier to the capital, must have been struck by the remarkable similarity between what he saw in India and what he knew of other lands; the Mauryan state stretched its right of eminent domain to its utmost limits and behaved as if it owned the land, and Megasthenes made the inference that was most natural in the circumstances.

But in reality, India knew nothing of the States ownership of its soil until she passed under the rule of foreigners who based their claims on the rights of conquerors.

Notes and References

1. Rajadharma, p. 133.
2. Bk. III, Ch. (1).
3. Contra *Rajadharma,* p. 82, where the passage is somehow understood as being in consonance with the doctrine of infallibility of the common source of both the Arthasastra and Dharmasastra. I am aware of the other interpretations of the last quarter of the verse—*tatra patho hi nasyati,* but I think the correct meaning is what I have stated above.
4. See *Rajadharma,* p. 133 ; *Some aspects of Ancient Indian Polity,* p. 170; and Ghoshal, *The Beginnings,* p. 141 and n. 8.
5. Social and Economic History of the Hellenistic World, pp. 1067-68.
6. Bk. II, Ch. 10, verse at the end,
7. *Op. cit.*, pp. 158-66.
8. *Mc. Crindle, Megasthenes and Arrian,* p. 42.
9. *Op. cit.*, p. 269.

11

The Yuvaraja in Ancient India

D.K. GANGULY

Although the office of the *Yuvaraja* is of earlier antiquity, we do not get any trustworthy account of it till we come to the age of the *Jatakas* where the crown-prince is generally called *Uparaja.* Usually the eldest son of the king was entitled to this post but there are indications that brothers were sometimes preferred to incompetent sons for heir-apparentcy. One of the *Jatakas,*[1] for instance, mentions two brothers of whom the elder was *Uparaja* and the younger, *Senapati.* The crown-prince helped the reigning king in the work of administration. We see Bimbisara taking the charge of Anga during the reign of his father.[2] At a still later date Bimbisara appointed his son Ajatasatru as the viceroy of the same province.[3] If the story of malevolence of the last-named king be regarded as genuine, it would follow that occasions were not few and far between when princes misused their power to usurp the throne for themselves.

Appointed as Viceroy

Literature and inscriptions prove that the practice of governing provinces with the help of princes continued in the Maurya period. The Pali tradition[4] speaks that when Bindusara was on the throne of Pataliputra, he appointed his two sons, Susima (or Sumana) and Asoka as viceroys at Taksasila and Ujjayini respectively. Later on the people of Taksasila rose in revolt and Asoka was deputed by his father to suppress the popular uprising. The *Divyavadana*[5] passage recording this incident has been translated as follows :

"Now Taxila, a city of king Bindusara, revolted. The king Bindusara despatched Asoka there. . . . While the prince was nearing Taxila with the four-fold army, the resident *Pauras* (citizens of Taxila), on hearing of it . . . came out to meet him and said: 'We are not opposed to the prince nor even to king Bindusara. But these wicked ministers insult us'."[6]

The following facts emerge from the above account.

First, the post of the *Kumara*-viceroys were subjected to transfer in the Maurya period.

Secondly, the *Kumaras* had their own council of ministers who, if allowed to act independently, would generally prove to be oppressive.

We may now turn to the edicts of Asoka for fuller information about princes, who were called both *Kumaras* and *Aryaputras.* Kalinga Edict I refers to a *Kumara* who was entrusted with the administration of Ujjayini (*Ujenite pi cu kumale*) and to a second prince who was in charge of Taksasila (*Takhasilate*), the headquarters of Gandhara, whereas, Kalinga Edict II informs us of one such prince, placed in charge of Kalinga with its headquarters at Tosali (*Tosaliyan Kumale*). The existence of another prince viceroy is indicated by Minor Rock Edict I which refers to an *Aryaputra* at Suvarnagiri (*Suvannagirite ayaputasa*). The testimony of the literary evidence about the appointment of the Mauryan princes as viceroys for outlying provinces is thus corroborated by the epigraphic evidence.

There are reasons for the belief that all the *Kumara-viceroys* did not claim the same status and position. The *Kumara-viceroy* at Tosali was not empowered to exercise unfettered power, as it was the case with those stationed at Ujjain and Taxila. This view is based on the three-fold arguments noted below:

1. The *Kumaras* of Ujjain and Taxila were to send on tour their own *Mahamatras* every three years to ensure the porper administration of justice, whereas, the *Kumara* of Tosali was not allowed to depute the *Mahamatras* who were to be sent by Asoka himself.
2. Secondly, in connection with the dispatch of such an officer the *Kumaras* of Ujjayini and Taksasila are mentioned by themselves and not associated with any state dignitaries,

whereas, in separate Kalinga Edict II (Dh. version) where alone the *Kumara* of Tosali is referred to, he is mentioned not by himself but associated with the *Mahamatras.*

3. And finally, Asoka issued orders to the *Nagara-Vyavaharikas* and others of Tosali directly when the *Kumara* remained in charge of the province, and not through the *Kumara* himself.

It would become clear from what has been said above that Asoka did not permit the *Kumara* of Tosali to enjoy a large measure of freedom in administration which he was pleased to grant to the *Kumaras* placed at Ujjain and Taxila. This disparity in position among princes justifies the assumption that the posts of viceroys for Taxila and Ujjain were reserved for the *Yuvaraja* and other important princes.

The *Arthasastra*[7] also gives us a good deal of information regarding the princes but when we compare the data gleaned from these diverse sources we find that the *Arthasastra* primarily deals with the upbringing and conduct of princes; it does not give us any idea about their role in administration, which can only be known from the Pali texts and epigraphic records.

Responsibilities of Crown-prince

Pusyamitra who succeeded the Mauryas on the throne of Pataliputra continued the Maurya tradition of associating the prince in administration. The *Malavikagnimitram* tells us that the crown-prince Agnimitra governed Vidisa (Besnagar in Eastern Malwa) as his father's viceroy. We do not know whether the example of Pusyamitra was followed by his successors or not.

The Hathigumpha inscription gives us an interesting insight into the education and responsibilities of a crown-prince in the first century B.C. The inscription tells us that Kharavela spent the first fifteen years of his life in games, befitting a young prince, and in the study of writing, coinage, accounting, administration and legal procedure. In his sixteenth year he was installed as *Yuvaraja* and held that position for a period of nine years. We thus see that serious attention was paid to the training of the crown-prince in order that, on his accession to the throne, he would be able to discharge the duties of Kingship efficiently.

Our knowledge about the *Yuvaraja* during the Gupta period is derived from the combined testimony of the contemporary inscriptions and the *Nitisara* of Kamandaka. We probably get an account of the selection of Samudragupta, probably as a *Yuvaraja,* by Chandragupta I. We are told that Chandragupta I selected him for the post in an open assembly. It is further stated that when this selection was announced his kinsmen of equal birth (*tulyakulaja*) became pale-faced with disappointment. This description leaves the impression that for heir-apparentcy the claims of the elder sons were sometimes overlooked in favour of those of the younger princes, otherwise the disappointment of kinsmen of equal birth would remain inexplicable. This supposition is corroborated by the fact that Chandragupta II, to judge from the expression *tatparigrhita,* 'accepted as his chosen successor' applied to him, was selected by his father to succeed the latter, though he was not the eldest son. The reason behind the selection of a younger prince as *Yuvaraja* was due not so much to the favouritism on the part of the father as to the character and ability of the candidate.

It is quite likely that the heir-apparent discharged a good deal of administrative work and led the Imperial army in the face of any attack from outside. When the Pusyamitra, who had great resources in men and money, invaded the Gupta dominions in the last years of Kumaragupta I's reign, Skandagupta fought hard with them 'to restore the fallen fortunes of his family'.

Some welcome light on the office of the crown-prince is thrown by a few seals from Basarh in which we have the following inscriptions:

(i) *Yuvaraja-padiya-Kumaramaty adhikaranam;* and
(ii) *Sri-yuvarajabhattaraka-padiya-kumaramaty-adhikaranasya.*

Unfortunately there is no unanimity among scholar as regards the meaning of the above legends: U.N. Ghosal[8] takes the word *Padiya* as equivalent to *padaimdhyata* and denoting the relationship between father and son. According to this interpretation, the *kumaramatyas* of the Basarh seals were related as sons to the Crown-prince. This theory does not appear to be conclusive'. Fleet has shown that the expression *padanudhyata* is used in inscriptions to mean different kinds of relations. The word *padiya* in the Basarh seals implies in all probability that the *kumaramatyas* in question were attached to the heir-apparents. The *Yuvaraja* had evidently a body of officers under him. While dealing with these inscriptions Dikshitar[9] observes: "This class of seals betrays clearly that the Crown-prince was distinguished from other princes of the royal family; while the Crown-prince was entitled

Yuvaraja Bhattaraka; ordinary princes were merely *Yuvarajas* and did not have the appellation *Bhattaraka*, attached to their names". It seems that both *Yuvaraja* and *Yuvaraja Bhattaraka* have been used indiscriminately in the sense of the heir-apparent, and that the expression *bhattaraka* is used in one case and omitted in the other because of some carelessness on the part of the scribes who incised the records.

Kamandaka who probably flourished in this age points out that the eldest among the princes should be made *Yuvaraja* (*avinitan Kumaran hi Kulamasu vivasyatijvinitamaurasan putran yauvarajye bhisecayet's*).[10]

Princely Curriculum

As regards the princely curriculum Kamandaka[11] says that he was to be well-versed in economics and politics as well as in the Vedas and philosophy. It may be noted that the Barhaspatya school holds that the king need not study the Vedas as it would act as a screen to observe the vision of a King who wanted to know the hard world around him. That the Gupta princes did not neglect the cultivation of fine arts is possibly indicated by the statement in the Allahabad inscription that Samudragupta 'put to shame the preceptor of the Lord of the Gods and Tumburu and Narada and others by his sharp and polished intellect and choral skill and musical accomplishments.'

The heir-apparent was an important member of the administrative machinery of the State in the age of the Harsavardhana. Rajyavardhana was sent by his father Prabhakaravardhana as the leader of the army to fight against the Hunas. If literature reflects the picture of the contemporary period, then Bana's account of Prince Candrapida, as found in the chapter entitled *Candrapidasya Yauvarajyabhisekah* of the *Kadambari* may be taken into consideration for knowing the condition of the princes in the seventh century A.D. Bana gives us the following details about Candrapida :

First, during his childhood days various rites such as tonsure, etc., were performed.

Then the prince was trained in all branches of bearing and crafts.

He took a period of ten years to complete his course of study, and then he was brought home. After that he was crowned as the heir-apparent. Bana vividly describes how Candrapida's coronation ceremony as *Yuvaraja* was observed with grandeur. The King himself, accompanied by his Prime Minister and many thousands of Kings, raised up the auspicious water-jar and crowned his son as heir-apparent by pouring the holy water on his son's head.

Dandin, who according to some scholars flourished at about the same age as the author of the *Kadambari,* speaks in *Ucchvasa* I of the *Dasakumaracarita* of the princes who acquired proficiency in all scripts (*sakalalipijnanam*), languages, *Vedas,* and then six *Angas, Puranas, Kavyas, Natakas, Akhyayanas, Akhyayikas, Itihasas, Citrakatha* (*Kavy anatakakhyanakakhyayiketihasa cilrakathasahitapuranaga-nanaipunyam*), *Dharmasastras, Vyakarana,* Astrology, Logic, *Mimamsa* (*Dharmasavdajyotiskeamimansadisamastasastranikaracaturyam*), treatise on politics of Kautilya and Kamandaka musical instruments, music, poetics, magical sciences, riding all vehicles, use of various weapons and different croocked arts such as thieving, gambling, etc.[12] The combined evidence of both Bana and Dandin would indicate that the princes of their times were not only trained in politics and military science, they had to be well-versed in all other branches of knowledge, not excluding fine arts also.

The *Yuvaraja* finds frequent mention in the Pala and Sena records. The King's eldest son, as usual, was selected as the heir-apparent, but as to his duties and functions during this period, we do not possess detailed information. Tribhuvanapala, who was the *Yuvaraja* under his father Dharmapala, acted as the *dutaka* or messenger in connection with the Khalimpur grant. Another Pala crown-prince, *viz.*, Rajyapala (*sthira yauvarajyan*) was entrusted with similar business in respect of the Monghyr grant.[13] The advice of the Crown-prince was some time solicited by the King on important issues, as would appear from the fact that Ramapala often held consultations with his son Rajyapala, in connection with his war-preparations against the Kaivartas.[14] The history of the Pala dynasty furnishes us with a few instances to show that the heir-apparents did not always succeed their fathers on the Imperial throne. Tribhuvanapala, as we have already seen was the Crown-prince during the regin of Dharmapala, but the prince who succeeded Dharmapala on the throne was Devapala. Are we to assume that the rightful claim of Tribhuvanapala was challenged by Devapala who occupied the throne after defeating his brother in a fratricidal struggle? Now, the possibility of an internecine war after the death of Dharamapala cannot be admitted in the presence of the statement in the Monghyr grant that Devapala ascended the throne peacefully (*nir-upaplavam*). Tribhuvanapala did not ascend the Pala throne probably for the reason that he predeceased his father. Again,

Devapala, after his demise, was followed by Surapala, and not by his worthy son Rajyapala (*atmanurupa-caritan*), probably because the latter died during his own life-time. The Crown-prince normally inherited the throne after the death of the King, but Narayanapala ascended the throne during the lifetime of his father Vigrahapala who abdicated the throne to adopt a life of austerities.[15]

Inscriptions do not help us much in knowing the position of the *Yuvaraja* in the contemporary Pratihara kingdom. But the little that we know about him would make it abundantly clear that generally the eldest son was selected for the post. We have, however, a few cases of younger brothers being elevated to the rank of the *Yuvaraja.* The Daulatpura copper-plates of Bhoja I mention Nagabhata as *Yuvaraja* and *dutaka* of the grant, but this Nagabhata was probably a brother of Bhoja.[16]

Powerful Yuvarajas

A perusal of the Gahadavala epigraphs reveals that the Gahadavala Crown-princes, called *Yuvaraja* and *Maharajaputras,* were more powerful than the heir-apparents in other contemporary kingdoms of Northern India. Unlike their contemporary princes in other kingdoms, they enjoyed the special prerogative of making grant of land, no doubt, with the approval of the ruling monarch, and issuing records of such gifts. When the *Yuvaraja* Jayacandra,[17] for example, made a grant, he did so with the consent of king Vijayacandra. They announced their grants in their own names unlike the queens whose gifts were to be announced by Kings.[18] The seals of these princes contain their own insignia or *lanchana* which consists of a conch-shell and an arrow below with the name of the *Yuvaraja* across the centre, as distinct from the royal seal which shows a *Garuda* above and a conch-shell below and the name of the king, written across the centre.[19] Sometime the Crown-prince seems to have been more closely associated with the Central Government as Govindacandra was during the reign of his father Madanapala, as may be guessed from the use of the royal seal in his own name in the inscriptions which he used during the lifetime of his father.

Notes and References

1. *Jat,* VI. 30.
2. Barua, *Asoka,* p. 35.
3. *PHAI,* p. 209.

4. *Dipavamsa,* VI. 15; *Mahavamsa,* XIII, 8.
5. P. 371.
6. *PHAI,* p. 363.
7. *Arthasastra,* I, 17.
8. *Historiography,* p. 186.
9. *The Gupta Polity*, p. 155.
10. *Kamandakiya,* VII, 5-6.
11. *Ibid.*, II, 2-5.
12. V. Satakopan, Dandin's *Dasakumaracarita* (Madras), 1966, p. 18.
13. *EI*, Vol. XVIII, p. 304 ff.
14. Sen, *Some Historical Aspects of the Inscriptions of Bengal,* p. 529.
15. *Ibid.*, p. 359.
16. D. Sharma, p. 314.
17. *EI*, Vol. IV, pp. 118, 120.
18. R. Neogi, p. 145.
19. *EI,* Vol. VIII, pp. 155-6; R. Neogi, p. 146.

12

Kingship and Republics in Ancient India

J.N. Samaddar

ORIGIN OF KINGSHIP

Protection—The Basis of Kingship

The *Mahabharata* thus speaks of the origin of Kingship.

"We have heard that a people without a king was perishing, devouring each ether like fishes. They, therefore, came together and made an agreement, to wit, that a voice-hero, a bully, an adulterer and a thief should be deserted; all the members of all the castes without exception (were to be punished thus). After they had made this agreement, they abode by it, but were nevertheless soon overcome by distress, and on this account they came to the grandfather and cried out for a king, saying, 'Without a king we perish; show us a king whom we may honour, who may protect us.' He indicated Manu, but Manu did not give them a kind reception, and said, 'I am afraid of the evil deed; it is harsh work to govern men, specially when they are wicked'. But the people answered, 'Fear not, the guilt shall rest on the criminals; we will agree to give the one-tenth of our income in grain and one-fifteenth in cattle and gold, a maid to wed and escorts to accompany thee, like gods Indra and Kubera; thou shalt have one-fourth of all the religious merit gained by the people, when they are protected by thee'. Manu, therefore, accepted the kingdom."[1]

The above, perhaps, *the most original idea of the origin of kingship;* lays special stress on the question of *protection,* necessity compelled them—as were, perhaps, the Hellanic invaders of Greece or the Teuton invaders of Britain—to strengthen the hands of one who would be able to protect them. "It is through fear of the king only, that men do not devour one another. As all creatures become unable to see one another and sink in utter darkness, if the sun and the moon do not rise, so fishes in shallow water and birds in a spot safe from danger dart and rove as they please (for a time) and repeatedly attack and grind one another, with force, and then meet with certain destruction, even so men sink in Utter darkness and meet with destruction if they have no king to protect them, like a herd of cattle without the herdsman to look after them.[2]

The *Ramayana* is also of the same opinion, for Valmiki says: "in a country where there is no king, nobody possess anything which is his own. Like the fish the people are always devouring one another."[3]

Manu also expressed the same idea of *Protection* when he said that everybody became afraid to live in a kingdom which had no king and so God created a king, for "if the king did not unwearily exercise the chastising rod on those deserving to be chastised, the stronger would kill the weaker like fish in water."[4]

Not only in religious books, but in books on polity as well, the same idea is echoed repeatedly. Canakya observes: "In the absence of the wielder of the chastising rod, the stronger devours the weak."[5] He writes further, "People afflicted with anarchy first elected Manu, son of Vivasvat, to be their king. They allotted one-sixth of their grains and one-tenth of their merchandise. Subsisting on their *wage,* kings become capable of giving safety and security to their subjects and removing their sins. Hence, hermits, too provide the king with one-sixth of the grains, gleaned by them, saying, 'It is a tax payable to him who protects us."[6] The *Sukraniti* also echoes the same sentiment by observing, "Though master in form (the king is) the servant of the people getting *pay* in the form of taxes and that was paid for the *protection* under all circumstances."[7]

The Buddhist books also bear ample testimony to *protection* being the root of kingship. The *Ulluka Jataka,* while referring to the system of election—which we will consider later on—speaks of thus, "Once upon a time, the people who lived in the first cycle of the world gathered together and took for their king a certain man, handsome, auspicious, commanding—altogether perfect." A similar principle is enunciated elsewhere.[8] Let us assemble together, and choose from our midst those who are the finest looking, the largest, the handsomest, the strongest and let us make them our lords over our fields and they shall recompense those of us who do what is praise-worthy and for the produce of our fields and for the fruits we gather, we will give them a portion." This punishing the wicked conveys consequently the idea of *protection,* a view endorsed by the *Mahavastu Avadana* that the king was called Kshattriya for protecting the people and maintaining them adequately.

Divine Origin of Kingship

Closely connected with the contract system or "Wage Theory" is the divine origin of kingship—a more popular theory. It also is referred to in the *Mahabharata* "Yudhisthira asked the grandfather, Bhisma, whence arose the word *Rajan,* which is used on earth? Possessed of hands, arms and neck like others, having an understanding and sense like those of others, subject like others to the same kinds of joy and grief, in fact, similar to others in respect of all the attributes of humanity, for what reason does one man, viz., the king, govern the rest of the world? Why do all men seek to obtain his favours?" And the great Bhisma replied that "at first" there was not sovereignty neither was there any king but all men used to protect one another righteously. But then *Moha* (infatuation) set in, the *Vedas* began to disappear, the Gods became frightened and went to Brahma and said, "O Lord of the three worlds, we are about to descend to the level of human beings. Men used to pour upwards, while we used to pour downwards. In consequence, however, of the cessation of all pious rites among men, great distress will be our lot." Brahma then composed a treatise containing one hundred thousand chapters for their guidance. The Gods then wont to Vishnu and said, "Indicate, O God, that one among mortals who deserves to have superiority over the rest," and the god of creation created a son born of him who was named Viraj.[9] The seventh in descent began to follow the rules of the treatise, his consecration was solemnly performed and Vishnu told him, "No one, O King, shall transcend thee". To give effect to this, the God himself entered the personality of the monarch, with the result that the entire universe offered divine worship to Prithi. Since then there has been no difference between a *deva* (god) and a

Naradeva (Man God), between a god and a god living as king on earth.[10] Nobody can vouchsafe the truth of the above statement but that to this is due the conception of the king as one "who is like a father when he is compassionate; a mother when he nourishes the wretched; fire when he consumes his enemies; Yama when he restrains the wicked; Kubera when he offers a sacrifice; a Guru when he gives instruction; a protector when he protects[11] his people," cannot be denied and, as a Hindu, I am prepared, whatever might have been its origin, to accept the view of Manu and say, "The King is the God living on earth."[12]

Election of Kings

How far was Kingship elective in ancient India? Zimmer is of opinion that while the Vedic monarchy was sometimes hereditary, yet in others the monarchy was elective, "though it is not clear whether the selection by the people was between the members of the royal family only or extended to members of all the noble clans". This view is not accepted by Professors Macdonell and Keith who are of opinion[13] that "It must be admitted that the evidence for the elective monarchy is not strong". They quote Geldner who argues that all the passages cited (*Rg.* X. 124, 174 and *Atharva* 19 iii. 4; iv. 22) can be regarded not as choice by the cantons (*Vis.*) but as acceptance by the subjects.

But, if, in the above, the learned Professors find only acceptance by the subjects, we find in other passages clear and conclusive evidence of election. We quote a few here :

(a) "Be with us. I have chosen thee"[14]
(b) "Let all the people wish for thee"[15]
(c) "Thy friends have chosen thee again"[16]
(d) "All elements have aided thee"[17]
(e) "Let all the clans desire thee"[18]
(f) "The tribesmen shall elect thee for the kingship"[19]
(g) "Let all of these in concert call thee hither"[20]
(h) "We as thy friends have chosen thee"[21]
(i) "The whole people want you. Do not fail from the states the people elect you to rulership"[22]
(j) "I have chosen thee."[23]

Not only in the Vedic age, but even afterwards also, later on when heredity was taking more and more prominent part, election was exercising its influence. In the *Ramayana,* King Dasaratha could think of consecrating and electing his son Rama as Crown-Prince only after he could secure the consent not only of Brahmans but of the people of the town and the country as well.[24] After the banishment of Rama, when Dasaratha died, the ministers called the *Sabha* and asked it to elect the king from among the descendants of *Ikshvakus.* The people unanimously empowered Vasistha, the royal priest, to elect one of the royal blood or some other person that was entitled in every way to wield the kingly sceptre.[25] Vasistha, according to will of people, sent for Bharata and Satrughna and the representatives elected the former. Also in the case of Sugrive represented as the monkey king, his tribe and ministers elected him when for one year no news of his elder brother Vali was heard.[26]

In the *Mahabharata,* when succession was being regulated by heredity to some extent, we find that "those who desire prosperity shall first elect and crown a king for the protection of all."[27] It was conclusive fact that even when the hereditary claims of the eldest were being considered supreme (excepting when the eldest happened to be an ascetic as in the case of Bhisma, or he was physically unfit as was Dhrtarasthra),[28] the people were exercising some right. In the matter of election of the king, Pandu got the kingship in supersession of Bhisma and Dhrtarasthra, but the choice had to be referred to and ratified by the people, though the former was practically an ascetic, having made a vow niether to marry nor to claim the crown, and the latter was blind.

But a change was gradually perceptible. In the Buddhistic age we do find election, though we note that herdity was gradually asserting itself. On one occasion, "the nobles and Brahmans and all classes combined, killed the king and elected another."[29] On another, the councillors elected[30] a king while at another time the people gathered together and took for their king a certain man.[31] After the death of Brahmadatta, king of Benaras, the elder son was refused and the younger was made king by the ceremonial sprinkling.[32] That the quadrupeds and other animals are also seen electing their kings, shows how far election had advanced.[33]

Indeed the eldest succeeding to the father was becoming the normal succession and any other transfer was becoming a crime. So, Canakya observed, "the sovereignty falls to the lot of the eldest son is to be respected."[34] With the growth of kingly power, it was becoming sharper and sharper. And, I venture to suggest that at this stage the Brahmans began to support the kingly powers. It was like the New Monarchy, when the church out of touch with the English nation, began to support the kingly power rigidly. Here also, the two religious revolutions had made the Brahmans lose their contact with the people. They found and knew that it was the kingly power which could alone rescue them from out of this oblivion and they began to side with the kings. They wanted to divert the attention of the people from Buddhism; they wanted to bring in a reaction against the Buddhistic condemnation of sacrifice and then we note the renaissance of Horse-sacrifice. And I may be permitted to add one interesting fact why Canakya who was all in all in the time of Chandragupta, could not or did not assume royal power though he practically wielded royal power. That Chandragupta, a man of low caste, could wield sovereign power was one of the effects of the levelling doctrine of the great preacher and the fact that he wielded it through a Brahman was the sign of the renaissance of Brahmanic power.

With the growth of kingly power, election disappeared altogether. In the time of Harsha "the royal house followed the law of heredity,"[35] while we find in *Vikramanikya* that when the king wanted to make the second son *Yuvaraja* (Crown-prince) the latter protested saying that the dignity of the Crown-prince belonged by right to his elder brother,[36] thus clearly showing what a turn things had taken.

REPUBLICS[37]

Hindu Shastras Generally against Democratic Government

In spite of the fact that there is very strong condemnation of ruling without kings, in all the Hindu Sastras in *Manu*[38] in *Ramayana,*[39] in *Mahabharata,*[40] in *Vayu Purana,*[41] in *Gautama,*[42] for the Republics inspired by the doctrine of equality of Gautama Buddha aimed at equality, we find frequently mention of and references to republics in all these very Sastras and literature. To me, it seems that these republics had their origin as early as the Vedic age.[43] *Rigveda*[44] mentions three kings, Varuna, Mitra, and Aryaman, ruling together, while the *Atharva* refers to "reign among the kings as a Sovran ruler."[45] Assemblies or Synods,[46] as they are called, were in the Vedic ages. It is quite likely that in their initial stage they were merely religious assemblies or congregation of worshippers, but with the advancement of progress, political questions were also discussed.

In *Atharvaveda* we find the following:

"Fair be thy words, O Father, at the meetings. We knew thy name, O Conference, thy name is interchange of talk. Let all the companies who join the Conference agree with me . . . make me conspicuous in all the gathered company."[47]

The word assembly is referred to clearly in the *Atharvaveda,*[48] which according to Griffith, was the assembly of the people of the village or hamlet.[49] Griffith, while referring to a hymn to the *Rg.*[50] speaks of the Samiti as the general assembly of the people, "meeting on some important occasion, such as the election of the king". Practically, the same thing is expressed again in the *Atharva* Book VI. Hymn 64:

"Agree, and be united, let your minds be all of one accord,

Even as the Gods of ancient days, unanimous await their share,
The rede is common, common the assembly, common the law,
so be their thoughts united. . . .
One and the same be your resolve, be all your hearts in harmony.
One and the same be all your minds that all may happily consent."

And, the expression "may Indra make all the tribes unanimous"[51] suggests the idea of a President of the Tribes meeting in the Assembly[52] with Indra as President.

At some period in the development of political institutions in ancient India, many of the assemblies grew more powerful and some of them began to usurp the royal power, leading finally to the establishment of republics. The process was hastened on, by the reaction against Brahmanism and the doctrine of equality preached by the Buddha, though it is peculiar that only certain places, e.g., the Punjab and the plains around Vais'ali showed a remarkable tendency for the development of non-kingly states. Many of these existed side by side with kingly states and their existence may be traced even from the days of the *Mahabharata.* It speaks of *ganas* which had treasury and army and which had also to do with foreign policy and certainly mere corporations could not have required or acquired all these paraphernalia of royalty.[53] Mr. K.P. Jayaswal very ingeniously (and perhaps rightly) suggests that "one of the reasons for the objection of Sis'upala to Krishna's presence amongst and assembly of crowned heads was that he was not a king and the story probably preserves an instance of kingly hatred towards the free communities."[54]

Grecian Accounts of Indian Republics

These republics or assemblies flourished in Northern India on the eve and at the time of invasion of Alexander the Great and some of them offered the stoutest opposition to the Macedonian hero. Megasthenes, to whom we owe so much relating to this period, clearly speaks of "self-ruled" cities in distinction to cities governed by kings.[55] The town of Nysa, he said, had an aristocracy with a President and governing body,[56] while the Kathians and other tribes of independent Indians are also mentioned. The Oxydrakai sent their leading men to Alexander,[57] while the Sambhasht dwelt in cities in which democratic form of government prevailed.[58] The Sabarce[59] had also a similar form of government. Nysa[60] which according to Megasthenes, had an aristocratic form of government, had according to Arrian,[61] an oligarchic form of government. Patala had a political constitution drawn on the lines of the Spartan government with two hereditary kings and a council of elders ruling the whole state with paramount authority.[62] Reference may also be drawn to the existence of autonomous tribes, dealt with by Cunningham and V.A. Smith.[63]

As already mentioned, the Buddhist Revolution exercised a good deal of influence on ancient Indian institutions. The many and abundant references found in the *Arthasastra* and the *Jataka* explain these. Kautilya who praises the sort of constitution observes: "Sovereignty may be the property of a clan, for the corporation of clans invincible in its nature and free from the calamities of anarchy, can have a permanent existence on earth.[64] He was of opinion that "the acquisition of the help of a corporation is better than the acquisition of an army, a friend, or of profits" and he strongly advises the reigning sovereign to secure and enjoy the services of such corporation by conciliation and gifts. He mentions many self-governing clans, e.g., Lichchavis, Vrijika, Mallaka, Madaraka, Kukuru, Kuru, Panchala, Kambhoja and Surasthra.[65] These evidently go to prove the existence of powerful republics side by side with kingly forms of government.

Republics in the Buddhistic Age

The Buddhist books afford ample materials about this. When King Pasenadi asked for one of the daughters of the Sakya Chief, the Sakyas discussed the question in the Mote Hall.[66] The administrative and judicial business of the clan being carried on in the Public Assembly in which young and old were present in the common Mote Hall.

The Republic of the Lichchvis is, of course, very well known. Buddha's conversation with Ananda, his favourite desciple, gives us a clear insight into the condition of the Vajjians. The very language of Buddha, as applied to the Vajjians and Bhikshus testify to this. The former is "So long, Ananda, as the Vajjians meet together in concord, and rise together in concord, as long as they exact nothing that has been already enacted and act in accordance with the ancient institutions of the Vajjians ... so long may the Vajjians be expected not to decline but to prosper and the latter is "So long, O mendicants, as the Bhikkus meet together in full and frequent assemblies, so long as they meet together in concord and carry out in concord the duties of the order—so long as the Bhikkus shall establish nothing that has not been already prescribed and abrogate nothing that has alredy been established and act in accordance with the rules of the order as laid down—so long as the Bhikkus honour and esteem and revere and support the elders of experience—so long the Bhikkus may not be expected to decline but to prosper." The Buddha in comparing his religious institution with a political institution expressed his regard for the latter.[67]

The *Vinaya Pitaka* reveals that the Buddhist *Samgha* was based and to a great extent governed on democratic principles. Resolutions were put to the vote and decided by a majority. As this vote-taking is interesting, I am describing the procedure in detail.

"Now at the time the Bhikkus assembled in *Samgha,* since they become violent, quarrelsome and disputatious and kept on wounding one another with sharp words, were unable to settle the disputed question. They told the matter to the Blessed one.

"I allow you, O Bhikkus, to settle such a dispute by the vote of the majority. A Bhikku who shall be possessed of five qualifications shall be appointed as taker of the voting tickets.

"And thus shall be appointed.

"First the Bhikku is to requested (whether he will undertake the office). Then some able and discreet Bhikku is to bring the matter before the *Samgha,* saying.

"Let the Venerable *Samgha* hear me. If the time seems meet to the *Samgha,* let the *Samgha* appoint a Bhikku of such and such name as taker of the voting tickets.

"This is the motion.

"Let the venerable *Samgha* hear me. The *Samgha* appoint a Bhikku of such and such name as taker of the ticket whosoever of the

Venerable one approves of the Bhikku of such and such a name being appointed as taker of the tickets, let him keep silence. Whosoever approves not thereof, let him speak. The Bhikku of such and such a name is appointed by the *Samgha* as taker of the voting tickets. Therefore, it is silent. Thus do I understand.

(And again), "I enjoin upon you, O Bhikkus, three ways of taking votes, in order to appease some Bhikku, the secret method, the whispering method and the open method.

"And, how O Bhikku, is the secret method of taking votes? The Bhikku who is the teller of the votes is to make the voting tickets of different colours and as each Bhikku comes up to him, he is to say to him thus, 'This is the ticket for the men of such an opinion. Take whichever you like'. When he has chosen he is to add, 'Don't show it to anybody'. If he ascertains that those whose opinion is against the *Dhamma,* are in the majority, he is to reject the vote as wrongly taken. If he ascertains that those whose opinion is in accordance with the *Dhamma* in the majority, he is to report the vote as well taken. This, O Bhikkus is the secret method of taking votes.

"And, now, O Bhikkus, is the whispering method of taking votes? The Bhikku who is the teller of the votes is to whisper in each Bhikku's ear. 'This is the ticket of those of such an opinion. Take whichever you like'. When he has chosen (he is to add), 'Don't tell anybody'. If he ascertains that those whose opinion is against the *Dhamma,* are in the majority, he is to reject the vote. If he ascertains beforehand that those whose opinion is in accordance with the *Dhamma* is in the majority he is to report the vote as well as taken. This is the whispering method. 'And, how, O Bhikkus, is the open method of taking votes?' If he ascertains beforehand, that those whose opinion is in accordance with the *Dhamma* are in the majority, it is to be taken undisguisedly, openly. Thus, O Bhikkus, is the open method of taking the votes." However, imperfect and doubtful the method be, there can be no denying the fact that in it we find the nucleus of the earliest method of taking and recording votes.[68]

Council of Ministers

While some of the Assemblies developed into powerful republics, other dwindled into kingly councils, and sank into insignificance. Too much prominence has been given to the existence of *Mantriparishad* or council of ministers corresponding to the modern-day Executive Councils to which I am not, however, prepared to pay so much importance. Manu recommends seven or eight councillors, we find but only one appointed.[69] In the *Mahabharata,* we find that Bhisma alone guarded the kingdom during the minority of the king.

Arthasastra's Views

Nowhere is this more evident than in the times of Canakya to whom great importance has been given by the nationalist school. Regarding this question, Kautilya advises that the king shall despise non but hear the opinion of all, for "a wise man shall make use of even a child's sensible utterance"[70] and he further advised the formation of a well-formed council in which all kinds of administrative measures are to be preceded by deliberation; but the authority which he exercised over Chandragupta hardly leaves any one in doubt about the establishment of a council. He agrees that[71] "a single minister proceeds wilfully and without restraint", but we find him always acting most wilfully and absolutely without any restraint in even trivial matters.[72] His object in getting hold of Rakshasa[73] justifies our statement and cannot make us accept his view that "in works of emergency, he shall call both his ministers—and the assembly of ministers. He shall do whatever the majority of members suggest or whatever course of action leading to success they point out". Further, what he speaks of in Book V, Chapter 17, also supports our theory that he was really averse to a council. The minister is to instal the heir-apparent, he is to conduct the administration and he is to invest himself with the powers of sovereignty."[74] His own idea was, as is expressed elsewhere, to be an all-powerful minister to whom the monarch was to delegate all powers.[75]

Kautilya in another place observes, "All activities depend upon the Prime Minister, such for instance, as the accomplishment of the works of the people, the security of the kingdom from foreign aggression and internal troubles, remedial measures against calamity, colonisation, improvement of the soil, maintenance of the army and the disbursement of the state revenue." Bhardwaja practically repeats the same thing saying, "In the absence of the Prime Minister, the King is absolutely incapable of doing any work like a bird deprived of its wing."

In later time though we occasionally hear of a body of Councillors, we are led to think of this body more for show than for exercise of any power. In *Harisacharita* we find mention of a council, but it *met once in five years* and that would go to prove our theory about the existence, at any rate, of the power of such a *Mantriparishad,* though there are references to it in various other places. Much of course depended on the power wielded by the respective kings, as it happened in England regarding the Witenagemot or even with the cabinet, but it is going too far to expect that the Mantriparishad was of such a powerful calibre as to withstand the wishes of all kings.[76]

Duties of Kings

My idea of the duties of kings in ancient India is that between the king and the people, the duty was reciprocal—there was the idea of contract—a view which Mr. V.A. Smith has so aptly described:— "Kings had duties as well as rights and that if he was, from one point of view, the master from another, he was the servant."[77] The king's mission was to succour the distressed[78] and for their general good he had to forego his own advantage.[79] The Hindu Sastras are very particular about it. The *Mahabharata* lays down that the kings who taking the sixth part of the produce from his subjects, fails to protect them, is said to take upon himself the entire burden of the sins.[80]

The *Bhagwat Purana* also echoes the same thing when it says: "Protection of his subjects is the highest of royal virtues by which in after life the king robs them of the sixth of their merits. Otherwise by exacting taxes from his subjects and yet failing to protect them, he is robbed by them of his merits and himself eats their sins."[81] The *Markandeya Purana,*[82]—also repeats the idea by observing, "If the subjects, after paying sixth of the produce as tribute to the king, have to be protected by others, the king is sure to go to hell; this tribute has been fixed by former jurists as the king's salary for protecting his subjects; if the king does not protect in return, he robs them and is guilty of theft." The king's dues have also been considered by Baudhayana.[83] *Arthasastra* speaks of the remuneration of kings,[84] a view endorsed by *Sukraniti* when it says : "Brahma created the king to be the servant of his subjects and he is remunerated by a share of the produce. He assumes the character of *king* only for protecting his subjects."[85]

The great king Ramchandra was severely blamed for the death of child, aged five years, for was it not due to his neglect of duty in consequence of which his subject suffered?[86] The *Mahabharata* had gone so far as to suggest that unrighteous king unmindful of his duties deserved capital punishment[87] and practically the same sentiment has been repeated in the same epic elsewhere.[88]

The great poet has also observed,

> "Honour to him who labours day and day;
> For the world's weal, forgetful of his own."[89]

The great writer on Hindu Polity in the *Arthasastra* has also observed the same thing when he has advised the king to devote only a part of his time for rest. Kautilya says : "The king shall divide both the day and the night into 8 nalikas."[90] During the first one-eighth part of the day, he shall post watchmen and attend to the accounts of receipt and expenditure; during the second part he shall look to the affairs of both citizens and country people. During the third, he shall not only bathe and dine, but also study; during the fourth, he shall not only receive revenue in gold but also attend to the appointments of superintendents; during the fifth he shall correspond in writing with the assembly of his ministers and receive secret information gathered by his spies; during the sixth he may engage himself in his favourite amusements or in self-deliberation; during the seventh; he shall superintend elephants, horses, chariots and infantry and during the eighth part he shall consider various plans of military operation with his Commander-in-chief. At the close of the day he shall observe the evening payer.

"During the first one-eighth part of the night, he shall receive secret emissaries; during the second he shall attend to bathing and supper and study; during the third, he shall enter the bed chamber and enjoy sleep; during the fourth and fifth parts, having been awakened by the sound of trumpets; during the sixth part he shall recall to his mind the injuction of sastras as well as the day's duties; during the seventh, he shall sit considering administrative measures, and send out spies; and during the eighth division of the night, he shall receive benediction from sacrificial priests."[91]

That is to say, for only 2 *nalikas*—one hour and a half—the king was to enjoy sleep—a very bard lot indeed. But all the same the king had to do it, "for in the happiness of his subjects lies his happiness; in their welfare his welfare; whatever please him, he shall not consider as good, but whatever pleases his subjects he shall consider as good.[92]

Speaking of the functions of the king, another jurist, Sukra, adds:

> "Having got up in the last *Yama,* he should for two minutes study the following points: How much is the fixed income and how much the certain expenditure? How much has been used out of

thing and materials in the treasury? What is the remainder after the transaction for the fixed income and expenditure?[93]

Perhaps the above, there is too much division of labour and what is more, more of theory than of practice but still countless, indeed, was the toil of "the lot of him who with his hands support the canopy that shields his subjects"[94] but it was a reciprocal relationship. In the words of the *Jataka*:[95]

"The bull through floods a devious course will take :
The herd of kine all straggling in his wake,
So if a leader tortuous paths pursue,
To base ends will be guide the vulgar crew,
And the whole realm age of license one.
But if the bull a course direct should steer,
The herd of kine straight follow in his rear.
So should their chief to righteous ways be true,
The common folk injustice will chew,
And through the realm shall holy peace ensure."

Dark Side of Kingship and the Controlling Agency

Though, we find, as in the *Ramayana* that "Rain fell in time, food could be readily had for the mere asking; the skies were clear; and the town and provinces crowded with a prosperous and well-fed population,"[96] all because of the virtuous king, instances are not rare of bad kings. Manu[97] speaks of bad and oppressive kings who perished with their supporters. The *Mahabharata* goes so far as to suggest the execution of kings. "The subjects should arm themselves for slaying that king who does not protect them, who simply plunders their wealth . . . and who is regarded as the most sinful of kings. . . . That king who tells his people that he is their protector, but who does not or is unable to protect them, should be slain by his combined subjects like a dog that is aflected by rabies and has become mad.[98] The *Kalika Purana* mentions seven deadily sins of a king, *viz.,* excessive sexual indulgence, drunkenness, financial extravagance, habitual use of harsh language and fondness of severe punishment.[99] Canakya mentions stupid,[100] greedy and extravagant kings. The other writer on polity, Sukra, writes: "The subjects desert a king who is uncharitable, who insults men, who practises deceit and uses harsh words and who is severe in punishments. People do not take to a king who is very cowardly procrastinating, very passionate and excessively attached to enjoyments through ignorance."[101]

The *Jataka* observes that "even the best of kings could be unjust"[102] and we read of Brahmadatta, the King of Benares, in whose time the country was without gold, for the king oppressed the country and so got treasure.[103] So Nagasena, in *Milinda Panha* says: "Kings are gasping. The princes might in the best of powers, subjugate, an extent of country twice or thrice the size of what they had, but they should never give up what they possessed."[104]

A list of bad kings, with a list of their various faults, which led to their overthrow is given in Manu[105] and a longer list in *Harisacharita.*[106]

Controlling Agency—How far Effective

The question naturally arises, had the people any means of making their influence felt on the misdeeds of the king? Was there a controlling-agency or what we would call, the voice of the people? If there was a *vox-populi,* was it effective? The question is one of great interest. For, while the "national" school of writers consider that "the king regarded himself as merely exercising a trust," and "the control of the administrative-machinery as the will of society," a writer of great eminence has asserted that the Hindu Sovereign was importent"[107] and that "the people were equally powerless and devoid of any apparatus for enforcing their will on the Government. They could enforce the royal mandate by passive disobedience."[108]

In the epic age, Dasaratha consulted the people with regard to his proposal to anoint Rama as his *Yuvaraja,* while the power of the people is manifest when we read in the *Ramayana* that even in his heart of hearts he was convinced of Sita's innocence, Rama banished her really in response to public will.[109] In the *Mahabharata,* the questioning by the people of the right of the king to instal Puru in supersession of the claims of the elder brothers is a tacit but clear admission by the king of the power of the people. Vidura, the half brother of Pandu and deemed to be a man of a great wisdom and foresight eulogized very highly that person who endeavoured to please the people by every means in his power, as they benefited him in the long-run. Even the great Sreekrishna advised Arjuna. to secure good will of the people. In the *Mahabharata, Artusas' anika Parva* section I, Yudhisthira summoned his subjects and informed them of his intention to leave the realm. The citizens of Hastinapur along with those of the provinces first disapproved of the proposal but at last they were persuaded to *sanction his proposal.* That would clearly show the extent of the power of *vox-populi.* It might not have been exercising the power of "Veto" but it cannot be said that it implied absence altogether of the power of the people.

I believe the above illustration proves our contention that there was a controlling agency, no matter the extent of control which was exercised, which must have varied in different times. It dose not matter whether it was banishment or punishment on this side of the world, or the threat of Hell, or the coronation oath which controlled, but the king was never above the law.[110]

Taxation

Balis or taxes to the king were in the existence even from the time of the Vedic age, the earliest reference informing us of the king's eating the rich.[111] The *Atharvaveda* follows by referring to the collection of "abundant tribute"[112] by the king. Very likely it was paid in kind. Regarding the question whether this tribute was free or voluntary, opinions differ. The *Vedic Index* in summing up this question observes : "*Bali* occurs several times in the *Rigveda* and often later in the sense of tribute to a king or offering to a god. Zimmer thinks that the offering in both cases were voluntary. He compares the notices of the Germans in Tacitus, where the kings of the tribes are said to have received gifts in kind as presents, but not a regular tribute. There seems to be no ground whatever for this view. No doubt in origin, the prerogatives of monarchy were due to voluntary action on the part of the tribesmen[113] but that the Vedic peoples who were essentially a body of conquering invaders were in this state, is most probable and the attitude of the Vedic Indian to his gods was at least as compatible with tribute as with voluntary gifts. Zimmer admits that in the case of hostile tribes, tribute is meant in the *Rigveda.*[114]

Manu advised the king to take moderate annual taxes[115] but the king was forbidden to oppress the people of his kingdom[116] and was to take only lawful taxes,[117] i.e. those sanctioned by custom and approved by the *Smrtis.*[118] Even in the time of the *Mahabharata* taxes continued, at least on occasions to be voluntary, for the great epic observes: *For love's sake,* the priest, warriors, men of the people, slaves, barbarians, all the folk, high and low, bring tribute to the king.[119] It is evident that with the progress of society and the growth of kingly power, the rate of taxes increased. The Buddhist books give abundance of references proving the above. On one occasion we find that "taxes sometimes could be so oppressive as would crush the subjects like sugarcanes in a mill and taxes them to the uttermost farthing." A king, named Panchala of the kingdom of Kampita began to oppress his subjects so much by taxation that they took their wives and families and wandered in forest like tribes. In the words of *Milinda,* "taxation always caused fear in the heart of subjects."

The *Jataka* speaks of a story from which we can evidently draw a moral. When Brahmadatta was ruling in Benares, he was anxious to know whether there was any one who would tell him of his faults. As no one spoke ill of him, either within or outside the city, he wandered about the countryside in disguise, where also nobody spoke to his dispraise. Then he went to a hermitage in the Himalaya region where a Sannyasi offered him fruits which were very luscious and sweet. On asking the reason why the fruits were so sweet, the *Sannyasi* replied that the king (not knowing that the person spoken to was the king, for he was travelling *incognito*) exercised his rule with justice and equity and so the fruits were so sweet. The king asked whether in the reign of an unjust king the fruits lost sweetness and an affirmative answer was given by the Sannyasi. Desirous of testing the words of the ascetic, the king began to rule unjustly, and after some time went back to the Sannyasi but the fruits offered this time were bitter. On being questioned about the cause, the ascetic replied that this was due to the unjust rule of the king. The story goes on. The king returned home and ruling righteously restored everything to its original condition.

Things however changed considerably and though in the words of Kalidasa "the king levies taxes on his subjects for their welfare, just as the sun draws up moisture from the earth only to return it a thousandfold," it represented only a pious wish in later times with the gradual growth of kingly power and the consequent ideal of divine right of kings.

Benevolences

It seems more than probable that Benevolences, like taxes were in existence even from the time of the *Mahabharata.* The prince's treasury was unable to pay a sum required suddenly. The minister advised him thus, "Let those who pay tribute to thee furnish thee with tributes and the gold." This advice was followed.

The *Jataka* speaks of a tax called Milk-money which was levied on the birth of a prince. This was evidently a benevolence.

The *Arthasastra* speaks of revenue by demand. In case of great financial stringency, "Wealthy persons" in such cases, "may be taxed with as much of their gold as they can". The *Arthasastra* suggests that "those who of their own cultivate and adopt intention of doing good, offer wealth to the needy are honoured with a rank in the court and get riches or some ornaments in return for their gold.

The following quotations from *Mudraraksha* will represent it very clearly :

Canakya—All kings expect to meet from those that may cherish some requital.

Chandanadasa—You need but speak it. Sir, and any sums what monies, may be needed?

Canakya—He get
This is the reign of Chandragupta, not of Nanda.
To his avaricious soul,
Your treasures were acceptable; but now
Your king esteem your happiness his wealth."

But in spite of this Canakya himself advocated the "policy of thinning the rich by exacting excessive revenue, or causing them to vomit their accumulated wealth". And he pithily observed, "Wealthy persons may be requested to give as much of their wealth as they can. These who of their own accord, or with the intention of doing good, offer their wealth to the king shall be honoured with a rank in the court, an umbrella, or a turban, or some ornaments in return for their gold."

Notes and References

1. *Mahabharata:* Santi Parvan, *Manu Samhita* also observed "Everybody becomes afraid to live in a kingdom which has no king and so God created a king".
2. *Mahabharata,* section 68, Santi.
3. *Ramayana* : Ayodhya Kand 67, 5.31. Also 3.10, 12-16, "A king may take one-sixth, provided he protects".
4. Vide also *Mahabharata* : Santi Parvan, Section 68.
5. *Arthasastra,* Page 9. This is perhaps the first reference in Indian Book on Politics to a political contract.
6. *Ibid.*, p. 22. *Vide also Sakuntala,* Act 2. The following incident from the same book may also be cited: When the king apprehends that he has been recognized by some of the ascetics, he asks the Vidusaka with what pretext he

would again visit the hermitage? The Vidusaka replies, "What the pretext for your kings ? Be it this—Let the anchorites bring over sixth part of wild grains". The king says, "The foresters give up the sixth part of their penance".

7. *Sukraniti*, p. 88—In pure literature also, there are references to *protection*, e.g. *Hitopdesa*. Hasti-Sigala says: "First seek out a *protector* (king), next seek for a wife and rext wealth. How can there be either wife or wealth if there be no king (i.e. there can be no security of enjoyment if there is no authority to preserve order) ?" It goes on "Like clouds pouring rain, the king is the support of all that live. Cloud falling, life may be possible; not so however, if the king fails."
8. Vide Rockhill's *Life of Buddha*, p. 6.
9. Also *Manu*, VII 3. "When the creatures being without a king, through fear dispersed in all directions, the Lord created a king for the protection of the whole creation." In this the idea of *divine origin of kingship* is very closely associated with protection.
10. *Mahabharata* : Santi Ch. 59.
11. *Ramayana*, Ajodhya Kand also says, "Truth and righteousness incarnate as being nobleness itself to the nobility, as the mother : nd father to his subjects and the benefactor of Mankind." Vide also *Agni Parana*, where the king is compared with various Gods.
12. *Manu* VII. The ancient Egyptians also had the same idea. Dr. Erman observes, "The king was the representative of the deity and his royal authority was directly derived from the gods". The Chinese also have such views. That such a view also played a prominent part in Europe is evidenced by the idea of the "divine right of Kings".
13. *Vedic Index*, Vol. 2. 211.
14. *Rg*. X. 173.
15. *Ibid.*
16. *Atharva* II. 3. The term "Rayakrita", i.e. makers of king (*Atharva*. III. 5, 8) has been interpreted to mean that there was a particular section of the people who had to do with the election of kings. Some have taken this to mean that they were only the Brahmans who elected the king and that no one else had the right to take part. To me it seems that just as in the attendance at the Witenagemot, every freeman, irrespective of position and wealth, had the right to attend, though gradually the difficulty of attending made many of them give up the right of attending, so every one formerly had the right of taking part in the elections, though gradually the number of those doing so dwindled and like the greater thegns and higher clergy, only those took *Rayakrita* part in the election of kings.
17. *Rg*. X.184.
18. *Atharva*, VI. 87.
19. *Ibid.*, III. 4.
20. *Atharva* III. 4. In his note on Atharva. Hymn 9, Griffith has properly observed, "The occasion of the hymn of a raja or a king who appears to have been elected among the members of a princely family".

21. *Samaveda,* 1, 2.
22. *Atharva.* V. 3, 1, 5.
23. *Ibid.,* VI. 8, 7.
24. King D saratha convened the peoples of his vast empire, represeniing the various classes and creeds, trades and guilds and the various representatives after the expressing their consent elected Rama. The Paura the Janapada and the nigama arc present respectfully waiting for Rama's consecration." Megasthenes (Frng. 1) writes of Indiars "Who elected their sovereigns on the principle of merit !"
25. *Ramayana,* 2.67.
26. *Ramayana,* 2.79 and 4.10 Sugriva says, "On my return I was forced by the people and the ministers to be installed king".
27. Santi Parva 67.3. The list of Kings of the solar and lunar lines shows that the eldest son was succeeding the father.
28. Long after *Sukraniti* also observed : "If in the king's family there be many males, the eldest among them is to be king, the others are to be his assistants and auxiliaries. If the e'dest however is deaf, leprous, dumb, blind, or . . ., he will not be eligible for the throne, the king's brother of the eldest son's son will be eligible" (*Sukraniti,* I, 684-88).
29. *Jataka,* pp. 1-180. The *Mahasammata* in the *Jataka* relates that the first king was elected by the people from among themselves to remove their want of ruler which they had been keenly feeling. The word *Mahasammata* meaning the great elect expressly puts before us election and it is still more clear in the *Mahavasth Avadana* which thus says : "O Bhikkhus the men hastened and assembled; after doing so, they held a consultation; we should select that person from among ourselves present here, who happens to be the most pleasing and powerful and who can punish those deserving punishment and support those worth supporting. We select you as the foremost of all beings; we give you a sixth of the produce of each of our paddy fields". Selected as he was by a large collection of people, he wis termed the Great Fleet.
30. *Jataka,* VI. p. 462.
31. *Jataka,* II. p. 270. It is curious to note that in this very *Jataka,* we find the quadrupeds, the fish and the birds choosing king; of their own. In *Jataka* I, p. 58 we find the monkeys also meeting together and choosing the *Bodhisatwa* their king. *Vide* below.
32. *Ibid.,* IV. pp. 46, 47. Even as late as the date of the Junagadh inscription, we find men of all castes electing one as their lord.
33. *Vide Ibid.,* II. p. 270, which begins thus: "Once upon a time, the people who lived in the first cycle of the world gathered together and took for their king a certain man, handsome, auspicious, commanding altogether perfect. The quadrupeds also gathered and chose for the king the lion; and the fish in the ocean chose a fish called Ananda. Then, all the birds in the Himalayas assembled and wanted to have a king, they did not like to live in anarchy. Then they chose an owl, and a bird made proclamation three times (*this is indeed significant, as it may be very well compared to the third reading of bills*) to

all. that there would be vote taken on this matter. After patiently hearing this announcement twice, on the *third time,* up rose a crow and objected to the election of the owl. 'I like not (with all deference be it said) to have the owl appointed as our head. Look at his face. If this, his good humour be, what will he do when he looks angrily?' The result was that the owl w»s rejected and a golden goose elected."

34. *Arthasastra,* Book XVII.
35. *Harshacharita,* Chapter 17 .
36. *Indian Antiquary,* Vol. XXXIII.
37. The mention of Republics was first made in 1903 by Dr. Rhys Davids. "In those parts of India which came very early under the influence of Buddhism, we find still surviving a number of small aristocratic republics. The earliest Buddhist records reveal the survival, side by side, with more or less powerful monarchies, of republics with complete or modified independence." (*Buddhist India,* pp. 19-20). It was Dr. Thorms who in the *Journal of the Royal Asiatic Society,* 1913, proved that the Sanskrit word *Gana* referred "to the existence in the ancient India of cities and tribes, not ruled by kings, but having republican or rather oligarchical institutions".
38. *Manu,* VII. 3. Manu advised the boycotting of a priest living in a republican country.
39. *Ramayana,* 2, 69, 28.
40. *Vide* also *Manu* VII. 5 and 123. And *Mahabharata* Santi I, 41, 27. "One shall not live in remains that have no kings." *Mahabharata* XII. 67, 4.
41. II. 37-321. "Faults are always engendered in a people that has no king".
42. Gautama laid down that a republican as well as an incendiary, a publican or a criminal should not be invited to public feast. XV. 9. He would even decline to take food offered by a republican. Yagnavalkya would go so far as to forbid a student to accept help from a republican though, at the same time, he "advised the king to punish those of his subjects who embezzled the money of the republicans and violated their constitution" (2. 187). The astrologer Varahamihir thought that an evil star presided over the leaders of republicans. More might be quoted, but above give sufficient indication of the Brahamanical feeling.
43. "The Vedas afford evidence of tribes in which authority was exercised by a family or even by a whole body of nobles who were actually designated kings."—Dr. Thomas. It may be interesting to note here that the Lichchavis were also ruled by rulers who were called Rajas.

    Athurvaveda V. 18, 10 gives us clear, conclusive and categorical evidence of the existence of non-monarchical states in those days.
44. Vide *Vedic Index,* Vol. 2, p. 210. "It is quite clear that the normal though not universal form of government, in early India was that by kings, as might be expected in view of the fact that the Aryan Indians were invaders in a hostile territory, a situation which as in the case of the Aryan invaders in Greece and of the German invaders of England, resulted almost necessarily in strengthening the monarchical element of the constitution." Vide *Atharva-*

veda, Book 1. Hymn. XLI, where the three Gods and distinctly mentioned as kings, "Whom they enrich", and "Whom they protect".

45. *Atharva* Book XX. *Cf. Rg.* 1, 31, where it means sacrificial assembly.
46. *Rg.* 1. 20 VI. 11. *Ibid.*, 1. 41, 1. 56 (where it means religious assembly); 1.117 (where it means congregation of worshippers). Also V. 96, VI. II. Also *Atharva* V. 31, 6; VII. 12, 1 and 2; VII. 10.5; XII. 1, 56; XIX. 55, 6. Also *Taithiriya Samhita* 1.7; *Maitrayani Samhita* IV. 7, 4; *Satapalha Brahmana* II. 3.2 and v. 3.1, 10. In a well-written article on "The State Council in Ancient India" (Modern Review, 1907) Mr. N. Law thinks that, "the assembly or a chosen body of its members performed Judicial works. We gathered this indirectly from the fact of *"Sabhachara"* being dedicated to justice (Dharma) at the *Purushamedha* in the *'Yayurveda'* from the use of the term *'Sabha'* to denote a law court and also from the word *'Sabha-Sad'* which denotes a member of the assembly which met for justice as well as for general discussion on public matters". *Cf. J.A.O.S.* Vol. XIII, p. 148.
47. *Atharva.* VI I. 22.
48. *Ibid.*, VIII, 10.
49. Vide Rhys Davids' *Buddhist India,* where he speaks of the villages mote halls.
50. *Rg.* Book X. Hymn 121.
    Cf. Atharvaveda, VI. 88, 3, V. 19, 15. These give clear signs that the monarchical power was controlled by the existence of the Assembly, while concord between them was essential for the prosperity of the former as also of the people at large. *Cf. Vedic Index,* 11, p. 31.
51. *Atharva,* Book VII. Hymn 95.
52. The first line of this hymn 'Quickened is this my priest rank' may well suggest the idea of a priestly president. Macdonnell and Keith referring to the *Samiti* in the Vedic time, observe *"Samiti* denotes an assembly of the vedic tribe. It is already mentioned in the *Rg. Veda* and often later, sometimes in connexion with *Sabha.* Ludwig considers that the Simiti included all the people, primarily the 'Visah' subjects, but also the Meghavans and Brahmans, if they desired, though the *Sabha* was their special assembly. This view is not probable, nor is that of Zimmer, that the Sabha was the village assembly. Hillebradt appears to be right in holding *Samitis* are much the same, the one being the assembly, the other primarily the place of assembly. . . . It was essential that concord between the king and assembly was essential for his prosperity. . . . It is reasonable to assume that the business of the assembly was general deliberation of policy including legislation, so far as the Vedic Indian cared to legislate." Mr. Jayaswal in his *Introduction of Hindu Polity* thought that (M.R. 1913) the *Sabha* looked after certain public matter, as distinguished from *Samiti* which was the most important institution in social system of the Hindus.
    I would venture to submit, that at first these were purely religious assemblies where only religious topics were discussed, but gradually other topics were also introduced. According to certain writers, there were three assemblies—(1) Sacrificial *Vidhatha,* (2) Rural and Social *Samiti,* (3) Political *Sabha.*

Sayana has defined *Samiti* as the assembly of the village-elders and *Sabha* as the assembly of the wise. If his definition is accepted, the Sabha or the assembly of the wise would be like the Witenagemot of the Anglo-Saxons.

53. Santi Parvan, 107. I have already drawn attention to the existence of the republican form of government even in the age of Vedas and the term "Swarajya" very likely nucleus of republics.
54. *Introduction to Ancient Hindu Polity* (*Modern Review,* 1913) *Mahabharata* has spoken of *ganas. Vishnupuran* part V. 16 speaks of *Gramabasinam* which may either refer to the existence of a republican village or of guilds.
55. In Frag. 9 Megasthenes speaks of 453 kings during 6042 years and amongst these "a republic was the thrice established". He continues, "After many generations the monarchy was dissolved and democratic government was established in the cities." He also mentions "a number of free cities having no kings occupying mountain heights". Megasthenes has also observed that "those who live near the sea have no kings" evidently referring to the existence of constitutions which were not regal. (*Vide* Indian Antiquary, Vol. VII, 340-1). Professor Hopkins, referring to these, truly observed : "Megasthenes plainly implies that self-ruled cities, in distinction from cities governed by kings, were common in his day,' (*J.A.O.S.*, Vol. 13).
56. *Alexander's Invasion,* Maccrindle, pp. 79, 81.
57. *Ibid.,* p. 134. Patanjali considered these as *Samgha* tribes. According to Curtius, the Oxydrakai was an independent tribe with leaders, while the Sabarcae was also a powerful Indian tribe whose form of government was democratic (and not royal). The Gedrosii were also spoken of as free people with a council for discussing important matters.
58. *Ibid.,* p. 92. Mccrindle identified these with the Ambashthas of *Mahabharata* (*Alexander's Invasion,* page 133). But *vide Indian Antiquary* 1.23, this people has been considered as powerful Indian tribe whose form of government was democratic not royal. Diodorus has written, "They dwelt in cities in which the democratic form of government prevailed". Mr. V.A. Smith thinks that "The Punjab, the Eastern Rajputana and Malwa were for the most part in possession of tribes and clans living under republican institutions. The Yaudeha tribe occupied both the banks of the Sutlej, while the Madrak's held the central part of the Punjab. (*Early History of India*). Mr. Smith was further prepared to admit that there were also autonomous tribes and nations in the south beyond Narbada. Arrian has spoken of Abastonoi, Xathroi and Arbitai as "independent tribes", though he has not mentioned their forms of government. *Anabasis,* 155.
59. *Vide* pp. 133, 232 and 292.
60. *Vide* note above "The Nysians sent out of him, their president, whose name was Akophis and along with him thirty deputies of their most eminent citizens to entreat him to spare the city. He confirmed the inhabitants of Nysa in the enjoyment of their freedom and their own laws—he praised them because the government of their state was in the hands of the aristocracy. He moreover requested them to send him 300 of their horsemen together with

]00 of their best men selected from the governing body which consisted of 300 members ... When Akophis heard this, he is said to have smiled at the request, and when Alexander asked him why he laughed, to have replied, "How, O King, can a single city, if deprived of a hundred of its best men continue to be well governed?" Mccrindle, pp. 79-81.

61. *Arrian*, p. 134.
62. Mention is made of a city of Brahmans both by Arrian and Diodorus. Dr. Fick, however, observes "what the Greek messenger said and what he tried to express was only the fact that in the immediate neighbourhood of great monarchies, such as the Kingdom of Magadha, whose capital town Pataliputra itself was, individual cities or small states maintained their independence and were autonomous. According to him, the difference between the constitutions of these small states and that of monarchies consisted only in the great or less part while the remaining members of the royal families took in the government by the side of the king and by which they more or less limited his absolute power." (English Edition published by the Calcutta University).
63. Cunningham's A.S.R., Vol. XIV and Journal of the Royal Asiatic Society, 1903, "Position of the Autonomous tribes of the Punjab". The best example according to Cunningham, of what resembled the republican or democratic state in ancient India was that of the Yaudehas (referred to by Panini) who continued till the days of Samudragupta (mentioned in the Samudragupta inscription at Allahabad). Mr. Kanakasabhai, in his "The Tamils 1800 years ago", refers not only to monarchies and democracies but also to constitutions in which there were hereditary monarchs, between whom and the subjects there were distinct organs to restrict the powers of the former and act as buffers. In this arrangement, there was no organized institution of the State to voice for the people's views. . . . The hereditary monarch along witn the "Five great assemblies" consisting of the representatives of the people, priests, physicians, astrologers, and ministers respectively wielded the sovereign power and not the monarch alone.
64. *Arthasastra,* 11-17. The commentator observes, "A clear proof of the existence of republican or oligarchic forms of government in ancient India". *Vide* also Book, XL, Chap. 1, Kautilya paid great importance to republics, for he advised the king to secure and utilize the services of those republics which on account of their union are invincible to the enemy and are favourably disposed towards himself.
65. *Vide Arthasastra,* and Rhys Davids' *Buddhist India,* 17-23 *Cf.* also Beal's *Buddhist Records of the Western World,* Vol. 2, and *Buddhist India.*
66. Mote Hall or *Santhaggara.* It is the hall where a clan mote was held and was used exclusively of places for the assemblies of the householders in the Free Republics of Northern India *Dialogues of the Buddha,* Vol. 2, Dr. Rhys Davids observes: "In it king Pasenadi's proposition was discussed. When Ambatha goes to Kapilvastu on business he goes to the Mote Hall where the Sakyas were then in session. And it is to the Mote Hall of the Mallas, that Ananda

goes to announce the death of the Buddha, they being then in session there to consider that very matter." (*Buddhist India*), *Vide* in this connection *Dialogues of the Buddha*, Vol. 3. The *Brahma-mangala Sutra* gives us an insight. Throughout the plural is used and Dr. Rhys Davids rightly points out: "The plural cannot be honorific, as the few great kings of that time are always spoken of in the singular. It is evident that we have to understand 'chiefs' and not the 'kings' and that not absolute monarchies, but republican institutions of a more or less aristocratic kind were in the mind of the composer."

67. Buddhist books speak of the 500 kings of Lichchavis and we find also mention of the Sakiyas of the Kapilvastu, Bullis of Allakappa, Koliyas of *Ramayana,* Mallas of Pava and the Moriyas of Pippalivana. Buddha compared the Lichchavi as "*Trayastrinsa* gods". Tradition in the *Jataka* says that there were 7,707 Lichchavis kings of Vaishali, each having his own Viceroy, General and Treasurer. The Lichchavis have been characterized by Canakya as having the profession of king (Chap. 1, Book XL). The kings were called "republican heads". Dr. Rhys Davids is of opinion that the Vajjans consisted of 8 confederate clans of which the Lichchavis of Vaishali and the Videhas of Mithila were the most important (*Buddhist India*). Hieun Tsiang observes: "The country of the Vrijjis or Samvrijjis was that of the confederated eight tribes of the people called Vrijjis, or Vijjis, one of which, namely that of the Lichchvis dwelt at Vaishali' They were republicans; they were confederation of Northern tribes who had at an early date taken possession of this part of India. They were driven back by Ajatsatru, king of Magadha" (Beal.,Vol. II.)

68. At Savathi, a family used sometimes to give alms to the Buddha and his friends, sometimes they used to give to the heretics or else the givers would form themselves into companies, or again the people of one street would club together or the whole of the inhabitants would collect voluntary offerings and present them. On this occasion all the inhabitants had made such a collection of all necessaries; but counsels were divided, some demanding that this be given to the heretics, some speaking for these who followed the Buddha. There it was proposed to divide upon the question, and accordingly they divided; those who were for the Buddha were in the majority. So this plan was followed.

    When a person wanted to be ordained, the proposal had to be made *thrice* and each time there was to be vote-taking, silence of the members indicated assent; similar procedure was followed where a monk was accused of an offence.

    Credit is due to professor B.S. Shastri of having first brought this matter to public notice.

    "Putting to the vote and deciding by the 'majority'"—in this phrase, the 'Majority' is not unqualified. By the 'majority' is to be understood the majority of those Bhikhus who are *dhammavddins,* i.e., who speak according to *Dhamm,* or law. *Cullavagga* IV, 14, 24 explains this clearly by stating, and "according as the large number of Bhikkus who are guided by the *Dhamma* shall speak, so shall the case be decided." *Cullavagga* IV, 10, refers to ten cases in which the taking of voting tickets is invalid.

69. *Monu,* VII. 54, "Let him appoint seven or eight ministers whose ancestors have been royal servants, who are versed in the sciences, heroes skilled in the use of weapons and descended from noble families and who have been tried. Let him daily consider with them the ordinary (business, referring to) peace and war, (the four subjects called) sthana, the revenue, the (manner of protecting himself and his kingdom) and the sanctification of, his gains (by pious gifts) (VII. 55). *But with the most distinguished among them all a learned Brahman, let the king deliberate on the most important affairs which relate to the six measures of royal policy* (VII. 58). Let him, full of confidence, always entrust to that (official) all business; having taken his final resolution with him, let him, afterwards begin to act." (VII. 59). From the time of the *Mahabharata,* the King's dependence upon the advice of the Brahmans becomes higher and higher. "The didactic portion of the *Mahabharata,* makes tutor and the family priest the controllers of the king's mind. The king is *enjoined* to abide by the judgment of the family priest, who is as much conversant with scared literature as with the principles of polity."
70. *Arthasastra.*
71. *Ibid.* It is interesting to observe that in this, Canakya summarizes the opinions of leading jurists, *viz.,* Manu who advocated an assembly of 12 ministers of Brihaspati who wanted 16 and of Usana who advised 20. But the many large numbers are suspicious; the quotation we have made from Manu may be considered significant.
72. *Cf. Mudrarakshasa.*

    "All public acts parses
    A threefold source. And from the king, the minister
    Or both can jointly emanate. What I have done,
    Is done by virtue of the state I hold;
    And to enquire of me why I did it,
    Is but to call my judgment or authority
    In question and designedly affront me."
73. *Rakshasa* is called the "Hereditary councillor".
74. *Arthasastra.*
75. Chandragupta ordered some rewards to be given but Canakya interferes.
    The king being offended says,
    "If this may highest mood is to canvassed,
    And thwarted by your excellency.
    My kingdom is but a prison to me."
    And Canakya answers,
    "It is eve thus.
    When monarchs reign with delegated sway."
76. Fick rightly observed, "The influence of particular ministers upon the course of internal and external politics depended upon the intelligence and energy of the then head of State."
77. The *Manusamhita* thus describes the duties of king, iike Indra, the sky god, showering rain on the earth during the four rainy months of the year, should

the king shower blessings, Indra—like over his Kingdom. Like Aditya, the sun god sucking up moistures from the earth during the eight dry months, should the king always realize taxes from his kingdom, therein imitating the sun god. Like Maruta, the wind god, pervading all things, should the king by his agents collect information of all kinds thus imitating the wind god. Like Yama, the death god, laying this hands, when the hour arrives, on friends and foes alike, should the king keep under control all his subjects thus imitating the death god. Like Varuna holding all things in his net, should the king keep the wicked ones in check thus imitating Varuna. Just as the sight of the Full Moon fill men with delight so should the sight of the king fill his subjects with delight, therein he should imitate the sun god. In dealing with wicked deeds the king should always show his power and indignation, punishing adequately the evil-doers even among his own chieftains, therein imitating the fire god (*Manu* IX, 304-310). Other references, to the duties of kings are to be found in *Satapatha Brahmana, Puranas* (specially the *Agni Purana*).

78. *Sakuntala,* Act 2, *vide* also *Jataka* III. 43 where a king is described as a "refugee to his people".
79. *Mudrarakshasa* Act III.
80. *Mahabharata,* Adi Parva 213.9. Yagnavalkya practically repeats this when he observes: "Uncared for by the king, whatever offences his subjects commit, half the guilt thereof is the king's for he takes from them." In his coronation oath the king had to take the swore to mentally, physically and verbally help on the advantage of the state. "Considering always as good whatever is law and whatever is in accordance with ethics and whatever is not opened to policy I will act according to that and will never act arbitrarily." The *Mahabharata* supported the wage theory, i.e., "the sovereign was to receive wages from people for the people we give you fines, forfeitures and taxes as wages" (*Shanti 61*).
81. *Skanda* 4, 2, verse 14.
82. *Skanda* 18, verse 6.
83. "Let the king protect his subjects, receiving as his pay a sixth part."
84. *Arthasastra* expressed the same sentiment. "As kings are remunerated by the people, it is their duty to look to the interest of the state". (Book II) Canakya also observes elsewhere, while discussing the spies "People suffering from anarchy as illustrated by proverbial tendency of a large fish swallowing a small one, first elected Manu, the Vaivasvata, to be their king; and allotted one-sixth of the grains grown and one-tenth of merchandise as sovereign dues: "Fed by this payment, kings took upon themselves the responsibility of maintaining the safety and security of their subjects and of being answerable for the sins of their subjects when the principle of levying just punishments and taxes has been violated." (XIII., Book I.)
85. *Sukraniti* I. 158 and 1. 255 Sukra also writes, "Though master in form the servant of the people getting pay in the form of taxes and that for the protection of the people under all circumstances" (I. 88).
86. *Ramayana;* Uttarkanda, 86.

87. *Mahabharata,* Santi Parva 92 5. 9.
88. "The subjects should arm themselves for slaying that king who does not protect them, who simply plunders their wealth and who is regarded as the most sinful of kings. That king who tells his people that he is their protector but who does not or is unable to protect them should be slain by bis combined subjects like a dog that is affected by rabies and has become mad." (*Anusasana* 61. 32-3)
    The *Aiterya Brahmana* says that the elected king before his consecration was to take an oath that he would forfeit everything if unjustly he would commit any injury to any of his subjects (VIII. 15). *Vide* also F.N., 121.
89. *Sakuntala.*
90. *Nalikas* = 45 minutes.
91. *Arthasastra,* Book I, XIX.
92. *Ibid.* The routine as set forth in the Samhitas is in substance almost the same as the one in the *Arthasastra.*
93. The time-table was like thus: The whole day consists of 30 Muhurtas:
    2 *Muhurtas*—Studying the budget.
    1 *Muhurtas*—Lavatory and Bath.
    2 *Muhurtas*—Religious performances.
    1 *Muhurtas*—Physical exercises.
    1 *Muhurtas*—Distribution of prizes.
    1 *Muhurtas*—State Business.
    1 *Muhurtas*—Dinner.
    1 *Muhurtas*—Study of old and new.
    2 *Muhurtas*—Constitution.
    2 *Muhurtas*—Hunting.
    1 *Muhurtas*—Parade.
    1 *Muhurtas*—Evening prayers.
    1 *Muhurtas*—Dinner.
    2 *Muhurtas*—Business with spies.
    8 *Muhurtas*—Sleep.
    It may be noted here that 4 hours are given to sleep as against 3 of Kautilya. *Cf.* the daily life of Emperor Shah Jahan was:
    4—Wakes—Prayer-Reading.
    6.45—Appears at Darshan Window—Elephant combats-review of cavalry.
    7.40—Public Darbar. 9.40—Private audience. 11.40—Secret consultation.
    12 p.m.—Harem—Meal—siesta—charity to women.
    4—Public audience—evening prayer.
    6.30—Evening assembly. 8—Secret consultation. 8.20—In the harem-music.
    10—Hear books read. 10.30 p.m.—Sleep.
94. *Sakuntala,* Act 3.
95. The *Jataka* v. 521, thus speaks of the duties of kings :
    "Keep ever thy folk well in hand, duly take stock of thyself.
    Never trust to another a loan or deposit but act for thyself.
    What is done or undone to thy profit and loss it is well thou shouldst know.

Ever blame the blameworthy and favour on them that deserve it, bestow.
Thou, thouself, O great king, should instruct thy people irt every good way.
Lest thy realm and thy substance should fall to unrighteous.
See that nothing is done by thyself or by others with overmuch speed.
For the fool that so acts without doubt will live to repent of tne deed.
To wrath one should never give way, for should it due bounds overflow.
It will lead to the ruin of kings and the proudest of houses lay low.
Be sure that thou never asking thy people mislead to their cost,
Lest all men and women alike in an ocean of trouble be lost.
When a king from all fear is set free, and the pleasures of sense are his aim.
Should his riches and all disappear, to that king it is counted as shame.
Herein is a text of thy duty to teach thee the way thou shouldest go.
Be an adept in every good work, to excess and to rot a foe.
Study virtue, for vice ever leads to a state full of suffering and woe."

In the same *Jataka,* the king is advised to put away all falsehood and anger and scorn, not to be slack, not to be untrue to his name and his frame, *to* be a friend to all, to be zealous to do right, to be earnest in efforts for good, never to be a sluggard.

96. *Ramayana :* Uttarkanda.
97. *Menu,* VII. 3 The ihoughtless king who through folly and recklessness oppresses his subjects forfeits his kingdom and he and his friends perish. The examples of Vena, Nahusa, Sudassa, Sanukha and Nimi are cited.
98. *Mahabharata,* Anusasana, 61 32.3.
    We find a similar thing in the *Jataka* 1.73.
99. Chapter 84, V. 42.
100. *Muhurtas—Arthasastra.*
101. According to *Sukraniti* the six enemies of kings are—sensuousness, anger, ignorance, cupidity, vanity and passion.
102. VI. 545.
103. IV. 478.
104. *Milinda,* p. 203.
105. *Manu,* Chap. VII.
106. *Harsacharita.*
107. That the Hindu Sovereign was impotent to a certain extent, is evident when we read the story of *Yakshini*, who when made the king's chief consort wanted him to give her unrestricted power over the whole kingdom. The king replied, "In no way do the subjects of my kingdom belong to me, nor am I their lord, only over those who rise against the king and do wrong, I am lord. Therefore, I cannot give you unrestricted power over the whole kingdom."
108. Professor J.N. Sarkar in "Oriental Monarchies" in *"Studies in Moghal India".* *Padakusalmanava Jataka* is very clear as showing that the people did express active disobedience. A young Brahman discovered the treasures stolen and concealed by the king. He called the king a thief in the presence of the assembled people and cried out: "May the householders and citizens

assembled here listen to me. What should be water is fire, where safety is expected, there come danger. The king plunders the land... Be on your guard, from your protector is generated your evil." The people determined to kill the bad king and with sticks and hammers they beat the king to death. The *Saccamkira Jataka* also gives us a second example of a king being driven out of the town by the enraged Kshatriyas, Brahmans and other citizens.

109. U*ttararamcharita* has observed that for the satisfaction of the public, Rama says, "I would sacrifice affection, kindness, nay even my very life, viz., Janaki, and still all this would not affect me in the least, if only my people should be contented thereby."
110. This is very clear when we bear in mind the story given by Hieun Tsiang about Bindusara who had passed a law to prevent fires, that wherever a fire was to break out, the owner was to be banished. When a fire took place in the palace itself, the king made his eldest son the king and banished himself saying, "I wish to maintain the law of the country. I am therefore myself going into exile." There was a coronation oath, referred to in the *Harsha-charita*. "And reviewing the whole army, under the pretext of showing him his forces, the base born general Pushyamitra crushed his master, Brihadratha, the Maurya, who was weak in keeping his *coronation oath*" (*Pratigna*).
111. *Rg.* 165. Professor Hopkins in J.A.O.S. XIII., observes: "The Brahman Literature appears to show the people-caste as a class existing mainly for the purpose of being levied upon and devoured." *Vide Aitareya Brahmana,* for the existence of taxes in the Brahmanicai period.
112. *Atharva,* III., 4. *Cf.* Also *Atharva,* IV., 22.
113. J.R.O.S., 1909. 760-62.
114. *Vedic Index. Vide* also Rigveda, VII., 6.5, 18-19.
115. *Manu,* VII., 80. "As the leech, the calf and the bee take their food little by little, even so much the king draw from his subjects realizing moderate annual taxes." *Cf.* also VII., 129.
116. *Manu,* VII., II.
117. S.B.E.,11., 64.
118. *Ibid.* Footnote.
119. The *Mahabharata* advised the king "to tap the resources of his kingdom as justly as the bee sucks honey from the flower, as men milk a cow without wounding the under and starving the calf, as the leech drinks the blood, as the tigress takes her cubs between her teeth and lifts them without inflicting pain, as the mouse bites the sole of the foot imperceptibly with its sharp teeth. From people in affluent circumstances the king should bring taxes on a gradually increasing scale," *Santi Parvan,* Section 88.

13

The Judiciary and Judicial Process in Ancient India

I
AN ANCIENT INDIAN COURT IN SESSION

PROFESSOR N.C. TYAGI

At the head of the judiciary in ancient India was the king who was the fountain of justice. He was not, however, the maker of laws which were codified in the Dharmasastras. He only adjudicated those cases which came before him. He was the highest court of appeal and there were smaller tribunals of justice which originally tried cases. Although minute details about the administration of justice are noticed in the law texts, they do not however present a clear picture of an ancient trial in a criminal court. The Mricchakatika of Sudraka probably of 5th to 6th century A.D. presents such a court scene with sufficient details, enabling us to have a clear conception of such an ancient Indian Court in Session. The Drama and its author have been the subject of discussion among the scholars, but the cultural data contained in the drama seem to be truthful and it may be presented here with reference to particular topic.

A Case of Rape and Gagging

Vasantasena, a pretty and rich damsel of Ujjayini, falls in love with Charudatta, a virtuous and poor Brahmana Sarthavaha, a caravan trader. One day while going to meet her lover she innocently accepts a lift in the cart of Sakara who, too, had an eye on her but was not encouraged by her; the result was the rape and gagging of the poor lady and her burial under the dried leaves. He goes a step further and lodges a complaint against Charudatta for the alleged murder of Vasantasena in order to pocket her ornaments, which she had already given to Charudatta's son who was weeping for having a gold cart to play with. Maitreya, a friend of Charudatta, comes with the ornaments in the court room, thus confirming the suspicion, and after the statement of the accused and the examination of witnesses, the poor Charudatta is found guilty by the judges who recommend for the Brahmana, according to the laws of Manu, the punishment of permanent exile from the country and not death, to the king. The king, however, condemns him to the gallows where he is actually carried by the Chandalas. In the meantime Vasantasena, rescued by a Buddhist monk appears on the scene and Charudatta is set free.

Bench of Judges and Jurors

The whole proceeding is described with details in the drama. The court-room or *Adhikaranamandapa* in the drama—a term also used in Gupta inscriptions as an office where transactions pertaining to land were decided and by Bana as a court of justice, was presided over by the judge (*Adhikaranika*) who assisted by several other judges (*Adhikarnikah*) and the jurors (*Niyuktah*). The presiding judge was the centre of attraction and his task was very difficult and responsible as he had to find out the true from untrue (Mri. IX Acts 3 and 4 Verse, pp. 456-57) and distinguish the real from the false. He was expected to be well versed in laws (Sastrajna), as protector of the poor (Klivan Palayita) chastiser of the offender (Sathan Vyathayita) devoted to the principles of Dharma (Dharmye-ti-lobhanvita) free from anger (na cha krodhana) impartial in deciding the cases of his son, friends and enemies (*Mitrapara svakesh tulya*) and eloquent (*vakta*).[1] He was helped by the jurors who were not necessarily the Brahmanas. In the drama the Sresthin, the head of the guilds and the kayastha, the court clerk, also seem to sit as assessors.[2] The kayastha also kept the record of the proceedings of the trial.

Undue Influence

The court proceedings actually began with the Sodhanaka, the court people, entering to arrange the seats in order.[3] The Sodhanaka's acts as described in the drama substantially represent what any one will find even today if one enters a court of law sometime before the court commences its work for the day. When the seats were ready the judge accompanied by the Sresthin, kayastha and others was conducted to the court-room by the Sodhanaka.[4] Once they were seated the judge ordered the Sodhanaka to go out of the hall and find out the persons who had come, to demand justice (Bhadra Sodhanaka ! bahirniskramya jnayatam—kah kah karyyarthi its). The complainants had already assembled before the court to lodge their complainrs.[5] Then the Sodhanaka had to go out of the court-room and enquire of them.[6] It depended upon the sweet will of the judge to heat a particular case on that very day or postponed it for the next day, but an influential person especially connected with the king, could have his that very day despite the reluctance of the judge. For instance in the drama when the judge came to know that the first complainant was the brother-in-law of the king, he considering it a bad omen postponed his case for the next day. But Sakara threatened to get another judge appointed in his place by the king.[7] Naturally the judge had to change his decision and take up his case that very day.[8]

Question by the Court

When the complainant or any other required person entered the court-room, his welfare was first enquired[9] and sometimes he was offered a seat.[10] Old persons gave their blessings to the judges. (*Sukham yusmakam bhavatu)* and others saluted them. Then the judge permitted the complainant to state his case. The complainant could not talk irrelevantly and if he did so he was interrupted by the judge who reminded him only to state the facts.[11] During this time while the complainant was making his statement, the judge put to him several questions in order to confirm or remove his suspicion.[12] In this drama Sakara stated that somebody brought Vasantasena to his garden and pressing her in his arms killed her for the love of her ornaments. This roused the suspicion of the judge, and immediately he asked him, 'How do you know the motive of the murder?' He replied that the absence of ornaments on her body hinted at the motive of the murder (Hamho! nunain—Parisuryaya moghasthanaya grivalikaya nissuvarukainabhpranasthavaistarkyami). At this Sresthin and the kayastha nodded their head (yujyata iva).[13]

Recording the Statement

Then the judge ordered the kayastha to write down the statement. The statement was first written down on the floor so as to make it easy for corrections, additions, improvements thereto being made in accordance with the answers of the Complainant to questions put to him by the court. For example, Sakara said in his statement "Vasantasena has been killed (but) not by me" (Kanapi Vasantasena ma ta, na maya).[14] The judge ordered the kayastha to write 'not by me' (na maya) first, for it had created a doubt in his mind.[15] At this Sakara clarified the position saying that he meant only 'seen by me' (Mayaiva drisht) and rubbed 'not by me' with his own foot.[16] It evidently shows that the statement was first noted down on the floor and then recorded.

Coercive Powers

After the statement being written before him, the judge began to consider the allegations and consult the jurors. In the drama the judge described Vyavahara as comprising two stages, the former—Vakyanusara, i.e. being the examination of the parties and the latter—Arthanusara, i.e. being the consideration by the judge.[17] After considering the allegations thoroughly the judge summoned the accused through the Sodhanaka and it is significant that when sending for Charudatta, the judge said, 'Summon him courteously' (*Sadaram ahriya).* The person thus summoned was put at his ease and then he was examined. During such an examination the judge could ask even most intimate and awkward questions, and the accused was made to answer them without reserve 'in the interest of Vyavahara'. In the drama the judge asked Charudatta whether the prostitute was his friend (Arya Charudatta! bruhi satyam, api ganika tava mitram). At first Charudatta hesitated to answer that question but the judge, the Sresthin and the kayastha made him understand that the question was asked in the interest of vyavahara and that he should not feel ashamed in answering it (Arya Charudatta! bhana alam lajjaya, vyavakara khalvesah dhairyyam chalam atra na grihyate). In extracting the truth from the parties the court adopted the policy of persuasion. Firstly, the accused was persuaded to speak the truth, but if he failed to do so, he was to be beaten with harsh canes. When Maitreya brought the ornaments to the court, the jurors asked Charudatta to speak the truth about the ownership of the ornaments.[18] They persuaded him repeatedly saying that solace was achieved only by truth, sin is not committed by the speaker of the truth (Satyam sukham labhyate satyalapam na bhavati pataki), but Charudatta kept mum. Then the judge warned him that he would be beaten with canes if he did not speak the truth.[19] It evidently shows that the court, to achieve its goal which was to arrive at the truth, could use its coersive powers. During the proceedings of the case, the judge could ask the police officers (*nagctr rakshaksh*) to make an enquiry or investigate into any point at issue. Horses were kept ready in the court, and they could be sent any time when required. As a principle, no other case could be heard till the decision of the first case was given. In the drama, when the judges are busy in deciding the case of Sakara, Virak, a police officer, came to the court to lodge a complaint against Chandanaka, another police officer, and he put his case before the court, but the judge asked him to wait till the case in hand was over.

In the present case, although no witness in the true sense of the term was called on by the court, yet Virak, the police officer, unknowingly became the witness and the statement of Sakara that Vasantasena was killed by Charudatta for ornaments, came to be confirmed by the statement of Virak who said in the court that he was beaten by Charudatta when he, according to the commands of the king, wanted to check up the bullock cart going out of the city. The judge asked him whose cart it was. Virak answered that the driver told him that it was Charudatta's cart and that it was carrying Vasantasena to Puspa Karandaka garden[20] where actually according to the statement of Sakara she was killed. Thus, he confirmed the statement of Sakara, and Charudatta was found guilty by the court of the alleged murder.

While the trial was going on, the court remained in charge of the royal guards (Rajapurushas) and after the decision the accused was handed over to these guards.[21]

Finding by the Court, Punishment by the King

It has already been stated that the duty of the judges was only to decide the guilt and find out the truth. In the drama the judges declared that their duty was only to give a finding and everything else rested with the king. (Nirnaye Vayam Pramanam sese tu raja).[22] After the decision the court sent its verdict to the king and he in his turn inflicted punishment. It is noteworthy that wh:n the court made its report about the guilt of Charudatta to the king, it reminded him that according to the laws of Manu, the Brahamanas could not be subjected to vadhadanda and could only be exiled from the country (*Ayam hi pataki viproh n vadhya manurabravita*).[23]

Principles and Procedures of Dharmasastras Observed

It shows that the cases are decided according to the laws of Manu and other Dharmasastras. Therefore to be well up in Dharmasastra for the judge was essential. The king was not bound to agree with the recommendations of the court and could overrule its decision and in the present case actually the king overruled the decision of the court and imposed capital punishment upon Charudatta while the court had only recommended the punishment of permanent exile. If the accused was sentenced to death he was handed over to the executioners who have been referred to in the drama as Chandalas. It is stated that the Chandalas beating the drum brought him to the burial ground where he was to be impaled. It was a common practice to proclaim at a number of public places the offence of the accused as well as the sentence imposed upon him, so that it could serve as a deterrent on the other members of the public. The conversation between the Chandalas is very natural and realistic and especially when one of them pleads to act upon the advice the had received from his father, namely, never to be in a hurry to carry out a sentence of death, because if there is some delay something may happen in the meantime and the convicted person may after all be set at liberty.

And in the drama this actually happens—the state revolution and the change of dynasty—and Charudatta is set free. Thus acted the Indian courts of the day.

In the end it may be said that the trial scene presented in the drama with all minute details shows the actual working of an ancient Indian Court of those days, and moreover it is in full conformity with the rules enunciated in the Smrtis, Dharmasutras, Nibandha granthas and other law texts. The Dharmasastras divide a litigation into four stages: Pratijna, i.e. plaint, Uttara, i.e. answer, Sadhana, i.e. evidence and Nirnaya, i.e. decision. The normal elements of judicial procedure are five—plaint, defence, proof, judgment and execution and in the Maricchakatika we notice that the case has been decided in accordance with the five above mentioned procedures. Not only this, how far the principles laid down in the Smritis were actually practised in the courts can be judged from the drama where the court makes its report to the king quoting Manu as an authority on law that a Brahmana cannot be executed, and he therefore should be exiled from the country with his property untouched.

NOTES AND REFERENCES

1. *Mri.* Act. IX pp. 446, 471; Sloka 34, p. 500.
2. *Ibid.,* Act IX, pp. 451-52.
3. Etadadhikaranam, tatpravishnam adhikarenabhojakah.
4. *Mri.* Act DC, p. 454.
5. *Ibid.,* Act IX, p. 459.
6. *Ibid.,* Act IX, p. 461.
7. *Ibid.,* Act. IX, pp. 469, 80.
8. *Ibid.,* Act IX, p. 480.
9. *Ibid.,* Act IX, p. 464.
10. *Ibid.,* Act IX, p. 464.
11. *Ibid.,* Act IX, p. 467.
12. *Ibid.,* Act IX, p. 465.
13. *Ibid.,* Act IX, p. 465.
14. *Ibid.,* Act IX, p. 466.
15. *Ibid.,* Act IX, p. 467.
16. *Ibid,* Act IX, p. 510.
17. *Ibid.,* Act IX, p. 512.
18. *Ibid.,* Act IX, p. 492.
19. *Ibid.,* Act IX, p. 519.
20. *Ibid.,* Act IX, p. 515.
21. *Ibid.*
22. *Ibid.*
23. *Ibid.,* Act X, p. 582.

II
JUDICIAL PROCEDURE IN ANCIENT INDIA[1]

We do not propose to go into details of ancient Indian judicial procedure. However, it would be apporpriatc to state that the rules of procedure and evidence in ancient India were sophisticated enough. In broad outlines there is considerable similarity between the system now in force. Let us mention some of the interesting rules of the ancient system. A civil judicial proceeding was commenced ordinarily by filing a plaint before a competent authority. A plaint, it was provided,[2] must be brief in words, unambiguous, free from confusion,[3] devoid of improper arguments and capable of meeting opposite arguments.

Rules of Pleading in Ancient India

There were elaborate rules about the contents of the plaint; for example,[4] plaints concerning immovable property were required to state, *inter alia,* the country and place (town or village), the situation (boundaries), name of the field and so on. There was to be a written statement to be filed by the defendant in reply to the plaint. The written statement must meet all points of the plaint, must not employ vague words, must not be self-contradictory and so on.[5]

Witnesses in Ancient India

Witnesses could be summoned by the order of the judge. According to the celebrated work Arthasastra:

> "The parties shall themselves produce witnesses who are not far removed either by time or place. Witnesses who are far away or who will not stir out shall be made to present themselves by the order of the judge."[6]

Consequences of Default

Manu[7] enumerates numerous situations in which a plaintiff may be non-suited or a defendant may lose his cause. According to Kautiliya, failure by a defendant to file the reply within three fortnights would mean the loss of the suit by the defendant.[8] A similar injunction is also to be found in Manu.[9]

Means of Proof

The various means of proof were classified as human or divine. The human means of proof were sub-divided into documents, witnesses and possession. There is the famous text of Yajnavalkya[10] enumerating three means of proof. There were even directions for comparison of handwriting.[11] In the absence of human proof, divine proof (ordeals) supplied the deficiency.[12]

After evidence had been led, a decision had to be rendered on the basis of certain recognised principles. These principles are enumerated in some of the smritis[13] as eight fold, namely, the three means of proof[14] (pramanas), logical inference, the usage of the country, oaths and ordeals, the edict of the king and the admissions of the litigants. The successful party was entitled to *ajayapatra* (document of success). Rendering of the judgment represented the fourth and the last stage of the law suit.[15] Several modes of execution were known.[16] These included, *inter alia,* imprisonment, sale, demand for additional security and fine.

Misconduct by Ministerial Staff

There are directions to the effect that if a clerk of the court makes errors in writing which lead to a miscarriage of justice, he should be punished.[17]

Res Judicata

The doctrine of res judicata was well-known.[18]

Criminal Justice in Ancient India

It would appear that the criminal justice system was equally sophisticated. Ancient Indian law-givers and commentators exhibit a richness of thought and variety reminiscent of modern legal systems.

Substantive Law

In substantive criminal law, for example, we find an elaborate classification of offences. The broad categories were five, namely, abusive words, assault, theft, adultery and crimes of violence.[19] There were, however, a number of variations or aggravations in each of these broad categories. For example, theft was classified into three kinds according to the value of the things stolen— trifling, middling and grave or high.[20] Another interesting refinement was the classification of thieves into open or patent thieves and secret thieves, reminding us to a certain extent of the modern discussions about white collar criminals and others. In open or patent thieves were included traders who employ false weights and measures, gamblers, quacks, persons giving bribes, persons who profess to arbitrate, persons who manufacture counterfeit articles and the like.[21] "Concealed thieves" are illustrated by persons who move about with tools for house-breaking without being observed. These were again sub-divided into nine categories.[22]

Learned discussions as to the right of private defence were not unknown.[23]

Punishment of Abetment

Detailed rules are to be found for the punishment of abettors. The rules relating to abetment and the penalties for various species of abetment as provided by Katyayana[24] offer an interesting parallel to the graded punishment in the Indian Penal Code for various species of abetment.

Offences

The range of offences itself was surprisingly large. Not only were offences such as murder, rape, dacoity and the like (which may be called conventional offences) punishable, but there were provisions punishing other crimes as well. For examples, not running to the rescue of another person in distress was an offence.[25] This is a surprisingly modern provision, as it should be noted that it is only during the last twenty years or so that the question whether such an omission ought to be made an offence has been seriously debated in common law countries.

Punishment is prescribed for causing damage to trees in city parks, to trees providing shade, to trees bearing flowers and fruits, to trees which are useful, to trees in holy places, or trees serving as boundary marks.[26]

Even the giving of a wrong decision, if done corruptly by a judge, was regarded as punishable.[27]

An interesting provision was the punishing a person who made a breach in an embankment.[28] Equally interesting is the provision punishing a person who, except in case of extreme necessity, drops filth on the king's high road.[29]

Criminal Procedure

As to judicial procedure in criminal cases, the law-givers seem to have been aware of the presumption of innocence; there are texts which forbid conviction merely on suspicion.[30] Rules for the evaluation of evidence of various classes of witnesses are met with. The famous Sanskrit play *Marichhhakatikam* has an interesting trial scene that reveals stages of procedure not very different from a modern criminal trial.

Perjury

Perjury and other offences by witnesses were punished severely by the criminal law,[31] the penalty being fine and banishment.

Punishment—Types of

There was six types of punishment,—fine, reprimand, torture, imprisonment, death and banishment.

The punishment was graded according to several factors. It was material to consider whether the offence was the first crime of the offender[32]—or whether it was his second criminal act, and so on. The time and place (of the offence) and the strength and knowledge (of the offender) were to be fully considered.[33]

Compensation to Victim

It is one of the justified complaints against the modern penal law that in criminal proceedings the injured party is generally neglected. In ancient Hindu law, the law-givers were fully aware of the necessity of directly compensating the victim of the crime. Thus, Manu says[34]—

> "If a limb is injured, a sound (is caused) or blood (flows, the assailant) shall be made to pay (to the sufferer) the expenses of the cure, or the whole (both the usual amercement and the expenses of the cure as a) fine (to the king)."

Manu adds—

> "He who damages the goods of another, be it intentionally or unintentionally, shall give satisfaction to the (owner) and pay to the king a fine equal to the (damage)." It would appear that on the basis of the injuctions contained in the texts, one could construct an entire code of criminal law.

Notes and References

1. Law Commission of India, Seventy-seventh Report, Chapter 5.
2. Brihaspati, cited by M.K. Sharan, Court Procedure in Ancient India (1978), p. 57 (300 A.D.—500A.D.).
3. *Cf.* Kane, History of Dharmasastra (1972), Vol. 3, p. 299 (words containing no coherent sense).
4. Katyayana, cited by M.K. Sharan, Court Procedure in Ancient India (1978), p. 57 (400 A.D.—600 A.D.).
5. Sukra, IV, 5.139, cited by M.K. Sharan, Court Procedure in Ancient India (1978), p. 57.
6. Kautilya, Arthasastra, Book 3, Chapter 11, verse 50; Kangle, Kautilya Arthasastra (University of Bombay) (1970), Part II, p. 230.
7. Manu, VIII, 53-58, Vol. 25, Sacred Books of the East (1967), pp. 263-64.
8. Kangle, Kautilya Arthasastra (University of Bombay) (1965), Part III, p. 218.
9. Manu, VIII, 58, Vol. 25, Sacred Books of the East (1967), p. 264.
10. Yajnavalkya, II, 22 (100 A.D.—300 A.D.); Kane, History of Dharmasastra, Vol. 3, p. 304.
11. Vishnu, VIII, 12; M.K. Sharan, Court Procedure in Ancient India (1978), p. 96.

12. Yajnavalkya, II, 22.
13. Sukra, IV, 5.271; Kane, History of Dharmasastra, Vol. 3, p. 379.
14. Documents, witnesses and possession.
15. Kane, History of Dharmasastra (1972), Vol. 3, p. 260 and p. 379.
16. M.K. Sharan, Court Procedure in Ancient India (1978), p. 183.
17. Kangle, Kautilya Arthasastra (University of Bombay) (1965), Part III, p. 221, referring to verse 4.9.17 of the Book on Arthasastra.
18. Kane, History of Dharmasastra (1972), Vol. 3, p. 301.
19. *Ibid.*, p. 515.
20. *Ibid.*, pp. 519-20.
21. *Ibid.*, p. 520.
22. Katyayana, Verses 832-34, as quoted by Kane, History of the Dharmasastra (1972), Vol. 3, p. 529.
23. Kane, History of the Dharmasastra (1972), pp. 507-08.
24. Katyayana, Verses 832-34, as quoted by Kane, History of the Dharma-saitra (1972), Vol. 3, p. 529.
25. Kangle, Kautilya Arthasastra (1965), Part 3, p. 230.
26. *Ibid.*, p. 229, citing Chapters 3.18 and 3.19.
27. Kautilya, IV. 9, Kane, History of the Dharmasastra (1972), Vol. 3, p. 271.
28. Manu, IX, 279; Vol. 25, Sacred Books of the East, p. 392.
29. Manu, IX, 282; Vol. 25, Sacred Books of the East, p. 392.
30. Kane, History of the Dharmasastra (1973), p. 521.
31. Manu, VIII, 120-23, Vol. 25, Sacred Books of the East, p. 275.
32. Manu, VIII, 129, Vol. 25, Sacred Books of the East, p. 276.
33. Manu, VIII, 16. Vol. 25, Sacred Books of the East, p. 218.
34. Manu, VIII, 287-88, Vol. 25, Sacred Books of the East, p. 393.

III
TRIAL BY JURY IN ANCIENT INDIA

RAM RAJ

The late Mr. Ram Raj was the Chief Judge of the erstwhile Mysore State, when he, in his letter dated 10th May, 1828 addressed to Mr. Graeme, the late Governor of Madras, gave his views on the introduction of Trial by Jury in the East India Company's Courts of Law. In 1806, Sir Alexander Johnston, the late Chief Justice, and President of His Majesty's Council in Ceylon, formed a plan for granting the right of sitting upon juries and of being tried by juries by their own countrymen, to all the natives of Ceylon. Having got a Charter from His Majesty's Government, the system came into operation in 1811 throughout the island of Ceylon. In 1827, the Governor in Council of Madras resolved to extend this right to all the natives living under the presidency of Madras. Following are the extracts from the above mentioned letter of Mr. Ram Raj concerning Trial by Jury in Ancient India. (*Ed.*)

Constitution of Ancient Courts

In order to a right determination of this point, it may, perhaps, be necessary to inquire into the details of the constitution of the ancient Hindu courts, as laid down in books of authority. *Sabha,* in Sanskrit, signifies a court, an assembly, a meeting. It is derived from *sa* together, and *bha,* to shine, and is applied to an association of respectable persons. *Subhas* are divided according to some, into four sorts, namely, *apratishthita,* temporary, *pratishthita* permanent, *mudrita* confirmed, and *sastrita,* constitutional. The first comprehends all assemblies occasionally convened for the purpose of deciding causes and disputes referred to them, the second includes all the established village and town-courts, the third is held by a chief judge, duly appointed by the king, and, in the last, the king presides in person.

Different Types of Courts

In the *Smriti Chandrika,* a work on Hindu law of great celebrity both in the northern and southern parts of India, are enumerated fifteen different descriptions of *sabhas,* courts or assemblies. They are as follows: 1. *Aranyasabha,* an assembly of foresters; 2. *Sarthikasabha,* that composed of merchants; 3. *Senikasabha,* the members of which were appointed from among military men; 4. *Ubhayanumatsabha* that chosen by the parties themselves; 5. *Gramavasisabha,* composed partly of the villagers and partly of strangers, or of civil and military persons together; 6. *Gramasabha,* a village court in which the *Mahajenams* or heads of castes are assembled to settle disputes arising in the village; 7. *Purasabha,* a town or city court; 8. *Ganasabha,* an assembly composed of all the four classes indiscriminately; 9. *Srenisabha,* an assembly composed of all the inferior classes, or castes such as washermen, barbers, etc. for deciding causes among their own tribes; 10. *Chaturvidyasabha,* that composed of persons learned in all the four *sastras;* 11. *Vargasabhi,* an assembly of irreligious men; 12. *Kulasabha,* a meeting composed of persons of the same family; 13. *Kulikasabha,* in which relatives of the plaintiff and defendant meet to discuss the matter; 14. *Niyuktasabha,* a court held by a deputy, or chief judge, regularly appointed by the king with the *sabhasads,* or assessors. This was sometimes called *mudritasabha,* as it was presided by the pradvivaka, or the chief judge, in virtue of the king's mudra, or seal with which he was entrusted; and sometimes also, *pradvivakasabha,* after the name of the presiding officer; 15. *Nripasabha,* or king's court, which is also called *sastrita,* because the king was assisted by persons skilled in *sastras,* and all desicions passed here were final. Of these fifteen descriptions of courts, the first three are called *apratishthita,* unsettled, because they were only occasionally held, and were liable to be removed from place to place; and all the rest excepting the two last, are called *pratishthita* fixed or permanent. An appeal lies from an inferior to a superior court in regular succession, or directly to the king's. The popular courts above described, from the number of persons of whom they were composed, and the facilities which they must have afforded in ascertaining the facts they were called to judge, present something like a jury, and appear to have produced all the advantages peculiar to that mode of trial, without the delay and vexation attending the forms introduced in more regular courts. But I am unable to assertain to what extent the inferior courts, took cognisance of criminal matters; there seems to be less doubt, however, as to their power trying civil causes without any limit. They often appear to have acted as mediators between the parties who could not proceed to higher tribunals without passing the lower.

Organisation of the Courts

As to the organisation of the two last-mentioned courts *sastrita* and *mudrita,* and the duties of the officers of whom they were composed, abundant information is to be gathered from our law books; but I will only quote a few extracts which bear on these points, from *Vijnyaneswariyam,* a commentary on the Intitutes of *Yajnyavalkya* which is consulted as the highest authority in southern India. This work, according to the practice of Hindu writers; on law, is divided into three heads; namely, *achara,* ceremonial rites *vyavahara* municipal law; and *prayaschitta,* expiations and purifications. The *vyavahara kanda,* or that part which treats of municipal law, opens with the following texts of *Yajnyavalkya:*

1. "Let the prince investigate judicial disputes, accompanied by learned Brahmans, in conformity to law, avoiding anger and avarice."
2. "Persons skilled in theology, well versed in law, who are

addicted to truth, and make no distinction between an enemy and a friend these (and such as these) ought to be appointed as assessors (*sabhasads*) by the prince."

3. "A Brahman experienced in all institutions, shall be appointed with the assessors (*sabhya*), by a prince who is engaged in other affairs, and not able personally to conduct judicial investigation."
4. "The prince shall examine causes in succession, attentively fixing his mind and adhering to law and opinion of the chief judge *[pradvivaka]*."
5. "On the assessors *[sabhya]* who deviate from law through fear, favour, or hope of reward, punishment shall be inflicted double that to which the parties are liable."

Eminent and Twice Born Assessors

It appears from the first, second, third, and fourth texts, as explained by Vijnyaneswara, that the king, with learned Brahmans, the chief judge (*pradvivaka*), and the assessors (*sabhasadas*), constituted the *sastrita;* and that the Brahaman, accompanied by the assessors, formed the *mudrita* court. The commentaries explain, they who sit in the court are termed *sabhasads,* assessors or judges, they ought to be selected from the sacerdotal class for Katyayana says—"He shall be accompanied by assessors (*sabhya*) who are eminent, twice born, and well versed in the art of reasoning." The term being in the plural number, the number of assessors ought to be three, at least as Manu has declared: "In whatever place three Brahmans, skilled in theology, meet with the very learned Brahman appointed by the king, the wise call that assembly the court of Brahma *with four faces*." But Vrihaspati says—"The court in which seven, five or three Brahmans, learned in theology and skilled in law, sit, is equal to an assembly for the performance of sacrifice." The distinction between the Brahmans mentioned in the first text, and the assessors (*sabhasads*) described in the second, is pointed out by Katyayana, who says,—"A king who investigates causes accompanied by his chief judge (*pradvivaka*) his ministers (*mantri*), his domestic priest (*purohita*) and assessors (*sabhasads*) shall by the power of virtue, obtain bliss in heaven." Vijnyaneswara further observes, that the Brahmans mentioned above are not constituted (*anyukta*), and the assessors are constituted members of the court (*niyukta*), as it is declared, "Whether constituted members (*niyukta*), or not constituted members of the court (*anyukta*), they who know the law or fact ought to declare it," and the commentator explains the passage by remarking, that the king should be admonished in the event of his acting contrary to justice by the constituted members of the court, and that, if they do not, they incur guilt, for Katyayana says—"The assessors who follow him who commits injustice become sharers in his guilt." But those who are not constituted members of the court, adds the commentator, incur guilt either by not giving information, or by not stating the truth, but not by not admonishing the king. The term "and such as these," in the second text, is explained as denoting a certain number of merchants of whom the court may be composed for the satisfaction of mankind.

The Brahman as Chief Judge

The Brahman mentioned in the third text, acted, in the absence of the king, as chief judge or magistrate, together with the assessors and Brahmans. It does not appear by what name his officer is designated; but a competent knowledge of the law, and established usages, an unblemished character, and a decent from a respectable family are the qualifications required in the person holding the office; for Katyayana says, "He must be capable of restraining his passions, well born, serious, not rash and violent. He must be in awe of the next world, benevolent, dexterous, and free from wrath." Where there is not an intelligent Brahman to be procured, says the commentary, a *Kshatriya or Vaisya,* may be appointed, but never a *Sudra;* for the same author says, "A *Kshatriya or Vaisya,* learned in law, may be employed where there is not an intelligent Brahman; but a *Sudra* is by all means to be avoided."

The officer mentioned in the fourth text is the *pradvivaka,* a term explained in the commentaries as signifying one who examines the pleading, and interrogates the parties in the suit; for Vyasa says—"He who inquires into disputes with attention, accompanied by the assessors, by reason of his investigating suits, is called *pradvivaka.*" His duties were somewhat analogous to those of the English judges, whether the king presided or not; but, when the king was not present, he sometimes presided in the king's court, and, according to the opinion of his assessors, determined finally all civil suits, whether original or in the last resort. All criminal cases, however, were either tried before the king personally, or referred to him for confirmation, for the *pradvivaka* is not authorised to inflict any punishment beyond reprimand. The duties of *sabasads are* to judge of the facts and law of any case, whether the king, the *pradvivaka,* or other officer, presided in the court. But there is a doubt whether, in criminal matters, the *sabasads* merely returned a verdict on the case, and the king, or the *pradvivaka,* passed the sentence, or, whether the former, or the Brahmans, mentioned before, explained the punishment and referred it to be confirmed and executed by the royal authority.

The Pandits are inclined to think that the king, or *pradvivaka,* merely carried the sentence into execution; many passage, to which I have consulted on the subject shew that the king may set the sentence aside at pleasure. There is a text quoted in the *Smriti Chandrika,* however, which clearly points out the functions of the several members of the court. "The chief judge interrogates, the king executes, the *sabhyas,* or assessors, judge of the facts (*karya pravartaka*), and the law determines the punishment." But some explain the word which I have translated *judge of the facts,* judge of the whole matter, and make it comprehend both the law and the fact. Be this as it may it is clear on the whole, that the *sabhasads* or *sabhyas,* so far as regards their verdict on the case, resemble the juries of the English court.

Trials in Ancient India Similar to the English by Jury

I hope I have shewn, by what precedes, that the Hindu law does contemplate trials similar to that of the English by jury, though differing in form and some non-essentials. Some might be disposed to think—and 1 have heard some persons maintain—that, as the *sabhasads* of the Hindu courts were composed of Brahmans, the jurors should be selected from among that class. But this is not correct, for it expressly ordained by Manu and others that protecting mankind shall be the duty of a *Kshetria* and Vijnyaneswara, in the course of commenting on the first text of *Yajnyavalkya,* quoted above, interprets the word, *nripah,* prince, as "not applicable to a *kshetryia* only, but to persons of any class of people in whom sovereignty rests." This exposition is founded on natural reason, why then may we not, in like manner, explain the following text which describes the qualifications of the *sabhasads,* or assessors, as applicable to all classes of people, who are possessed of the abilites required. We cannot so explain it, the objector says, because the commentator interprets it differently, that "although it is only mentioned that they must be skilled in theology, yet they ought to be Brahmans, for Katyayana rises the epithet 'twice-born'."

'Twice Born' Signifies Three Higher Classes

Now, the term, *dwija,* 'twice born' may signify any of the three higher classes, viz. Brahman, Kshatryia, and Vaisya; so that still the exposition of the text, as relating exclusively to Brahmans, is objectionable. Moreover, the commentator explains the term "such as these," in the foregoing text, as implying "a certain number of merchants, of whom the court may be composed, for the satisfaction of mankind," and quotes a passage from Katyayana to the same purport in support of his interpretation; which clearly shews that the office of *sabhasads,* or assessors, was never intended by the legislature to be confined to Brhamans alone, but to all the three higher classes, at last, who were the most respectable in the age in which the law was promulgated. But, a worldly point of view, it must be remarked, that society has now assumed a different character from what orignally bore; many of the priestly class have abandoned their sacerdotal functions, and follow secular profession; while *sudras,* have become more enlightened than formerly, follow the professions ordained for higher classes, and, in most respects, are in better circumustances than their priests generally are. In this state of the community, I do not see any objection to the juries being selected from all the respectable castes of Hindus; that is Brahmans, Kshatriyas, Vaisyas, and Sudras indiscriminately as is now done in the supreme court at Madras. These classes do not shew the least scruple to associate together, on a footing of equality, in temporal matters.

Popular Tribunals once Prevailed in India

A few words with respect to the courts at present existing, or which have lately existed, under Hindu dynasties, would, perhaps, be desirable. I have not been able to obtain much detailed information on the subject; but as far as I could collect, there is every reason to conclude, that popular tribunals once prevailed all over India, and still exist in many parts of the country. In the commencement of the Mahratta power in the Dekkan, a supreme court was established in the capital of the empire, presided by one of the eight *pradhuns,* or ministers, in his capacity of *nyaydtthipati,* or judge; and this office, though usually held by Brahmans, was not altogether confined to that class of people. This court was abolished after the usurpation of the royal power by the prime minister, or as he was commonly called, the *peshwa.* Latterly, the administration of justice and the collection of revenue were united into one department. Almost all the civil affairs, such as loans, contracts, inheritence, etc. were decided by the awards of *panchayet,* or arbitrators, regularly summoned from among the classes of merchants, and all criminal cases were determined by local authorities, excepting such as were capital, which were regularly referred to the head of the government, who alone retained the power of inflicting capital punishments and heavy penalties.

Nearly the same mode of administering justice is said to prevail at the present day in the dominions under the Raja of Mysore. I am personally acquainted with several instances in which the *faujdar* at Bangalore, an officer who, as his name implies, must have originally belonged to the army, but at present acts as collector and judge of an extensive district summoned an assembly called the *panchayet,* composed of all classes of people indiscriminately, to attend at his *kachahri* for the purpose of deciding civil causes. Adultery, rape, etc. are commonly tried by a similar assembly of the people, often of the same class as that to which the offender belongs.

A digest of Hindu law, entitled *Sataswativilasa,* attributed to Prataparudradeva, one of the Princes of the Kalinga dynasty, who reigned in the commencement of the forteenth century of Salivahana, attests the existence of regular courts in his dominions; and it is well known that the rajas of Vijayanagara established tribunals, and administered justice under certain modifications, according to law, in their once flourishing empire; and it was under the auspices of its founder that the *Madaviyam,* a commentary on the Institutes of Parasara, and *Dattamimansa* a tract on the law of adoption were composed. That it appears that, after the destruction of the Vijayanagara empire, the viceroys of Madura and Trichinopoly abolished the courts which existed during the prosperity of the government to which they were tributaries: and though they substituted in their place some mode of judicial investigation, not exactly according to law, yet the memory of some of the princes of this dynasty is still held in high estimation for their justice and equity.

The constitution of the courts in the south under the Chola monarchs must have been strictly conformable to law, for the *Vijniyaneswariyam* is supposed to have been the standard of justice which they established throughout their kingdom, but these institutions did not survive the dynasty under which they were reared. The present Raja of Tanjore has for some years past established four different descriptions of courts, called *pratishthita Sabha, adhyaksha Sabha, mudrita sabha, and uttara sabha,* which have jurisdiction over the fort of Tanjore and the villages attached to it. The proceedings are conducted partly according to the Hindu law and partly according to certain regulation framed in imitation of the practice of the Company's courts. The officer who presides in the *pratishthita* court is not a Brahman but a Mahratta of a different class. The *sabhasads,* or assessors, are said to act both as jurors, in finding a verdict, and as expounders of law, in passing sentence. In so limited a jurisdiction as that of Tanjore, cases of capital crimes must seldom occur. It was once the custom in Tanjore to refer most civil cases that were brought before the raja to the *mahajenams,* or the assembly of the inhabitants of the village in which the cause of action arose; and their decisions, if approved by the raja, were carried into execution. Much can be gathered in this way to prove the existence, in this country of trials similar to that now proposed to be introduced. The *Asiatic Journal,* Vol. XXIII, No. CXXXV, from page 329 to page 339, in speaking of the judicial system observed in the Dekkan, adverts to decisions by Panchayet, through whom a tolerable dispensation of justice among the people is said to have been effected. I have known several instance in which the trial of civil causes established in the Company's territories, subject to this presidency, has given more satisfaction to the parties than they might have otherwise had; and I can safely say, that it has produced all the benefits contemplated wherever the parties had recourse to the system, and made a judicious choice of an honest and respectable body of inhabitants for the purpose. But, after all it is, I presume, altogether unnecessary to trace through the books on law and history for a pattern of any measure that is newly proposed for the good of the public. It is for the government to alter, improve, or originate such measures, from time to time, as are best calculated to forward the due administration of justice; and when the objects contemplated by such measures are known to the people, it is impossible they can dislike them the flimsy ground of their not being sanctioned by former usages and customs.

14

Local Self-Government in Ancient India

C. Hayavadana Rau

Ancient Indians, Well Versed in Local Government

At the present time, when political ideals are discussed with considerable earnestness all over India; it is not inopportune to consider whether in ancient days, (even before the advent of Muhammadans into India) the people of this country enjoyed any sort of local self-government and if so, how far it was real. Before considering these questions, it must be remarked that even academic discussions of this sort are not altogether out of place for clearing up a great many misconceptions Foreigners have grown into the habit of speaking of the inferiority of Indians in this mater; perhaps the chief cause of this is the great mystery and doubt in which the early history of this country is enveloped in. That this is one of the gross errors that ever was perpetrated (and is being perpetrated), nobody, who pretends to a knowledge of Indians and their mental and moral character, can deny. It is unfortunate that this should be so, for it affects the advancement of Indians at every step and Government, which is, to speak in the langauge of a distinguished writer, composed of human units with their usual defects and idiosyncracies, is equally in the dark. Ignorance is thus allowed free play and one reason for the failure of modern Municipal institutions is the vigour with which higher officialdom interferes and intervenes into the conduct of local affairs.

Three Types of Local Management

Municipal officers, indeed, could do little with the nightmare of Governmental prinpricks on their chests. The Government intends to do the best; but the best is unfortunately outcome of the darkest ignorance imaginable, ignorance both of Indian character and of Indian political institutions. That is the reason why it has failed to popularise modern Municipal work in India. "In countries, where the organs of Local Government," as a recent English writer has well put it, "are under the thumb of the Central authority, although the efficiency of administration may be great, the political character of the people will be unsatisfactory; it will be apathetic for long periods and then dangerously excited, with the result of instability and corruption in the Central Government. On the other hand, a country of strong Local Government may be slow to move, but it will be a country of steady progress, and of political stability and honesty." It is proposed to pass in review below three different types of local management, exercised by Indians in olden days, to show how far the natives of this country have been accustomed to manage their own local affairs in the past and even to a certain extent at the present day.

A Nation of Panchayatdars

First, we shall take the orgnisation of the various castes. A study of the same, even in its present disintegrated state, cannot but make us pause a little and consider how far the charge, that the Indians are incapable of managing their own affairs, can be sustained.

Every Indian caste is democratically organized; though each recognises a headman, yet his powers are so far limited that he cannot exercise them without summoning to his assistance a council of elders. This is the well-known Panchayat and Indians have been called a nation of Panchayatdars. These Panchayatdars are very like jurymen, summoned for the settlement of civil, criminal and marital disputes. They are usually brought together by a caste or tribal servant corresponding to the Beadle of Teutoni history. The headman sets out the facts before them and with them the customary mode in which disputes have hitherto been settled amongst them. On this, the Panchayatdars proceed to hear the case, the statement of the parties and of their witnesses. The trial partakes the character partly of a judicial trial and partly (in some cases) of a religious inquiry. At. the end, the Panchayatdars deliver their verdict, which binds the parties. The headman of the caste sees that the verdict is given effect to. Some of the castes in Southern India even elect their headmen by a highly complicated system of voting at a general meeting of the whole caste. Amongst all castes, questions affecting the caste, as a whole, are determined by the caste itself summoned together for the purpose. The whole caste, then, goes, in Parliamentary language, into Committee and then resolves upon a definite course. Its powers were not restricted in olden days by the nature of the dispute in question; the Hindu rulers of the country (and even to a certain extent their Muhammadan successors) do not appear to have interfered with them in these matters. On the other hand, the rulers encouraged the system of local settlement of affairs by themselves, by associating their own agents in the eventual adjudication of civil and criminal affairs. In the settlement of disputes relating to rights of property and the like, the caste was enlarged as it were by the election of Panchayatdars from amongst other castes as well, if there be any necessity for the same. Each of the disputing parties chooses an equal number of persons and in olden days the Ruling Chief appointed one of his own men as the President of the Panchayat to act as umpire. This man may be objected to by either party, if suspected of partiality or the like. Another is nominated instead and the affair is satisfactorily settled. In some places (or in some cases) both parties agree to refer the disputed question to a Panchayat for determination and before them, they lay the evidence and their decision binds both parties. "The members of a Panchayat are selected," writes a distinguished authority, "by the general suffrage of their fellow-citizens, and whether in the lower or higher ranks, a person who has once established a reputation for talent and integrity in these courts is deemed a permanent member. It is popular distinction, and becomes, therefore, a point of fame. A person is estimated in proportion as he is free from suspicion of being retracted by influence or corruption and to have fame as a Panchayat is an object of ambition with the poorest inhabitant of the hamlet as well as the highest and wealthiest citizen. To sit upon these courts is conceived a duty which every man is bound to perform. The members receive no pay; their attendance is regulated with attention to general convenience; but after consenting to sit, it is not to be evaded." These words of Sir John Malcolm apply with as much force to South as to Central India. The simple settlement of local disputes has been gradually going out of existance; not so much through its inherent weakness as by the want of Governmental countenance to it. So long ago 1823 Malcolm proposed to retain these Panchayats with certain modifications to suit the "cold and rigid" though just character of British administration of India. "It" (our administration), he writes, "creates no alarm, it inspires little, if any, emulation. The people are protected but not animated or attracted. It is rare that any native of India, living under it can suffer injury or wrong; but still more rare that he can be encouraged or elevated by favour or distinction. Our rules and regulations contribute a despotic power which is alike imperative upon the Governors and the governed. Its character compells it to generalize and its forms as well as principles, are unyielding. To indraft upon this system an instiutions such as the Panchayat is no easy task; but if satisfied of its excellence, we should not be deterred from its introduction by any difficulties of our own creation." The curious will find Malcolm's scheme of reforming the Panchayat system to suit modern requirements in the Second Volume of his *Memoir of Central India.* In the Panchayat system there was (and there is yet) ample material to restore and develop on modern lines a form of local autonomy that would confer a great blessing on Indians in general. It is a pity that the whole system has been grossly neglected by a Government which, proceeding upon a defined general system, has rejected as Malcolm himself observes, everything personal. That is a blame that Government must itself bear before it charges Indians with being absolutely unacquainted with the idea of managing their own affairs.

In Buddhist Times

The Second type of Local Self-Government refers to Buddhist times. Here we shall see how the Panchayat was utilised in working the Municipal institutions of great cities. For this purpose we examine the form of Local Government enjoyed by the people of India during the times of Chandragupta, the grand-father of Asoka, the great Buddhist Emperor. Chandragupta, the founder of the Mauryan dynasty, ruled over what is now India (including Afghanistan and excluding Burma), from Himalayas in the North to roughly Madras in the South, from 321 B.C. to 297 B.C. He was succeeded by his son, Bindusara, who ruled up to 272 B.C. He was, in turn, succeeded by his son, the great King Asoka. His descendants, according to the latest authority, bore rule up to about 184 B.C. The Mauryan dynasty thus lasted for a period of about 137 years. During the time of Chandragupta, all except the East Coast of India and the country south of Madras belonged to the Mauryan Kingdom. Asoka conquered Kalinga in 261 B.C. and annexed the East Coast in his dominions. We have an exceedingly interesting account left to us by Megasthenes, which has come to us in a fragment of Strabo, which gives us an excellent glimpse of the system of Municipal Government enjoyed by a big town like Patna, the capital of the Mauryan Kingdom. Whatever may be said of other portions of Megasthenes that have been rescued by Dr. Schwabeck from classical authors, it is undoubted that this fragment, containing as it does administrative details of the capital town, is reliable and trustworthy. It is exactly with these details that an ambassador like Megasthenes would, as remarked by Dr. Rhys Davids, "be better acquainted." As Mr. Vincent Smith rightly says, Megasthenes' vivid accounts of Chandragupta's civil and military administration "may be accepted without hesitation as true and accurate".

Megasthenes Account

"Those who have charge of the city," says Megasthenes, "are divided into six bodies of five each. The members of the first look after everything relating to the industrial arts. Those of the second attend to the entertainment of foreigners. To these they assign lodgings, and they keep watch over their modes of life by means of those persons whom they give to them for assistants. They escort them on the way when they leave the country or in the event of their dying, forward their property to their relatives. They take care of them when they are sick, and if they die, bury them. The third body consists of those, who inquire when and how births and deaths occur, with the view of not only levying a tax, but also in order that births and deaths among both high and low may not escape the cognisance of Government. The fourth class suprintends trade and commerce. Its members have charge of weights and measures, and see that the products in their season are sold by public notice. No one is allowed to deal in more than one kind of commodity unless he pays a double tax. The fifth class supervises manufactured articles, which they sell by public notice. What is new is sold separately from what is old, and there is a fine for mixing the two together. The sixth and last class consists of those who collect the tenths of the prices of the articles sold. Fraud in the payment of this tax is punished with death. Such are the functions which these bodies separately discharge. In their collective capacity, they have charge both of their special departments, and also of matters affecting the general interest, as the keeping of public buildings in proper repair, the regulation of prices, the care of markets, harbours and temples."

It is clear from the above passage that in the time of Chandragupta, the administration of Patna was entrusted to a Municipal Commision of 30 members divided into six Boards or Committees of five members each. "These Boards," as Mr. Vincent Smith appositely remarks "may be regarded as an official development of the ordinary non-official *Panchayat,* or Committee of five members, by which every cast and trade in India has been accustomed to regulate its internal affairs from time immemorial." These six Boards were in their individual capacities entrusted with the care of (1) the industrial arts; (2) foreigners, who must have come in large numbers to require a Board for themselves; (3) Vital Statistics including the systematic registration of births and deaths both for the information of Government and for levying the taxes; (4) Trade and Commerce, with the duty of regulating sales and enforcing the use of duly stamped weights and measures; (5) Manufactures, charged with the duty of seeing that old goods were not mixed with new; and (6) Tithe on Sales. Speaking of the third of these Boards, Mr. Vincent Smith, who writes with commendable appreciation of the Mauryan kings of India, says that "nothing in the legislation of Chandragupta is more astonishing to the observers familiar with the tax methods of ordinary Oriental Governments than this registration of births and deaths. The spontaneous adoption of such a measure by an Indian native state in modern times is unheared of and it is impossible to imagine an old fashioned Raja feeling anxious 'that births and deaths among both high and low might not be concealed'. Even the Anglo-Indian administration with its complex organization and European nations of the value of statistical information did not attempt the collection of Vital Statistics until very recent times, and has always experienced great difficulty in securing reasonable accuracy in the figures." We might note here that the first scientific attempt to record Vital Statistics was made in England after the introduction of printing.

'Provincial Edict' of Asoka

Though this is stated by Megasthenes as applying to the capital city of Patna, it is reasonably infered (by Mr. Vincent Smith) that it applied equally well to all the principal cities of the Mauryan Kingdom, such as Taxila, Ujjain and the other great cities of the Empire. The 'Provincials Edict' of Asoka is addressed to the officers in charge of the city of Tosali. This Tosali was in the Kalinga country, the country between the Mahanadi and the Godavari, where was stationed as Viceroy, a prince of the Royal blood. Its site is not known, but as Mr. Smith suggests, "it may be represented by Jaugada," in the modern Ganjam District, where the Edicts of Asoka, inluding the one in question, are to be seen yet engraved on the face of a rock about 120 ft. high. A copy of the same Edict is found at Dhauli, about 4 miles west of south of Bhuvanesvar in Cuttack. In this Edict, Asoka thus instructs the Municipal Commissioners of Tosali:

> "I desire my views to be practically acted upon and carried into effect by suitable means; and, in my opinion, the principal means for accomplishing this object are my instructions to you, for you have been set over many thousands of living beings to gain the affection of good men."
>
> "All men are my children, and, just as far my children I desire that they should enjoy all happiness and prosperity both in this world and in the next, so for all men I desire the like happiness and prosperity."
>
> "You however, do not, gain the best possible results. There are individuals who heed only part of my teaching and not the whole. You must see to such persons so that the moral rule may be odserved."
>
> "There are, again, individuals who have been put in prison or to torture. You must be at hand to stop unwarranted imprisonment or torture. Again, many there are who suffer acts of violence. It should be your desire to set such people in the right way."
>
> "There are, however, certain dispositions which render success impossible, namely envy, lack of perseverance, harshness, impatience, want of application, idleness, indolence."
>
> "You, therefore, should desire to be free from such dispositions, in as much as the the root of all this teaching consists in perseverance and patience in moral guidance. He who is indolent does not rise to his duty, and yet an officer should bestir himself, move forward, go on. The same holds good for your duty of supervision. For this reason I must repeat to you, 'consider and

know that such and such are His Majesty's instructions'. Fulfilment of these orders bears great fruit, non-fulfilment brings great calamity. By officer's who fail to give such guidance neither the favour of Heaven nor the favour of the King is to be hoped for. My special insistance on this duty is profitable in two ways, for by following this line of conduct, you will both win heaven and discharge your debt to me."

"This edict must be recited at every Tishya Nakshatra festival, and at intervals between Tishyas, as occasion offers, it should be read to individuals. And do you take care by acting thus to direct people in the right way."

"For this purpose has this edict been inscribed here in order that the officers in charge of the city may display persevering zeal to prevent unwarranted imprisonment, or unwarranted torture of the citizens."

For the same purpose, he caused to be summoned at his Capital once in every five years to the assembly "those men who are mild, patient, and who respect life, in order that hearing these things they may act according to my instructions". With the same end in view, he directed the Viceroys of Taxila and Ujjain (in the Punjab and Malwa respectively) to summon assemblies of the same kind, "every three years without fail".

That is a remarkable edict. It not only sums up admirably what a Viceroy should be to his subjects, like a father unto his children, but also testifies to us that the system of civic administration inaugurated by Chandragupta continued down to his grandsons' days. "The mere extent of the Empire," remarks Mr. Smith, "which was transmitted from Chandragupta to Bindusara, and from Bindusara to Asoka, is good evidence that the organisation of the Government, which was strong enough in military force to defeat foreign attacks, and to subdue an extensive kingdom, was also adequate for the performance of civil duties."

The system of Local Self-Government that obtained during Chandragupta's time was thus in full force in Asoka's time as far south-east as modern Ganjam. It is not known for certain when peninsular India (or Deccan) was conquered by the Mauryas. It was either the work of Chandragupta or of his son, Bindusara, and not of Asoka. Mr. Smith inclines to the view that it was an achievement of Chandragupta himself. This formed the Southern province of Asoka (extending from the banks of the Narbada to very near Madras) and was under a Viceroy who was stationed at Suvarnagiri. To him and to the magistrates at his place is addressed the first of the minor rock edicts of Asoka (232-1 B.C.) in which the Emperor proclaims the precept—'Let small and great exert themselves to this end' (of winning for themselves much heavenly bliss). It is reasonable to suppose that the same mode of managing local affairs was in vogue in this part of the Empire as well. Also, that it continued down to its disruption itself about 184 B.C.

Third Type of Local Self-government

We now pass on to the third type of Local Self-government that existed in olden days in India. Here, we have mainly to do with Southern India, though it is not improbable that the same conditions obtained in Northern India as well. I refer to the system that was in vogue all through Southern India during the Pallava and Chola days. It is necessary to impress on the reader the important fact, almost generally overlooked, that, there is a continuity of history from the time of Asoka to the time of the Cholas of the 10th Century A.D. The Cholas are, with the Pandyas and Keralas, mentioned in Asoka's inscriptions and by Pliny (1st Century A.D.), the author of the *Periplus Maria Errythrae,* who wrote very shortly after Pliny and Ptolemy, the Greek Geographer (2nd Century A.D.). But there is evidence to believe that during the period immediately preceding the ascendancy of the Cholas (i.e. roughly from the 4th to the 10th Century A.D.), the Pallavas were dominant in the South. Sivaskandavarman, one of their earliest known Kings, must have been the ruler of a considerable tract of country since he addresses one of his grants to "Lords of provinces, Royal Princes, Generals, Rulers of districts, Custom House Officers, Prefects of countries," and others. One of his successors was Narasimha Varman, during whose reign, (first half of 7th Century A.D.), Hiouen Thsang, the Chinese Buddhist traveller, visited Kanchi in the course of his perigrinations through India. During this time also lived the Great Saiva Saints, Tirugnanasambandar and Appar who wandered though the country singing hymns in honour of the shrines they visited. But the other dynasties, Cholas, Pandyas and Cheras make headway apparently with the help of the northern Chalukyas. We are in the middle of the 7th Century A.D., a period contemporaneous with the rise of English local institutions, 'the unconscious adaptation' as it has been said, 'of primeval Teutonic custom to the conditions of new settlement'. We may as well note here that the Central Government of England—represented by the Treasury, the King's Bench and Parliament—dates from the 12th Century, the period of the Angevin and Plantagenet Kings.

Settled Conditions in South India

During the next Century, the eighth, Southern India, was still under the Pallavas, though they shared the country with the other dynasties. Their successors ruled in different parts of the country until the commencement of the 10th Century. But their exact relationship to each other is not yet definitely known. However, when the Cholas replaced the Pallavas in Southern India at the beginning of the 10th Century, they became the possessors of a country that was fully settled in every aspect of its life. They were in no sense the organisers of any system of Government in it, and their predecessors had been rulers over a wide area, they had 'Lords of provinces', 'Prefects of countries' and 'Rulers of district', under them. In all probability these divisions of the Central Government were the successors of others that the Pallavas themselves found in the country when they rose to prominence. How old they were really at that time, there is no evidence at present available to say. But it may be supposed—at any rate in countries that came under the sway of the Mauryan Kings—that they were as old as the 4th Century B.C. In other parts of Southern India, we may not be wrong if we said that substantially the same conditions prevailed.

Internal Governance of Local Units Entirely Independent

These divisions of the Central Government, which was entirely Hindu in nationality down to the middle of the 16th Century when the disruption of the Vijayanagar Kingdom took place, attempted to bring together into a cohesive whole the local units, the villages. They continued, it may be added, in some form or another, until in the fulness of time they developed into what they are at the present day. During the times of which we write these units were, so far as their internal governance was concerned, entirely independent of the rulers and their representatives in the province and the district. In other words, we find the functions of Government during the times exercised by two district bedies,—first the Central, by the ruling King and his representatives over defined areas, and second the Local, by the village in its corporate capacity having jurisdiction only within its four corners. It must be firmly grasped that a number of these villages or rather townships, for they were often something more than mere villages, were grouped together to form a sub-division; a number of sub-divisions went to form a division; a number of divisions again into a province; and a number of provinces into the Kingdom. During the height of Chola prosperity this was the case. We have reason to believe that a similar division of the country for carrying on the general administration existed during the time of their predecessors, the Ganga Pallavas and the Pallavas. The basis of the Central Government daring those days was thus in the locally orgnised village; in other words the Central Government grew out of the Local Government. The autonomous village was not the creation of the Pallavas or the Cholas, any more than it can be described to be that of the Muhammadans or the British. They have existed from time immemorial and, wisely enough, like Archbishop Theodore (who by the way came from Tarsus in Macedonia) in England and the Romans in their Provinces, successive rulers in Southern India recognised it and the other older divisions that grew out of it and shaped the Central Government on that basis. Even the British Government, which had completely destroyed organised village life, even to a large extent had, to reckon with the village as an established fact. Therein lies the solidarity of the Indian village and the opportunities it offers to the rulers of the land to turn it to practical advantage in the evolution of a popular system of Local Self-Government. In olden days it mattered very little to the villager whether the Central Government of the time was a Monarchy or a Despotism of the most absolute sort; for he was left secure in the management of his own internal affairs. The Central Government refrained from actually interfering into its affairs except for the sole purpose of obtaining its revenue. The average citizen had thus ample scope left to him in the work of government. During the worst times of the 'tax-gathering' Muhammadan rule, the village or the township had been left to itself. It was reserved to the British to slowly but surely undermine its very corporate character, despite, it must be added, the protests that were raised against such a ruinous revolution by far-seeing Anglo-Indian Statesmen. No less an authority than Sir H.S. Maine felt compelled to raise his voice against it. 'The most beneficent systems of Government in India,' he said nearly fifty years ago, 'have always been those which have recognised the village community as the basis of administration. . . . To the attempts of English functionaries to separate the ideas involved in it may be assigned some of the most formidable miscarriages of Anglo-Indian administration'.

Prefectures, Townships and Districts

During the Pallava and the Ganga Pallava times, Southern India was, as we have seen above, divided into Prefectures, Townships and Districts—Mandalams, Kottams and Nadus. Each Nadu contained a number of villages and towns, the latter being usally nothing more than the combination of several villages. Each village had a Mahasabha or assembly which governed it according to its own wishes. The Pallava and Ganga Pallava inscriptions that have been found so far do not allow us to set out in full detail the mode in which members were elected to these assemblies, how they conducted their business; what were all the powers they exercised; the committees into which they usually divided for purposes of administrative convenience and so forth. But there is some evidence to believe that those must substantially have been the same they were during the time of the Cholas, who succeeded them. Thus we see from cerain inscriptions of the 9th Century A.D. found at Uttaramallur (belonging to the reign of the Ganga Pallava King, Danti Vikramavarman) that the assembly of that village took property in trust for the purpose of removing silt annually from its tank. An inscription of the time of the Ganga Pallava King Kampavarman found at Ukkal records a similar assumption of trust property and informs us that the management of the same was entrusted to the 'annual supervision' committee of the village. This committee, with others of its kind, came into greater prominence, during the Chola times. But to say that they originated with them, would be as unphilosophical as contrary to ascertained facts. They were in existence when the Cholas rose to eminence; but to them belongs the credit of purging them of some of the abuses that had grown upon them.

Assembly Consisted of Several Committees

That being so, we may easily understand the nature of the control exercised by these assemblies over their local affairs even during Pallava times. That must have been as real as that exercised by the assemblies of Chola days. The Cholas rose to power in the beginning of the Tenth Century A.D. Parantak I was the first distinguished King of the new (their connection with those mentioned in the Asoka Edicts is not yet known) Chola line. He is spoken of in his inscriptions as the conqueror of Madura and of Ceylon. He ruled between A.D. 900 and 940 (? 906 to 946 A.D.). Two inscriptions dated the 12th and 14th years of his reign (or A.D. 912 and 914) and found at Uttaramallur, in the modern Chingleput District, which figures also in inscriptions of the Ganga Pallava period, give interesting details of these assemblies and the mode in which members were elected to it and how they formed themselves into Committees for purposes of carrying out the practical duties of administration. These and some others found at Ukkal and in the Kistna District (also first half of 10th Century) have been considered in quite a scholarly manner by Rai Bahadur V. Venkayya, Government Epigraphist, Madras. The conclusion to which be comes to in brief about them is that these inscriptions did not bring into existence the assemblies and committees referred to in them, "which are referred to in records undoubtedly more ancient than the first quarter of the 10th Century A.D." Also, that these institutions were as much common in Telugu as in Tamil Districts. "In fact," he writes, "until the contrary is proved, it may be assumed that the system prevailed over a considerable portion of Southern India." According to these inscriptions the assembly consisted of several committees, four of which are specifically mentioned, viz.—'Annual supervision', Tank supervision', 'Garden supervision' and 'Supervision of justice'. These Committees were chosen every year and the names by which they were known seem to indicate roughly their spheres of work. The first apparently looked after all affairs which did not fall within the scope of the other committees. From an inscription dated 916 A D., we might infer, for instance, that the acquisition of land for purposes of making local roads was left to this Committtee. Some other inscriptions add the names of two more Committees, viz., Gold Supervision and Panchavara-Variyam. Mr. Venkayya thinks that the former in all probability regulated the currency. This might have been so, for Southern India had no silver coinage before the advent of the Muhammadans into it. The other Committee, according to him, was perhaps a body which supervised the work of the five Committees of the village. From a study of several inscriptions, he infers, that though each of these Committees as a body was subordinate to the village assembly, yet the members of the former were not debarred from taking part in the deliberations of the latter. Both the Uttaramallur inscriprions set out in some detail the rules for the appointment of Committees, the qualifications and disqualifications for membership and the mode of selecting members to the Committee. "This is the way" says the the record of 914 A.D., "in which (we, the members of the assembly) made rules for choosing once every year, 'Annual supervision', 'Garden supervision' and 'Tank supervision' (committees): (1) There shall be thirty groups (or wards) in Uttaramallur; (2) In these thirty wards those that live in each ward shall assemble and shall choose men for 'pot-tickets'." As regards qualifications, if a man wanted his name to be entered on the pot-ticket and put into the pot, the inscription says:—(a) He must own more than a quarter (veli) of tax-paying land; (b) He must have a house built on his own site; (c) His age must be below 70 and above 35; (d) He must know the Mantrabrahmana—i.e. he must know it himself and be able to teach (it to others); and (e) Even if one owns only one-eighth (veli) of land, he shall have (his name) written on a pot-ticket and put into (the pot; in case he has learnt one Veda and one of the fair Bhashyas and can explain it to others.

Committee Members must Submit their Accounts

Among those possessing the foregoing qualifications, "only such as are well conversant with business and conduct themselves according to sacred rules" shall be chosen; and those who have acquired their wealth by honest means, whose minds are pure and who have not been on (any of) these Committees for the last three years shall also be chosen. However, "those who have been on these Committees but have not submitted their accounts and their relations specified below shall not have (their names) written on the pot-tickets and put (into the pot): the sons of the younger and elder sisters of their mothers; the sons of their paternal aunts and maternal uncles; the brothers of their mothers; the brothers of their fathers; their brothers; their fathers-in-law (?); the brothers of their wives; the husbands of their sisters; the sons of their sisters; the sons-in-law who have married the daughters of disqualified persons; their fathers; their sons." Again, "those against whom illicit sexual intercourse or the first four of the five great sins," (killing a Brahman, drinking intoxicating liquors, theft, committing adultery with the wife of a spiritual teacher and associating with anyone guilty of these crimes) "are recorded; and all their various relations above specified shall not have (their names) written on the pot-tickets and put into (the pot)". Others disqualified included those who have been outcaste for association with low people, fool-hardy people, those guilty of theft or plunder of property belonging to others, those who have partaken of forbidden dishes, those who had been declared "village-pests," those guilty of adultery and those guilty of other expressly mentioned sins. These were excluded to the end of their lives.

"Excluding all these thus specified," goes the inscription, detailing the mode of selection, "names shall be written for pot-tickets in the thirty wards and each of the thirty wards in the twelve hamlets (of Uttaramallur) shall prepare a separate (packet) with a covering ticket (specifying its contents) tied to it. (These packets) shall be put into a pot. The pot-tickets shall be opened in the midst of a full Meeting of the Village Assembly including the young and old (members), convened (for the purpose). All the temple priests who happen to be in the village on the day in question shall without any exception whatever, be seated in the Village Hall (?) where the assembly shall meet. In the midst of the temple priests one of them who happens to be the oldest shall stand up and lift an (empty) pot so as to be seen by all the people present. Any young boy who knows nothing about the matter shall hand over to the standing priest one of (the packets from) the thirty wards. The contents (of the packet) shall be transferred to the (empty) pot and (well) shaken. From this pot shall be taken out (by the young boy?) and made over to the arbitrator. While taking charge of the ticket the arbitrator shall receive it on the palm of his hand with the five fingers open. He shall read out (the name on) the ticket thus received. The ticket read by him shall also be read out by all the priests then present at the hall. The name thus read shall be put down (and accepted). Similarly one man shall be chosen for each of the thirty wards."

Composition of the Committees by Pot Tickets

From these thirty persons were chosen the Committees "Of the thirty persons thus chosen, those who had previously been, on the 'Garden supervision' (Committee) and on the 'Tank supervision' (Committee) and those who are advanced in learning and those who are advanced in age shall be chosen for (the Committee of) 'Annual supervision'. Of the rest, twelve shall be taken for the 'Garden supervision' (Committee) and the remaining six will form the 'Tank supervision' (Committee). The last two Committees shall be chosen after an oral expression of opinion (?). The great men who are members of these three Committees shall hold office for full three hundred and sixty days and then retire. If any one who is on the

Committees is found guilty of any offence, he shall be removed (at once). For appointing the Committees after these have retired, the members of the Committee for 'Supervision of justice' in the twelve hamlets (of Uttaramallur) shall convene a meeting with the help of the arbitrator. The selection shall be by drawing pot-tickets according to this order which lays down the rules (thereof)." As regards the two other Committees the inscription makes due provision. "For the Pancha-Vara-Variyam and the Committee for 'Supervision of gold'," it says, "names shall be written for pot-ticket in the thirty wards, thirty (packets with) covering tickets shall be deposited in a pot and thirty pot-tickets shall be drawn (as previously described). From these thirty tickets twelve men shall be selected. Six out of these twelve shall form the 'Gold supervision' (Committee) and the (remaining) six constitute the Pancha-Vara-Variyam. When drawing pot-tickets for (the appointement of) these (two) Commitees next year; the wards which have been already represented (during the year in question) on these Committees shall be excluded and the appointments made from the remaining wards by an oral expression of opinion(?). Those who have ridden on assess and those who have committed forgery shall not have (their names) written on the pot-tickets and put into (the pot)." After some of other provisions the inscription ends with the words: "Thus, from this year onwards as long as the moon and sun endure Committees shall always be appointed by pot-tickets alone. To this effect was the Royal order received."

The last sentence is significant. It must be read with the commencement of the inscription. It would seem that a Royal order could take effect only after it had been approved by the village assembly. The other inscription of the 12th year of Parantaka's reign gives similar particulars about these assemblies but on an examination it would appear that the later one set out in detail above made certain alterations in the rules then in force to purge off "wicked men" from the Committees. The Village Assembly itself was, what we might term now-a-days a primary body; though its constitution is not yet definitely known, it is fairly-certain that it is consisted of all the residents of the village, both young and old. These Committees were chosen, partly by election and partly by lot, from it. The rigorous rules of exclusion would have permitted only the most capable and eligible men to get into them. Their tenure of office was only one year, and this would have given every deserving man an opportunity to serve his village or township. In passing, we may note the theocratic tinge about certain of the rules set out in the inscription, but then we must not forget that the village for which it provides was an Agraharam or Brahman village. Other rules might have obtained in other villages. Also, we may note, that Uttaramallur in these days consisted of 12 hamlets, which were divided into 30 wards for civic purposes. We might in these days term it a town, at least from the census point of view.

15

Aspects of Ancient Indian Society

I
MANNERS AND CIVILIZATION

JOHN ADAM

Ancient Hindus—An Agricultural Community

Wherever the Aryan conquerors came, they cleared forests and introduced agriculture, which was the main industry of the ancient, as it is of modern Hindus. The very name, *A'rya,* by which the conquerors called themselves, is derived from a root which indicates tilling, and there is a beautiful short hymn on ploughing, which may be quoted as the oldest pastoral in the Aryan world.

1. "We will till this field with the Lord of the Field; may he nourish our horses; may he bless us thereby."
2. "O Lord of the Field! bestow on us sweet and pure and butter-like and delicious and copious rain even as cows give us milk. May the Lords of Water bless us."
3. "May the crops be sweet unto us; may the skies and the rains and the firmament be full of sweetness; may the Lord of the Field be gracious to us. We will follow him unharmed by foes."
4. "Let the oxen work merrily; let the men work merrily; let the plough move on merrily. Fasten the traces merrily; ply the goad merrily."

5. "O Suna and Sira! accept this hymn. Moisten this earth with the rain you have created in the sky."
6. "O fortunate Sita (Furrow)! proceed onwards, we pray unto thee. Do thou bestow on us wealth and an abundant crop."
7. "May Indra accept this Sita; may Pushan lead her onwards. May she be filled with water and yield us corn year after year."
8. "Let the ploughshares turn up the sod merrily; let the men follow the oxen merrily; let the god of rains moisten the earth with sweet rains. O Suna and Sira! bestow on us happiness."
—*Rig Veda,* IV. 57.

This ancient agricultural song is marked by that simplicity and joyousness in active pursuits which mark all the most ancient effusions of the Hindus.

Agriculturists and Warriors Both

But cultivation on the Punjab on an extended scale was impossible, except by means of sinking wells and digging irrigation channels, and it is not remarkable that we find allusions to such contrivances in the songs of the Rig Veda. Pasture land too was extensive; chiefs and leaders of men owned large herds of cattle, and warriors and poets prayed to the gods for increase of cattle and of wealth. Society was yet in its infancy, and was not yet marked by a hard and fast division into ranks; and we find in the Rig Veda, as in the pages of Homer, that the same chiefs who owned broad acres and pastured large herds of cattle in times of peace, distinguished themselves as leaders of men in times of war, and returned home after victories to worship their gods at their own firesides with copious libations, and with cakes or the fresh of victims. The earliest records and traditions of all Aryan nations point to this simple stage of civilization, when communities lived by agriculture and by pasture, when division into classes was little known, when all able-bodied men were warriors, and when great chiefs and leaders returned with their people to the plough after the war was over. Such is the picture of early Hindu life which the Rig Veda presents to us.

Animal Food and Drinks

Barley and wheat were the principal produce of the field; and rice was as yet unknown. Animal food was however also largely indulged in, the bull and the ram were frequently sacrificed, and even the flesh of the horse was relished by the earlier Hindus, although in later times the sacrifice of the horse was reserved for imperial festivities only. The juice of the soma plant was a favourite drink, and was copiously used at sacrifices, and the poets of the Rig Veda go into ecstasies over the virtues and powers of this exhilarating beverage. In the end Soma was worshipped as a deity.

Technicians of Gold Ornaments and Iron Weapons

The simpler arts of civilized life were practised by the Punjab Hindus. Carpentry and weaving were well known, and considerable progress was made in the working of metals, of gold and silver and of iron. The weapons of war and various gold ornaments of which we find frequent mention show the progress made in these arts.

Armour and helmets, javelins, swords and arrows, and three thousand warriors covered with mail are spoken of in one remarkable verse (VI. 27, 6). In other places we are told of necklaces and bracelets and anklets, of golden plates for the breast, and of golden crowns for the head (V. 53 and 54, etc.). All these allusions show that a considerable advance was made by the Punjab Hindus in the working of metals.

Architecture too had made some advance, and there are allusions to "mansions with a thousand pillars". But we find no distinct mention of sculpture; and the religion of the early Hindus, which was not idolatrous, did not foster that art.

Religious and Patriarchal Society

The rules of social life were simple and patriarchal. The father of the family was its head, his sons and grandsons with their wives often lived under the same roof, and owned their lands and herds in common. The sacred fire was lighted in the house of every pious householder, the women of the family prepared the soma wine and other sacrificial requisites, and the benignant gods of the sky, firmament, and earth were invoked in simple hymns to be present at the sacrifices and to bestow health and progeny and wealth on the sacrificers. Wives joined their husbands at these domestic sacrifices, and some beautiful hymns are still preserved to us which are said to have been composed by female worshippers.

High Status of Hindu Women

There were no unhealthy restrictions upon Hindu women in those days, no rules to keep them secluded or debarred from their legitimate place in society. A girl generally selected her own husband, but her parents' wishes were for the most part respected. We have frequent allusions to careful and industrious wives who superintended the arrangements of the house, and, like the dawn, roused every one in the morning and sent him to his work. Girls who remained unmarried obtained a share in the paternal property. Widows could re-marry after the death of their husbands.

The ceremony of marriage was an appropriate one, and the promises which the bride and the bridegroom made were suitable to the occasion. We will quote a few verses from a remarkable hymn on this subject:

> (Address to the bride and bridegroom.) "Do ye remain here together; do not be separated. Enjoy food of various kinds; remain in your own home, and enjoy happiness in company of your children and grandchildren."
>
> (The bride and bridegroom say.) "May Prajapati bestow on us children; may Aryaman keep us united till old age."
>
> (Address to the bride.) "Enter, O bride! with auspicious signs the home of thy husband. Do good to our male servants and to our female servants, and to our cattle."
>
> "Be thy eyes free from anger; minister to the happiness of thy husband; do good to our cattle. May thy mind be cheerful, may thy beauty be bright. Be the mother of heroic sons, and be devoted to the gods. Do good to our male servants and to our female servants, and to our cattle."
>
> "O Indra ! make this lady fortunate and the mother of worthy sons. Let ten sons be born of her, so that there may be eleven men with the husband."
>
> (Address to the bride.) "May thou have influence over thy father-in-law and thy mother-in-law, and be as a queen over thy sister-in-law and brother-in-law."
>
> (The bride and bridegroom say.) "May all the gods unite our hearts; may Matarisvan and Dhatri and the goddess of speech unite us together."—*Rig Veda, X*, 85, 42 to 47.

Devoted to her Husband and Family Gods

These few verses give us a clear insight into the patriarchal family system of the olden days. The bride was a new-comer into her husband's family, and she was received with appropriate injuctions. The male servants, the female servants, and the very cattle were of the family, and the bride was asked to be kind and considerate and good to them all. Free from anger, and with a cheerful mind, she must not only minister to her husband's happiness, but be devoted to the gods worshipped in the family, and be kind to all its dependants. She must extend her gentle influence over her husband's father and mother, she must keep under due control his brothers and sisters, and be the queen of the household. And thus she must remain, united to her husband until old age, the virtual mistress of a large and patriarchal family, and respected and honoured as Hindu women were honoured in ancient times.

Polygamy Allowed

Polygamy was allowed in ancient India as it was allowed among all ancient nations; but it was probably confined to kings and great chiefs only. The ordinary people were content with one wife. Sons inherited the property of their father, and in the absence of sons, the daughter's son or some other boy might be adopted.

Hopes of a Future World—No Hell Mentioned

Burial was probably the first form of funeral ceremony among ancient Hindus; but this was soon followed by cremation, and the ashes were than buried in the earth. A few verses from the funeral service will interest, and will show that the hopes of a future world cheered the last moments of a Hindu's life in ancient times, as they do at the present day.

"O thou deceased ! proceed to the same place where our forefathers have gone, by the same path which they followed. The two kings Yama and Varuna are pleased with the offerings; go and meet them.

"Proceed to that happy heaven and mix with our forefathers. Meet Yama, and reap the fruits of thy virtuous deeds. Leave sin behind, enter thy home.

"O ye shades ! leave this place, go away, move away. For the forefathers have prepared a place for the deceased. That place is beautiful with day, with sparkling waters and light. Yama assigns this place for the dead."—*Rig Veda,* X, 14, 7 to 9.

It is remarkable that there is no mention of hell and its tortures in the Rig Veda.

II
ANCIENT SOCIETY AS REVEALED IN THE DHARMASUTRAS*

DR. SURES CHANDRA BANERJI

The Dharmasutras constitute one of the most valuable literary sources for the reconstruction of the social history of ancient India. Prof. P.V. Kane is inclined to place the period of composition of the principal works on Dharmasutra between 600 and 100 B.C. There may be differences of opinion about the period of their composition. But, their high antiquity admits of no doubt whatsoever.

From a study of the major Dharmasutra treatises, hitherto available in print, we propose herein to deal with the following aspects of Indian society reflected in them:—

(1) Varnasrama-dharma,
(2) Administration of secular law and royal duties,
(3) Manners, morals and customs,
(4) Superstitions,
(5) Apaddharma.

1. VARNASRAMA-DHARMA

Introductory Remarks

The DS. literature deals with the rights and duties of men belonging to the four castes and four stages of life. We propose here to systematise the information, scattered all over the works, in a critical manner, making, at the same time, a comparative study of the contents of the different works on particular topics. Such a survey will enable

*The following abbreviations have been used in this article:
A—Apastamba-Dharmasutra, Banaras, 1932.
B—Baudhayana-Dharmasutra, Banaras, 1934.
DS.—Dharmasutras.
G—Gautama-dharmasutra, Mysore, 1917.
HG.—Haradalla's Com. (Mitaksara) on Gautama-dhannsutra, Poona, 1931.
MB.—Maskari-bhasya, Com. on *G* above.
U—Ujjvala, Haradalla's Com. on *A* above.
V—Vasistha-dharmasastra, Bombay, 1883.
Vai.—Vaijayanti (See Nand., above).
VI— Visnu-smrti, Calcutta, 1881.
V.K.—Vaikhanasa-smarta-sutra, Calcutta, 1927.
Vna.—Vivarana, Com. of Govindasvamin, on *B* above.

us to have glimpses of the social, cultural and religious outlook of the people of those remote times, if not of the actual conditions prevailing in those far-off ages.

Different Castes

The four principal castes, viz., Brahmana, Ksatriya, Vaisya and Sudra, constitute the social set-up. The mixed castes owe their origin to the intermixture of these castes either in the regular (*anuloma*) or in the reverse order (*pratiloma*). All people, outside the pale of the caste-system, are regarded as casteless and impure with whom association of those belonging to one or other of the castes is condemned. A place, where the rules of castes and of the four stages of life are not observed, is branded as *'mleccha-desa'* a sojourn to which renders a member of any of the castes liable to expiation.

According to *A.*[1] in the list of castes enumerated above, each preceding is superior to each succeeding one. Besides the four principal castes which may be called pure, the DS. mention a number of sub-castes or rather mixed castes. The various castes originating from all kinds of permutation and combination of castes may be classified as follows:

Anuloma—One begotten by a man of the higher caste from a female of the lower caste.

Antarala—Begotten by a *anulomaja* man on an *anulomaja* woman.

Pratiloma—The reverse of *anuloma.*

Vratya—Begotten by a *pratilomaja* male upon a *pratilomaja* female.

We name the various mixed castes below, and describe them according to the different works on DS.

Abhisikta[2]: Son of a Brahmana father begotten secretly upon a Ksatriya maiden.

Adhonapita[3]: Son of an Ambastha by a Ksatriya. (Ambastha defined below).

Ambastha[4]: Born of the union of Ksatriya and Vaisya[5]. Issue of a Brahmana and a Vaisya[6].

Ayogava[7]: According to *MB.*, born of a Sudra male and Vaisya female (G). Issue of a Vaisya by a Ksatriya[8].

Bhrjyakantha[9]: Issue of a Brahmana by a Vaisya wife.

Bhoja[10]: Son of a Ksatriya by a Ksatriya, born secretly, the sacred rites not having been performed.

Cakrin[11]: Son of a Vaisya paramour by a Brahmana girl.
Candala[12]: Born of a Sudra and a Brahmani.
Carmakara[13]: Son of a Vaidehaka and a Brahmani. (For Vaidehaka, see *infra.*)
Cucuka[14]: Son of a Vaisya and a Sudra.
Dausyanta[15]: Issue of a Ksatriya and a Sudra.
Dhivara[16]: Born to a Vaisya by a Ksatriya wife.
Karana[17]: Issue of a Vaisya by a Sudra.
Karmakara[18]: Son of a Madgu and a Ksatriya.
Ksatta[19]: Born of a Vaisya and a Brahmani.[20] Born of a Sudra and a Nisadi (B). (For Nisadi, see *infra.*)
Manikara[21]: Son of a Vaisya by Vaisya wife, the marriage rite not having been performed.
Matsyahadku[22]: Son of a Cucuka by a girl of the Ksatriya caste.
Magadha[23]: Born of the union of a Vaisya and a Ksatriya (*MB.*). *G.*[24] defines this as an issue of a Brahmani and a Vaisya. Born to a Sudra by a Vaisya (*B.*).
Son of a Vaisya father and a Brahmana mother (*VK*).
Malavaka[25]: Son of a Sudra paramour by a Sudra female.
Mahisya[26]: Issue of a Ksatriya by a Vaisya wife.
Murdhabhhisikta[27]: Born of the union of a Brahmana and a Ksatriya.
Navika[28]: Son of an Ambastha father and a Brahmana mother.
Nisada[29]: Born of a Brahmana and a Vaisya[30]. Born of the union of a Brahmana and a Sudra (*B.*).
Parasava[31]: Issue of a Brahmana and a Sudra.[32]
Pulinda[33]: Begotten by a Vaisya paramour on a Ksatriya.
Pulkasa[34]: Born of the union of Sudra and a Ksatriya[35].
Issue of a Nisada by a Sudra (*B.*).
Rajaka[36]: Born of the union of a Pulkasa and a Brahmana woman. (for *Pulkasa* see above.)
Rathakara[37]: Son of a Ksatriya paramour by a Brahmani (*VK.*). Born of the union of a Vaisya and a Sudra (*B.*)
Savarna[38]: Son of a Brahmana father and a Ksatriya mother.
Sucika[39]: Son of a Vaidehaka by a Ksatriya woman.
Sulika[40]: Begotten by a Ksatriya paramour of a Sudra girl.
Suta[41]: Born of a Ksatriya and a Brahmani[42].
Son of a Ksatriya father and a Brahmani mother.
Svapaka[43]: Issue of an Ugra by a Ksatta wife.
(For *Ugra,* see *infra.*)
Svapaca[44]: Son of a Candala by a Brahmani girl.

Taskara[45]: Son of a Cucuka and a Brahmana maiden. (For *Cucuka,* see *supra.*)

Tamra[46]: Begotten by an Ayogava on a Brahmani maiden. (For *Ayogava* see *supra*).

Udbandhaka[47]: Son of a Khanaka and a Brahmani maiden.

Ugra[48]: Issue of a Ksatriya and a Sudra[49]. Issue of a Vaisya and a Sudra (*G.*).

Vaidehaka[50]: Born to a Vaisya by a Brahmani woman (*B.*). Born of a Sudra and a Vaisya woman.[51]

Vaina[52]: Born to a Vaidehaka by an Ambastha wife.

Velava[53]: Begotten secretly by a Sudra on a Ksatriya woman.

Venuka[54]: Son of a Madgu and a Brahmani maiden.

Yavana[55]: Born to a Ksatriya by a Sudra.

Duties of Castes

The general duties of the four castes are clearly laid down by *V.*[56] Those of a Brahmana are:

(i) Vedic study, (ii) Teaching, (iii) Performance of sacrifice for ownself as well as for others, (iv) Making gifts, and (v) Acceptance of gifts.

The duties of a Ksatriya consist in (i) Study, (ii) Sacrifice, and (iii) Making gifts.

Protection of people by weapons is the means of livelihood of Ksatriyas.

Besides the above, a Vaisya has the following to do:—

(i) Agriculture, (ii) Commerce, (iii) Rearing of cattle, and (iv) Lending money at interest (*Kusida*).

For the Sudra, the only duty is the service of the higher castes.

V. lays down that a member of a particular caste, when unable to maintain himself by his own avocation, may take to the occupation of the next inferior caste, but never to that of the higher one. But a Brahmana or a Ksatriya, if compelled to adopt the occupation of a Vaisya, is debarred from dealing in the following commodities:

Stones, salt, jewels, hempen cloth (*sana*), silk (*Kauseya*), linen cloth (*ksauma*) and skins, dyed cloth of all kinds (*tantavam, raktam*), prepared food (*Krtanna*), flowers, fruits, roots, perfumes for flavouring food, water, juice extracted from plants, *soma,* weapons, poison, flesh milk and its preparations, iron, tin (*trapu*), lac (*jatu*), lead, tame animals with uncloven hoofs and having an abundance of hair, wild animals, birds, beasts having tusks, sesamum produced by others.

The practice of lending money at interest is also condemned for Brahmans and Ksatriyas.

Vi. points out that the three regenerate classes (*dvija*) are distinguished from the other caste by this that the rites, connected with the former from *niseka* (impregnation) down to funeral practices, are accompanied by the recitation of incantations (*mantravat*).

But for certain minor differences, *Vi.* generally agrees with the previous works on the occupation to be followed by the different castes. The innovations, introduced by *Vi.*, are as follows: *'Yoniposana'*, i.e., storing seeds,[57] has been mentioned as an additional duty of the Vaisya. Another thing that deserves mention is that *Vi.* allows a Sudra to resort to all kinds of art (*Sarva*[58] *-silpani*)[59]; besides the service of the higher castes.

Besides the specific occupations of the particular castes, the following are mentioned by *Vi.* as duties common to all the castes:—

Forbearance, truthfulness, restraint (*dama*), purity, liberality, self-control, non-violence (*ahimsa*), service of Guru (*guru-susrusa*), visiting places of pilgrimage, kindness, straightforwardness (*arjava*), freedom from covetousness, reverence towards gods and Brahmanas, freedom from jealousy (*anabhyasuya*).

As regards the duties and occupations of the castes, *VK.* agrees substantially with the previous works. In the case of Sudras, if adds agriculture only besides the usual service of the three superior castes.

Stages of Life

The four well-known stages of life are recognised. It must, however, be pointed out that there is no agreement among the works with regard to the name and order of the four stages. The number and order of the stages, according to *G.*[60] are:

> (i) that of the student (*brahmacari*), (ii) that of the householder (*grhastha*), (iii) that of the ascetic (*bhiksu*), and (iv) that of the hermit (*vaikhanasa*).

B.[61] agrees with *V.* in designating a person in .the third and the fourth stage as *vanaprastha* and *parivrajaka* respectively.

A.[62] enumerates the stages in the following order:—

(i) Garhasthya, (ii) Acarya-kula, (iii) Mauna, and (iv) Vanaprastha.

A. prescribes duties for *a parivrajaka,* i.e., one who renounces the world in quest of the soul (*atman*). This, however, does not appear to have been a compulsory stage if life to be resorted to by all, but one that might be adopted by one at one's option, because *A.* provides that one can take recourse to this life just after studenthood.[63] A man, resorting to this mode of livelihood, shall forsake all kinds of *agnikarya* (rites to be performed in fire), renounces home (*aniketa*), and give up all desires for wordly pleasures (*asarma*), shall not seek anybody's shelter (*asarana*), shall observe silence except while performing Vedic studies, beg in villages only as much food as is necessary for keeping alive (*pranavarttl*).[64] He shall abandon all things conducive to meterial welfare or to benefit in the life hereafter (*anihomutra*). He shall wear things thrown away by others[65] or go naked.[66]

From the trend of *A.'s* discussion on the different stages of life, it appears that, according to him, it was not compulsory for one to go through all the stages in succession. In other words, *A.* does not seem to have divided the life of a *dvija* into these stages. What *A* appears to mean is that one might choose any one of these modes of life; *brahmcarya,* however, was the basis of all of them.[67] Thus, directly from *brahmacarya* one might proceed to the life of *parivrajaka*[68] or of a *vanaprastha.*[69]

The order of the last two stages in *G's* list is reversed by *VK.* which also replaces the designation *vaikhanasa* by *vanaprastha.*

Duties in Different Stages

The general rules to be observed in the stages irrespective of caste, are as follows:—

Brahmacarya

The entrance to this stage is marked by the ceremony of initiation to Vedic studies (*upanayana,* lit. "taking near", i.e., near the preceptor).[70] The chief rules, to be observed by a student, consist in regular Vedic study, implicit obedience to the preceptor, begging alms,[71] and strict discipline in daily life.[72] The great importance, attached to *upanayana* by the *DS.,* can be gauged from the restrictions imposed on an uninitiated person who is debarred from offering oblations to the fire (*agni-havana*) and from giving offerings (*baliharana*). Such a person is not allowed to recite most of the Vedic texts.

Rules of rigid self-control are to be strictly observed by a student.

He must abstain from rich and intoxicating food such as *mamsa, madhu,* articles of luxury like perfumes, garlands, etc. He is debarred from participating in amusements of all kinds including dancing, music, etc. He cannot sleep by day, must avoid conveyances, umbrellas and footwears. Association with women, nay, even gazing at them, must be shunned by all means. *G*[73] sums up the rules of self-control by saying that the student should keep in subjection his speech, arms and stomach.

It is interesting to add the that, as a rule, corporal punishment is prohibited for a pupil.[74] When no other course is possible (*asaktau*), he may be punished with a thin rope or cane.[75] Teachers are forbidden from striking their pupils with any other thing on pain of punishment to be inflicted by the king.[76]

As regards the period of stay at the preceptor's house, *G.* does not appear to have fixed any limit,[77] although it prescribes twelve years' stay for one Veda or twelve years each for the other Vedas. From *G.* it appears that, for a person, the study of one of the Vedas only was required and that of the others was optional. A fee was to be paid to the teacher on the completion of instructions. Then the pupil was to perform ablution marking the completion of the period of his studenthood.

The teacher, according to some, or, the mother, according to others, is regarded as the chief among all the *gurus.*

B. declares that one is on a level with the Sudra before one's *upanayana.*

With regard to the period of studentship, *B.* says that it is forty-eight years according to the ancients.[78] *B* appears to have allowed the following alternatives in the matter:

> (i) Twenty-four or twelve years for each Veda, (ii) At least one year (*samvatsaravama*) for each *kanda*, and (iii) Until the Veda has been learnt.

According to *B.*, the persons fit to be approached by a student for alms are the Brahmanas and so forth (*brahmanadyah*) who follow their own occupations (*svakarmasthah*).

B., like *G*, ordains strict obedience on the part of the student to his teacher. But the former, unlike the latter, does not assume a teacher to be above all faults, and provides for the impunity of a student transgressing such order of the teacher as, if followed, will cause loss of his caste.

As a measure of self-control, the student, after reaching puberty, is debarred even from saluting the young wives of brothers and of teachers.

The rule that one may study under a non-Brahmana teacher in times of distress[79] implies that normally one was required to study under a Brahmana.

A. clearly explains the significance of the term *'dvija'. A.*[80] declares that a teacher gives the student his intellectual birth which is far superior to the physical birth given by his parents. The initiation to Vedic studies was regarded as indispensable, so much so that all kinds of social intercourse was prohibited with a man whose two immediate ancestors remained uninitiated or the initiation of whose ancestors up to the great-grandfather and of one's ownself was not remembered.

According to *A.*, the shortest period of a student's residence at his teacher's house is twelve years (*dvadasavarardhyam*). But, the following alternatives are also allowed:

(i) Forty-eight years, (ii) Thirty-six years, and (iii) Twenty-four years.

As regards the rules to be observed by a student, *VK.* generally agrees with the other works. Of the *brahmacarins. VK.* distinguishes four kinds,[81] viz.,

(1) Gayatra, (2) Brahma, (3) Prajapatya, and (4) Naisthika.

Garhasthya

This stage of life has been described by *G.* as the source (*yoni*) of the other stages, because others do not produce any offspring. *V.*[82] holds that this stage of life excels all others. *V.*[83] gives a very happy analogy. It compares a grhastha to a sea. Just as all rivers flow into the ocean, so also people in all other stages of life resort to the *grhastha. V.*[84] further says that, as all creatures live by resorting to their mother, so also all those who live by begging (*bhiksukah*) live by resorting to the *grhastha.* The life of a householder, as described in *DS.*, does not appear to be one of ease and luxury. The householder is required to spend his days through a round of duties prescribed by the *sastras.* Of his various daily duties, the most important are the following:

(1) Performance of the sacrifices in honour of gods, Manes and human beings,[85] and Vedic study. Of these sacrifices, the first

is the performance of the rite, known as Vaisvadeva[86]. The second, the *pitryajna* as it is called, consists in feeding Brahmanas for the benefit of the Manes. The third, the *manusya-yajna* or *nr-yajna,* means the performance of the rites of hospitality towards guests. Vedic study is called *rsi-puja* or *brahma-yajna.*

(2) *Bali-karma* also called *bhuta-yajna.*
This consists in offerings to the presiding deities of the different directions after the performance of the rite known as Vaisvadeva.

(3) Giving water to the gods, the Manes and the *rsis.*

All domestic rites (*grhyani*) are to be performed in the sacred fire which must be preserved either from the time of one's marriage, or from the partition of one's family property.

While making gifts is generally commended by *G.,* for a householder it has been said to particularly meritorious when made to a Brahmana who has mastered all the Vedas (*veda-paragah*). The following classes of people have been especially recommended as deserving gifts:

(1) Persons begging for their preceptors, (2) Those who are in need of money for defraying expenses of wedding, (3) The sick requiring medicine, (4) Destitute, (5) Those who want to perform a sacrifice, (6) Those engaged in study, (7) Travellers, and (8) Those who have performed the *Visvajit*[87] sacrifice.

But, gifts for an unlawful purpose have been expressly condemned even though one may have promised to make such a gift.[88]

The householder is required to lead a life of self-restraint. Besides being abstemious in his food and drink, he must be restrained in enjoying his wife. He must meet his wife after her monthly illness[89] and must avoid sexual intercourse on festive occasions.[90]

Besides showing due consideration to all the members of his family, particularly the females and the children, the householder is to accord cordial reception to his guests. A guest is described by *G.*[91] as one who, belonging to a different village and intending to stay for one night only, arrives when the sun's rays pass over the trees (*adhivrksa-suryo-pasthayi*).[92] The status of the guests and their castes and relationship with the *grhastha* are factors which determine the manner of reception deserved by them. *Madhuparka*[93] should be used in welcoming one's priest, teacher, father-in-law, paternal or maternal uncles and in entertaining them in a sacrifice or wedding ceremony. A Brahmana guest is to be especially honoured. Among other things, he must be given water for washing his feet (*padya*), special offerings (*arghya*) and food of a superior quality (*anna-visesa*).

With regard to the duties of a householder, *B* substantially agrees with *G.* Unlike *G., B.* ordains that the sacred fire, in which all the religious ceremonies are to be performed, must be kindled at the wedding[94] ceremony.

A. gives very elaborate rules about the life of a householder. We note below only the chief rules in which it differs from *G. A.,* prohibits connubial intercourse in the day-time. It allows this act subject to the restrictions imposed by the *sastras,* but allows it in the interval also provided the wife's consent is obtained.

The slave of a Brahmana householder should fetch rice from the royal store, and honour a Sudra guest. *A.* also lay great stress on the proper reception of guests.[95] But, according to *A.*, a guest is one who approaches a *grhastha* for the fulfilment of religious duties and not for any other purpose.[96] The prevalence of beef-eating, at the time of the composition of Apastamba's work is clearly proved by the rules[97] which provide for the offering of cows to distinguished guests, e.g., one who has mastered the Veda, preceptor, the priest known as *rtvik,* a *snataka,* a king, father-in-law.

V. does not add materially to the above rules. It however, defines a guest as 'a Brahmana who stays for one night only.'[98]

Vi. classifies the property, acquired by a householder of any caste, into[99]:

> (1) White—what has been acquired by the mode of livelihood prescribed for his caste, (2) Mottled—what has been acquired by a man by the made of livelihood of the caste next inferior to his own, (3) Black—what has been acquired by the mode of livelihood of the caste lower, by two or three degrees, than his own.

Each preceding in the above list is better than the succeeding one.

Vi. gives elaborate rules to be observed by the householder in his daily life. An important rule deserving mention is that he must not converse with *mlecchas, antyajas* and *patitas.*[100]

Vi. agrees with *V.* in the definition *of 'atithi'* or guest, and, like the other works, dwells, at considerable length, on the mode of reception to be accorded to various kinds of guests.

The duties, prescribed by *VK.* for a householder, are substantially the same as those found in the other works. But, *VK.* introduces an innovation by classifying householders into four kinds[101], viz. (1) *Varta-vrtti,* (2) *Salina-vrtti,* (3) *Yayavara, and* (4) *Ghoracarika.*

Bhaiksva[102] : Life of ascetic—

The rules, to be observed by a man in this stage of life, are not ro elaborate as those prescribed for the preceding stages. The chief rules are that an ascetic cannot possess any store. Living at one place during the rainy season, he will enter a village only in order to beg. He will live a life of strict discipline and self-restraint and be kind and sympathetic to all creatures.

V. the *'parivrajaka'* of which coıresponds to this stage, allows an ascetic to live in a village at his option.[103] *Vanaprastha* : Life of a hermit:

The chief rules to be observed by a hermit are as follows:— Dressed in bark, he will dwell at a place outside the village, and sustain himself by roots, fruits, leaves and grass and by gleaned corns.

B. classifies *Vanaprasthas* in the following manner:

A. Pacamanakas —those who cook their food—

(a) *Sarvaranyakas*—those who eat everything available in the forest, (i) *indravasiktas*— those subsisting on forest produce generated by Indra, e.g., lianas, shrubs, creepers, (ii) *retovasiktas*— those subsisting on forest produce generated from semen, e.g., flesh of animals slain by tigers, wolves, and other carnivorous beasts, (b) *Vaitusikas*— those who live upon unhusked grains, (c) *Kanda-mula-bhaksah*— those who live upon bulbs and roots, (d) *Phala-bhaksah*—those who eat pot-herbs and fruits.

B. Apacamanakas—those who do not cook their food.

(a) Unmajjakas—those who avoid the use of instrument made of iron and stone, (b) Pravrttasins—those who eat their food with their hands, (c) Mukhenadayins—those who take their food with the mouth only (like beasts), (d) Toyaharas—those who subsist on water only, and (e) Vayubhaksas—those who eat nothing.

VK. however, gives the following classifications of *Vanaprasthas*[104]:

(1) Sapatnika—with wife, (i) Audumbara, (ii) Vairifica, (iii) Balakhilya, (iv) Phenapa, (2) Apatnika—without wife.

Of this class there are numerous sub-divisions[105] which are as follows:

Kalasika, uddata-samvrtta, asmakutta, udagraphali, danto-lukhala, unchavrttika, samdarsana-vrttika, kapota-vrttika, mrga-carika, hastadayi, saila-phalakadi, arka-dag-dhasi, baivasi, kusumasi' pandu-patrasi, kalantara-bhoji, eka-kalika, catus-kalika, kantaka-sayi, virasana-sayi, pancagni-madhya-sayi, dhumasi, pasana-sayi abhyavagahi, udakumbha-vasi, mauni, avak-siras, surya-pratimukha, urddhva-vahuka, eka-pada-sthita.

2. ADMINISTRATION OF SECULAR LAW AND ROYAL DUTIES

Administration of Justice

G. lays down that the administration of justice shall be regulated by the Veda, the Institutes of the sacred law, the Angas and the Purans.

The king is advised to come to a decision regarding a matter concerning a class of people after consulting those who have authority'over that particular class. Of such classes of people are mentioned cultivators, traders, herdsmen, money-lenders, artisans, etc.

In the cases of conflicting evidence, the king will have to arrive at a decision after consulting Brahmanas versed in the Vedas,

Rural Administration

Vi. lays down a very interesting system of administration. A village has been taken as the unit of administration. A man will be appointed at the head of each village. Ten villages together will have one chief. Every hundred villages will have one higher chief, and a whole district will have a lord. A wrong done in a village will be righted by the village-chief. On his failure, he will bring it to the notice of the chief of ten villages. Each succeeding chief in the above order will have higher authority.

Departmental Officials

The king should appoint able officials to look after his various departments, viz., Mines, Taxes, Fares to be paid at ferries, Elephants,

Forests, etc. Persons, placed in charge of different departments, must be endowed with requisite qualities. Thus, for financial business, skilled men will be appointed; for fighting brave men. and so on. It is interesting to note that enunchs are recommended for protecting the harem of the king.

Taxation

The rates of tax, to be levied by the king, should be as follows:

1. Sixth part of annual produce in the case of grains and seeds. 2. Two per cent, in the cases of cattle, gold and clothes, 3. Sixth part of flesh, honey, clarified butter, herbs, perfumes, flowers, roots, fruits, liquids, condiments, wood, skins, earthen pots, stone vessels, things made of split bamboo.

A tenth part of the marketable commodities, sold within the country of the king, shall have to be paid as duty. A twentieth part is fixed on exported commodities. The goods of a man, fraudulently avoiding the toll-house, are to be forfeited.

Subversive Activities

Proper punishment is ordained for those who try to subvert the constituent elements of a state, viz., Monarch, Council his Fortress, Treasury, Army, Realm, King's ally.

Espionage

Vi. provides for the appointment of spies to secure information both in the king's realm as well as in that of his enemy.

Political Expedients

Towards his neighbouring kings, who may be allied to him, neutral or inimically disposed, the king should adopt, according to the exigencies of the situation, the four modes of obtaining success, viz., negotiation (*sama*), division (*bheda*), presents (*dana*), and force of arms (*danda*).

According to the exigencies of the situation, the king should have resort to the six measures, viz., alliance (*sanahi*), war (*vigraha*), marching to battle (*yana*); sitting encamped (*asana*), seeking the protection of a more powerful king (*samsraya*), and distributing his forces (*dvaidhibhava*).

Conquered Territory

A very practical piece of advice has been given by *Vi.* to the king by holding that, after conquering the country of his foe, he should not abolish all the laws prevailing there.

Treasure-trove

Of a treasure-trove, the king should give one-half to the Brahmanas, and take the other half himself. A Brahmana, coming across a treasure-trove, may keep the whole of it.

Minor's Property

The king is required to protect the properties of minors, of helpless persons having no guide and of women having no guardians.

Recovered Stolen Goods

Regarding recovered stolen goods, *Vi.* ordains that the king must restore the entire property to the owner. That the recovery of a stolen thing was regarded as a bounden duty of the king is clearly proved by *Vi's* rule that a king, failing to recover such a property, must make good the loss sustained by the owner.

3. MANNERS, MORALS AND CUSTOMS[106]

The *DS.* yield a good deal of information on the manners and morals of the society which they represent. We propose herein to note the salient features in their practices and moral outlook. For the sake of convenience, we shall deal with the subject under each of the four stages of life.

The Stage of a Brahmacarin[107]

The *acarya* is held in high esteem. He is to be saluted every morning. Before proceeding to study, the student is to request the teacher to begin his lecture. This request is to be made by the pupil after touching one foot[108] of the preceptor. The pupil, seated on the *darbha* grass to the right of the teacher, facing east or south, shall proceed to study only when asked by the teacher to do so. If anybody passes between the teacher and the taught, the student has to follow anew the procedure necessary for commencing his study. The names of the preceptor, his son and his wife must not be uttered by the pupil. The bed or seat of the pupil must be lower than those of the preceptor.

The student should retire to bed after his preceptor, but get up before him.

The reply to a question, asked by the preceptor, must be given by the pupil after rising from his seat. He should always engage himself in doing what is pleasant and beneficial not only to the preceptor but also to the preceptor's wife and sons. But he must not eat the leavings of the food of the preceptor's wife and son, nor should be bathe them or help them in toilet, nor wash their feet and salute them by touching their feet.[109]

Daily prayers are to be said at both junctures of the day, in the standing posture in the morning and sitting till stars are visible in the evening.

In the presence of superiors, he should avoid the following practices:

> Putting a piece of cloth on the neck, placing a foot on the knee (avasakthika), sitting on a raised spot, stretching the feet.

The following are to be avoided in the presence of all: spitting, laughing, yawning, cracking the fingers (avasphotana).

A student is forbidden to use harsh words to anybody, and is required to practise control over his speech, arms and the stomach.

A brahmacarin may beg food of members of "all the castes" (*sarva-varnika*) excepting those who are known as abhisasta[110] and *patita* (degraded or apostate). It is not very clear as to whether by 'all castes' *G.* includes Sudras also. The following sutra[111] provides that, in begging, the word 'bhavat' should be used at the beginning, in the middle and at the end (of the address at the time of begging) by the members of the three castes in order. If alms be not obtained from the persons noted above, a brahmacarin should approach the following persons in the order in which they are mentioned[112] preceptor, *jnati* (sapinda, according to commentators/guru (=matula, etc.). The food, obtained by alms, must at first be given to the preceptor and then taken for himself with his permission. In the absence of the preceptor, such food should be made over to the preceptor's wife, son or fellow-students. The brahmacarin shall drink water before eating, keep silent throughout the process of eating, and avoid over-eating.

The preceptor should refrain from inflicting corporal punishment on his students. In exceptional cases, however, where the student proves extremely unruly, and otherwise unmanageable, he may be given slight physical punishment.[113] Heavy physical punishment for a student has been condemned as a crime.[114]

At the conclusion of Vedic studies, the student should ask his preceptor what he should do for him (preceptor). Having acted up to his order, the student should, with his permission, take the ablution marking the completion of Vedic studies.

B.[115] gives us the additional information that, in begging, the word *'Bhavat'* should be used in the beginning, 'bhiksa' in the middle and a word indicating 'prayer' at the end.[116] This, together with the subsequent sutra, appears to have been meant for the Brahmana alone. In the case of Ksatriyas and Vaisyas, the word 'bhavat' should be used in the middle and at the end respectively. *B.*[117] clearly provides that members of all the castes (sarvesu varnesu) may be approached for begging. The immediately following sutra requires that the persons, to be approached for the purpose, must be Brahmanas, etc., following their own occupations.[118] Govindasvamin, presumably in consonance with the practice prevalent in his time, says that here Sudras are excluded; what is meant is that the members of the regenerate classes alone are to approached, and among them those who follow their own avocations (sva-karma) are to be preferred to others.

B. does not push devotion to one's preceptor too far. *B.*[119] requires the student to obey the preceptor, but not as implicity as *G.* appears to ordain. The same sutra of *B.* allows the student to transgress his preceptor's order when, if carried out, this may lead to the student's degradation. According to *B.*[120] while saluting the teacher, the student is to announce his own name besides touching the ears. Another person, of pure conduct, shall also be saluted at the order of the preceptor. With sacrificial wood, a pitcher of water, flowers and rice in hand, one should neither salute others nor be saluted by others.

A student should hold the umbrella on his teacher, help him in toilet, bath, etc., and eat the leavings of his food.[121] For the teacher's son also he should do all these things except eating the remnants of his food. For the wife of the preceptor, however, he shall do none of these.

In times of emergency (apat), when Brahmanas are not available (brahmanabhavah-*Vna.*), one can study with a person 'other than a Brahmana'. Govindasvamin explains *abrahmana* as a member of any of the two other higher castes but not Sudras Such a teacher shall be served and obeyed like the regular teacher.

The[122] additional information that *A.* gives us is that a brahmacarin should not partake of what has been offered in a Sraddha or to a deity. He should avoid day-sleep.

The student is required by *A.* not to be angry with or jealous of anybody.

A. also provides for the pupil's eating the leaving of such food of his preceptor as is not condemned by Sruti.[123] He can also take the leavings of the food of his father and elder brother.

A. gives an additional rule that a pupil should carry a pitcher of water in the morning and evening.[124] Blind obedience to the preceptor is forbidden by *A.*[125] who allows a student to point out to him, in private, any breach of rule that may have been committed by the latter either inadvertently or wilfully. The next two sutras ordain that, if the preceptor does not desist even after that, the student himself shall perform the duty neglected by the former, or dissuade him.[126]

Strict discipline on the part of the student is very strongly advocated in *A.*[127]

Regarding the castes, from which food can be begged, *A.*[128] is absolutely clear. If allows a *brahmacarin* always to beg food, for his *Acarya,* of not only Sudras but also of Ugras.[129] This is the opinion of others (*eke*) cited, apparently with the approval by *A.* In the previous rule, *A.* provides for such a measure in times of emergency.

A.[130] forbids a student to indulge in self-applause and censure of others.

A. requires a student to treat his preceptor's wife just like the preceptor himself subject to the restriction that the former should not be saluted, and that the leavings of her food must not be taken. Apart from the remnants of food, the rules of a student's conduct towards his preceptor's son are exactly like those towards the preceptor. The same rules to be observed by a student towards his preceptor's wife should also be observed by him with respect to one who teaches him at the direction of the preceptor, and to a fellow-student who is superior to him in age and learning.

They[131] hardly prescribe any noteworthy additional rules. Of them, Visnu adds one noticeable innovation. He maintains that, for purposes of begging, a brahmacarin shall approach qualified persons (gunavatsu) excepting those who belong to the family of the guru.[132] It should be noted that none of these writers imposes any restriction on the caste of the person to be approached for begging.

THE STAGE OF A GRHASTHA

General Rules, Especially with Regard to Guests

G.[133] ordains that one should feed the following persons, first of all:—guest, a child, diseased person, a pregnant woman, daughter and sister.[134] The proper reception and entertainment of guests is regarded by the authors of DS. as a bounden duty of a householder. For example, *A.*[135] maintains that the honouring of guests leads to peace on the part of the host in this life, and to the attainment of heaven after death. There is some divergence of opinion among the authors about the technical meaning of the term 'atithi'. The definition given by *V.* is very clear. According to this work, an *atithi* (< na tithi) is so called because of his not staying permanently (anitya). *V.*[136] defines *atithi* as a Brahmana who stays for one night. This definition does not take non-Brahmanas into account. It may be that *V.* defines an atithi in relation to Brahmanas alone. The next verse of *V.* excludes a co-villager from this category. *G.'s* definition of atithi[137] substantially agrees with that of *V.* with this difference that the former does not specify the caste of the atithi.

If the preceptor, father or friend comes to the house, the householder should offer him food and follow his bidding. According to *G.* such distinguished guests as rtvik, acarya, svasura, pitrvya (uncle), matula, etc. must be welcomed with madhuparka. A king, who is a *srotriya* (lit. a Brahmana versed in the Vedas), is entitled to the same honour. A king of other castes shall be offered a seat and water. A srotriya Brahmana must be offered water for washing feet, (arghya) and special kinds of food (anna-visesa). A householder, who is unable to receive a guest in the manner described above, shall welcome him with sweet words.[138] To guests, who are either superior or equal to the host, the latter must offer bed, seat, place in the house (avasatha), etc., which should be like those used by the latter himself.[139] Besides, the host shall move behind such a guest and honour him in other ways.

A guest of the Brahmana or the Ksatriya caste is to be welcomed with the words *kusala* and *anamaya* respectively. A Vaisya and a Sudra are to be addressed with the word 'arogya'.[140] *A.*[141] provides that a Brahmana guest, who has not studied the Vedas, should not be welcomed by rising from the seat. He should, however, be offered a seat, water, food, etc. If he is otherwise worthy of this honour,[142] he should be welcomed in this manner. Guests of the Ksatriya and Vaisya castes also are to be treated similarly.[143]

G.[144] appears to mean that, of a Brahmana, no other person than a Brahmana can be an atithi in the technical sense of the term, except when the non-Brahmana guests are invited to a sacrifice. Of the non-Brahmana guests, who are not entitled to as respectful a reception as the Brahmana guests, the Ksatriya is to be fed after the Brahmana gueet. The guests of the other castes are to be fed along with the servants. *A.*[145] ordains that a Sudra guest should be engaged (in drawing water, etc.) and then fed. *A.*[146] refers to the interesting custom that the servants of the host used to bring food from the king's house (raja-kula) for the entertainment of Sudra guests.[147]

G.[148] hints at the fact that the guests of the castes other than Brahmana and Ksatriya are to be entertained merely from the point of view of humanity, because these people, not being atithis properly speaking, are not legitimately entitled to such reception.

Manner of Salutation

After returning from abroad, one should salute, by touching the feet, of the parents, their bandhus[149] who are older in age, teacher and the teacher of the father, etc.[150] When these superiors are present together, the one who is the most revered should be saluted first. In saluting, one should, first of all, announce one's own name, Superior women, excepting mother, aunt and sister, should not be saluted on any occasion other than on returning from abroad.[151] *G.*[152] prohibits the salutation, by touching feet, of elder brother's wife and mother-in-law.[153] The rtvik priest, father-in-law, uncle maternal and paternal—these persons, if younger in age, should be respected merely by rising from the seat.

THE STAGE OF A VANAPRASTHA

General Rules

The movements of a vanaprastha are restricted within the forest. He cannot live on a piece of cultivated land, nor can he enter the village.[154] He will wear matted locks, cira (he., made of darbha grass, etc.) and ajina (i.e., carma or skin). *A.*[155] inform us that a man, intending to resort to this mode of life, may go to the forest either alone or with his wife and children. *Vi.* attempts to fix a particular time in the life of a grahstha for his taking to this stage of life, although it does not specify the age. *Vi.*[156] lays down that a grhastha should enter the third stage of life when wrinkles and grey hair are visible on his person. Or he may do so after the birth of a grandson.

Food, Habits and Manners

A.[157] ordains that a vanaprastha shall not only subsist on forest-produce but shall also entertain guests, and perform religious observances with those things. He will offer caru (i.e., preparation of rice, barley and pulse boiled with milk). *G.* while allowing a vanaprastha to live on roots and fruits alone, definitely forbids him[158] to take anything grown in a village. He has to perform the five great sacrifices (maha-yajna) prescribed for the householder. He has to entertain all[159] the guests excepting those who are expressly prohibited.[160]

A man, in this stage of life, is not debarred from eating the flesh of animals killed by wild animals, such as tigers, etc. It is interesting to note that *Vi.*[161] allows a'vanaprastha to gather his food from a village even an entrance to which is forbidden by some of the authorities.[162]

B.[163] adds that a vanaprastha should abstain from injury even to insects, and be capable of enduring cold. *A.*[164] prohibits the acceptance of gifts for a vanaprastha. *A.*[165] ordains that he shall lie and sit on bare ground. *A.*[166] further provides that a vanaprastha, desiring to observe greater discipline, should beg only as much food as is necessary for bare maintenance.[167]

From *V.*[168] we learn that a vanaprastha should practise continence. *V.*[169] provides that he shall live at the roots of trees after six months.[170] It is interesting to note that *V.*[171] appears to enjoin upon a vanaprastha the performance of only three yajnas, viz. deva, pitr and manusya yajnfia out of the usual five.

Vi. lays stress on the extreme self-mortification of the vanaprastha.[172] As an example of the severe austerities prescribed by *Vi.*, we may cite the practice of the 'five austerities',[173] in summer, lying under the sky in the rainy season and putting on vet clothes in the dewy season (hemanta).

THE STAGE OF A PARIVRAJAKA OR BHIKSU

General Rules

G.[174] lays down that a man, in this stage of life, should not accumulate anything. Practising self-restraint, he shall fix his abode at one particular spot (dhruva-sila) during the rains. He shall enter the village for begging. *B.*[175] fixes afternoon as the proper time for begging. After the expire of the rainy season, he is not to stay for more than one day in a village. *V.* ordains that he shall not live permanently at any place; he may fix his abode at any one of the following paces: outskirts of village, temple, empty house (sunya-gara) and foot of a tree.

A.[176] adds that he shall renounce all worldly pleasures, shall not take resourse to any body's help or perform any act conducive to temporal well-being (aniha) and spiritual benefit derivable in the other world (anamutra).[177] This work further provides that such a person shall renounce even all that is ordained in the sastras, not to speak of what is prohibited, shall keep above pleasure and pain, and meditate upon the Soul (atman), such meditation being conducive to happiness.[178] *V.* does not lay so much strees on the renunciation of all work both ordained and prohibited—as *A* does. But it agress with the latter in holding the acquisition of knowledge of the Supreme Soul as a bounden duty of a parivrajaka. The subjects to be meditated upon, according to *Vi.*[179] are chiefly these:—transitoriness of life, impure character of the body (asuei-bhava), the effect of old age on appearance, distress in the shape of diseases—physical, mental and extraneous (agantuka), the woeful condition in the mother's womb, the various miseries of the mundane existence and its worthlessness, the lamentable stage of rebirth as lower animals, etc. *V.*[180] lays down that a man, in this order of life, shall renounce all work excepting the study of the Vedas the giving up of which reduces him to the status of a Sudra. With regard to begging. *V.*[181] appears to imply that he should go to seven such houses as may come on his way and not selected previously. *V.* expressly prohibits begging as a profession. *V.*[182] appears to imply that begging at the houses of Brahmanas alone, is allowed. The vessels, to be carried while begging, are, according to *Vi.,*[183] to be made of earth, wood or pumpkin.

Food, Habits and Manners

He is debarred from eating fruits and leaves not falling down spontaneously from trees.

He shall wear as much of cloth as is necessary to cover his nakedness. *A.*[184] cites the opinion of 'some' who advocate nakedness. *G*[185] refers to the view of 'some' according to which he should wear a piece of cloth, for saken by others, after washing it.[186] *V.* appears to differ, to a great extent, from other writers in allowing a parivrajaka to wear a single piece of cloth[187] As an alternative, it prescribes ajina or grass (?).

He may either have a shaven head or keep the sikha.[188]

The parivrajaka will have equanimity towards all creatures. *A.*[189] prescribes silence (mauna) except when studying the Vedas. According to *V.*, he should avoid the following:

> Wickedness, jealousy, pride or vanity, egoism, faithlessness, crookedness (anarjava), self-applause, censure of others, boasting, greed, delusion (moha), anger, envy.

Vi.[190] lays down that such a person should not bow down[191] to anybody.

Morals

Although the *DS.* do not teach moral principles as a separate topic, yet we can have an idea of the moral outlook of their authors, and, for the matter of that, of the then society, from a critical study of the contents of these works.

From what we have said above about the life of a brahmacarin, it is clear that the formulators of the Sastras were quite alive to the fact that the life of the student was the foundation of the life of the man in making. In course of the rules and regulations regarding the training of a student, the authors of *DS.* lay great stress on the principles of morality to be inculcated into him. The chief features of the moral training of a student consist in his relation to women. He is forbidden to touch or even look at such a woman with whom his sexual intercourse may be suspected by others.[192] Although the wife of the preceptor must be saluted after returning from abroad, yet such salutation is prohibited if she is younger than the pupil.[193] The same prohibition applies, according to *B.*, to the wife of a brother also. *B.* further adds that he should speak with women only as much as is necessary.[194] Besides these restrictions, the student is debarred from indulging in gambling, and falsehood on his part is strongly deprecated.

Implicit obedience to the teacher, as we have seen above, is a bounden duty of the student according to most of the authorities.

Coming to second stage of life, we find that a grhastha has to perform a series of duties not only towards the members of his family, viz., the women and children, but also towards others, particularly guests.

The general position of the woman in the society was exalted no doubt, but certain passages bear testimony to the fact that lasciviousness of men, in their enjoyment of women, was not only condoned but also indirectly encouraged by the formulation of social law. For example, among the various kinds of sons, having a legal status, we find Gudhaja, Sahodha, Kanina, etc. The description of the origin of these kinds of sons betrays very loose morals of the society.

Clear evidences of the existence of the institution of levirate, contained in the *DS.*, testify to the fact that the moral outlook of the society was not very high, at least judging by modern standards. That men were allowed great licence, in their enjoyment of women, is sufficiently proved by such remarks as—na stri dusyati jarepa, i.e., a women is not defiled by a paramour.

There may be some who would try to find out a deeper significance underlying these practices; but one, going through the pages of the *DS.* with the spirit of a historian, feels constrained to brand them as moral laxities prevalent in the society of India at a time when civilisation did not reach a high degree of refinement.

4. SUPERSTITIONS[195]

Preliminary Remarks

The *DS.* contain references to certain practices, presumably prevalent in the society reflected in them, which appear to us to be based on sheer prejudice or superstitious ideas. The most prominent and interesting of them are noted below.

Classification of Superstitions

References to these practices are scattered all over the literature. For the sake of convenience, we broadly classify them as follows: —

(1) Superstitions relating to study, (2) those connected with food, (3) those concerning sins and their expiation, (4) miscellaneous superstitions.

(1) Superstitions relating to study. The following are some of the occasions when study had to be suspended:

> Passing of a dog, an ichneumon, a snake, a frog or cat between the teacher and his pupil, blowing of 'lust-carrying wind, sound of certain musical instruments, cries of dogs, jackals and asses, sight of unseasonal cloud surcharged with water, incessant downpour, falling of a thunderbolt or a meteor, eclipse and so on.

It will be seen that most of these rules are based on superstitious ideas.

An interesting rule is that the learning of the language of Mlecchas is forbidden.[196]

(2) Superstitions about food.

One should not eat, at night, anything brought by a servant (presya).[197]

B.[198] mentions, *inter alia,* the custom of eating with women prevalent in the southern regions. *B.*[199] says that this practice is reprehensible to the northerners. It is not clear whether *B's* striya saha bhojanam means eating in the company of women or eating from the same vassel with them. *V.,* with the same vagueness, condemns the practice of eating with one's wife.

The leavings of the food of the preceptor are believed to cure the pupil of his disease.[200]

B.[201] forbids eating on a stool or chair (asanadi). *A.* prohibits eating on a boat and on a palace (prasada).[202]

Vi.[203] forbids eating during solar and lunar eclipses.

V.[204] on the authority of the Vajasaneyins, condemns the practice of eating with one's wife. He says that such a practice result in the birth of weaklings (aviryavat) to them.

(3) Superstition concerning sins or impurities, and modes of their expiation and removal.

According to *G.*[205] taking to Mleccha, unholy or impious persons, is supposed to taint a man with impurity which can be expiated by meditating upon pious persons. Gautama further lays down that bath, with all the clothes on, removes the impurity caused by the touch of a fallen person (patita, Chandala, a woman delivered of a child before the usual period of impurity is over), a woman in her monthly illness, Sava[206] (corpse) and of one who has touched the preceding person, etc.

Samudra-samyana is regarded as one of the sinful practices causing degradation (patana). This word has been explained by Govindasvamin[207] as going to another island by boat.

Minor Superstitions

Besides the above, we meet with a number of other superstitious ideas and practices throughout the *DS.* The principal among them are noted here.

Euphemistic expressions are to be used to indicate certain objects whose real descriptions are unpleasant. A dry cow is to be referred to as dhenubhavya and an inauspicious thing as bhadra (auspicious).[208]

Indra-dhanu should be referred to as mani-dhanu. A cow, feeding its calf, should not be told of to others.[209]

With shoes on, one should avoid sitting greeting others or saluting the elders (abhivadana) and salutation of gods.[210] A person should not salute another who is carrying samit (sacrificial wood), a pitcher of water, flower or rice, nor should he allow himself to be saluted by others in these conditions.[211]

The rope, with which a *vatsa* is tied, should not be crossed over.[212] *MB.* interprets vatsa as go-jatyupalaksanam.

A.[213] prohibits the practice of counting birds remaining in a flock.

Riding a cart, drawn by asses, is prohibited by *A.*[214]

According to *Visnu,*[215] the performance of sraddha should not be seen by a women in her monthly course, dogs, pigs, village cocks (gramakukkuta); but the performer of Sraddha should carefully show it to an aja (goat).

5. APAD-DHARMA
(Rules to be observed in times of distress)

General Remarks

From what has been stated under Varnasrama-dharma above, it is clear that the authors of *DS.* fixed the duties of the different castes with great rigidity. It was considered to be a gross violation of social discipline for a member of one caste to take the occupation of another. But the authors were not devoid of practical considerations. They took into account the exigencies of an adverse situation when it might not be possible for a person to follow his own calling. Below we collect the information, contained in the *DS.*, about the rules to be observed by one in times of danger as also the restrictions imposed on the person concerned in such circumstances.

Brahmanas

In times of danger, a Brahamana is allowed to study under a non-Brahmana. In such a circumustance, however, the service (susrusa) of the teacher consists merely in the pupil's following him (anugamana), and the elaborate rules of attending upon the former will not be observed by the latter. After the completion of studies, the Brahmana pupil will be treated as the guru by the non-Brahmana teacher.

At such times, a Brahmana is allowed to carry on his usual duties of yajana (performing sacrifice for others), adhyapana (teaching) and pratigraha (acceptance of gifts) without such caste distinction as is to be usually observed. He can perform sacrifices on behalf of members of any of the castes. Likewise, he can teach all, and from all he can accept gifts.[216] Of these three kinds of work, each preceding in the list is superior to the succeeding one, so that the inferior one should be taken to at first; and on failure of that the next one should be chosen.

If the means of livelihood, set forth above, be not possible, a Brahmana xan even take to the occupation of Ksatriyas and Vaisyas, the latter on failure of the former. But a Brahmana is debarred from dealing in unguents, oil. krtanna (prepared food), sesamum, hemp, flax and leather, dyed and washed cloth, milk and curd, roots, fruits, flowers, medicine, honey, flesh, grass, water and poison, beasts when there is the likelihood of their being killed, slaves, cows of the following descriptions:—barren, she-calf, one that has destroyed the foetus. G.[217] cites the opinion of 'some' who prohibt also *bhumi,*[218] paddy, barley, goat, sheep, horse, bull, milch-cow and cart-drawing ox. *G.*, however, allows a Brahmana in distress to barter the following in exchange of similar things:—rasa, i.e., oil, etc., beasts.

G.[219] ordains that, in times of extreme distress, a Brahmana may, in violation of the above restrictions, subsist by any means (*sarvatha*) provided, however, he does not take recourse to the occupation of a Sudra. In the next sutra, *G.* cites the opinion of 'some', obviously with approval, that even the occupation of a Sudra may be adopted by a Brahmana when there is the risk of loss of life, the only restriction in this case being that he cannot eat garlic, etc. nor sit together with a Sudra nor can his body come in contact with the Sudras.

When there is any risk of life, a Brahmana may use arms[220] for self-protection.

B.[221] allows a Barhmana at such a time to take to the occupation of a Ksatriya, on its failure to that of a Vaisya, but does not impose the restrictions as described above.[222]

Ksatriyas

In times of distress, a ksatriya can take to the occupation of a Vaisya.

Vaisyas and Sudras

It is interesting to note that the authors of *DS.* do not show any anxiety to formulate rules to be observed by Vaisyas and Sudras in times of distress. Even in the case of a Ksatriya no restrictions are imposed. These facts tend to demonstrate that the non-Brahamanas, particularly the Vaisyas and Sudras, were at liberty to take recourse to any means of livelihood without the risk of being degraded.

Notes and References

1. I.1.5.
2. *VK.* X.12
3. *VK.* X. 15.
4. *G.* IV. 16; *B.*I.16.7; 1.17.2; *VK.*X.12, 15.
5. *M.B,* on *G.*
6. *B, VK.*
7. *G.*IV.17; *B.*I.16.8; *VK.*X. 14, 15.
8. *B. VK.*
9. *G.*IV.20.
10. *VK.*X.11.
11. *VK.*X.13.
12. *G.*IV.17; *B.*I. 16.8; *VK.*X.14,15.
13. *VK.*X.15.
14. *VK.*X.13, 14.
15. *G.* IV. 17.
16. *G.* IV. 19.
17. *G.* IV.21.
18. *VK.* X. 15.
19. *G.*IV.17; *B.*I.16.8.12; I.I7.14.
20. *MB.* on *G.*
21. *VK.*X.11.
22. *VK.*X.14.
23. *G.* IV. 17; *B.*I.16.8; I.17.6; *VK.*X.13.
24. *G.*IV.18.
25. *VK.*X.12.
26. *G.*IV.20.
27. *G.*IV.19.
28. *VK.*X.15.
29. *G.*IV.17; *B.*I.16.7.
30. *MB.* on *G.*
31. *G.*IV.17.21; *B.*I.17.3; *VK.*X.13; II.3.30.
32. *MB. on G.*
33. *VK.* X. 14.
34. *G* IV.19; *B.* I. 16.8; 11, 1. 17.13; *VK.* X. 14, 15.

35. *G., VK.*
36. *VK.*X.15.
37. *VK.*X.13; *B.*I. 17.5.
38. *VK.* X. 12.
39. *VK.* X.15.
40. *VK.* X.13.
41. *G.*IV.17; *B.*I.17.8; *VK.*X.13.
42. *MB.* on *GB.*
43. *B.*I.16.9, I.17.11.
44. *VK.*X.15.
45. *VK.*X.14.
46. *VK.*X.15.
47. *VK.*X.15.
48. *B.*I.167, I.17.4; *G.*IV.17; *VK.*X.13.
49. *B. VK.*
50. *B.*I.16.8, I.17.7; *G.*IV.17, 20.
51. *G. VK.*
52. B.I.16.8, 10; 1.17.12.
53. *VK.*X.14.
54. *VK.*X.15.
55. *G.*IV.21.
56. II.14-20.
57. Jolly's rendering as "growing seeds" appears to be inaccurate, in view of the fact that Nand. explains the word as *'raksanam'.* Nand. explains the seeds as those of barley and paddy.
58. Sarva-sabdena vaisya-vrttinam krsyadinamapi grahanam. Nand. that is to say, *sarva* (all) implies the occupations of the Vaisya also, e.g., tillage, etc.
59. 'Silpani citra-karanadini'—*Nand. 'Silpa'* means painting, etc.
60. III. 2.
61. II.11.14.
62. II.21.1.
63. II.21.8.
64. Haradatta comments (on II.21.10) that such a man will enter the village only for the sake of alms, but usually live outside.
65. II.21.11.
66. II.21.12.
67. II.21.3-4.
68. II.21.8.
69. II.21.19.
70. He is usually called *acarya* the etymology of which word has been given in *A.*I.1.14 thus:

    Yasmaddharmanacinoti, i.e., one from whom a person 'gathers' the knowledge of religious duties.
71. *G.* allows begging from all castes excepting *abhisastas* and *patitas.* The former is explained by *HG.* and *MB.* as one who has committed a sin technically

known as *upa-pataka.* But, *U.* on *A.* I.21.8, in conformity with *A.* I.24.7, interprets it as one who has committed brahma-hatya.

72. We refrain from recording the minutiae of the manner of saluting the preceptor, the mode of sitting near him, the rules about begging alms, etc., but indicate the broad rules only which are important for the purpose of drawing the picture of the society of those times.
73. II.28.
74. *Cf.* Sisya-sistir-avadhena—*G.* II. 49.
75. *G.*II.50.
76. *Cf.* anyena ghnan rajna sasyah—*G.* 11.51.
77. *Cf.* sarvesu grahanantam va—G.II.54.
78. 'pauranam' (*B.*I.3.1).
    This word has been interpreted by Vna. as follows: (i) Practised in the golden age (krta-yuga). (ii) Ordained and practised by the ancients like Manu, etc.
79. *B.*I.3.42.
80. I.1.16.
81. For duties of each kind, see Caland's Eng. tr. of *VK.* pp. 185-86.
82. VIII. 14.
83. VIII.15.
84. VIII.16.
85. *G.*V.9.
86. Name of a particular religious ceremony performed morning and evening, and especially before the midday meal.
87. This is the name of a sacrifice in which one has to give away one's all as sacrificial fee.
88. *G.*V.24.
89. *G.*V.I.
90. *G.*V.2.
91. V. 41.
92. This time has been said to be *'madhyahna'* (midday) by *MB.* Haradatta, however, suggests that the word of the text may mean either midday or evening.
93. A mixture of curd and honey or of milk and honey. In some Puranas and works on Smrti, it has been described as an admixture of curd, ghee, water, honey and sugar.
94. II. 4.22.
95. *A.*II.4.21. While commenting on this, Haradatta says that this *sutra* implies that a king should set up stores of paddy, etc., in the villages for honouring the Sudra guests.
96. *A.*II.6.5. The "religious duties" (dharmapuraskarah) have been explained by Haradatta as begging for the preceptor, etc.
97. *A.*II.8. 5-7. Haradatta, in his *U.*, takes the word *'go'* in these rules as daksina or fee. But, his interpretation is not-plausible in view of the fact that 'goghna' (lit. meaning one in whose honour a cow is killed) is found in the sense of 'guest' in many branches of ancient Indian literature. *Cf.*, for instance, *Panini,*

III.4.73; commenting on this Bhattoji explains *'goghna'* as *'gam hanti tasmai goghno' tithib'.* The practice of beef-eating presumably became obsolete in Haradatta's time.

98. VIII.7.
99. LVIII. 2-8.
100. *VI.* LXIV.15. *'Mleccha'* is generally used to denote those who do not follow the *varnasramadharma. 'Antyaja'* means low-born people and *'patitas'* outcaste.
101. For the description of each kind, see Caland's Eng. tr. of *VK.,* p. 187.
102. This corresponds to *'pravrajya'* mentioned by *B.* as the last stage.
103. *X.*26.
104. For details about each class, see Caland's Eng. tr. of *VK.,* pp. 189-90.
105. For descriptions of the sub-divisions, see Caland's Eng. tr. of the *VK.,* p. 191.
106. Care has been taken to avoid repetition of the above rules dealt with under *varnasrama-dharma.*
107. *Gautama.*
108. See Haradatta on *G.* (*A. A..* ed., I. 1. 49). But, *MB.,* on the same *sutra,* appears to mean that the preceptor's hand should be touched.
109. *G.* II. 39. Both Haradatta and *MB.* point out that this rule, by implication, provides for these things to be done by a pupil for the teacher.
110. The word has been explained by both *HG.* and *MB.* (on *G.* II. 43) as one who has committed a sin technically known as *upa-pataka.* On *G.* XVII. 15, *MB.* explains it as one who is declared as having committed a fault. In this context, *HG.* explains it as one who is declared either rightly or wrongly, to be a wrong-doer. But, *A.* (I. 24-6-7) clearly defines *abhisasta* as one who has killed either a Brahmana or a man of either the Ksatriya or the Vaisya caste who has completed Vedic studies (*Vedadhyaya*) or is engaged in performing *Savana* (*=soma-yaga,* ace. to *U.*) *A.* (I. 28. 17), however, describes such a sinner as one who kills one's ownself or any other person. On *A.* (I. 29. 8), *U.* explains the word as *patila;* on *A.* (II. 2. 6), *U.* says that the word means 'murder of a Brahmana'. The word also occurs in *A.* I. 3. 25 and I. 24. 15; in the latter case, *U.* explains it as *brahmaha.*
111. II.43.
112. II.44-45.
113. II. 50.
114. II.51.
115. *Baudhayana.*
116. I. 3. 17.
117. I. 3. 18.
118. *Cf.* brahmanadayah svakarmasthah, I. 3.19.
119. I. 3. 23.
120. I. 3. 27.
121. I.3.36.
122. *Apastamba.*
123. I.4.1.5.
124. For the preceptor's drink and bath—*Vna.*

125. I.4.25.
126. Either directly or through the student's superior, like father, etc.
127. I. 5. 2.
128. I. 7.21.
129. *Cf.* Sarvada sudrata ugrato vacaryarthasyabaranam dharmyam (*Vna.*) *B.* (I. 17. 4) defines Ugra as one born of a Ksatriya father and Sudra mother.
130. I.7.24.
131. *Vasistha, Visnu* and *Vaikhanasa.*
132. What precisely is meant by this word is not clear. From the trend of the discussion, however, it seems to mean the preceptor. *Vai.* adds that, for this purpose, one's own family is excluded.
133. V. 26.
134. Sva-vasini (V.L. Su-vasini, according to *G.* On this *MB.* comments—garbhayukta duhita).
135. II. 6. 6.
136. VIII.7.
137. V. 41.
138. *G.* V. 37.
139. *G.* V. 34.
140. This is Haradatta's interpretation. But, according to *MB.* on *G. V.* 42, this sutra does not relate to Sudra guests the mode of addressing whom is to be learnt from other works.
141. II. 4.16-18.
142. See *A.* I.14. 12.
143. These rules must be taken to apply to a Brahmana host.
144. V. 43-45.
145. II. 4.19-20.
146. II. 4. 21.
147. Haradatta comments that this hints at the prevalence of the system of the king's keeping stores of paddy, etc., in every village for the entertainment of Sudra guests.
148. V.45.
149. Matula-matamaha-pitrvya-pitamahadayan—*MB.* rr. atula-matrsvasr-pitr-svasradayah—*HG.*
150. *G.* VI. 3.
151. *G.* VI. 7.
152. *G.* VI. 8.
153. *Svasru*—this prohibition does not carry conviction unless we take the word to mean 'mother-in-law who is younger in age'. The Anandasrama ed., of the *Gautama-dharmasutra* reads *Svasrnam* which again contradicts *G.* VI. 7; the latter provides for the constant salutation of the sister.
154. G. HI. 32-33.
155. II. 22. 8-9.
156. 94.1-2.
157. II. 22. 17.

158. III. 28.
159. The commentators point out that the restrictions of caste, etc., with regard to guests, imposed on a *grhastha,* e.g., a non-Brahmana, cannot be the guest of a Brahmana, do not apply to a *vanaprastha.*
160. *E.g.,* thieves and people born in the reverse order of castes (pratilomaja).
161. 94-94.
162. *E.g. G.*III. 33.
163. III. 3. 19.
164. II. 22.11.
165. II. 22. 23.
166. II. 23. 1.
167. *U.* explains that begging should be resorted to instead of gleaning corns. It further points out that a vanaprastha should beg of other vanaprasthas.
168. IX. 5.
169. IX. II.
170. The meaning of the passage is not very clear. Does it provide for his living in the open after six months from the entrance to this order of life ?
171. IX. 12.
172. *Vide Chap.* 93.
173. Sitting in the midst of fire on four sides with the sun overhead.
174. III. 11 ff.
175. II. 11.24.
176. II. 21. 10.
177. *Cf.,* iharthah krsyadayah paralokarthasca japahomadayo yasya na santi so'nihonamutra ityuktah—*U.*
178. *Cf,* atmani buddhe.. . . tadeva juanam sarvamasubham praksalya ksemam prapayati—*U.* on *A.* II. 21.14.
179. Chap. 96.
180. Chap. X.
181. X. 7.
182. X. 24.
183. 96.7.
184. II.21. 12.
185. III. 19.
186. The commentators point out that this provision is necessary for obviating the fault that may be committed by the acceptance of gifts. This, however, seems incompatible with *G.* III. 14 which allows such a person to beg. The conflict may, perhaps, be reconciled by taking this rule as a manner of self-mortification on the part of the person taking to pravrajya.
187. Perhaps excluding the upper garment which is to be worn by other people.
188. *B.* II. 11. 20, provides for the shaving of all the hair excepting the sikha. *V.* X. 6, advocates complete shaving of the hair.
189. II. 21. 10.
190. 96.22.
191. *Vai.* construes it to mean that, though greeted with namaskara by others, he

should not return the namaskara, but should simply remember Narayana. According to others, referred to in *Vai.*, he should not bow down to anybody for alms.

192. *G.* II. 22.
193. *G.* II. 41.
194. I.3.24.
195. Some people, who look upon *DS.* with a spirit of reverence, may take exception to this word. They may argue that, though seemingly superstitious, these ideas are based on scientific principles. To assess their scientific basis, if any, is the work of specialists. It is, therefore, our concern here to note such of the practices as appear to be based on prejudice or superstitious belief according to modern outlook. (The references to Gautama in this section are taken from the Anandasrama ed., of this work, unless otherwise stated.)
196. *V.* VI. 4.
197. *G.* I.9. 57.
198. I. 2. 3.
199. I. 2. 5.
200. *B.* II. 1. 25.
201. II. 6. 6.
202. *A.* I. 17. 6. 7. This word is explained as darumaya manca (wooden platform) by Haradatta.
203. 68.1.
204. XII. 31.
205. IX. 17-18.
206. Explained by *MB.* us a corpse or one who has touched it.
207. On *B.* II. 2.2.
208. *G.*
209. *G.*
210. *G.*I. 9. 45.
211. *B.* I. 3. 32,
212. *G.*
213. I. 31. 19. na patatah sa caksita. The word 'patatah' is taken by Haradatta to mean birds in a flock. He refers to other views according to which it means luminaries falling from the firmament.
214. I.32.25.
215. 81.6.9.
216. *G.* VII. 4. As an alternative interpretation of this *sutra,* the commentators suggest that the three-fold occupation of the Brahmana can be resorted to by members of all other castes.
217. *G.* VII. 15.
218. Commentators explain it as grha (house).
219. VII. 22.
220. *G.* VII. 25.
221. II.4.16,19.
222. It is interesting to note that, according to *B.* II. 4. 17, Gautama does not

allow a Brahmana to take to the occupation of a Ksatriya on the ground that the latter is too difficult for the former. Curiously enough, the extant work of Gautama does not contain this prohibition—a fact that has led Govindasvamin to suppose that another version of Gautama's work existed.

III
RELIGION AND RELIGIOUS PRACTICES

ROMESH CHUNDER DUTT

The religion of the ancient Hindus in the first or Vedic epoch was the worship of Nature leading up to Nature's God.

The hardy and enterprising conquerors of the Punjab were a warlike race with a capacity for active enjoyments, and an appreciation of all that was lovely and joyous in nature. They looked up to the beauteous and bright sky, and worshipped it under the name of *Dyu,* equivalent to the Greek *Zeus* and the first syllable of the Latin *Jupiter.* They also called the sky of day by the name of *Mitra,* corresponding to the Zend *Mithra;* and they called the sky of night *Varuna,* corresponding to the Greek *Ouranos.* These common names under which the sky-god was worshipped by the different Aryan nations of the ancient times prove that the sky was worshipped under these names by the primitive Aryans in their original home.

Worship of Nature's Gods

But while the Hindu Aryans of the Punjab continued to worship the ancient sky-god under the ancient names of Dyu, Mitra, and Varuna, they paid special homage to the *sky that rains,* which they called *Indra.* For in India the rise of rivers and the luxuriance of crops depend on the rain-giving sky; and in course of time Indra became the most prominent deity in the Hindu pantheon. He was conceived as a warlike deity, battling with the clouds, called Vritra, to obtain copious torrents of rain for man, and fighting with the demons of darkness, called Panis, to restore to the world the light of the morning. The Maruts or storm-gods were supposed to help Indra in his contest with the reluctant clouds, for in India the first showers or the rainy season are often attended with storms and thunder. And the deity, at once so beneficent and so warlike, was naturally a favourite with the martial and conquering Hindus; and as we have seen before, they constantly invoked him to lead them against the retreating barbarians, and to bestow on the conquerors new lands and wealth, cattle and progeny.

It will help us to enter into the spirit of the warlike and simple Hindu worshippers of the olden times if we read some verses describing the battles of Indra with the cloud.

1. "We sing the heroic deeds which were done by Indra the thunderer. He destroyed Ahi (clouds), and caused rains to descend, and opened out the paths for the mountain streams to roll.
2. "Indra slew Ahi resting on the mountains; Tvashtri had made, the far-reaching thunderbolt for him. Water in torrents flowed towards the sea, as cows run eagerly towards their calves.
3. "Impetuous as a bull, Indra quaffed the soma juice; he drank the soma libations offered in the three sacrifices. He then took the thunderbolt, and thereby slew the eldest of the Ahis.
4. "When you killed the eldest of the Ahis, you destroyed the contrivances of the artful contrivers. You cleared the sun and the morning and the sky, and left no enemies behind.
5. "Indra with his all-destructive thunderbolt slew the darkling Vritra (clouds) and lopped his limbs. Ahi now lies touching the earth like the trunk of a tree felled by the axe.
8. "Glad waters are bounding over the prostrate body as rivers flow over fallen banks. Vritra when alive had withheld the waters by his power Ahi now lies prostrate under the waters." —*Rig Veda,* I. 32.

Let us contrast with this the following verses addressed to Varuna the sky-god of righteousness, and we shall perceive how the ancient Hindus worshipped the sky in its different aspects under different names, now as the Lord of tempests and of rain, now as the Lord of mercy.

3. "O Varuna! with an anxious heart I ask thee about my sins. I have gone to learned men to make the inquiry; the sages have all said to me, 'Varuna is displeased with thee'.
4. "O Varuna! for what deed of mine dost thou wish to destroy thy friend, they worshipper?' O thou of irresistible power, declare it to me, so that I may quickly bend in adoration and come to thee.
5. "O Varuna! deliver us from the sins of our fathers. Deliver us from the sins committed in our person. O royal Varuna! deliver Vasishtha like a calf from its tether, like a thief who has feasted on a stolen animal.

6. "O Varuna! all this sin is not wilfully committed by us. Error or wine, anger or dice, or even thoughtlessness has begotten sin. Even an elder brother leads his younger astray. Sin is begotten even in our dreams.
7. "Freed from sins, I will serve as a slave the god Varuna, who fulfils our wishes and supports us. We are ignorant; may the *Arya* god bestow on us knowledge. May the wise deity accept our prayer and bestow on us wealth."—*Rig Veda,* VII. 86.

Sky and Sun most Prominent Objects of Worship

Next to the sky, the sun was the most prominent object of the worship of the ancient Hindus. *Aditi* was the limitless light of sky, and her sons, the *A'dityas,* were the suns of the different months of the year. *Surya,* answering to the Greek Helios, the Latin Sol, and the Teuton Tyr, was, however, the most popular name by which the sun was worshipped. *Savitri* is another name of the same deity, and the sacred hymn, the Gayatri, which is still repeated every morning by pious Biahmans all over India, as the first act of their daily devotions, is a verse addressed to their deity. It runs thus in translation:

"We meditate on the desirable light of the divine Savitri who influences our pious rites."—*Rig Veda,* III. 62, 10.

Viewed in other aspects the sun had other names. Pasture was still extensively followed by the Punjab Hindus as a means of living, and the simple shepherds looked on the sun as their guide and protector in all their migrations, and called him *Pushan.*

1. "O Pushan! help us to finish our journey, and remove all dangers. O son of cloud! do thou march before us.
2. "O Pushan! do thou remove from our path him who would lead us astray, who strikes and plunders and does wrong.
3. "Do thou drive away that wily robber who intercepts journeys.
7. "Lead us so that enemies who intercept may not harm us; lead us by easy and pleasant paths. O Pushan! devise means for our safety on this journey.
8. "Lead us to pleasant tracks covered with green grass; may there not be excessive heat by the way, O Pushan! devise means for our safety on this journey."—*Rig Veda,* I. 42.

One more name of the sun it is necessary to mention. *Vishnu,* which in later Hindu mythology has become a name of the Supreme

Preserver of all beings, was a name of the sun in the Vedic age. The rising sun, the sun at zenith, and the setting sun were considered the three steps of Vishnu striding across limitless space.

Agni—The Priest among Gods

Fire or *Agni* was an object of worship. No sacrifice to the gods could be performed without libations or offering to the fire, and Agni was therefore considered to be the priest among the gods. But Agni is not only the terrestrial fire in the Rig Veda; he is also the fire of the lighting and the sun, and his abode was in heaven. The early sages Bhrigus discovered him there, and Atharvan and Angiras, the first sacrifices, installed him in this world as the protector of men.

Vayu, or the wind, is sometimes invoked in the Rig Veda. The *Maruis,* or storm-gods, are oftener invoked, as we have seen before, and are considered the helpers of Indra in obtaining rain for the benefit of man. *Rudra,* the loud-sounding father of the Maruts is the Thunder, and in later Hindu mythology this name has been appropriately chosen for the Supreme Destroyer of all living beings.

We have said that Agni, or fire, received special homage because he was necessary for all sacrifice. The libation of soma juice was similarly regarded sacred, and *Soma,* was worshipped as a deity. Similarly, the prayer which accompanied the libations or offerings was also regarded as a deity, and was called *Brahmanaspati.* In later Hindu mythology, Brahman is selected as the name of the Supreme Creator of all living beings.

Gods of Rigveda

We have now enumerated the most important gods of the Vedic pantheon, but it is necessary to add a word about the twin-gods of the Rig Veda, Morning and Evening. Light and Darkness naturally suggested to the early Aryans the idea of twin gods. The sky (Vivasvat) is the father, and the Dawn (Saranyu) is the mother, of the twin *Asvins,* and the legend goes on to say that Saranyu ran away from Vivasvat before she gave birth to the twins. We have the same legend in Greek mythology; and Erinnys (answering philologically to Saranyu) ran away from her lover, and gave birth to Areion and Despoina. The original idea is that the ruddy nymph (Dawn and Gloaming) disappears, and gives birth to Light and to Darkness.

But whatever the original conception may have been, the Asvins have lost their primitive character in the Rig Veda, and have simply become physician gods, healers of the sick and the wounded, tending morta's with kindness. Similarly the twins, *Yama* and his sister *Yami* (children of the same parents, Sky and Dawn, and originally implying Light and Darkness), have also acquired a different character in the Rig Veda. Of Yami we hear little, but Yama is the ruler of the future world, the beneficent king of the departed. Clothed in a glorious body, the virtuous live in the future life by the side of Yama, in the realms of light and speaking waters. Two short extracts from hymns to Yama and to Soma respectively, will illustrate the idea of future life and future felicity which the Hindus of the Vedic age entertained.

1. "Worship Yama, the son of Vivasvat, with offerings. All men go to him. He takes men of virtuous deeds to the realm of happiness. He clears the way for many.
2. "Yama first discovered the path for us. That path will not be destroyed again. All living beings will, according to their acts, follow by the path by which our forefathers have gone."— *Rig Veda,* X. 14.
7. "Flowing Soma ! take me to that immortal and imperishable abode where light dwells eternal, and which is in heaven. Flow, Soma ! for Indra.
8. "Take me where Yama is king, where are the gates of heaven, and where mighty rivers flow. Take me there and make me immortal. Flow, Soma ! for Indra.
9. "Take me where is the third heaven, where is the third realm of light above the sky, and where one can wander at his will. Take me there, and make me immortal. Flow, Soma ! for Indra.
10. "Take me where every desire is satiated, where Pradhma has his abode, where there is food and contentment. Take me there and make me immortal. Flow, Soma ! for Indra.
11. "Take me where there are pleasures and joys and delights, and where every desire of the anxious heart is satiated. Take me there, and make me immortal. Flow, Soma ! for Indra."—*Rig Veda,* XI. 113.

The deities named above are the most important gods of the Rig Veda. Of goddesses there are only two who have any marked character or individuality, viz., *Ushas* or Dawn and *Sarasvati* the river-goddess.

Lovely Description of Dawn

There is no lovelier conception in Rig Veda than that of the Dawn, and there are no fresher or more beauteous passages in the lyrical poetry of the ancient world than some of the hymns dedicated to Ushas. She is described as the far-extending, many-tinted, brilliant Dawn, whose abode is unknown. She harnesses her chariots from afar and comes in radiance and glory. She is the young, the while-robed daughter of the sky, the queen of all earthly treasures. She is like the careful mistress of the house who rouse every one from his slumbers and sends him to his work. And yet she is radiant as a bride decorated by her mother for the auspicious ceremony, and displaying her charms to the view.[1] Such are the fond epithets and beautiful similes with which the Hindu Aryans greeted the fresh and lovely mornings of a tropical sky.

It is remarkable that the Hellenic Aryans of the time of Homer regarded the lovely Eos with much the same feeling of poetic fondness. But the mystery is explained when we learn that Eos is the same name as Ushas, and that the other Greek names of the Dawn correspond philologically to Hindu names of the same deity,[2] and there can be little doubt, therefore, that the Hindu and the Hellenic Aryans alike derived their conceptions and their names of the Dawn-goddess from the primitive Aryans.

This remark does not apply in the case of Sarasvati, who is purely a Hindu goddess. Sarasvati is the name of a river in the Punjab,[3] deemed to be holy because of the religious rites which were performed on its banks and the sacred hymns uttered there. By a natural development of ideas she came to be considered the goddess of those hymns or the goddess of speech, in which character she is worshipped in India to the present day.

Difference Between Hindu and Greek Gods

From the foregoing account the reader will perceive that there was an essential difference between the Hindu gods of the Vedic age and the Greek gods of the Homeric age. The Hindu conceptions go nearer to the original Nature-worship of the primitive Aryans, even as the Sanscrit language is nearer and closer than the Greek to the original Aryan tongue. Among the Greeks of the Homeric age, the gods and goddesses have already attained a marked individuality; their history, their character, their deeds, engage our attention; their connection with the powers and manifestations of Nature almost escape us. The Hindu gods of the Vedic age, on the contrary, are obviously still Nature's powers and manifestations; they have scarcely any other character or history. We can more clearly identify Dyu with the sky than Zeus, and Ahana and Dhana are more obviously and manifestly the Dawn than Athena and Daphne. The Hindu conceptions are more ancient, more archaic, more true to their original sources. The Greek conceptions are more developed, and have passed farther from the domain of Nature-worship to that of Polytheism.

It is probably owing to this difference that the Hindus attained to a conception of the one supreme God sooner than the Greeks. It was an easy step from the worship of natural powers to the conception of Nature's God; but it was not easy for the Greeks, who had already invested their gods with distinct characters and histories, to set them aside and rise to the conception of one God. The Greeks of the Homeric age failed, therefore, to rise to the worship of the Supreme Deity, which the Hindus succeeded in doing even in the Vedic Age.

Hindu Monotheism

In some of the latest hymns of the Rig Veda we find that the worshipper correctly interpreted the names of the different gods as only different names of the same great Power, the Father of all, the Creator of all.

1. "The all wise Father saw clearly, and after due reflection created the sky and the earth in their watery form, and touching each other. When their boundaries were stretched afar, then the sky and the earth became separated.
2. "The Creator of all is great; he creates and supports all; he is above all, ard sees all; he is beyond the seat of the seven Rishis. So the wise men say, and the wise men obtain fulfilment of their desires.
3. "He who has given life, he who is the Creator, he who knows all the places in this universe,— *he is one, although he bears the names of many gods.* Other beings wish to know him."—*Rig Veda,* X. 82.

This is the earliest indication of Hindu monotheism, that monotheism which has continued to be the true religion of the Hindus for over three thousand years, in spite of the legends and allegories and "the names of many gods" with which the popular mind has been fed from age to age.

One more extract, a sublime hymns to the same supreme God, will enable us to understand this the earliest phase of Hindu monotheism.

1. "In the beginning the Golden Child existed. He was the Lord of all from his birth. He placed this earth and sky in their proper places. Whom shall we worship with offerings?
2. "Him who has given life and strength, whose will is obeyed by all gods, whose shadow is immortality, and whose slave is Death. Whom shall we worship with offerings?
3. "Him who by his power is the sole King of all the living beings that see and move; him who is the Lord of all bipeds and quadrupeds. Whom shall we worship with offerings?
4. "Him by whose power these shadowy mountains have been made, and whose creations are this earth and its oceans; him whose arms are these quarters of space. Whom shall we worship with offerings?
5 "Him who has fixed in their places this sky and this earth; him who has established the heavens and the highest heaven; him who has measured the firmament. Whom shall we worship with offerings?
6. "Him by whom the sounding sky and earth have been fixed and expanded; him whom the resplendent sky and earth own as Almighty; him by whose support the sun rises and gains lustre. Whom shall we worship with offerings?"—*Rig Veda,* X. 121.

It will thus be seen that the religion of the sturdy conquerors of the Punjab was a progressive religion, leading from Nature up to Nature's God. We see the entire journey of the human mind in the Rig Veda—a work unique in the world for this reason—from the simple, child-like admiration of the ruddy dawn or the breaking storm, to the sublime effort to grasp the mysteries of creation and its great Creator.

Caste System Unknown in Vedic Age

While a few of the advanced spirits of the age rose to this height, the nation still continued to invoke their beloved gods, and poured libations and offered cakes to them with their prayers. There were no temples and no hereditary priests. Each pious householder, each patriarch of his family, lighted the sacrificial fire in his own home, poured the soma juice in libations, and prayed to the gods for health and crops, for cattle and progeny.

Great kings and chiefs, however, performed their religious sacrifices with ostentatious prodigality, and families of priests were supported by such chiefs and presided at all royal observances. In course of time such families, who followed the same vocation from generation to generation, became known for their skill in composing or reciting hymns and performing rites. Different collections of hymns were preserved in such families, handed down from father to son, and preserved by memory alone, and it is to this pious custom that the Aryan world owes the preservation of the earliest of Aryan compositions now extant, i.e.. the hymns of the Rig Veda.

But although certain families followed the vocation of priests from father to son, and were therefore rewarded by princes and respected by the people, there was no hereditary distinction yet between the priest and the people, and the caste system of India was unknown in the Vedic Age. The only insuperable distinction which existed in that age was between the conquerors and the conquered, the Hindus and the Aborigines, the *Aryans* and the *Dasyus,* as they are styled in the Rig Veda. Among the Aryan Hindus themselves no such distinction was yet known, and the patriarchs and leaders of the Punjab Hindus composed their hymns, fought their battles, and ploughed their fields before the castes of the Brahmans, Kshatriyas, and Vaisyas were formed.

Forms and Ceremonials Gain Importance

The increase in wealth and civilization, and the comparatively settled and easy life of the people, gave birth to a taste for great and pompous sacrifices; and a hereditary priestly caste naturally attached great importance to the forms and ceremonials which accompanied these rites. And in the performance of these elaborate sacrifices the attention of the worshipper was to a great extent diverted from the deities, who were the true objects of devotion, to the minutiae of rites, the erection of altars, the fixing of the proper astronomical moments for lighting the fire, the correct pronunciation of prayers, and to the various requisite acts accompanying a sacrifice.

The literature of a nation is but the reflection of the national mind; and when the nation turned its religion into forms and ceremonials, religious literature became to some extent inane and lifeless. We miss in the voluminous Brahmanas of this age the fervency and earnestness of the Vedic hymns. We find, on the other hand, grotesque reasons given for every minute rite, dogmatic explanations of texts, penances for every breach of form and rule, and elaborate directions for every act and movement of the worshipper. The works show a degree of credulity and submission on the part of the people, and of absolute power on the part of the priests, which remind us of the Middle Ages in Europe.

Legends of Brahmanas

We willingly leave this subject and turn to the legends contained in the Brahmanas, some of which are interesting. That which is the best known in Europe is one resembling the account of the deluge in the Old Testament. Manu the mythical progenitor of man, was washing his hands when a fish came unto him and said, "Rear me; I will save thee". Manu reared the fish, and it told him, "In such and such a year the flood will come. Thou shalt then attend to me by preparing a ship." The flood came, and Manu entered into the ship, which he had built in time, and the fish swam up to him and carried the ship beyond the northern mountain. The ship was fastened to a tree, and when the flood subsided Manu descended. "The flood swept away all the creatures, and Manu alone remained here,"—*Satapatha Brahmana.*

In some of the legends of the Brahmanas we notice how poetical similes used in the Rig Veda were transformed into mythological tales. The simile of the sun pursuing the Dawn-goddess lent itself easily to a tale of Prajapati seducing his daughter, and thus creating and peopling this universe. Hindu commentators saw the origin of this myth, and the learned Rumania, who lived some five centuries after Christ, thus explains it:

> "Prajapati, the Lord of Creation, is the name of the sun, and he is called so because he protects all creatures. His daughter Ushas is the dawn; and when it is said that he was in love with her, this only means that at sunrise the sun runs after the dawn."

Various other accounts of the creation are given in the different Brahmanas. We are told in the *Taittiriyaka Brahmana* that in the beginning nothing was except water, and a lotus leaf stood out of it. Prajapati dived in the shape of a boar and brought up some earth, and spread it out, and fastened it down by pebbles. That was the earth.

In the *Satapatha Brahmana* we are told that the gods and the Asuras (enemies of gods) both sprang from Prajapati, and the earth trembled like a lotus leaf when the gods and Asuras contended for mastery. And elsewhere ill the same Brahmana we are told, "Verily in the beginning Prajapati existed alone." He created living beings, and birds and reptiles and snakes, but they all passed away for want of food. He then made the breasts (of mammals) teem with milk, and so the living creatures survived.

These examples will suffice. We have seen that the Hindus of the Vedic Age were led from the worship of Nature up to Nature's God, and were able to conceive the great idea that in the beginning nothing existed except the Deity, and that the whole universe was his handiwork. The more speculative Hindus of the Epic Age reproduced the same idea, and their various guesses as to the way in which God created the universe are among the earliest conjectures of man into the mysteries of creation. But nobler and more earnest efforts were made in this Epic Age to know the unknown God, and these strivings of Hindu mind are imbedded in the works called the *Upanishads,* which are among the most remarkable works in the literature of the world.

Universal Soul of Upanishads

The idea of a Universal Soul, of an All-pervading Breath, is the keystone of the philosophy and thought of the Upanishads. This idea is somewhat different from monotheism, as it has been generally understood by other nations. The monotheism of other nations recognizes a God and Creator as distinct from the created beings, but the monotheism of the Upanishads, which has been the monotheism of the Hindus ever since, recognizes Gcd as the Universal Being;—all things have emanated from him, are a part of him, and will resolve themselves into him.

This is the truth which the poor fatherless boy Satyakama learnt from the great book of Nature. He was a poor child of a poor servant-girl, and did not know who his father was. When he came to a Guru to learn according to the custom of the times, and the Guru asked after his family, the truthful boy replied, "I do not know, sir, of what family I am. I asked my mother, and she answered, 'In my youth, when I had to move about much as a servant, I conceived thee. I do not know of what family thou art'." The Guru was pleased with the truth-loving boy, and kept him in his house.

And the boy, according to the custom of the times, served his teacher menially, and went out to tend his cattle; and in course of time he learnt the great truth which Nature, and even the brute creation, teach those whose minds are open to instruction. He learnt the truth from the herd which he tended, from the fire that he lighted, from the flamingo and diver-bird that flew around him when in the evening he had penned his cows and laid wood on the evening-fire. His teacher was struck, and asked, "Friend, you shine like one who knows God; who then has taught you?" "Not men," was the young student's reply. And the truth which he had learnt was that the four quarters, and the earth, the sky, the heavens beyond, and the ocean, and the sun, the moon, the lightning and the fire, and the organs and minds of living beings-yea, the whole universe, was God,—*Chhandogya Upanishads.*

This is the truth which the learned priest Yajnavalkya explained to his beloved wife Maitreyi when she refused all wealth which her husband offered to her, and thirsted for that which would make her immortal; and the priest, gratified by the noble wish of his spouse, then explained to her that the Universal Soul dwells in the husband and in the wife and in the sons, in Brahmanas and in Kshatriyas, and in all living beings, in the gods above and in the creatures below—yea, in all the universe.—*Brihadaranyaka Upanishad.*

This is the truth which is inculcated in numerous passages in the Upanishad in language simple and fervent and solemn, the like of which has never been composed by Hindus of later times.

"The intelligent, whose body is spirit, whose form is bright, whose thoughts are true, whose nature is like ether (omnipresent and invisible), from whom all works, all desires, all sweet odours and tastes proceed;—He who embraces all this, who never speaks and is never surprised.

"He is my soul within the heart, smaller than a corn of rice, smaller than a corn of barley, smaller than a mustard-seed or kernel of a canary-seed. 'He also is my soul within my heart, greater than the earth, greater than the sky, greater than the heavens beyond, greater than all these worlds.

"He from whom all works, all desires, all sweet odours and tastes proceed, who embraces all this, who never speaks and is never surprised, He—my soul within my heart—is God. When I shall have departed from hence, I shall mingle with him."—*Chhandogya Upanishad,*

This is the truth which is explained in a hundered beautiful similes. The Universal Sou! is like the honey, in which drops collected by bees from distant trees mingle; it is like the ocean, in which rivers coming from distant regions are lost; it is like the saline water, in which particles of salt can no longer be discerned.

"At whose wish does the mind, sent forth, proceed on its errand?" asks the pupil. "At whose command does the first breath go forth? At whose wish do we utter this speech? What god directs the eye or the ear?"

The teacher replies: "It is the ear of the ear, the mind of the mind, the speech of the speech, the breath of the breath, the eye of the eye. . . . That which is not expressed by speech, but by which speech is expressed. . . . that which does not think by mind, but by which mind is thought, . . . that which does not see by the eye, but by which one sees, . . . that which does not hear by the ear, but which by the hearing is heard, . . . that which does not breathe by breath, but by which breath is breathed,—that alone is God—not that which people here adore."—*Kena Upanishad.*

It is esay to see in the above passage all effort made by the sages and thinking men in the ancient age to shake themselves from the trammels of meaningless ceremonial and the fanciful gods whom "people here adore," and to soar to a higher region of thought, to comprehend the incomprehensible, the breath of the breath and the mind of the mind. It was a manly and fervent effort made by the Hindus three thousand years ago to know the unknown God; and the daring but pious thinkers thus describe the Diety whom they tried to conceive:

> "He, the Soul, encircled all bright, incorporeal, scatheless, without muscles, pure, untouched by evil, a seer, wise, omnipresent and self-existent,—He disposed all things rightly for eternal years."—*I'sa Upanishad.*

Such were the earliest efforts made by the Hindus to discern the attributes and nature of the unknown Diety. They are among the earliest efforts of man to comprehend his maker, and we find them in the imperishable works of the Hindus, the Upanishads.

Transmigration of Soul

Another new and startling idea is also first met with in these works. Other nations have believed in the resurrection of the soul;

the Hindus believed in the past as well as in the future existence of the soul; and this idea of the transmigration of souls is first taught and explained in the Upanishads.

The idea is that the same soul passes through various bodies according to its acts, before it can be freed from all its imperfections and mingle in the Diety. "According to his deeds and according to his knowledge, he is born again as a worm, or as an insect, or as a fish, or as a bird, or as a lion, or as a boar, or as a serpent, or as a tiger, or as a man, or as a something else in different places." And after passing through various worlds, the purified soul approaches God.—*Kaushitaki Upanishad.*

This doctrine of transmigration of souls, which was first taught in India, and which other ancient nations borrowed from the Hindus, is explained in many beautiful similies. The progress of the soul through different bodies is like the progress of the caterpillar moving from blade to blade, or like the changes in the gold which the goldsmith turns into newer and more beautiful forms. And when at last the soul is thus purified of all its imperfections, it finally casts off the body and mingles with God. "As the slough of the snake lies on an anthill, dead and castaway, thus lies the body; but the disembodied immortal spirit is God, it is Light."—*Brihadaranyaka Upanishad.*

Creation of the World

The creation of the world also puzzled the sages of the Upanishads. We are told in the *Chhandogya* that the Self-existent grew into an egg, and the egg burst itself into two halves, the heaven and the earth. And elsewhere in the same work we are told that the Self-existent first sent forth-fire, and the fire sent forth water, and the water sent forth the earth.

The *Aitareya A'ranyaka* discusses the first material from which the universe was created; and, as in the Rig Veda and in the Jewish account of the creation, water is said to be the first material cause.

And in the *Brihadaranyaka Upanishad* we are told that the self-existent Soul formed himself into the male and female, and the creation proceeded therefrom.

Mysteries of Death

The mysteries of death were no less strange to the early sages than the mysteries of creation, and a beautiful legend is told of a sage,

Nachiketas, who asked Death to reveal his mysteries. But Death was unwilling to reveal his secrets, and said:

> "Choose sons and grandsons who shall live a hundred years, herds of cattle, elephants, horses, gold. Choose the wide abode of the earth, and live thyself as many harvests as thou desirest.
>
> "If you can think of any boon equal to that, choose wealth and long life. Be king, Nachiketas, on the whole earth. I make thee the enjoyer of all desires.
>
> "Whatever desires are difficult to attain among mortals, ask for them, anything to thy wish. These fair maidens with chariots and musical instruments, such are indeed not to be obtained by men,— be waited on by them whom I give thee, but do not ask me about dying."

But Nachiketas said, "These things last till to-morrow, O Deaih ! for they wear out the vigour of all the senses. Even the whole of life is short. Keep thou thy horses, keep dance and song for thyself."

Pressed by the pious inquirer, Death at last revealed his great secret, which is the cardinal idea of Hindu monotheism.

"The wise who by mediation of his own soul recognizes the soul . . . as God,—he indeed leaves joy and sorrow far behind.

"A mortal who has heard this and accepted this,—who has separated it from all qualities, and has reached the subtle Being,— rejoices because he has cause for rejoicing. The house of God is open, I believe, O Nachiketas."—*Katha Upanishad.*

Such were the efforts of the Hindus of the Epic Age to learn the mysteries of the Diety and of the soul, of creation and of death. And though in these ancient ideas we find much that is fanciful, and though they are clothed in quaint similes and legends, yet it is impossible not to be struck with the freshness, the earnestness, and the vigour of thought which mark these yearnings after the truth. A great German philosopher, Schopenhauer, has recorded his high admiration for the Upanishads in striking words which have been often quoted. "From every sentence, deep, original, and sublime thoughts arise, and the whole is pervaded by a high and holy earnest spirit. Indian air surrounds us and original thoughts of kindred spirits. . . . It has been the solace of my life; it will be the solace of my death."

Notes and References

1. *Rig Veda,* I. 30, 21; I. 48. 7; I. 113. 7; I. 124. 4; I. 123.11.
2. Argynoris is Arjuni of the Veda, Daphne is Dahana, Athena is Ahana, Erinnys is Saranyu, etc.
3. Some identify the Sarasvati with the river Indus itself.

16

The Role of Gambling in Ancient Indian Society

DR. M.M. PATKAR

The vocabulary of a language records the state of civilization and culture of a particular society during its existence. For example, the words for food and drink in ancient literature show what type of commodity was used by the people of those times. Similarly, the names of games that were in vogue in historic and pre-historic times are an indication of the role they played in society at different times and places. The present paper is an attempt in this direction.

Anthropologists distinguish between games of chance and games of skill. Since their outcome is always a matter of luck, games of chance offer obvious opportunities for wagering and gambling. Man's interest in gambling has never subsided. A student of cultural anthropology is amazed to find numerous kinds of games of chance such as card-games, dice-games, question games and lotteries. Such games are usually accompanied by high stakes and the gambler, in the heat of excitement, even goes to the extent of gambling away not only all his wealth but even his beloved wife, as is evident from the story of the *Mahabharata,* where Yudhisthira, the eldest of the Pandavas, gambled away not only his kingdom but his brothers and wife Draupadi. The lament of the gambler narrated in the *Rgveda* (X.34) is well-known. Sometimes gamblers repented for what they had done and improved their conduct later. In the *Mrcchakatika* we find an instance of this type. There the samvahaka, a shampooer by profession and formerly in the service of Carudatta, later turned to gambling, is persecuted for the debts he owes to another gambler and takes refuge in the house of Vasanrasena, who pays-off his debts. Bitten with remorse due to the humility to which he is put by the gamblers, he repents for his folly and resolves to be a monk (*cf. aham dyutakarapamanena Sakyasratnanako bhavisyami*).

Gambling during the Vedic Period

During the Vedic period the game of dice seems to have attained a high place in society. Numerous references to the game of dice are to be found in Vedic and post-Vedic literature. Dicing was as much loved by the Vedic Aryans as horse-racing. They were extremely fond of dice-playing and the word *aksa* in the sense of 'die' is frequently used in the *Rgveda.* The dice seem to have been made of the *vibhitaka* nuts and were brown in colour.[1]

Names of throws and dice: In the later Samhitas and Brahmanas the names of the throws are said to be of four kinds named as *krta, treta, dvapara* and *askanda.* Some of these names are traced in the *Rgveda* and the *Atharvaveda.* For example the word *kali* occurs in *AV* VII. 114.1 and a number of passages where the word occurs are recorded by Luders.

The *krta* was the name of a die or the side of a die marked with four points or dots. This was supposed to be the most lucky or winning die. *Krta* was also the collective name of the four dice in opposition to the fifth die called *kali.* The *treta* was a throw of a die as well as the side of a die marked with three dots (*VS.* XXX. 18; *TS.* IV). A die or the side of the die marked with two spots was called *dvapara.* The name of the fourth die was *askanda.*

The names of some of the throws are to be found in the *RV* and the *AV. Kali* occurs in *AV* VII. 114.1 इदमुग्राय बभ्रवे नमो यो अक्षेषु तनूवशी। घृतेन 'कलिं' शिक्षामि सनो मृडानीदृशे।।

Luders has shown in several places that *krta* means a 'throw' (not a 'stake' or 'what is won'), in which sense the word is usedin the *AV*.[2]

Although dicing was condemned by thoughtful men it appears that in the Vedic times it was not a disreputable game, as even kings indulged in it, and there was even a royal officer called *'Aksavapa"* or a Superintendent of gambling. In spite of its evil effects, known to all and loudly lamented, the gambling house was regarded as a useful institution in certain respects and was supposed to be a meeting place for social intercourse.[3]

It is extremely doubtful if during Vedic times or even in later periods ladies ever visited gambling houses. In this connection Prof. Dass observes: There is a verse in the *RV* (I. 124.7) of doubtful sense, which seems to imply that sometimes widows visited the dicing hall with a view to gain wealth by gambling. Such conduct on their part was, of course, not approved, as the conduct of a brotherless young woman, who sought the company of young men met with public disapprobation.[4]

Post-Vedic Period

In the Dharmasutras we find scanty references to the game of dice. Apastamba states that the king should provide for a gambling house which was to be open to all the twice-born men. Here men played with wooden dice. Gautama, Baudhayana and Vasistha are all silent so far as the topic of gambling or play at dice is concerned. In *Visnusmrti* provision is made for the punishment of persons who play false game and indulge in other fraudulent practices.[5] However, it states that a king should not indulge in dice-playing and forbids the game for the king along with wine, women and hunting.[6]

It is only in the Smrti works that gambling finds a detailed treatment and a place in the topics of law. Although there are divergent views on the topic of gambling the consensus of the opinion of the Smrti writers seems to be that gambling should be permitted under certain circumstances, particularly because it is helpful in the detection of thieves. Manu's attitude towards the same of dice is uncompromising. In his opinion gambling should find no place in the kingdom because gambling and prize-fighting are the causes of destruction of a kingdom. He declares *dyuta* and *samahvaya* to be open thefts and all those indulging in such games should be corporally punished irrespective of their castes.[7] He further states that gamesters like dancers are secret thieves, who should be banished. He prescribes that gambling should not be resorted to even in joke as it leads to enmity.

These views of Manu are not subscribed to by other writers like Kautilya, Yajnavalkya, Narada, Brhaspati and others. They not only allow gambling, though under certain circumstances, but lay down rules for the proper conduct of the gambling houses. They speak elaborately about the place of gambling, the keeper of the gambling house, settlement of disputes among gamblers, the share to be paid to the king, the punishment for fraudulent practices at the game and so on.

It will thus be seen that the attempted reform in Manu's time was rendered futile. In later Smrtis laws regarding play at dice reappear in all their glory. Manu's emphatic prohibition against gambling was reduced to a regulated gaming, and gambling flourished as before in the times of his successors. The rules laid down by the later Smrti writers indicate a larger prevalence of gambling leading to relaxation of restrictions. Although gambling was permitted as a means for the detection of thieves, in course of time it became a source of revenue for the State.

The Place for Gambling or the Gambling House

Ordinarily the game of dice was to be played in a Gambling Hall (*sabha*) prescribed for the purpose and supervised by an officer called *sabhika.* The earliest reference to the gambling hall is to be found in the *Ap. Dh. Sutra* where it is stated that the gamblers should play the game in a gambling hall using a table for the throws of dice.[8] It appears that in Apastamba's time gambling was to be carried on only in the gambling hall; otherwise the person playing elsewhere was liable to fine.[9] But Narada (17.8) provides that gambling might take place also in an open place outside the gambling house, in which case the gamblers were required to give the king his share in the stake and then would incur no punishment. The general rule, however, seems to be that the game of dice should be played in a place provided for the game. This place according to Katyayana should have an arch erected near the door of the gambling hall so that respectable people might not mistake about its real nature.[10] Yajnavalkya mentions two different kinds of gambling houses. One was a public (*prasiddha*) gambling house, where gambling took place, not secretly, but in an assembly of gamesters supervised by a keeper of a gaming house, and in the presence of the officer of gaming appointed by the king. The other was a secret gambling house without a keeper.

The Officers of the Gambling House

It will appear from Kautilya's *Arthasastra* and also from several other works that gambling was under State control and that the gambling house was supervised by officers such of the *sabhika* and the *sabhapati.* The former was the keeper of the gambling house to whom belonged the house for the residence of gamesters.[11] The *sabhapati* was the other officer, whose duty was to make provision for all the instruments of gambling such as dice, arrangement for play, etc., and he was to maintain himself on the income derived therefrom.[12]

The duty of the keeper of the gambling house was to superintend the play in the hall and to pay to the king a fixed portion.[13] He was to recover the amount of the wager from the losing party by accepting a pledge or by arrest. Having recovered the amount he should pay it to the successful party. Similarly, being impartial, he should always declare a true decision to the gamblers.[14] Narada (16.2) also ordains the same duties to the keeper of the gambling house.

The keeper was to receive 5% when the stake was for 100 panas or more and 10% when it was for less than 100 panas. Aparарka explains that the keeper was to receive as his fee 5% from the victorious gambler and 10% from the losing one. Narada prescribes a flat rate of 10% on the stake as the fees of the *sabhika.* Kautilya allows the *sabhika* to charge hire for supplying gambling accessories such as dice, leather pieces as also for supplying water and accommodation.[15]

Disputes Regarding Gambling

The gambling house was a meeting place for the rogues and dishonest people. The work of deciding the cases between the gamblers was therefore naturally entrusted to persons who knew very well the fraudulent practices of the gamblers. Yajnavalkya (2.202) therefore lays down that both the judges for settling the disputes about gambling as also the witnesses shall be the gamesters themselves in spite of the injunction that the gamblers could neither be witnesses in law suits nor sit in an assembly as assessors. They were to be appointed by the king and the usual rule that a judge shall be accomplished in learning and study, etc., was not made applicable to the persons who decided disputes arising in the gambling houses.[16] Katyayana provides the same rule but Brhaspati adds a proviso that where the gamblers are alleged to be inimical to the disputants the king may himself decide the matter.[17]

Although gambling was permitted by the Hindu lawgivers they not only condemned deceitful or fraudulent gambling but ordained severe punishment in such cases. Narada provides that when gambling is carried on secretly and without the king's permission on with false dice or other deceitful tricks, the gamblers and the keeper of the gambling house were not entitled to their profit or gain and would be liable to punishment. He further states that wicked men who play with false dice were to be driven out of the gambling house with a wreath of dice hung round their neck.[18] Yajnavalkya also prescribes that persons gambling with false dice or other instruments should be branded and banished by the king.

Formation of Words Relating to Gambling

As already observed gambling or playing with dice must have been a very common game in ancient Indian society, with the result that numerous words pertaining to the game of dice crept into the Sanskrit language (see Appendix). Even Panini, the well known Sanskrit grammarian, could not avoid using the formations of words pertaining to gambling. In this behalf Mm. Dr. P.V. Kane observes: "Panini teaches the formation of many words relating to gambling. In II. 1.10[19] he teaches the formation of *avyoyibhava* compounds like *'aksapari'* or '*salakapari'* in the sense 'that loss was caused by one dice being cast in a way different from the way in which it was cast in a prior game'. In 4.4.2[20] he teaches that *'aksika'* means one who uses dice in gambling or wins by using dice, and in 4.4.19[21] he states that *'aksadyutika'* means '(enmity) brought about by using dice in gambling'. *Vide* also Panini 3.57.58." (*History of Dharma Sastra,* III. 541).

Gambling with dice appears to have been an institution in vogue even before the Aryans penetrated the Indian soil. It had assumed considerable importance in the earliest times in India as also in the other parts of the world. Tacitus speaks of the influence of the game among the Germanic tribes where pawning away not only one's own belongings but also one's liberty was not uncommon. He states that strong and powerful young men overcome by the sway of the game meekly followed as slaves the winners at a game of dice at which the gambler's personal liberty was at stake. A parallel at once strikes in Yudhisthira's pawning his kingdom, his brothers, himself and even his wife at the game of dice[22] and although Manu emphatically condemned such games of chance, calling upon the king to abolish gambling, his attempt to reform was only shortlived. In later times Manu's strict prohibition gave way to regulated gambling which in course of time flourished as before. To quote Dr. N.C. Sen Gupta: "The strict supervision at public gambling place for the public benefit too was in time relaxed, so that by paying a fee to the king anybody was enabled publicly to play any game for a wager. The public benefit professed to be sought from controlled gaming ultimately yielded to a scheme for getting revenue out of this vice."[23]

APPENDIX

Some Sanskrit Words for Gambling

[The list is enumerative and not exhaustive.]

अक्ष[24] m. a die for gambling. *Nar.* 19. 1 : अक्षवध्रशलाकाद्यैः।

अक्षस् m. a die for gambling. *RV.* 10. 34. 6 : अक्षासो अस्य वितरन्ति कामं प्रतिदीव्ने।

अक्षकाम mfn. fond of gambling. *MW.* 3a.

अक्षकितव m. a gambler *MW.* 3a.

अक्षकुशल mfn. skilled in dice. *MW.* 3a.

अक्षगोप्तृ m. keeper of a gambling house.

अक्षग्लह m. gambling, playing at dice. *MW.* 3a.

अक्षतत्त्व n. science of dice. *MW.* 3a.

अक्षतत्त्वविद् mfn. skilled in the science of dice. *MW.* 3a.

अक्षदाय m. handing over the dice in gambling. *MW.* 3a; moving a piece on hand.

अक्षदेवन n. gambling. *MW.* 3a.

अक्षदेविन् or अक्षद्यु m. a gambler or dice-player. Af *W.* 3a *Dhk.*

1911.15; *Viv. Rut.* p. 614: एकरूपा द्विरूपा वा द्यूते यस्याक्षदेविनः।

अक्षद्यूत n. gambling. *MW.* 3a. Sayana on *RV.* 1. 41. 9: अक्षद्यूतं कुवतोर भयोर्मध्ये 4. 4. 19 : निवृत्तेऽक्षद्यूतादिभ्यः।

अक्षद्रुग्ध mfn. hated by (unlucky at) dice.

अक्षधर mfn. holding dice. *MW.* 3a.

अक्षधूर्त्त mfn. a gambler, a dice-rogue.

अक्षनैपुण्य n. skill in gambling. *MW.* 3a.

अक्षपराजय m. defeat at the game of dice. Sayana on *RV.* 10.34.10:

अक्षपराजयादृणवान् कितवः।

अक्षपराहित mfn. defeated in gambling. *Nar.* 4.203: यां चैवाक्षपराजितः।

अक्षपरि ind. with the exception of one die. *MW.* 3b.

अक्षपात m. throw of dice. *MW.* 3b.

अक्षपातन n. the act easting dice. *MW.* 3b.

अक्षप्रक्षेप m. throw of dice. *AV.* com. 7.52.2: अहमेव प्रथमः अक्षप्रक्षेपेण प्रतिवादिनं जेष्यामि।

अक्षप्रिय mfn. fond of dice, favoured bydice. *MW.* 3b.

अक्षभूमि f. gambling-place. *MW.* 3b. *Kaut.* 3.20 अक्षभूमिहस्तदोषाणां चाप्रतिषेधने द्विगुणो दण्डः।

अक्षमद m. passion for dice. *MW.* 3b.

अक्षमात्र n. anything as big as dice: *MW,* 3b.

अक्षमाला f. garland of dice. *Nar.* 19.6: कण्ठेऽक्षमालामासज्य स ह्येषां विनयः स्मृतः।

अक्षराज m. king of dice; the dice called *Kali.* *MW.* 3b.

अक्षवृत्त n. anything that happen in gambling.

अक्षवेदिन् mfn. one acquainted with gambling. *Nar.* 19.3: द्विरभ्यस्ताः पतन्त्यक्षा ग्लहे यद्यक्षवेदिनः।

अक्षावपन n. dice-board. *MW.* 3b.

अक्षातिवाप m. keeper or superintendent of a gambling house. cf. अक्षावाप।

अक्षावाप m. keeper of a gambling house. *Mait. Sam.* 3.6.3: अक्षावापस्य च गृहभ्यः।

अक्षावापन n. case for keeping dice in *Sat. Br.* 5.3.1.11.

अक्षिक m. gambler. Com. on *RV.* 10.34.8: अक्षिकाः प्रायेण तावद्भिरक्षैर्दीव्यन्ति हि।

अदूत्य n. unlucky gambling; not derived from gambling; honestly earned. *RV.* 1. 112.29.

अधिदेवन n. a table or board for gambling; *MW.* 21a. *Mait. Sam.* 4.4.6; तेन स्फ्येनाधिदेवनं कुर्वन्ति तत्र षष्ठौही विदीव्यन्त।

आदिनवदर्श n. vie of (another's) misfortune or want of luck in dice. *Tait. Br.* 3.4.16.1: त्रेताया आदिनवदर्शम् (com. आदिनवदर्श मर्यादायां देवस्य परीक्षकम्।)

अधिदेविन् mfn. playing false at dice. *Yaj.* 2. 202: राज्ञा सचिह्नं निर्वास्याः कूटाक्षोपधिदेविनः।

कटप्रू m. gambler; dice-player. *MW.* 243c.

कितव m. 1. gambler, *Kaut,* 3.20: प्रायशो हि कितवा कूटदेविनः। *Nar. 19.3 :* द्विरभ्यस्ताः पतन्त्यक्षा ग्लहे यद्यक्षदेविनः। जयं तस्यापरस्याहुः कितवस्य पराजयम्।। *RV.* 10.34.6: सभामेति कितवः पृच्छमानः। Com. on *RV.* 10.34.2: मां कितवं न मिमेथ।

2. expert in gambling. Com. on *Tait. Br.* 3.4.16.1: कितवं द्यूतकुशलम्।

कितवसमाज m. assembly of gamesters. *Mit.* on *Yaj.* 2.201: सभिकसहिते कितवसमाजे।

कूटदेविन् mfn. a false gamesters. *Viv. Rat.* p. 616: निर्वास्या कूटदेविनः। *Kaut.* 3.20: प्रायशो हि कितवाः कूटदेविनः।

कूटाक्ष m. a false dice.

कूटाक्षदेविन् mfn. one who plays false at dice. *Nar.* 16.6: कूटाक्षदेविनः पापान् राजा राष्ट्राद्विवासयेत्। *Yaj.* 2.202: राज्ञा सचिह्नं निर्वास्याः कूटाक्षोपधि देविनः।

कृत m. name of a die or a part of the marked with four dots. *Tait. Br.* 3.4.16.1: यथा कृतादविजितायाघरेयाः संयन्त्येवमेनं।

ग्रह m. or ग्राभ m. a throw of dice.

ग्लह[25] m. a game at dice; a die, dice-box. असं 4.38: ग्लहे कृतानि कृण्वानाम्। *Yaj.* 2.199. ग्लहे शतिकवृद्धेस्तु सभिकः पञ्चकं शतम्।

जितग्लह mfn. one conquered in gambling. *Mit.* on *Yaj.* 2.199: जितग्लहस्य विंशतितमं भागं गृह्णीयादित्यर्थः।

दीव् to play at dice. *RV.* 10.34.3: अक्षैः मा दीव्यः। *mit* on *Yaj.* 2.202: मतिवञ्चनहेतुना मणिमन्त्रौषधिना ये दीव्यन्ति तान् श्वपदादिनाङ्कयित्वा राजा स्वराष्ट्रान्निर्वासयेत्।

दुन्दुभिः f. a particular throw of dice in gambling. *MW.* 484a.

दुर्द्यूत n. bad or unfair gambling: देविन् mfn. cheating at gambling.

देवन[26] n. gambling. *Manu.* 9.222. प्रकाशमेतत्तास्कर्य यद् देवनसमाह्वयौ।

देवनकर्माधिपति m. superintendent of gambling. Com on *AV.* 7.52.3: अग्निः देवनकर्माधिपतिः नः अस्माकं दीव्यताम्।

देवनसाधन n. means of gambling. Com. on *AV.* 7.52 1: अक्षैः देवनसाधनैः।

देवितव्य n. gambling.

देवितृ mfn. a gambler.

देविन् mfn. a gambler.

द्यूत n. gambling, play at dice. *Nar.* 16.2: सभिकः कारयेद् द्यूतम्। *Manu* 9.233: अप्राणिभिर्यत्क्रियते तल्लोके द्यूतमुच्यते।

द्यूतकर m. a gambler. Com. on *RV.* 10.34.9: द्यूतकराणां कितवानां हृदयस्योपरिं स्फूरन्ति।

द्यूतकरमण्डली f. a gambler's circle.

द्यूतकर्तृ mfn. gambler. *Aparaka* on *Yaj.* 2.199: धूर्तो विजयी वा कितबो द्यूतकर्ता स धूर्त्तकितवः।

द्यूतकार m. a gambler.

द्यूतकारक m. a keeper of a gambling house.

[(द्यूतकारिता (वृद्धि)] f. (interest) on debt for gambling. *Nar.* 19.2; दशकं च शतं तस्य वृद्धिः स्याद् द्यूतकारिणः।

द्यूतकारिन् m. a keeper of gambling house. *Nar.* 19.2: दशकं च शतं वृद्धिस्तस्य स्याद् द्यूतकारिणः *Mit.* on *Yaj.* 2.200; तथा क्षमी भूत्वा सत्यं वचो विश्वासार्थ द्यूतकारिणां दद्यात्।

द्यूतकिङ्करी f. a female slave won at dice.

द्यूतकृत् m. a gambler.

द्यूतक्रिया f. play at dice; gambling. Com. on *AV.* 4.38.1: तदुक्तं द्यूतक्रियामधिकृत्यापस्तम्बेन।

द्यूतक्रीड़ा f. playing with dice.

द्यूतजय m. victory in gambling. Com. on *AV.* 4.38.1: कृताय लाभो हि महान् द्यूतजयः।

द्यूतजयकर्मन् n. victory at dice. Com. on *AV.* 4.38.1: अस्मिन् द्यूतजयकर्मणि अहं हुंवे।

द्यूतजयकामिन् mfn. desirous of victory at dice. Com. on *AV.* 7.52.2: द्यूतजयकामिनं मामिति शेषः।

द्यूतजयचिह्न n. mark of victory at dice Com. on *AV.* 4.38.1: तस्मिन् ग्लहे निमित्ते कृतनि द्यूतजयचिह्नहानि।

द्यूतजित mfn. won at dice. Com. *AV.* 4.38.3: द्यूतजितंन पय (?) उपलक्षितेन।

द्यूतता f. playing with dice; gambling. *MW.* 500 b.

द्यूतदास m. a slave won at dice. *MW.* 500 b.

द्यूतधर्म m. rule or law re. gambling. *Manu.* 9.220: क्रमशः क्षेत्रजादीनां द्यूत धर्म निबोधत।

द्यूतपति m. Superintendent of gambling.

द्यूतपलायित mfn. one who has run away from the game of dice. *MW.* 500 b.

द्यूतपूर्णिमा or पौर्णिमा f. the day of full moon in Karttika (spent in games of chance in honour of Lakshmi). *MW.* 500 b.

द्यूतप्रतिपद् f. the first day of the bright half of the month of Karttika (celebrated with gambling). *MW.* 500 b.

द्यूतप्रिय mfn. fond of gambling. *MW.* 500 b.

द्यूतफलक n. gambling board. *MW.* 500 b.

द्यूतबीज n. a cowrie (small shell used as a coin and in gambling). *MW.* 500 b.

द्यूतभूमि f. gambling place.

द्यूतमण्डल n. a circle or party of gamblers; a gambling house; a circle drawn round a gambler to make him pay.

द्यूतलेखक mn. a gambling bill.

द्यूतवर्त्मन् n. method of gambling. *MW.* 500 b.

द्यूतविशेष m. pl. different kinds of gambling. *MW.* 500 b.

द्यूतवृत्ति m. a professional gambler; a keeper of a gambling house. *Manu.* 3.160.

द्यूतवैतंसिक m. one who lives by gambling and bird-catching.

द्यूतव्यवस्था f. rule re. gambling. Kulluka on *Manu.* 2.220.

द्यूतव्यवहार m. Judical proceedings re. gambling. *Mit.* on *Yaj.* 2.202: द्यूतव्यवहाराणां द्रष्टारः सभ्यास्त एव कितवा एव राज्ञानियोक्तव्याः।

द्यूतव्यसनवत् mfn. addicted to gambling. Com. *AV.* 7.52.2: सर्वदा द्यूतव्यसनवतीनामित्यर्थः।

द्यूतशाला f. a gambling house.

द्यूतसदन n. gambling house.

द्यूतसभा f. a gambling house.

द्यूतसभाधिकारिन् m. a keeper of a gambling house. *Mit.* on *Yaj.* 2.1999.

द्यूतसभायोजक m. a keeper of a gambling house.

द्यूतसमाज m. a gambling house; an assembly of gamblers.

द्यूतसाधन n. means of playing of dice. Com. on *AV.* 4.38.4: अक्षेषु द्यूतसाधनेषु प्रमोदते। Com. on *RV.* 7.86.6: विभिदको द्यूतसाधनोऽक्षः।

द्यूताधिकारिन् m. keeper of a gambling house. *Mit.* on *Yaj.* 2. 200: य एवं क्लृप्तवृत्तिंद्यूताधिकारी स राज्ञा धूर्त्त कितवेभ्यो रक्षितः।

द्यूताधिदेवता f. the goddess presiding over the play at dice. Com. on *AV.* 4.38.3: सा द्यूताधिदेवता पयस्वती।

द्यूताध्यक्ष m. superintendent of gambling. *Kaut.* 3.20: द्यूताध्यक्षो द्यूतमेकमुखं कारयेत्।

द्यूताभियोग m. plaint re. gambling. *Kaut.* 3.20; द्यूताभियोगे जेतुः पूर्वः साहसदण्डः।

द्यूतसक्त mfn. addicted to gambling. Com. on *AV.* 4.38.4: द्यूतासक्ताश्च।

द्यूतोपकरण n. means of playing at dice. *Apararka* on *Yaj.* 2.199: काकिन्यो वध्रिकाश्चैव शलाका मौर्य एव च। अक्षाः सबीजाः कुहका द्यूतोपकरणानि पट्।

धूर्त्त m. a gambler.

धूर्त्तकितव m. a gamester. *Yaj.* 2.119: ग्लहे शतिकवृद्धेस्तु सभिकः पञ्चकं शतम्। गृह्णीयाद्धूर्नकितवात्। *Napararka* explains धूर्त्तकितवाद्धूर्तो विजयी वा द्यूतकर्ता स धूर्त्तकितवः।

धूर्तमण्डल n. assembly of gamesters. *Yaj.* 2.201: प्राप्ते नृपतिना भागे प्रसिद्धे धूर्त्तमण्डले।

धूर्त्तमण्डलाधिपति m. leader of gamesters Visvarupa on *Yaj.* 2.199: तां सभिको द्यूतसभायोजकः धूर्त्तमण्डलाधिपतिर्गृह्णीयात्।

पणक्रीडा f. gambling; play at dice. *Nar.* 14.1: पणक्रीडावयोभिश्च पदं द्यृतसमाह्वयम्।

पाश m. a die, dice. *MW.* 623c.

पाशक mn. a die. *MW.* 6723c.

पाशकपीठ mn. a gambling-table. *MW.* 623c.

पाशक्रीडा f. dice-play; gambling *MW.* 623c.

प्रतिकतव m. an adversary in gambling. Com. on *AV.* 7.52.1: प्रतिकितवपराजये मम सदृशोऽन्यो नास्तीत्यर्थः।

प्रतिदिवन् m. an adversary in gambling. *RV.* 10.34.6: अक्षासो अस्य वि तिरन्ति कामं प्रतिदीव्ने दधत आ कृतानि।

प्रतिदेवितृ m. an adversary in gambling. Com. on *RV.* 10.34.6: तत्र प्रतिदीव्ने प्रतिदेवित्रे कितवाय etc.

विज् to stake. *Rc.* 229.

विभीदक m. a die for gambling. *RV.* 7.86.6: सा सुरा मन्युर्विभीदको अचित्तिः (Com. विभीदको द्यूतसाधनोऽक्षः।

सभा f. a gambling house. *RV.* 10.34.6: सभामिति कितवः पृच्छमानः।

सभानायक m. keeper of a gambling house.

सभापति[27] m. keeper of a gambling house.

सभापाल m. keeper of a gambling house. *Tait. Br.* 1.7.10.5

सभाविन m. keeper of a gambling house. *Tait. Br.* 3.4.16.1: कृताय सभाविनम् (Com. सभाविनं सरसभाता अधिष्ठातारम्)।

सभास्थाक्ष[28] m. aricer.

सभिक m. keeper of gambling house. *Nar.* 19.1: सभिकः कारयेद् द्यूतम् *Yaj.* 2.199: ग्लेह सभिकवृद्धेस्तु सभिकः पञ्चकं शतम्। (Visvarupa: द्यूतसभायोझकः, *Mit.* explains सभिक as a person to whom belongs the house for the residence of gamesters. *cf.* सभा कितवनिवासार्था यस्यास्त्यसौ सभिकः।)

सभ्य m. keeper of a gambling house. *MW.* 1151c.

साधुदेविन् mfn. playing skillfully at dice. *AV.* 4.38.1. उद्भिन्दन्तीं सजयन्तीमप्सरां साधुदेविनीम्।

NOTES AND REFERENCES

1. Macdonell and Keith, *Vedic Index,* I.P. 2.
2. For fuller information see *Vedic Index, ibid.* I. *s.v. aksa,* pp. 2 ff.
3. R. C. Dass, *Rgvedic Culture,* p. 325.
4. *Ibid.*
5. *Cf.* 5.134.35. द्यूते कूटाक्षदेविनां करच्छेदः। उपषिदेविनां संदंशच्छेदः।
6. Cf. 3.50, मृगयाक्षस्त्रीपानाभिरतिं परिहरेत्।
7. *Manu,* 9.221-28.
8. Cf. 2.25.13, सभाया मध्येऽधिदेवनमुद्धत्यावोक्ष्याक्षान्निवपेद्युग्मान्वैभीतकान् यथार्थान्।
9. *See com.* on *Apastamba,* 2.25.13. स एव च स्थानान्तरे दीव्यते दण्डयेत्।
10. *Katyayana Smrti Sarodhara,* P.V. Kane, verse, 935.
11. *Mitaksara on Yajnavalkya,* 2.199, सभा कितवनिवासार्था यस्यास्त्यसौ सभिकः।
12. *Ibid.,* कल्पिताक्षादिनिखिलक्रीडोपकरणस्तदुपचितद्रव्योपजीवी सभापतिरुच्यते।
13. *Yajnavalkya,* 2.200.
14. *Mitaksara* on *Yaj.* 2.200, तथा जितं यद्द्रव्यं तदुद्ग्राहयेत् बन्धकग्रहणेनासेधादिना च पराजितसकाशादुद्धरेत् उद्धृत्य च तद्धनं जेत्रे जयिने सार्थको दद्यात्। तथा क्षमी भूत्वा सत्यं बचो विश्वासार्थ द्यूतकारिणां दद्यात्।

15. *Arthasastra,* 3.20.
16. *Cf. Mitaksara* on *Yaj.* 2.202, द्यूतव्यवहाराणां द्रष्टारः सभ्यास्त एव कितवा एव राज्ञा नियोक्तव्याः। न तत्र "श्रुताध्ययनसम्पन्ना" इत्यादिर्नियमोऽस्ति। साक्षिणश्च द्यूते द्यूतकारा एव कार्याः।
17. *History of Dharma Sastra,* III. 540, उभयोरपि सन्दिग्धौ कितवा स्युः। यदा विद्वेषिणस्ते तु तदा राजा विचयारयेत्।
18. *Narada,* 19. 6-7, कूटाक्षदेविनः पापान् राजा राष्ट्राद्विवासयेत्।
कण्ठेऽक्षमालामासज्य स ह्येषां विनयः स्मृतः।।
19. अक्षशालासंख्याः परिणा। on which the *Mahabhasya* quotes the *karika.*
अक्षादयस्तृतीयान्ताः पूर्वोक्तस्य यथा न तत्।
कितवव्यहारे च एकत्वेऽक्षशलाकयोः।।
20. तेन दीव्यति खनति जयति जितम्। अक्षैर्दीव्यति जयति वा आक्षिकः।
21. निर्वृत्तेऽक्षद्यूतादिभ्यः। अक्षद्यूतेन निर्वृत्तमाक्षूतिकं वैरम्।
22. N.C. Sen Gupta, *Evolution of Ancient Indian Law,* 281.
23. *Ibid.,* 285.
24. For a ditailed note on *aksa* Macdonell and Keith, *Vedic Index,* I.2ff.
25. *Vedic Index* I, 248: *'Glaha'* denotes the 'throw' at dice, like *Grabha,* of which it is a later form occurring in the *Atharvaveda.*
26. *Devana* is mentioned in the *Rgveda* (10.43.5) in connection with dicing. According to Macdonell and Keith (*Vedic Index* 1.375) the word designates the place on which the dice are thrown (elsewhere called *adhidevana*)
27. *Mit.* on *Yaj.* 2.199, explains सभापति as one who makes provision for all the instruments of gambling, such as dice, etc. and maintains himself on the amount received therefrom. *Cf.* कल्पिताक्षादिनिखिलक्रीडोपकरणस्तदुपचितद्रव्योपजीवी सभाहतिरुच्यते)
28. *MW.* 11151c explains सभास्थानु as 'a post at a gambling house', either a 'gambling table' or a man who sits like a post at a gambling table. It also means 'a persistent gambler'.

17

International Law and Conduct in Ancient India

DR. P.N. BANERJEE

Introduction

Eminent jurists and disinterested publicists regard International Law as the product of modern European culture. They do not deny that the ancients—by the ancients they mean exclusively the Greeks and the Romans—had a distinctive civilisation of their own; but obsessed with the Austinian conception of law they refuse to believe that the constitution of ancient societies was at all favourable for the development of a body of systematic rules. Sir F.E. Smith, the Attorney-General of England, in his book on International Law gives the following testimonial to ancient societies:

> "The constitution of ancient societies was little favourable to the development of International Law. Since states are its units, International Law can only exist where a number of communities acknowledge a mutual equality before the law and make common submission to its authority." Such conditions, says the great lawyer, did not prevail amongst the nations of antiquity in general. He rates the ancients—meaning of course the Greeks and the Romans—because certain rules or customs which guided the relations between people of cognate race were not observed with regard to people

outside that pale. "For the most part a state of hostility characterized the relationships between a nation and alien races. Might was regarded as right. Neither person, nor property was considered sacred."[1]

Kent,[2] in his Commentary on International Law held the same view. Even the most civilized states amongst the ancient, according to him, had no conception of the moral obligations of humanity and justice between nations, and that no such thing as International Law obtained among them. Wheaton[3] was no less disparaging in his opinion concerning International Law in Greece. "In the ancient world," says he. "the law of might was universal .... that even Aristides the Just was guided by state-interest rather than by justice." According to Oppenheim,[4] the ancients could not possibly have any regard for man as man, or for territorial rights; the stranger was regarded by them as a spy and the normal condition of things was war, during which everything was permissible.

In the "well-considered" opinions of the above jurists therefore, very little of a systematic body of rules governing interstatal relationships could be looked for in antiquity, even among the Greeks and. the Romans who have admittedly bequeathed a rich legacy of culture to the modern European nations. International Law therefore, has until quite recently, been regarded as a tardy offshoot of modern civilisation. Imbued with imperialistic ideas, Hall[5] considers International Law as a 'favoured monopoly' of the European family of nations and he regards with great complacence and philosophic satisfaction, "the tendency which has shown itself of late to conduct relations with states, which are outside the sphere of International Law, to a certain extent in accordance with its rules." "A tendency has also shown itself on the part of such states to expect that European countries shall behave in conformity with the standard which they have themselves set-up."

Hall was obviously referring to the cases of China and Japan. The case of India, stood on a different footing as she was neither a sovereign state, nor a "civilised" state. Such a considerate publicist like Lawrence[6] would regard the Indian troops as "semi-civilised or imperfectly civilised troops" and he recommended their "use against border tribes and in warfare with people of the same degree of civilisation as themselves." To such people saturated with the theory of the European origin of International Law, the admission of India in the peace conference was regarded as either an "eye wash", or as the legitimate exercise of the right of "self-determination". The signing of the peace treaty by two Indian agents of the Government of India—not the accredited representatives of the people—was regarded by most Indians "as a parting of the old ways", the herald of a brighter dawn, when the westernised education of the Indians would have a distinct though late recognition by the civilised nations of the world. To them India was a:

> ". . . Sad relic of departed worth,
> Immortal, though no more, though fallen, great."

It is, however, the object of the present thesis to establish the apparently incredible fact that the *ancient Indians had a definite knowledge of the rules af International Law according to which they regulated their international conduct.* Warfare was conducted according to such customs and usages, and the rule of might and the doctrine of state-necessity had no more elaborate applications with them as with the 'moderners', in their cynical disregard of the rights of others as has been evidenced during the great World War, in the utter disregard for all rules of civilized warfare and in the curtailment of the rights of the non-combatants to the lowest limits. The ancient Indians had two thousand years before a Grotius, a Rachel or an Ayala recalled Europe to humanity, propounded a body of rules governing the relations between different states into which the continent of India was generally divided.

Nor could we, in the face of modern researches, attribute the rules of International Law solely to modern European ingenuity, to modern European thought, to modern European culture and to the powerful writings of European jurists like Grotius, Rachel, Ayala, Puffendorff, Bynkershoeck or Vattel. We have a dim perception of the rudiments of International Law in ancient Egypt. To Mr. Petrie is due the undying gratitude of every orientialist because of his discovery and interpretation of what we now call the Tel-el-amarna and the Boghazkoy inscriptions. They clearly prove the international consciousness of ancient Egypt. Intercourse between Egypt and the countries in Syria was maintained by diplomatic agents; hostages were demanded and kept and lastly, the Egyptians entered into elaborate extradition treaties with the Hittites for the protection of their national industries.

Mr. Martin[7] in his "Traces of International Law in China" has pointed out the existence of International Law in China long before the dawn of the Christian era. Diplomatic agents maintained interstatal relationship in China : they were immune from personal violence and the sanction of religion was invoked to militate the rigours of Chinese warfare.

Mr. Philipson has clearly established the existence of International Law in ancient Greece. Apart from rules relating to "naturalisation" and "aliens" the Greeks had rules relating to hospitality, asylum, extradition, diplomatic agents and intervention. They firmly grasped the principles of the theory of the Balance of Power and actually used them in practice. They had also rules relating to the declaration and cessation of hostilities, rules relating to the treatment of combatants, to maritime jurisdiction, embargo, blockade and neutrality. Similarly, the Romans had a variety of international rules relating to various topics dealt with by modern International Law; alliances, arbitration; naturalisation, extradition, immunity of ambassadors, procedure and formalities in the conclusion of treaties, right of asylum, treatment of enemy person and enemy property. They had a clear cut conception of protectorates and territorial sovereignty; they knew the position of hostages and the doctrine of *post-liminitum* owes its origin to them. With the gradual expansion of Rome, all these rules of International Law were frequently violated till the Roman foreign policy was summed up in one word—the triumph of expediency. The foreign policy of the later Roman Republic and the Roman Empire has been admirably described by Ortolan[8] thus:

> "To sow discord among different nations in order to array one against another—to assist the vanquished in conquering the conqueror—to husband its own resources, to use those of its allies to invade the territories of its neighbours—to interfere in the disputes of other states, so as to protect the weaker party and finally to subjugate both—to wage unnecessary wars and prove itself stronger in reverses than in success—to evade oaths and treaties by subterfuge—to practice every kind of injustice under the specious guise of equity—this was the policy which gave Rome the sceptre of all Italy and which was destined to secure for it that of the entire known world."

If Europe owes the invention of gunpowder to the Saracens, it owes also its first systematic war code to them. Thus, precepts of kindness and chivalry abounded in the Quoran and in the decisions of Mohammad and his successors. There were injunctions against the making use of incendiary projectiles, cutting trees belonging to the enemy, intercepting his water-supply or poisoning wells and water courses, while the killing of women and children or the insane and the mutilation of prisoners without order was absolutely forbidden. Women and minors of both sexes became the immediate property of captors. The disposition of adult male persons was reserved to the commander. They could be sent back, released on ransom, exchanged or reduced to slavery. The giving of food to the prisoners was compulsory, and their torture was prohibited. Captured enemy property became the property of the whole Mussalman community. Booty could not be appropriated till after a fifth had been taken from it for religious purposes. These rules were very frequently violated in actual practice even by the Saracens themselves; but the Turks who succeeded them did not perceive the utility of observing any rules whatsoever in their dealings with non-Mussalmans and betrayed their Turanian origin by habitual disregard of them.

From what has been said above, it would appear that rules of International Law are not exclusively of European origin. The rules of interstatal relationships followed in ancient India were much more humane and much more elaborate than the rules followed by all nations of antiquity and even by nations of modern Europe down perhaps to the time of the French Revolution.

The Origins

The geographical configuration of India, her early political development and her intellectual expansion all helped in origin, growth and the frequency of regularised interstatal relations. Unlike Greece, the various states of India were not isolated from each other. Hills and dales were in plenty in this vast continent of India, but they did not help the development of autonomous city states as in ancient Greece. Although city republics were in existence, they did not form the ideal of political organization in ancient India: on the contrary, the country state was the prevailing type of advanced political organisation. The territories of these country states were contiguous to each other and political development as well as commercial intercourse necessitated the observance of a body of rules governing such intercourse. India could not therefore develop what is called in the case of Greece "inter-municipal law". Her geography stood in her way.

Difference Between Modern and Ancient International Law

The political development of the ancient Indians also helped the growth of interstatal rules. The chief accusation brought against the Indians has been their utter lack of a perfected and lasting imperial organisation. The idea of imperialism had no doubt ruled the minds of men in India in the distant past long before the vista of a vast imperial organisation was opened up to the Indian eye by the invasion of the Persian Emperor Darius or the Macedonian conqueror, Alexander the Great. But the establishment of an empire in India was the exception and not the rule. This lack of an imperial organisation in India, however reproachful to the imperialistic school, was helpful to the establishment of a body of rules guiding the conduct of states in their daily intercourse with the other states, either in times of profound peace or in anxious times of war. Behind this fortuitous concourse of circumstances stood the ever present sanction of religion or *Dharma* which differentiated modern International Law from ancient International Law. Followers of Austin have denied the title International Law to rules based on religious sanction. They put their case too high. All laws are not *laws* according to the positive theory of Austin. Thus Jenks in his "Law and Politics, in the Middle Ages" has shown that in mediaeval times there existed a body of rules propounded by merchant guilds, by the Church, or based on feudal customs which were laws but could not be regarded as "laws" according to the Austinian sense of the term. If that is the case with municipal law how very different would be the case with International Law? International Law has not ceased to be law because admittedly up to the present day, it has lacked the element of sanction, or coercion in cases of infringement. Rules of International Law have been in the past based on moral persuasion followed by physical compulsion in cases of grave infringements. No common superior has yet enforced the sanction of International Law.

The ancient Hindus did not lack in the idea of the positive sanction of law but they preferred to base the rules relating to interstatal relationship on *Dharma* or religion as the sheet anchor of common humanity. They had no special code of International Law but as will be seen later, their Dharmasastras and their Arthasastras lay down a body of rules guiding their interstatal relations under the title, *Deshadharma.* A careful study of *Niti* was particularly recommended by the Arthasastras as conducive to all-round prosperity.

Thus, belief in the efficacy of a Science of polity as a condition precedent to progress leads to increased intercourse between states on approved lines. Thus says Kautilya :

वृग्डि क्षयं च स्थानं च कर्शनोच्छेदनं तथा
सर्व्वोपायान् समादध्यादेतान्यश्चार्थशास्त्रवित्।।
एवमन्योन्यसचञ्रं पाड्गुण्य योऽनुपश्यति।
स वृव्डिनिगलैर्व्वैरिष्टं क्रीड़ति पार्थिवैः।।[9]

True it is that the exponents of the theory of expediency in the ancient India declared :

तावत् परो नीतिमान् स्यादुयावत् मबलावन् स्वयम्।
मिचं तावच्च भवति पुष्टाग्नेः पवनो यथा।।[10]

But does not this doctrine of political morality contain certain and universal truth? In spite of the tangled mass of rules of International Law, is there any respectable state in Europe to-day which does not live in a perpetual armed peace? And where is that rule of International Law which in the stern realm of fact concedes equality of status to a tiny little state, or a rather weak state, along with any of the "Big Five"? In the past retention of Egypt by England, the subordinate treaty of alliance entered into with Persia, Japan's persistent refusal to return Shantung to China are forceful illustrations of the statement of Sukracharyya.

International Consciousness in Ancient Books

As observed before, International Law in ancient India was based largely on religion and tacit consent but in numerous treaties and alliances entered into by various states, and in the developed conception of the Balance of Power we have also express sanctions of International Law. We have a definite idea of international consciousness in Kautilya's Arthasastra. In a passage the Vijigisu is advised to incite the "Circle of States" or मण्डल (a theory which probably owes its origin to the love of symbolism of the ancient Indians), to preserve the balance of power against the over-rapid growth of a *Madhyama King.*[11]

Although this international consciousness has for its basis interests of a sordid types till the force of public opinion is duly regarded by the Vijigisu or the conquering King in his dealings with the other states included within the circle of states. Thus, if he thinks that the circle of states would be enraged against a friendly state, for giving up its "sovereign" state, then the conquering King should keep quiet.[12]

King—First Servant of State

If it is conceded that "laws" governed the relations between different states, the further question arises whether International Law in ancient India was a law regulating the relation between states or the conduct of Kings? The answer to this question depends upon the general character of ancient Indian monarchy. It has been repeated many times that Grotius' Law of Nations was a law regulating the conduct of princes while the inestimable services of Vattel towards International Law consisted in his advocacy of the rules of International Law as guiding not princes but states in their mutual dealings, as also in his presentation of a developed body of rules relating to Neutrality. Hindu monarchy has been sanctified by the halo of divinity but the Hindu King could not at any time, like Charles I of England, declared that *Rex is Lex* and not *Lex is Rex,* nor could he proclaim like Louis XIV at the height of his power, *"L'etat c'est moi".* Though divine origin was attributed to him, the Indian monarch remained a mere servant of the Community, "the first servant of the state"; unlike the Roman "imperator", he was to all intents and purposes a trustee of the state. That was his position from the time of the Atharvaveda to the days of Kautilya when imperialism was at the noontide of its power and a ruthless policy of conquest and further conquest was urged upon the monarchs, by the Arthasastras. The King had to take a coronation oath in which he had to promise without mental reservation that he would see to the prosperity of the country, look upon it as Brahma and undertake to abide by all laws dictated by ethics or not opposed by politics.

The conception of the King as a salaried official of the state is an established truth according to Manusamhita, Sukracharyya and the Agnipurana.[13] Even an avowed imperialist like Kautilya recommended a virtuous king to address his army just on the eve of a battle thus:

> "I am a paid servant like yourselves; this country is to be enjoyed by me together with you; you have to strike the enemy specified by me."[14] This theory about the trusteeship of the monarch receives further confirmation from the various theories about the origin of the state—even the "social contract theory" being clearly discernible in the Mahabharata, the Agnipurana and the Arthasastra of Kautilya. Thus, International Law in ancient India dealt not with the princes alone but with the subjects of all states as well. It is interesting to

note here that in a voluminous dissertation, Grotius argued against the view that sovereignty, always and without exception, belonged to the people. Just as an individual may give himself up to slavery, he says, so may a people subject itself completely to one or more persons. In certain cases such submission will be advantageous. If it is objected that free men are not articles of commerce, Grotius replies that the liberty of an individual is one thing and the liberty of the nation of which he is a part another. According to Hindu ideas on the other hand, the personality and the sovereignty of the state stood for the personality and the sovereignty of the prince.

International Law Existed in Ancient India

An account of International Law and practice in ancient India given here show that rules of International Law in various forms existed in ancient India. Admittedly, these rules were not perfect, nor did they cover rules relating to few important subjects and topics of International Law, but the imperfections, in certain respects, of International Law in ancient India should not blind one to the very fact of its existence. The translation of the Code of Manu into various European languages has led to the reluctant admission by some European writers that mitigations of horrors in warfare were advocated by the whole of the Aryan family of nations. To some authors like Philipson, the idea of warfare set forth in Manu's Code was not actually followed in practice and he therefore condemned the ancient Indians to eternal perdition : their conception was high, their practice was low. The following account will prove that practice generally confirmed to the ideal excepting when the supreme need of the state overbore all moral considerations. Protection of state interest ought not condemn a nation to hell.

Sources of International Law

Interstatal relations owe the English title "International Law" to Jeremy Bentham. Hugo Grotius called his book "De jure belli ac pasis" : Puffendorff christened his work, "De jure natural et gentium"; Balthazar Ayala named his work, "De jure et officis Bellicis"; while Vattel wrote on "the Law of Nations or the Principles of Natural Law'". Bentham in his "Introduction to the Principles of Morals and Legislation" (1789) made the following observations:

"The word 'International Law', it must be acknowledged, is a new one, though it is hoped sufficiently analogous and intelligible. It is calculated to express in a more significant way that branch of law which goes by the name of the law of nations; an appelation so uncharacteristic that were it not for the force of custom, it would apply rather to internal jurisprudence. The Chancellor D'Aguesseau has already made, I find, a similar remark : he says that what is commonly called *droit des gens* ought rather to be termed *droit centre les gens"* (XVII, 25). The Hindus gave no special name to the science of interstatal relations or the modern science of International Law. They were firm believers in *"Desadharma",* they knew that a regulative science of international rules alone could accelerate interstatal intercourse and consequently internal prosperity; but the rules of international law according to their ideas had a better place in a science of polity, directing the activities of the sovereign of a sovereign state rather than in a separate treatise like the *Consolato del Mare* of the mediaeval ages.

The four "eternal divisions of knowledge" according to the *Arthasastras,* "were *Anvikshikee, Trayee, Varta* and *Dandaniti,*"[15] paving the way to happiness. Some of the great thinkers went so far as to assert that *Dandaniti* was the sole[16] source of knowledge and within this *Dandaniti* were included the rules and customs governing international intercourse and interstatal relations.

Basis of International Law

International Law in ancient as well as in modern times is based upon the sociability of the human nature directed by specific human needs and interests. The guiding motive of International Law, locked at from this point of view, is the utility or the satisfaction of collective needs and interests of states whether intellectual, moral or material. This theory of utility has been very forcefully brought out by the *Agnipurana;*[17] "No king becomes a friend or foe without sufficient cause, or without a due regard to his own interests for the sake of amity or discord." This then is the *basis* or foundation of International Law.

Writers frequently confuse the *sources* of International Law with its *basis* or *foundation* on the one hand and the *evidences* or witnesses to its existence on the other.[18]

'Dharma' Meant Law

The primary sources of International Law, according to modern jurists are: (1) custom based on tacit consent and imitation;[19] (2) conventions or express agreements by means of treaties of an international character. The ancient Hindus understood the first source by *Desadharma* or *Dharma* in general, for example, Sukracharyya defines Desadharma as "custom which may or may not owe its origin to the Srutis but is always followed by the people in different climes"[20] . . . Various meanings have been attached to the expression *Dharma.* Dhammapada was so bewildered with their vastness and complexity that he exclaimed, "for those that are enveloped there is gloom, for those that do not see, there is darkness, and for the good it is manifest, for those that see there is light; even being near those that are ignorant of the way and the *Dharma* do not discern anything."[21] One thing at any rate is certain : that from the time of the Rigveda onward, *Dharma* meant both "Law" and "Custom."[22]

The well-known definition of Dharma given in the Raja-dharma-Prakaraa of the Santiparva of the Mahabharata bears repetition : "No one in discoursing on righteousness can indicate it accurately. Righteousness was declared for the advancement and growth of all creatures. Therefore, that which leads to advancement and growth is Righteousness. Righteousness was declared for restraining creatures from injuring one another. Therefore, that is Righteousness which prevents injury to creatures. Righteousness is so called because it upholds all creatures. Therefore, that is Righteousness which is capable of upholding all creatures". Some say that Righteousness consists in what has been inculcated in the *Srutis.* Others do not agree to this. I do not censure them that say so. Everything again has not been laid down in the *Srutis.*[23]

No student of Indian antiquity has yet suggested this all-embracing definition of Dharma to be a subsequent interpolation and it very forcibly points out that Dharma or custom is indeed the basis of all righteousness whether in the dealings of a man towards his fellowmen or that of one sovereign state towards another sovereign state. Thus, the ancient Hindu recognized the truth of the well-known maxim of Pindar "that custom is the king of all things."[24]

Conventions and Treaties

The second primary source of International Law has been stated as conventions or express agreements by means of *treaties* of an international character. Unfortunately for us, like the treaty of an international character between Rameses II, King of Egypt ("the Pharaoh who knew not Joseph")[25] and Khitasir, the King of the Hittites, we have no treaty of an international character in ancient India. We have various kinds of treaties defined and classified in the Arthasastras between the sovereign states of a *mandala,* we have instances of treaties or alliances and intercourse with foreigners, e.g., Selukos Nikator, Antiochos Soter, Ptolemy Philadelphos, but they do not bequeath to us treaties with the stamp of International Law. Probably the ancient Hindus trusted too much to custom and probably they looked upon Dharma with the eyes of an ancient Hellene towards "the law of Nature". Thus Aristotle says :

> "Customary laws have intrinsically more force, and pertain to more important matters than written laws; and that a man may well be a safer ruler than the written laws, but not safer than the customary law."[26] Thus when Creon accused Antigone of breaking the laws of the state, she replied that those laws were not ordained by Zeus, or by Justice who dwells with the Gods below :
>
> Cr. Now, tell me thou—not in many words, but briefly—knewest thou that an edict had forbidden this?
> An. I knew it; could I help it ? It was politic.
> Cr. And you didst indeed dare to transgress that law?
> An. Yes; for it was not Zeus that had published me that edict ; not such are the laws set among men by the Justice who dwells with the Gods below; nor deemed I that thy decrees were of such force, that a mortal could override the unwritten and the unfailing statutes of heaven. For their life is not to-day, or yesterday, but from all time; no man knows when they were first put forth."[27]

The evidences or witnesses of International Law in ancient India are many and various. These may broadly be classified into (i) the evidences of the Dharmasastras, (ii) the evidences of the Arthasastras, (iii) those of the Puranas and lastly (iv) of inscriptions. We have very little trace of interstatal relations during the Vedic times. We have only glimpses of a state in formation in the Vedic age—the Vedic monarch stood midway between a tribal chief and a territorial king, but the negative evidence of the Vedas stands us in good stead in proving the existence of International Law in ancient India. We get no examples of blood-curdling warfare, nor do we find the *Dasyus* or the *Dasas* absolutely outside the pale of law. Although the Aryan conquerors and colonizers called them "अकर्म्मन्" (a-karman), अब्राह्मण (a-brahmana) and अब्रत[28] (a-brata, i.e., "lawless") still their struggle for existence was not embittered by the use of inhuman methods of warfare; the sacred pages of the Vedas are not disfigured by cannibalism and although we have absolute proof of the use of "poisoned arrows,"[29] still it is not proved that they were exclusively reserved for the aborigines.

Morality and Expediency

Rules of International Law based on *accepted principles of morality* were promulgated in the Dharmasastras, e.g., Manu Smriti, Yagnavalka, Apstamba, etc. Thus, in Chapter VII of the Code of Manu we have a glimplse of the Kautilyan theory of the "Mandala", or "the circle of states," an evidence of international intercourse in the appointment of diplomatic agents and we have also the accepted rules of humane method of warfare fully stated as well as rules relating to chivalry, enemy person and enemy property. We have humane laws of warfare as well as rudiments of what we now call "a Science of Politics" stated in the Santiparva of the Mahabharata, while warfare in the two Epics, the Ramayana and the Mahabharata, seems to have been conducted on the accepted principles of interstatal morality of a very high order.

Various Writers of 'Arthasastras'

Rules of International Law drawn from principles of expediency broadbased upon 'political considerations' find their suitable place in the Arthasastras. Almost the same rules relating to the "circles of states", intercourse between them, and rules relating to the six-fold policy, viz. *sandhi* (peace), *vigraha* (war), *asana* (observance of neutrality), *yana* (marching),[30] *samsraya* (alliance) and *dyaidhibhava* (making peace with one and waging war with another) have been stated and re-stated in almost all their works. There were other writers of the Arthasastras (besides Kautilya, Kamandaka and Sukra) dealing with the same topics or allied topics but their works have been lost. We can gather scraps of information about them from the authors of various extant Arthasastras, such for instance, Kautilya, Kamandaka and Sukracharyya. Prof. Bhandarkar of the Calcutta University has framed a list of the authors of the Arthasastras preceding Kautilya[31]:

Schools: 1. Manavah. 2. Barhaspatya. 3. Ausanashah. 4. Parasarah. 5. Ambhiyah.

Individual Authors : 6. Bharadvaja. 7. Visalakha. 8. Parasara. 9. Pishuna. 10. Kaunapadanta. 11. Vatavyadhi. 12. Bahudantiputra. 13. Katyayana. 14. Kaninka Bharadvaja. 15. Dirgha Charayana. 16. Ghotamukha. 17. Kinjalka. 18. Pishunaputra.

Kautilya—The Most Outstanding Author

The most outstanding witness of International Law and Custom of ancient India is Kautilya, who has been identified by scholars with Chanakya, the Prime Minister of Chandragupta Mauryya. His Arthasastra is interesting from many points of view—not the least among them is its close analogy to rules of International Law laid down by mediaeval jurists, for example, Grotius, Ayala and Rachel. As an evidence of International Law, Kautilya's Arthasastra has two obvious limitations : Firstly, he is a ruthless exponent of the principle of expediency, although it will be shown in subsequent chapters that Kautilya's diplomacy is based on the universally followed doctrine of state-necessity. Secondly, the Arthasastra of Kautilya deals exclusively with warfare on land and does not therefore enable us to construct a body of rules relating to important topics such as blockade or contraband. It does not also deal with subjects of vital interest such as naturalisation and extradition. The Arthasastra of Kautilya was followed by Kamandaka and Sukracharyya, who along with Kautilya were the advocates of the utilitarian school of political philosophy. Many references relating to peace and war are to be found in their works as well as in the Agnipurana which from its own evidence is a book written at a time when the Tantricism was at its height.

Besides the rules directly relating to interstatal relations in the Arthasastra, we have in the Sukranitisara, evidence of private instructions given by individual states to their armed forces—rules of military discipline[32] some of which are followed by the civilised nations of the world even to-day, e.g.:

(1) The king should station troops near the village but outside it. And there should be no relationship of debtor and creditor between the village-folk and the soldiery.

(2) The troops should always forsake violence, rivalry, procrastination over state affairs.

(3) They should never enter the village without a "royal permit".

(4) They should never point to the defects of their commander, but should always live on friendly terms with the whole staff.
(5) The troops will remain not only responsible for their personal arms and uniforms but also for their provisions and their cooking utensils.
(6) They were subjected to martial law if they intrigued with the enemy and were required to take an oath of allegiance which ran thus—"I shall kill the troops who will actt otherwise."

Notes and References

1. F.E. Sm th. *International Law*, p. 1.
2. P. 11.
3. Introduction.
4. *International Law*, I, 37.
5. *International Law*, p. 40.
6. Lawrence: International Law.
7. History of Roman Law : Curtis Ed., 181.
8. *Ibid.*
9. Arthasastra, VII. 18. Whoever is acquainted with the science of polity should clearly observe the conditions of progress, deterioration, stagnation reduction and destruction, as well as the use of all kinds of strategic means. Whoever thus knows the inter-dependence of the six kinds of policy plays at his pleasure with kings, bound round, as it were, in chains skilfully devised by himself.
10. Sukra, IV., vii, 89 : One should follow *Niti* or moral rules so long as one is powerful. People remain friends till then : Just as the wind is the friend of the burning fire.
11. Arthasastra, VII., 18.
12. *Ibid.*
13. *Vide* Carmichael Lect., III (*b*), 191g.
14. Arthasastra, X., 3.

15 & 16. Kamandaka, ii, 5,

17. Agnipurana, GCXXXIII, 20.
    Cf. also Story (Conflict of Laws, 35) on p. 62 and Bentham's Works, VIII., 538.
18. For example, Westlake (I., 14-15) makes "custom and reason," the two sources of International Law. He confuses one of its sources with a means of interpretation. And Oppenhein (I., n. 22) justly remarks that "reason is a means of interpreting law, but it cannot be called into existence."
19. Pollock: Sources of International Law, 2 Col. L.R. (1902), 511-24, Pomeroy. 31-46.
20. Sukra, IV., iii., 64.
21. The S.B.E.X. (ii), 144.

22. McDonald and Keith : Vedic Index.
23. Mahabharata, Santi-Raj, CIX, 8-13, Pratap Ray's translation.
24. Attributed to Pindar by Herodotos, Bk, III., 38.
25. Brugsch : Egypt under the Pharaohs, Vol. II, pp. 71-76.
    Petrie : History of Egypt.
    See Breasted : Records of Ancient Egyptian History.
26. Politics, III., 16-9.
27. Sophocles : Antigone, 450 *seq.* tr. Philipson.
28. R. V., I., 51, 8; I., 175, 3.
    R. V., VI., 14, iii.
    R. V., IX., 41, ii.
29. R. V., VI., 75, xv.
    A. V., VI., 6, vii.
    A. V., V., 18, viii.
30. There is a difference of opinion as to whether all these six expedients should govern the interstatal relations of the circle. Kautilya however votes for all the six.
31. Carmichael Lectures, pp. 89-90.
32. Sukra, IV., vii., 379, 381-83.

18

Administration of Justice to Aliens in Ancient India

S.L. MALHOTRA

The problem of administering justice to foreigners always demands the special consideration of a State. In modern times a nation is under obligation to follow rules of Public or Private International Law in dealing with the citizens of other States. Public International Law governs the jurisdiction of a state over aliens and determines the rights and duties of the latter. Private International Law, more appropriately called the Choice-of-Laws or the Conflict of Laws, decides as to which territorial system of law, should be chosen for the adjudication of a case which has contact with more than one territory.

But the position was quite different in ancient times. There was no single body of laws, recognized by all or a large number of states, that governed the relations between the states and consequently a state was independent in laying down rules for dealing with foreigners. A state could even disown responsibility towards them and could deal with them arbitrarily. For instance, the Greeks did not accept any moral or legal obligation towards aliens until and unless bound by a treaty.[1] The Romans manifested the same attitude. The life and property of the citizens of a state which had no treaty of friendship with Rome were not safe in the Roman territory; such persons could be made slaves and their property seized.[2]

Such principles cannot be harmonized with the rising contacts of a state with the members of other political communities and so must sink before the needs of the time. The intermingling of the people of diverse nations and distant lands is a powerful solvent of prejudices aganist other nations and races. It is evident from the development of the Stoic philosophy in Greece though it found its true expression in Rome.

Moral and Legal Norms

But the mode of adjudication of cases involving foreigners could be evolved only out of the moral and legal norms of a political community. For instance, law among the ancients was usually considered as personal and not as territorial which meant that the conduct of a person could be judged only by the law he observed or the law of the community to which he belonged. So in conformity with this principle the Ptolemies, the Greek ruler of Epypt, appointed different judges in Alexandria for administering justice to the members of different communities.[3]

This principle also implied that separate arrangement must be made for deciding cases between aliens since they observed different systems of law. So Aristotle felt the necessity of instituting a separate court for that purpose.[4]

Conception of a Universal Law

Of course, the problem became difficult whenever parties to the dispute followed different sets of law. It again demanded special arrangement. Thus in Egypt a special court was created in the 3rd century B.C. to judge disputes between the Greeks and the Egyptians taking into account the laws of both.[5] Similarly one of the divisions of the court dealing with the cases of aliens, recommended by Aristotle, decided disputes between foreigners and citizens. The Romans attempted to tackle this problem by developing the conception of a Universal Law which was applicable to all mankind. It was called the law of nature and was identified with the law of Nations. It was defined as a moral code implanted in men by 'natural reason'. Cicero described it in the following words: "True law is right reason in agreement with nature, world-wide in scope, unchanging, everlasting—we may not oppose or alter that law, we cannot abolish it, we cannot be freed from its obligations by any legislature, and we need not look outside ourselves for an expounder of it. This law does not differ for Rome and for Athens, for the present and for the future—it is and will be valid for all nations."[6] Such ideas helped in the development of a separate body of laws called *jus gentium* and was applied in cases involving foreigners.

Justice Based on Principles in Ancient India

In line with the practice of the ancients, the Indians too, evolved the mode of adjudication of cases involving aliens out of their own moral and legal norms. Administration of justice in ancient India was based on a number of principles.

First, it was considered as a rule of absolute virtue which no other factor or sentiment could qualify or alter. There was even divine sanctity attached to it. According to Kautilya, it is verily the power of the ruler when exercised with impartiality and in proportion to guilt, whether it be his enemy or his son, which sustains this world and the next.[7] So a violation of this principle was sure to be visited by divine punishment. In the Silappadikaram, the poet depicts how the capital of the Pandya king was destroyed because of the execution of an innocent person who had just come from Puhar, the capital of the Chola king.

So the ancient Indians acquired high reputation among foreigners for being very just. Ktesias speaks of them as being extremely so.[8] Similarly, other Greek writers pay glowing tributes to the system of administrating justice to the foreigners in India.[9]

Secondly, law was regarded as personal. It was the recognized principle that proper justice could not be done until and unless it was administered in accordance with the laws of the parties to the dispute. No law or custom was considered as beneficial to all. An action of an individual could be best judged in the light of the notions and standards of morality or conduct observed by the community to which he belonged since his character was formed largely in that environment. Thus the customs recognised by the community were accepted as authoritative in matters relating to the administration of justice. Kautilya gives expression to this principle when he admits that it is no crime for Mlechhas to sell their own offspring though it was crime in the case of Aryas.[10] Similarly, all the writers of the Hindu Law Books recognize the customs obseved by different communities and professional groups and the king is asked to follow them while administering justice.[11]

Further, once it was accepted that the parties to the dispute had the right to appeal to the laws of their own community, the king was advised to take into confidence some one from that community who was well versed in its customs and usages. Thus, Gautama advises the king that "Having learned the (state of) affairs from those who (in such class have the authority to speak, the king shall give) his legal decision."[12] This means as Hardadatta explains that the king's decision must be given in accordance with that which is declared to be established custom in a community by its authorised and accredited spokesman and representative who alone is entitled to pronounce on it. It virtually meant that the king was to seek the advice of the leader of that community. It is for this reason that Katyayana declares that "In the cases of Mlechchhas, Chandalas, rogues, gamblers, ascetics, the decisions against those who (are alleged to) have violated the conventions, dose not rest with the king."[13] It was more expedient for him if he assigned the task of deciding such cases to a prominent person among them. According to Bhrigu, the members of caravan of merchants were to settle dispute among themselves.[14] The reason for this is quite obvious. The local ruler was not conversant with their practices.

Such legal norms enabled a king to allow all the foreigners, whether they had settled in his realm or had established commercial colonies, to settle their disputes among themselves in accordance with their own laws. The grant of Sthanu Ravi Gupta in the 9th century A.D. conferred on a Syrian Christian the right of administering justice among his followers.[15] Similarly, the grant of Bhaskar Ravivarman in the 10th century conferred certain privileges on a particular Jew.[16] These privileges were of the nature of the feudal lordship including jurisdiction over his followers.

Justice to Muslim Sojourners

Like the Jews, the Muslims were bound by their religion to settle their disputes in accordance with their own laws. The Prophet ordered the non-resident Muslims to observe the Muslim Law wherever they might be. Hence the dictum of Abu-Yusuf that "a Muslim is to regulate his conduct according to the laws of Islam wherever he may be."[17] Accordingly, wherever the Muslim merchants went they had an understanding with the local ruler that they should be governed by their own laws. Usually, someone among them was appointed to administer their affairs on behalf of the ruler. In India this function was performed by Hunermah who was generally an influential Muslim merchant. Apart from administering justice to the Muslims he also advised the king in all cases in which Muslim interests were involved. The following account will show how justice was administered to the Muslim sojourners in India in the 9th century A.D.

Buzurg-ibn-Shariyar relates that "theft is generally punished in India by death. If the thief be Muslim he is adjudicated by the Hunermah of the Muslims who pronounces sentences according to the Muslim Law."[18] He narrates a case in which a Muslim sailor was involved. "Once", according to him, "a new comer, a Muslim sailor, violated the sanctity of a temple in Saimur. One of the priests caught hold of his hand and look him before the king of Saimur and related to him the whole affair. The sailor confessed his guilt. The king asked the people around him : "what should we do with him ?" Some said, 'Let him be trampled by elephants'; other said, 'Vivisect him,' 'No' said the king, "this is not permissible since he is an Arab, and there are pacts between us and them. So one of you should go to al-abbas-ibn-Mahan, the Hunerman of the Muslims and ask him what he would do if he found a man in similar conditions in a mosque."[19]

Similarly we learn from Masudiy[20] and Ishtakhari[21] that a Muslim ruled over the Muslims on behalf on the king in Hindu kingdoms. Ibn Hawq-ual while giving similar information, adds some details, "this is the same practice that I found in most of the cities ruled over by infidel kings like Khazar-al-sarir, al-lan, Ghana and Kugha. In these cities the Muslims, however, few they will not tolerate the exercise of authority, nor the imposition of punishment, nor the testimony of a witness except by Muslims. But in some parts I have seen Muslims seeking witness among non-Muslims who have reputation for honesty and the other party is satisfied. Sometimes the other party refuses to accept the witness, and Muslim takes his place and so the decision will be reached."[22]

It appears that this arrangement was found very beneficial by the foreigners and so they had all praise for it. But it must not be interpreted to mean any limitation to the authority of the king in whose territory they either settled or stayed for a temporary period. It was the logical result of the principles governing administration of justice in ancient India that we have already pointed out.

Conflict of Laws

But such a system involves another problem. How could a dispute be settled if the persons involved followed different sets of law? The problem was not difficult if the parties to the dispute were Indian or Aryan. It could be settled on the basis of rules laid down in the Dharmasastras as they were regarded as higher than the customs of the different communities. According to Katyayana, "In disputes between the residents of the same country or capital, hamlet or cowherd, town or village, the decision should be based on their own conventional usages, but in disputes between the inhabitants of these and others the decision must be in accordance with the sacred texts."[23]

But what would be the position if the dispute was between an Indian and non-Indian or an Aryan and a Yavana. Justice in such cases, required of a judge to set before himself a standard higher than that of a particular code. The Romans looked to the Law of Nature or Natural Reason for guidance in such matters. Natural reason, in fact, was the enlightened judgement of a judge formed by humanitarian and liberal ideas. Kautilya suggests a similar criterion. According to him whenever sacred law or the law contained in the Vedas and the Dharmasastras is in conflict with Dharmanyaya, then nyaya or justice shall be held authoritative.[24] Dharmanyaya here means any decision that is consistent with reason or the decision which the conscience of the judge take to be right or true even when it is not in conformity with the Dharmasastras.

Further, a liberal judge could seek common basis in the legal codes of different communities and could pronounce judgement according to the common standards. It was not unusual for the writers of nitisastra to find common rules of behaviour between the codes of the Indians and the non-Indians. According to Sukra, "The Yavanas have all the four castes mixed together. They recognise authortity other than that of the Vedas.... Their sastras have been framed for their welfare by their own masters. But the rules that are followed for ordinary purposes are the same in the two cases."[25]

This attitude manifests respect for the laws of the foreigners and assures them just treatment at the hands of Indian judges.

Such ideals and principles enabled an Indian ruler to extend special consideration to the interests of an alien whenever he was involved in a dispute with an Indian. We are told by a Greek writer that "the (Indian) judges also decide cases in which foreigners are concerned, with the greatest care and come down sharply on those who take unfair advantage of them."[26] Kautilya affords even ampler concessions to the outsiders in cases of civil disputes. He lays down the rule that foreigners (importing merchandise); shall be exempted from civil suits.[27] Probably it means that civil disputes involving foreigners may be settled by a special authority, may be by some high administrative body entrusted with the work of looking after the foreigners like the one existing in Pataliputra under Chandragupta Maurya.

But this concession was not extended to the employees of foreigners. In their case civil disputes were permissible. This is because they were mostly citizens.

Similarly, the sixth century inscription of Visnusena states among other customary laws that a stranger merchant from another kingdom is not to be implicated in a case in which he is not directly involved.[28]

Conclusion

Our enquiry reveals that foreigners in ancient India were not at a disadvantage in matters relating to the administration of justice. They were often extended certain concessions in view of their special position. They were not fully aware of the local conditions and so needed sympathetic treatment by the Indian judges. Their short stay often demanded speedy justice by such persons as were in touch with them and so could appreciate their difficulties.

Further, Indian legal philosophy was flexible enough to adjust to the legal norms of the foreign communities and the conception of justice was sufficiently liberal to accommodate reason and equity.

Notes and References

1. Will Durant, *The Story of Civilization, Part II; the Life of Greece,* p. 263 (1039).
2. Oppenheim, *Public International Law,* Vol. I, pp. 59-61 (4th edition).
3. Rostovzeff, M., *Social and Economic History of the Hellenistic World,* Vol. I, p. 323.
4. Baker, *The Politics of Aristotle,* Bk. IV, ch. xvi, p. 201 (1946).
5. Tarn, Hellenistic Civilization, p. 157.
6. Will Durant, *The Story of Civilization, Part III; Caesar and Christ,* p. 405 (1944).
7. Jolly & Schmidt, *Arthasastra of Kautilya,* III, i. 55.
8. McCrindle, *Ancient India as described by Ktesias,* p. 12 (1882).
9. See Below p. 351.
10. Jolly, *Arthasastra of Kautilya,* III, xiii, 5-6.
11. Narada lays down the rule that "the aggregate of the rules settled amongst heretics, followers of the Veda (naigarmas) and others, is called samay (a compact or established usage). Thus arises a title of law, termed transgression of a compact. He further says, "Among heretics, followers of the Veda

(Naigmas), guilds (of merchants) (Pugas), troops of soldiers, assemblages (of kinsmen) and others, the king must maintain the usages settled among them." (*Narada and Brihaspati,* Jolly, X, i, p. 153).

Yaj., provides that the varying usages and conventions of srenis (guilds) of artisans, naigamas, traders, heretics and associations (soldiers and the like), should be respected by the king in the same way as he honours the usages of learned Brahmanas (II., 132).

12. Buhler, *Sacred Laws of the Aryas,* Vol. II, Part I, xi-22 (Sacred Books of the East).
13. Kane, P.V., *Katyayanasmriti on Vyavahara.* 943 (1933).
14. *Ibid., History of Dharmasastra,* Vol. III, p. 283.
15. Thurston, *Castes and Tribes of South India,* Vol. VI, p. 415; Logan, *Manual of Malbar,* Vol. I, p. 270.
16. *Indian Antiquary,* Vol. III, p. 333; *Epigraphica* Indica, Vol. III, 1894-95; Thurston, *Castes and Tribes,* Vol. II, p. 496.
17. Hamidullah, *Muslim Conduct of State,* p. 104 (1945).
18. Devic, Marcel, *Kitabe-Ajaib-ul-Hind,* Story XCIX, pp. 137-38.
19. *Ibid.,* LXXXIV, pp. 120-21.
20. Hamidullah, *Muslim Conduct of State,* pp. 109-10.
21. Elliot, *History of India,* Vol. I, p. 27.
22. Nainar, S. Muhammad Husayan, *Arab Geographers' Knowledge of Southern India,* p. 163.
23. Kane, P.V., *Katyayansmriti,* 47.
24. *Arthasastra of Kautilya,* III, i, 57.
25. Sarkar, *Sukranitisara,* IV, sec., i, 74-77.
26. McCrindle, *Ancient India as described by Megasthenes and Arrian,* p. 44.
27. *Arthasastra of Kautilya,* II, xvi, 17.
    In this connection also see Bhattasvamin's commentary (J.B.O.R.S., Vol. XII, Part I, 1926). Ganapati Sastri follows Bhattasvamin's Interpretation (*Arthasastra,* Vol. I, p. 243). Shamasastry interprets the passage as follows : "Foreigners importing merchandise, shall be exempted from being sued for debts, unless they are (local), associations and partners." (*Kautilya's Arthasastra,* II, xvi, p. 105 (1951).
    (anabhiyogascharthesshvagantunamanyatassabhyopakaribhyah)
28. J.R.A.S.B., Vol. XVI, No. 1, 1950, rule 16.

19

Kautilya and Machiavelli

PROF. NARENDRAKRISHNA SINHA

Kautilya—Disciple of None

In a comparative study of Kautilya and Machiavelli, the first relevant point is the respective methods of the two writers. Kautilya's work is to a certain extent professedly a summary of the work of the previous writers on political science. "Learning from many he became the disciple of none and was thoroughly independent." His quotations are made in order to present all possible views, on a problem subject to differences of opinion. He ably; refutes the views of his predecessors in most cases and advances his own, with reasons adduced. His method, however, is philosophical rather than historical. But he is not ignorant of the historical method. In some cases, his empiricism is supported by references to history.

Machiavelli—More Scientific but Empirical

Machiavelli relies much more on the historical than on the philosophical method. Apparently, therefore, he appears more scientific than Kautilya, but his method also is none the less, empirical. As Dunning says, 'his conclusions were reached empirically and were then supported by references to history'. Moreover, his picking and choosing of facts from past history was very much disjointed. As one writer has said, "His was not the valuation of a historian. He rather prized an event as a chemist prizes his acid or his salt for the reactions he could obtain by projecting it into the elements of a particular combination in politics at which he seemed to be working."

Heat and Light

Machiavelli wants to see Italy unified under one supreme ruler much like an 'Avatar' whereas Kautilya writes for the guidance of one who is already established as a supreme ruler of an unified country. As such, Machiavelli writes with all the ardour of a passionate patriot. His objectivity was overshadowed by his subjectivity. In the case of Kautilya, we have no such fiery enthusiasm, no sentimental background. In Machiavelli, we have both heat and light, in Kautilya only light.

State to be Feared than Loved

Machiavelli's theory of the state is very different from that of Kautilya. He relieved the state from the dominion of the church. In his theory of the state even the individual and the society do not count. "He delivers men over to the political power as helpless, almost imbecile slaves." His state is the all-embracing Leviathan whose highest duty is to assert itself and whose most contemptible sin is weakness. Machiavelli's state is an end not a means. Its chief foundations according to Machiavelli are laws and arms and not so much laws as arms. He inculcates the doctrine that it is much safer for the state to be feared than loved, when of the two either must be dispensed with. His state also is a combination of the fox and the lion. It has no beauty or grace. "It is a fearsome thing ruling by intrigue and by ruse * * *. There is no limit to the state thinking—undeterred by any fear except the fear of physical punishment."

Commensuration Between State and Society

But in Kautilya's book there are definite bounds on the state. It is going too far to assert that the chief duties of the state described by Kautilya 'were the punishment of crime and the filling of the king's treasuries and it maintained only the irreducible minimum of political organisation—caste, custom and religion squeezing the state into a very small corner of Indian public life'. Caste, custom and society were certainly alive; but that does not necessarily mean that the state was only half-alive. "There is always a continual interaction between the state and the society". "The ideal aim is that the two should be commensurate and that every living social force should find a place in the constituted order of things." The state of Kautilya strives to realize this ideal so far as it is realizable.

Machiavelli is not alive to this problem, of the relations between the state and the society and its importance. The state is kept confined in its proper sphere by Kautilya. It is not to be the dreary and appalling Sparta, but at the same time there is to be no *imperium in imperio.* Whatever may be said to be the position of the Brahmins in ancient India, in Kautilya's book they do not have an exaggerated importance politically in spite of their immunities. The functions of Kautilya's state include internal and external protection, the promulgation of laws, maintenance of judicial tribunals, maintenance of the Varnashrama Dharma. It gives relief in times of famine, relief to the poor even in normal times, spends munificently in public works and charities and patronises learned men. It collects taxes for all these purposes. Such a state cannot certainly be described as half-alive.

Failure of Centralisation

In fact as Mr. K.P. Jayaswal has shown the most pre-emient characteristic of the Mouryya state as we find in Kautilya—is centralisation. "Justice had become royal, even law tended to be royal. The village came under the royal officer. All ships were owned by the state. Virtues alone did not come under the focus of the crown. Also vices were brought under the imperial vigilance. Prostitutes were placed under a royal department, gambling was centralised in goverment buildings, or in buildings licensed by the government. Hotels and wine-shops were placed under imperial departments. Mines were monopolised, * * * Centralisation was against the genius of the race and it failed."

Means to be Acquired by the King and the End of Government

What are to be the relations between the government and the governed ? What is to be the end of gevernments ? On this point, we should note first how the two writers desire their Kings to prepare for their task. Kautilya wants his King to have Vidya Samarthyam (i.e. to read Puranas, Itivritta, Akshyaika, Udaharana Dharmasastra, Arthasastra, Itihasa, etc). 'He is to give up lascivious tendencies if any, and anger, greed, vanity and overjoy. He is to restrain the organs of sense, acquire wisdom, see through spies, establish safety and security by being over-active, exercise authority, keep up his personal discipline and endear himself.

Machiavelli wants his Prince to have 'no other aim or thought, nor select anything else for his study than war and its rules and discipline, for this is the sole art that belongs to him who rules. In peace, he should addict himself more to its exercise than in war. For this, he is to keep men well organised and drilled, to follow incessantly the chase and to read histories.'

Thus it is quite apparent that Machiavelli takes the end of government less seriously than Kautilya. Unlike Kautilya he does not regard his Prince's calling as a sacred one. He is so much taken up with the question of the safety of the state that the welfare of the governed, the end of the state does not keep him engrossed at all. But as Kautilya regards the calling of his Prince to be sacred, he recommends elaborate preparations for the task.

Kautilya very distinctly lays down that the end of government is the welfare of the governed. "In the happiness of his subjects lies his happiness, in their welfare his welfare, whatever, pleases himself he shall not consider as good but whatever pleases his subjects."

As against this strong assertion of Kautilya, we have a bold statement by Machiavelli. The motive of Machiavelli's Prince is mere enlightened self-interest and he is to do good to his people 'as he can never secure himself against a hostile people because of their being too many'—'A Prince ought to show himself a patron of ability and honour, the proficient in every art. At the same time, he should encourage the citizens to practise their callings peacefully both in commerce and agriculture.'

Machiavelli brushes away all idealism in his statement "how one lives is so far distant from how one ought to live." He lays more emphasis on the 'show' than on the fact itself. Herein he compares unfavourably with Kautilya. The Indian was certainly far from an idealist. But so far as the aim of the state is concerned, Kautilya had glimmed enough of idealism to make him cognisant of the fact that the best way to convince the people, that their Prince loves them is really to love them.

Clear-sighted but not Far-sighted

Machiavelli is certainly clear-sighted but 'clearness is not necessarily the only or the most important aspect of a truth.' Most probably he had the same opinion as Trietscke later. 'The question of the material condition of the subjects is secondary from the political point of view and the essence of the state is power directed both inward and outwards.'

In view of all these facts the following accusation does not seem unjustified. 'Machiavelli was clear-sighted but not far-sighted. He never saw things as they might be,—he saw them as they were and hence missing possibilities he missed statesmanship. He understood cunning for the craft of the statesman in the largest sense of the term.' His doctrine of power for its own sake stands self-convicted.

Both much Alike in 'The Art of Government'

In their treatment of the art of government, Kautilya and Machiavelli are much alike, but within the limited perspective, the Italian surpasses the Indian. Kautilya reserves his questionable methods for extreme cases. But so much has been said of bad measures, and in this Machiavelli is more guilty than Kautilya, that it is a wonder if good measures would at all be adopted. The "Gresham's law" is operative no less in politics than in economics.

Kautilya speaks at length about the institute of espionage, of the different kinds of spies and how it is necessary to examine the character of the ministers by different allurements, religious, military, love and fear. Even the queen is not above suspicion and the sons of the King, are not to be free from the attention of spies. In reading through the pages of Kautilya we are pretty often reminded of Aurangzeb who once wrote to one of his sons that a monarch should fear even his own shadow. In the case of royal officers, we have the same policy of mistrust. 'Just as it is impossible not to taste the honey or the poison that finds itself at the tip of of the tongue, so it is impossible for a government servant not to eat up at least a bit of King's revenue.'

'When in concert, they eat up
When in disunion they mar the work.'

'Without bringing to the knowledge of their master they shall undertake nothing but remedial measures against imminent danger.' Kautilya recommends that the heads of different departments shall at first be temporary. Then when their fidelity had been tested by different allurements should they be made permanent. But he recommends handsome remuneration knowing it full well that wealth is the best means of ensuring loyalty. According to him about one-fourth of the total revenues should be set apart for maintaining the servants though recommending a spirit of suspicion, Kautilya is not obvious of the fact that this alone will not do to make a good ruler. 'A single wheel can never move.' He must have a few very trusted ministers. Suspicion is not thus carried to such an extent as to make goverment an impossibility.

Machiavelli is of opinion that the qualifications essential for success in the art of government are 'combinations of audacity with diplomatic prudence, adroit use of cruelty and fraud, self-reliance, avoidance of half measures, empolyment of native troops and firm administration in the conquered provinces. He recommends that in order to do great things Princes should hold faith of little account, they should have the qualities of the fox and the lion, should appear merciful, faithful, humane, religious and upright, but should know and be always ready if necessary to turn opposite. 'Everyone sees what you appear to be, few know what you really are.' Princes cannot avoid hatred altogether, but they should avoid being hated by everyone and should in particular avoid the hatred of the most powerful. A wise prince should also foster some animosity against himself so that crushing it he may increase his reputation. Like Kautilya, Machiavelli says that a prince ought always to take counsel, but the Italian is of opinion that the prince should take such counsel only when he wishes and not when others wish.

Low Opinion about Human Nature

Both Machiavelli and Kautilya have very low opinion about human nature. Kautilya opines that men are naturally fickle-minded and like horses at work exhibit constant changes in their temper. Machiavelli makes a like assertion. 'Men are ungrateful, fickle, false, cowards and covetous, and only as long as you succeed, they are yours entirely.' Elsewhere he say, 'men will always prove untrue to you unless they are kept honest by constraint.' Both hold the doctrine of the total depravity of human nature. The unblest gospel taught by both Machiavelli and Kautilya is that 'whatever policy demands justice will allow." The squareness which imagination looks for in eminent men receives a rude shock when we go through the pages of Machiaevelli and Kautilya. The unremitting craft of Kautilya's King and Machiavelli's Prince seems inconsistent with upright conduct even under normal circumstances. In spite of his ultimate failure, Caesar Borgia was chosen by Machiavelli as the ideal ruler who tried ably to carry out the principles of the art of government inculcated by Machiavelli. But that man was nothing but a devil with all the arts of devilry. His talent was 'to slay fellow citizens, to deceive friends, to be without faith, without mercy, without religion !' In spite of his reservation of doubtful measures for extreme cases, the environment of Kautilya's state, in its gloom is surpassed only by that of Machiavelli.

Conclusion

We do not assert that the strictest morality of the Sermon on the Mount should have been recommended by Kautilya and Machiavelli. But that does not necessarily mean that the alternative is the policy that 'the end justifies the means.'

The differences between Kautilya and Machiavelli are considerable. The Italian is apparently more scientific but not really so. He is certainly more ardent. He excels Kautilya in his treatment of the art of government, though that excellence is limited in its range to that aspect of policy specifically known as Machiavellian. But the Indian is certainly superior, in dealing with foreign policy. There is, however, a world of difference between the two so far as the aim of the government is concerned. Machiavelli is not interested in the problem at all. The art of government engages too much of his attention. He forgets that the state exists for the sake of good life. What has been said of Trietscke is also true of Machiavelli. 'The dreary and appalling Sparta was to be imposed upon the world, not the culture of artistic and scientific world. . . . This would reduce the world from the comparative civilisation, it has reached to the level of the ocean, where mighty sharks and gigantic devil fishes struggle with each other for survival—the human refinement in the warfare would be found in the astuteness of the spies and the mendacious representatives.'

To the credit of Kautilya, however, we must admit that with all his defects, he does not after all, present the picture of a dreary and a desolate Sparta. The atmosphere may not be pure, clear and sunny but certainly his world is not without vegetation.

20

Game of the Science of War

I
THE GAME OF CHESS

PARMESHWAR LALL

The English word chess like the French *Echees,* Italian *Scacchi,* German *Schach* is a corrupted form of the Persian *Shah*=king. The origin of this game is lost in obscurity. Its invention has been variously ascribed to almost all the nations of antiquity comprising the Greeks, Romans, Babylonians, Scythians, Egyptians, Jews, Chinese, Persians, Hindoos, Arabians, Arancanians and even to Castalinians, the Irish and the Welsh. Not content with the claims of nations and races, some have even endeavoured to fix upon particular individuals as the inventors of this noble game. Among the recipients of this honor might be mentioned Japhet, Shem, Solomon, Mandodari—the wife of Ravana, King of Lanka, —the Philosopher Xerxes, the Grecian Prince Palmedes, Hermes, Aristotle, the brothers Lydo and Tyrrhene, Semiramis, Zenobia, Attalus, who died in B.C. 200, the Chinese mandarin Hansing, the Brahmin Sissa and the celebrated Persian astronomer Shatrenscha. Many of these assumptions are of course fabulous, some rest upon little authority and some proceed from easily traceable errors.

The three most formidable rivals for the honor of originating this game are the Hindoos, the Persians and the Chinese.

The Chinese Claim

The Chinese claim is urged in a letter of Mr. Eyles Irwin to the Earl Charlmount written in 1793. This letter was published in the *Transactions* of the Royal Irish Academy. Mr. Irwin states that Chess was invented by the Mandarin Hansing to amuse his soldiers in their winter quarters while invading the Shensi country in the reign of the Emperor Lin Pang about the year 174 B.C. Irwin states the Chinese name for Chess is "Chang Ki" which means literally "royal game". Captain Hirman Cox, however, commenting on Irwin's letter gives the Chinese name for chess as "Choke-Choo Hong" which implies the "play of the science of war".

The Persian Claim

Mr. N. Bland, M.R.A.S., in his book "Persian Chess" endeavours to prove that the Persians were the inventors of the game of chess and he maintains that the game after being born in Persia found a home in India, whence after a series of ages, it was brought back to Persia and thence spread over Europe by the Arab conquerors.

The Indian Claim

But the veiw, however, which has been most seriously put forward and has gained the greatest amount of credence, is the view that attributes the origin of chess to the Hindoos. Abul Fazl, the celebrated minister of Akbar the Great, states in one of his works that chess along with the Hitopadesha was carried to Persia by the ambassadors of Nowsherwan. In Europe the Hindoo origin of chess was put forward for the first time in 1694 by Dr. Hegdean, Oxford Professor, who, however, was unacquainted with Sanscrit. The theory was taken up by Sir William Jones, the celebrated orientalist, in an Essay published in the second volume of the "Asiatic Researches". Sir William argues that Hindoostan was the cradle of chess; the game having been know there from time immemorial by the name of "Chaturanga" = the four "angas" or members of an army which was composed according to the "Amarakosha" of elephants, horses, chariots and foot soldiers. His essay is substantially a translation of and a commentary upon a passage in the "Bhavishya Purana", in which is given a description of four hundred games of chess played with dice. This account claims for chess an antiquity of four thousand years. Sir W. Jones does not ground his opinion of the origin of chess upon the Purana account, which he considers to be a later form of the game. His opinion is based upon the testimony of the Persians. The famous Persian poet, Firdausi, in his Shah-namah states that to Nowsherwan (chosrais), King of Persia, came ambassadors from the sovereign of Hind with a chess board and men asking him to solve if he could the secrets of the game or pay tribute. From this Sir W. Jones lays down that the Sanskrit name Chaturanga was exported from India to Persia in the sixth century A.D.; that by a natural corruption the old Persians changed the name into "Chatrang", but their country being soon afterwards conqured by Arabs who had neither the initial nor the final letters of the word in their alphabet, wherefore they changed it into Shatranj, which name found its way into modern Persian and ultimately into the dialects of India.

The theory of Sir William Jones continued almost undisturbed for about a hundred years. Receiving support from the writings of Professor Duncan Forbes, who among other points urged apparently with justice that the word Shatranj is a mere exotic in the language of the inhabitants of Persia defying all the ingenuity of their grammarians to make it their own.

Various Theories

The Dutch scholar Van deer Liande examined all the theories concerning the origin of chess in an exhaustive treatise which was published in 1874. He agrees with those that consider that the Persian received the game from India, but the elaborate theories about "Chaturanga" receive scant courtesy at his hands. "Chaturanga" he argues, is always used of an army by the poets of ancient India and of a game never. All Sanskrit scholars agree that chess is never mentioned in any of the really ancient Hindu records. The Puranas were considered works of remote antiquity formerly, but recent criticism has shown that their date cannot be beyond the 10th century A.D. Nor is the passage in "Bhavishya Purana" relied on by Sir William Jones and Forbes to be found in the copies of the work preserved in the British Museum and the Berlin Library—a fact which throws doubt on the genuineness of the passage. The ultimate outcome of Vandeer Lindi's studies is that chess certainly existed in India in the 8th century and was probably invented there. While nothing definite can be said as to the origin of chess, facts appear to point to the game having been invented in India about the 2nd or the 3rd century A.D., at the time when the religion of the Buddhists was prevalant in the country. War and the slaying of one's fellowmen being

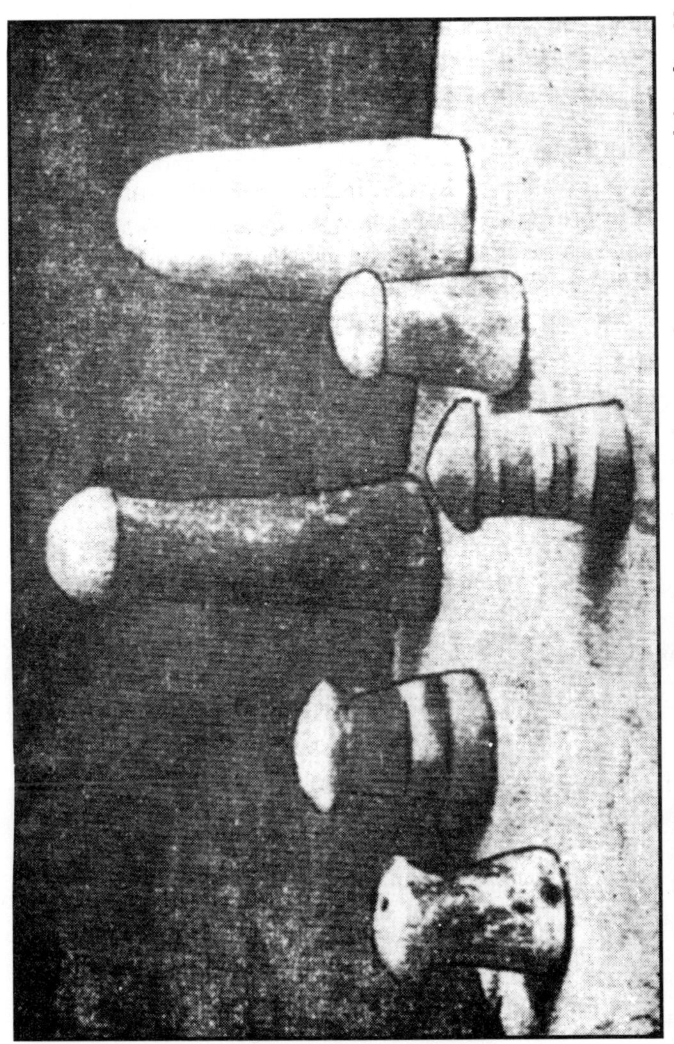

The world's oldest chess pieces unearthed from Moenjodaro and now preserved in the National Museum of Pakistan

strongly condemned by the Buddhist religion, chess was invented as it ministered to the combative propensities of human nature by providing a bloodless warfare as a substitute for the carnage of the battle-field.

Chess, invented in India, was sent out to Persia, whose conquerors, the Arabs, also conquered parts of Europe and introduced this noble game along with many other elements of civilization into that Continent. At first the game was not well received by the Roman Catholic clergy. Like most things new it was condemned as an invention of the devil. In the third volume of the "Councils of Spain" we find "Clerks playing at dice or chess shall be *ipso facto* excommunicated." Similar condemnation of the game is to be found in the ecclesiastical records of other European nations. But wiser counsels prevailed latterly and this noble game, as it deserved, became the most popular of intellectual recreations—a position which it has since maintained undisputed.

II
CHESS ORIGINATED IN MOENJODARO

F.D. DOUGLAS

Chess, in its original form, was played in ancient India 5,000 years ago in Moenjodaro and Harappa, cities of the Indus Valley Civilization of 3000-2400 B.C. located in what is today Pakistan.

This was revealed in Karachi in 1948 by the late Dr. Sir Mortimer Wheeler, then Archaeological Adviser to the Government of Pakistan, who showed me the pieces illustrated in this articles (now in the National Museum in Karachi) which were excavated at Moenjodaro.

It was the first scientific judgment on the origin of chess, backed by archaeological evidence. It disproved the Western writers' theory, repeated in numerous publications, that the game originated in the Indian subcontinent as late as the 6th century A.D.

Moenjodaro is 17 miles south of Larkana in Sind. It is 200 miles north of Karachi. Harappa is in the Punjab, about 300 miles from Rawalpindi.

Relics

The twin cities of Islamabad and Rawalpindi are located on the Potwar Plateau, where Sir Mortimer Wheeler discovered relics of the

Stone Age of 500,000 years ago, when early man dwelt in this area, before the Himalayas were born.

As Deputy Principal Information Officer in the Government of Pakistan (the post I had held in the Government of India when I opted for Pakistan in August 1947) I was discussing with Sir Mortimer publicity for his book "Five Thousand Years of Pakistan", dealing with the Indus Valley Civilization.

Sir Mortimer showed me Stone Age "axes" from the Potwar Plateau svhich I had mistaken for paper-weights and was gruffly rebuked. Then he surprised me with a display of what he described as the earliest known chess pieces—relics excavated at Moenjodaro, which in the Sindhi language means "Mounds of the Dead". In 1922, an Indian surveyor had pointed out the significance of this legendary name to Sir John Marshall, then Director-General of the Archaeological Survey of India, who began excavations at the site and uncovered the ruins of a civilization possessing a high standard of art and craftsmanship and a well-developed system of pictographic writing of between 3000-2400 B.C. which had existed long before the arrival of the Indo-Aryans in the Indus Valley. It was contemporary in part with the Early Dynastic Sumerian Civilization in the Middle East. Significantly, the decorative elements included the checker-board design.

These facts have been gleaned from "The Glory That Was Moenjodaro" by Dr. F.A. Khan, who, on the retirement of Sir Mortimer Wheeler, was appointed Director of Archaeology and Museums Ministry of Education, Government of Pakistan. In his slim illustrated pamphlet, Dr. Khan styles the chess pieces "gamesmen". Similar pieces were uncovered at Harappa.

While inaugurating Chess Championships and lesser tournaments in Pakistan, I have spoken of Sir Mortimer Wheeler's discovery, but unfortunately this has not found mention in the world Press and I see from that fascinating collection "Evans on Chess" (p. 30), that Dr. Henry Davidson in "A Short History of Chess" repeats the erroneous belief that chess originated in India in the 6th century A.D., when it was known by its Sanskrit name "Chaturanga", literally "four arms" or "four members". These were the four components of ancient armies : Elephants (now Bishops), Cavalry (Knights), Chariots (Rooks or Castles), and Infantry (Pawns). It was, of course, originally a military game and the ancient version in Burma (now replaced by the European or International game, evolved through the centuries) had the opposing forces ranged against each other in the centre of the board.

Larry Evans, Gerald Abrahams, Leonard Barden, I.A. Horowitz, Harry Golombek, Henry Davidson and other notable authorities on chess will be pleased to learn that the barrier of lime concealing the origin of the world's most popular game was penetrated by one of the world's most famous archaeologists.

Dr. Sir Mortimer Wheeler was of the definite opinion that chess in its original form with the checker-board was played in ancient India 5,000 years ago, making it the world's oldest game.

When Mr. A. Sattar Gabole, then a Minister in Mr. Bhutto's Government, who also hailed from Sind, inaugurated the Sind Chess Championship at the Karachi Press Club in 1972 I was also called upon to speak. I repeated what Sir Mortimer Wheeler had told me in Karachi in 1948.

Mr. Gabole said if I could obtain evidence to support Sir Mortimer's theory he would stage a World Chess Championship at Larkana, extending invitations to Bobby Fischer and other Grandmasters. After over three years as Information Officer (now styled PIO) with the Colombo Plan, I had retired as Pakistan's PIO and was on contract as Chief Editor, National Press Trust. The same week the Government of Pakistan recalled me as a Deputy Director to train Federal Grade 17 Officers at the Civil Service Academy (later the Academy for Administrative Training) at Lahore. On returning to Karachi in 1975, I was appointed Editor in the National Book Foundation, an autonomous body under the Ministry of Education, from which I retired once again in 1978. Sir Mortimer has passed away but Dr. F.A. Khan has confirmed these pieces in the National Museum as "gamesmen". Research requires time and resources.

Sir Mortimer was a recognised authority on the Indus Valley Civilization and to my mind there is not a shadow of doubt that these are the world's oldest chess pieces. Today they are a priceless national asset.

Thanks mainly to Arab and Iranian sponsorship in Europe in the 11th century A.D., chess is now played in every country in the world, completely eclipsing any other indoor or outdoor sport. It is also played by post, phone, cable and radio and there is a World Correspondence Chess Championship. It is impossible to estimate the number of chess buffs, ranging through all strata of society from the poor man to the millionaire.

Devotees

It has 35 million devotees in the USA alone and at least 70 million in Russia, including one million school children (from 5 to 14 years of age) who participate in an All-USSR Children's Championship in the world's most scientific game. Chess is also taught in schools in many other developed countries and in India and is studied in military academies, following the example of that military genius, Nepoleon Bonapart, who was a chess addict.

As many as 110 nations are members of FIDE (Federation of Internationale des Echecs), the International Chess Federation. Only United Nations Organisation has a much bigger membership.

The famed Mona Lisa, the 15th century painting in the Louvre has earned for France enormous sums in foreign exchange. And Leonardo da Vinci's masterpiece has many rivals in the realm of art. These chess pieces have none. They are unique.

21

Art of War in Ancient India

Major S.P. Sharma

State (*Rashtra*)

War is an instrument of State policy. The capacity to wage war and win it, is in proportion to the strength and structure of State itself. The modern concept of State is related to land, government and ethnic unity. In *Atharva Veda,* State is described thus:

अहं रुद्रेभिर्वसुभिश्चराम्यहमादित्यैरुत विश्वेदेवैः।
अहं मित्रावरुणोभा विभर्म्यहमिन्द्राग्री अहमश्विनोभा।।1।।
अहं राष्ट्री संगमनी वसूनाँ चिकितुर्षा प्रथमा यज्ञियानाम्।
ता मा देवाब्यदधु पुरुत्रा भूरिस्थात्रां भूर्याशयन्तः।।2।।
अहमेव स्वयमिदं वदामि जुष्टं देवानामुत मानुषाणामृ।
यम् कामये तन्तमुग्रं कर्णोमित तं ब्रह्माणं तमृषिं तं सुमेधाम्।।3।।
मया सोऽन्नमत्तियो विपश्यतियः प्राणातियः ईशृणोत्युक्तम्।
अमन्तवो मात उपत्तियन्ति श्रुत श्रद्धेयं ते वदामि।।4।।
अहम् रुद्राय धनुरा तनोमि ब्रह्मद्विषे शखे हन्तवा उ।
अहं जनाय समदं कृणोम्यहं द्यावापृथ्वी आ विवेश।।5।।
अहं सोममाहनसं विभर्म्यहं त्वष्टारमुत पूषणं भगम्।
अहं दधामि द्रविणा हविष्मते सुप्राव्यायजमानाय सुन्वते।।6।
अहं सुवे पितरमस्य मूर्धन्मम योनिरप्स्वन्तः समुद्रे।

ततो वितिष्ठे भुवनानि विश्वोतामूद्यं वर्ष्मणोप स्पृशामि।।7।।
अहमेव वात इव प्रवाम्यारभमाणा भुवनानि विश्वा।
परोदिवा पर एना पृथिव्यैतावती महिम्ना सं बभूव।।8।।

(षष्ठोनुवाक।। अष्टमः प्रपाठकः)

"I, (i.e. statehood or power of State) stay with the brave soldiers, industrialists, teachers and wise people. I install the patriots, soldiers, scientists and men of medicine in the State. I am the power of State. I alone am responsible for bringing together the riches and industrialists of the country. I (nationalism) am the noblest ideal in man and am the foremost to be worshipped. I stay in every nook and corner of the country and defend the State from internal and external aggression. I inspire the brave and the learned for the country. I am available to the rich and to the poor alike. Those who do not worship me are soon destroyed. It is I who inspire people to prepare the various munitions of war. My sovereignty extends from the earth to the skies. My power is inherent in the scientists, industrialists and wise of the land. I inspire people to elect a suitable head of State. All national endeavour for progress and unity is endowed in me. It appears that I am pervading the country like air. I initiate the birth of all people's (democratic)! institutions in the country and conduct them. This is my glory."

The basic factors on which the power of State is dependent are beautifully stated in the *Rig Veda* as under:

इला सरस्वती मही त्रिस्रो देवीर्मयोभुवः।
वर्हिः सीदन्त्वस्रिधः।।

(*Rig Veda 1-13-9*)

"National language, own culture and devotion to motherland are the three elements which are essential for the well-being of the people."

Much has been written in the *Vedas* describing the qualities of administration and the administered. Suffice it to say here that such a people and their State were capable of producing unlimited war effort. The many-sided development of the country was inherent in the full attainment of statehood. The nationalist sentiment was foremost in the Aryan way of life.

The Citizen Army

The vedic way of life does not contemplate huge standing armies. Every able bodied citizen was psychologically trained to be a soldier. Military training was freely available to every citizen provided he proved his aptitude for the training to his guru (instructor). The *gurus* themselves were looked after by the State and the demands of their dedicated lives were few and no burden on the State. Although *kshatriyas* normally adopted the military career others were not barred because of their birth or caste (*varna*).

The standing armies were small in size and were meant to meet the threat of the enemy from within. Once war was contemplated, the case for which the war was to be fought was made known to the people and citizen volunteers would swarm the rank and file of the army swelling it to the required size. There was no conscription. Citizens who approved of the propriety of the cause would volunteer to defend the motherland as a matter of duty. This system, apart from its other virtues, reduced the State expenditure on defence on the one hand and, on the other, cut down the tail to the minimum. The administration, apart from the maintenance of the small standing army, amounted mostly to procurement agencies during an emergency. Responsibility for military training was vested in the hands of those who were considered the best military thinkers of their time by the State. As such, the uniformity of military training was ensured. War games were occasionally organised to practise commanders in handling large bodies of troops.

Morale and Discipline

With the army trained and organised as mentioned in the preceding paragraphs, a doubt arises as to how the morale of fighting forces was kept at the desired level. The factors now considered essential for the maintenence of high morale, e.g. pride in the Unit, and confidence in the leaders and weapons, were not applicable then as they are today. However, the Aryans solved this problem more efficiently but from a different angle. The military leaders won their followers by personal example and by proving their worth as leaders of men. Discipline of the followers was solely achieved through voluntary allegiance rather than by the wooden rank structure as at present. Punishment was awarded and accepted more as a result of a universally accepted code of conduct and self-discipline than by force, although force had to be used to bring the offender to book, at times, and then the offender was treated as an anti-social element.

Education in self-culture and mental descipline formed an essential part of any vocational training and seeds of moral and mental discipline were ingrained from the very childhood when the education of the child started. The importance of cultural training to the child was given the pride of place in his education. This played a vital role in the formation of his character and ensured deep devotion to his motherland and a determination to sacrifice himself for the betterment of the society as a whole. The pride, therefore, was already built up in the soldier not in his Unit, but in the Vedic way of life for which he fought and died. *Atharva Veda* contains numerous verses ordaining people to live, work and die for the *Rashtra* (State) अस्मान राष्ट्राय अभिवर्धय, i.e. let us live and progress for the State. We should progress and develop to be able to serve the motherland so that our country may shine in the world. Whatever we do or achieve should be dedicated to the betterment of our motherland. राष्ट्राय मह्यं वध्यतां। सपत्नेभ्यः पराभुवे।। "Let me be tied down to my country so that I may defeat and destroy her enemies. My own interest and that of my country may never clash. I should live and die for the country." Verses of this kind are found interspersed in all prayers and formalities of worship.

On morale, as on discipline, *Atharva Veda* is full of verses. In *Veda* the word *"Manyu"* (मन्यु) is used for morale. *Atharva Veda sukta 31* and *32* describe morale (मन्यु) as follows:—

> "When high morale is well established on the chariot of a man's heart and mind, he is always happy, never feels despondent. He is able to carry out his duties cheerfully. Even when he is dying, he is keen to get up and be active. He is always full of enthusiasm and optimism even in adversity and takes steps to fight it out. It is morale that makes a man powerful as fire. Morale in leaders makes them invincible military commanders (नः सेनानी) who can then (मृधः विनुदस्व) destroy the enemy with confidence, (विशं विशं युद्धाय सं शिशाधि). Every man must be able to sound the bugles of victory and never get bogged down in the mire of dependency. Therefore (अस्माकम् अधिपा) let this high morale be enshrined in our heart and mind, as our strength is eternally wedded to this morale."

Approach to War

The fundamental principle of Indian culture is love of peace and righteousness. It is in this context that we can appreciate warfare in ancient India. In modern times we have given *Panchashila* to the world. This love of peace is in our blood from times immemorial.

We in ancient India realised the terrible loss of men and material in war and hence tried to avoid war in general. Bernhardt's characterisation of war as a "biological necessity" and as "an indispensable regulator in the life of mankind" is typical of the modern culture revealing the dominance of materialistic values of life.

Sukta 7 in *Atharva Veda* states that the responsibility for maintaining peace internally and defending the motherland from external aggression devolves upon two sections of society, *brahman* and *kshatriya.* First the *brahmans* must try their best to persuade the enemy to desist from evil through their reasoning, preaching and practice. If this method fails, then they should direct the *kshatriya* to use force against the enemy. The amount of force to be used is to be decided and directed by *brahmans,* i.e. the wise and the learned. Manu, the great lawgiver, states : "Since victory or defeat in war among contestants is seen to be impermanent, war shall be avoided. Enemies should be overcome by any other means but never by war." It is thus evident that the Aryans abhorred war and tried to avoid it as far as possible.

However, there are occasions in the life of nations when war becomes an unavoidable necessity, when its avoidance not only leads to the sacrifice of all that is worthwhile, but also defeats the very purpose for which war is desired to be avoided. Such wars are described as *"Dharam Yudha"*. Even then, war was resorted to only when other means of reconciling or desisting the enemy from aggression were exhausted. Up to the period of *Mahabharat,* there were six instruments of State policy, which were known as शडगुण्य (*Shadgunya*) and were universally accepted in India. These six instruments were as follows:

(a) सन्धि (*Sandhi*)—As far as possible peaceful relations were maintained with neighbouring States. The principles enunciated in modern *Panchshila* were strictly adhered to.

(b) आसन (*Asan*)—If it appeared that the enemy was rearing its head and intended aggression, the call for preparation was given to the country and armed forces deemed necessary to meet the aggression were raised and organised. For this step to succeed, it was vital that the intelligence services of the State were kept at the highest pitch of their efficiency so that sufficient notice of the enemy's intentions was obtained and the country was not caught napping by a surprise attack.

(c) समाश्रय (*Samashraya*)—If the military leaders appreciated that the resources of the country were not enough to cope with the enemy, efforts were made through diplomatic channels to enter into peace treaties with powerful neighbouring States. This was evidently done to augment one's own meagre resources.

(d) द्वैधिभाव (*Dwedhibhav*)—Concurrently efforts were made through national agents operating in enemy country to create a split in the enemy's ranks. If this succeeded, it weakened the enemy and either he deserted the idea of aggression or was easily defeated.

(e) यान (*Yan*)—If the steps mentioned above did not deter the enemy and it was found that the enemy still contemplated aggression, military manoeuvres on an impressive scale were carried out on the borders. This was a warning to the enemy that the country was well prepared and aware of his intentions. It was hoped that the enemy would be impressed by a show of might and bloodshed thus avoided.

(f) विग्रह (*Vigrah*)—If all these steps failed, then a decision in favour of war was taken as a painful necessity. A suitable area was selected and the time for starting the battle was mutually agreed upon. This system of starting a war appears to be queer and ridiculous in modern times when surprise, camouflage and concealment are vital keys to success. In those days, it was universally accepted that war is a trial of physical force and it was considered cowardly and against the accepted code of conduct to strike the opponent if he was any other than a fighting soldier. Surprise, camouflage and concealment were used in the battlefield to entrap or extricate the fighting troops. Indiscriminate destruction of non-combatant civilian population was considered repugnant and contrary to the code of conduct in war. Numerous instances are found where cultivators would plough their land just adjacent to the battlefield without any fear or danger. This evidently required a high sense of moral and mental discipline on the part of the fighting troops which was extensively prevalent in those days.

Organisation of the Army

In modern times, the armed forces of a country are organised into three services, viz., Army, Navy and Air Force. In Vedic days, no other country except India was powerful enough or even civilised enough to commit aggression over the seas. Merchant ships and pleasure yachts were in existence. Trade, diplomatic and cultural relations with countries as far flung as the Americas were in force. However, naval warfare was not much in vogue. Air Force was not kept on such a large scale nor were the strategical roles now allotted necessary in those days. Aircraft were few and were used either in a tactical role or for transportation of VIPs. Hence, the burden of war was borne by the land forces.

In modern times, the army is composed of fighting arms, supporting arms and services. Units from the three elements are grouped together to constitute an organic formation. Considering the mobility required in a nuclear war, the post-World War II trend is to cut down the tail of the army to the absolute minimum. The American idea of pentomic divisions is the result of this thought. In ancient India, the various fighting and supporting arms were integrated down to the lowest rung of the ladder. In the absence of mechanised transport, the army was composed of the following:

(a) Chariot Corps (*Rath Vahini*)
(b) Elephant Corps (*Gaj Vahini*)
(c) Cavalry (*Vaji Vahini*)
(d) Infantry (*Padati*)

Chariot Corps

Chariots were used as we use armour these days. The characteristics of the chariot were mobility, fire power and armour protection. The tasks allotted to the chariots were:

(a) to resist attacks or counter-attack
(b) to suddenly occupy or abandon positions
(c) to break out
(d) to threaten the enemy's rear.

Oxen were used as tank transporters to carry chariots over long distances. Horses were used only on the battlefield.

Elephant Corps

Elephants were used in the role of armour and engineers. The tasks allotted to elephants were:

(a) as armour

(i) Flank protection
(ii) Produce shock effect
(iii) Break-in

(b) as engineers

(i) Building roads and camping grounds
(ii) Water crossing
(iii) Destruction of field defences.

Cavalry

Horse was the queen of the battle and not infantry as at present. The characteristics of cavalry were speed and obstacle clearance. Horse was used in the role of light armour and signals. Tasks allotted to the cavalry were:

(a) as light armour

(i) Breaking through obstacles
(ii) Pursuit
(iii) Flank protection

(b) as signals

(i) Communications.

Infantry

Foot soldiers were more of a supporting arm than basic fighting arm as now considered. They were used in the escort roles and close contact. Infantry was an integral part of a fighting formation, the detailed organisation of which is given hereafter.

Commissariat (Service)

There were no separate Corps like AOC, ASC, EME. Except as nucleus to cater for the standing army, these services were manned by the civilians and were raised according to needs in an emergency. Most of these services were made available on a voluntary basis and formed no drain on the public exchequer.

Medical

According to the prevalent code of conduct in battle, fighting was normally conducted from dawn to dusk. Most of the evacuation of casualties was done during lull periods at night. Hospitals were established near the battlefield under the guidance of eminent men of medicine. Medical services were mostly manned by women volunteers. Casualties were evacuated and attended to, irrespective of considerations of being friend or foe. Instances were not uncommon when wounds were healed overnight to make the soldier fit for the next day's battle.

The largest composite field formation even up to the days of *Mahabharat* was called *Akshauhini.* The outline organisation of an *Akshauhini* was as given below:

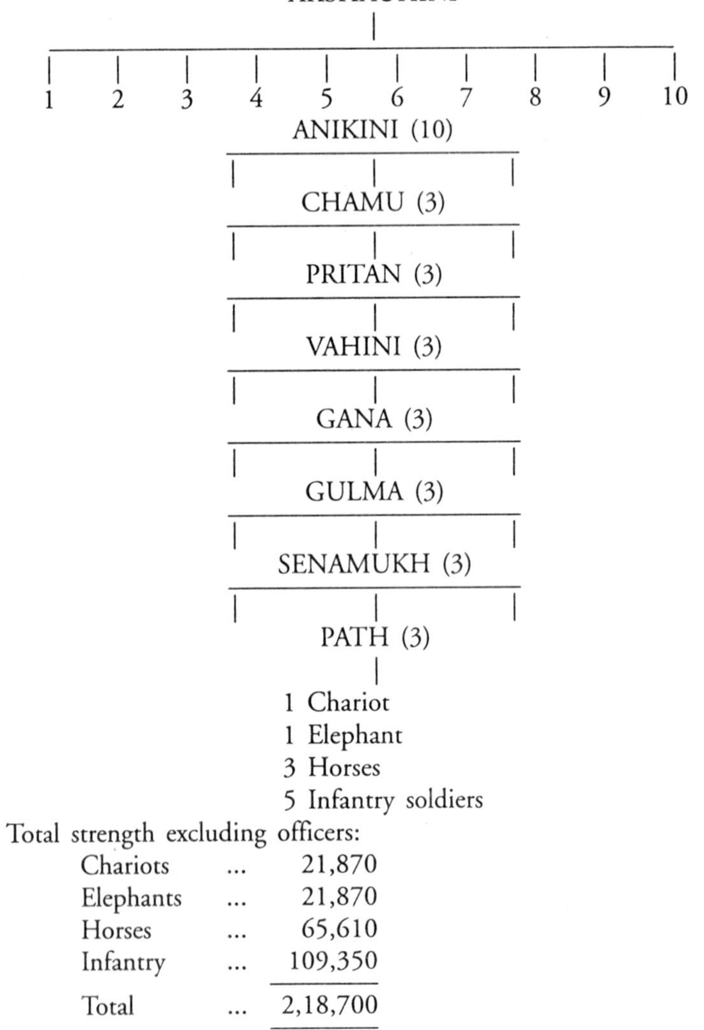

Total strength excluding officers:

Chariots	...	21,870
Elephants	...	21,870
Horses	...	65,610
Infantry	...	109,350
Total	...	2,18,700

Equipment

Bows, arrows, swords and other personal arms are well known to us. That these were the equipment in ancient India is our concept which is apparently erroneous. The battle of *Mahabharat* was fought for 18 days only and fighting was confined only to daylight hours. The Kaurawas had 11 *Akshauhini* force and the Pandavas had 7. This meant that a total of 39,36,600 men were involved, excluding officers and the services. At the end of the battle only 35 individuals were left. Compare this with the casualties of Word War II, which carried on for nearly six years day and night, and it will stand to reason that such a magnitude of casualties could not possibly have been the result of mere bows and arrows.

We will now deal with armaments which are considered to be a monopoly of our times.

Incendiaries

We read a lot about *Agniban* (अग्निवाण) in *Ramayana* and *Mahabhharat.* This वाण here does not mean the arrow of our conception. It was a missile. As late as Chandra Gupta Maurya, Kautilya describes three types of incendiary missiles known as *Agniban:*

(a) अग्निधारण (*Agni Dharan*)
(b) क्षेप्य अग्नियोग (*Kshepya Agniyog*)
(c) विश्वासघाती (*Vishwas Ghati*) having a fragmentation effect.

Explosives

Sir A.M. Elliot says, "Arabs learnt the manufacture of gunpowder from India." The turkish word *'top'* and the persian word *'tufang'* are derived from the Sanskrit word *dhoop. Agni Purana* describes *'dhoop'* as a type of rocket, which was later called *Naaldipika* by Kautilya.

Guns

Guns are known from the days of *Ramayana* and *Mahabharat.* The main types mentioned are शतघ्नी (*Shataghni*), कुणप (*Kunap*) and तूलगुण (*Toolguna*). *Shataghni* was a gun used in static emplacements, whereas *Kunap* and *Toolguna* were portable field guns.

Nuclear Weapons

Atharva Veda describes *Agni Dhraji* (अग्ने: ध्राजी) having the same heat and flash effects as are known of a nuclear bomb. *Vatasya Dhraji* (वातस्य ध्राजी) was a missile having the same blast effect as our present day nuclear bomb. *Tamasasra* (तमसास्र) was a weapon to create temporary blindness in the enemy forces. *Apva* (अप्वा) was a missile that would paralyse human limbs temporarily. In *Ramayana* and *Mahabharat* are described such weapons as had the effect of nuclear tactical weapons, e.g., *Auravagni* (औरवाग्नि), *Pashupatasra* (पाशुपतास्र) and *Shakti* (शक्ति). It can, however be stated definitely that these weapons were used in the tactical role only.

Strategy and Tactics

Strategy is defined as the art of moving and disposing troops or ships so as to impose upon the enemy the time, place and conditions for fighting that are preferred by one's own commander. Tactics is the application of this art to the troops in contact. In ancient India, movement of forces was not on such a vast scale because of the limited nature of communications and the nature of wars. Strategy was confined only to the dispositions of a field force on the march. Kautilya, *skandhparva* of *Mahabharat* and *Agni Purana* give detailed order of march when the army was on the move.

Tactics was preferred as a science to its last details. After considering all possible situations, a number of battle arrays were evolved. These battle arrays, called व्युह (*Vyuha*) were not rigid and were improved upon from time to time depending upon the genius of the force commander. Manu details eight types of battle, arrays, namely, दण्ड (*Dand*), शकट (*Shakat*), वाराह (*Varah*), सूची (*Soochi*), गरुड़ (*Garuda*), मकर (*Makar*), पद्म (*Padma*) and वज्रहार (*Vajr Har*). Kautilya refers to four principal types, viz., दण्ड (*Dand*) in which forces were disposed in transverse sections; भोग (*Bhog*) which was a snake like formation, one force following the other; मण्डल (*Mandal*) where forces were disposed in a circular pattern, and lastly असंहत (*Asamhat*) which was a diamond formation of detached divisions. The names of battle arrays were not fixed, but the same type has been given different names at different periods. Thus *Mandal* was probably the famous *Chakra Vyuha* of *Mahabharat.*

Conclusion

In conclusion it can be said that whether in equipment or in organisation, the Indian Army as late as the Mauryas, was second to none in the whole world, and judged by contemporary standards it was a highly efficient instrument of warfare which contributed to maintain peace at home from internal disorders and freedom from attack by external aggressors.

Select Bibliography

A History of India from the Earliest Times to the Present Day (M. Edwardes).
Ancient India (R.C. Majumdar).
Ancient Indian Polity (Aiyanger).
Arthasastra (Shama Sastri).
Aspects of Political Ideas and Institutions of Ancient India (R.S. Sharma).
Cambridge History of India—Ancient India (E.J. Rapson).
Civil & Military Law Journal.
Cyclopaedia of India (Dr. E. Balfour).
Evolution of Ancient Indian Law (N.C. Sen Gupta).
Handbook of Oriental History (Dr. C.H. Philips).
Hindu Law and Custom (Jolly).
Hindu Law : Past and Present (J.D.M. Derrett).
Hindu Polity (Indopadhaya).
India (Stanley Wolpert).
India in the Vedic Age (P.L. Bhargava).
Indian Chronology (D.S. Triveda).
Indian History Congress.
Journal of (the) Asiatic Society of Bombay.
Journal of (the) Bihar and Orissa Research Society.
Journal of (the) Bihar Research Society.
Mahabharata (C. Rajagopalachari).
Origin & Development of Legal & Political System in India (H.S. Bhatia).
Ramayana (Sudha Mazumdar).
Rgvedic Culture (R.C. Dass).
State and Government in Ancient India (Altekar).
The Epic of the Ancients (K.M. Munshi).
The Indian Review.
The State in Ancient India (Beni Prasad).
Studies in Hindu Political Theories (Sen).
Vedic Index (Macdonnel and Keith).
Vishveshvaranand Indological Journal.

Index